Before Taliban

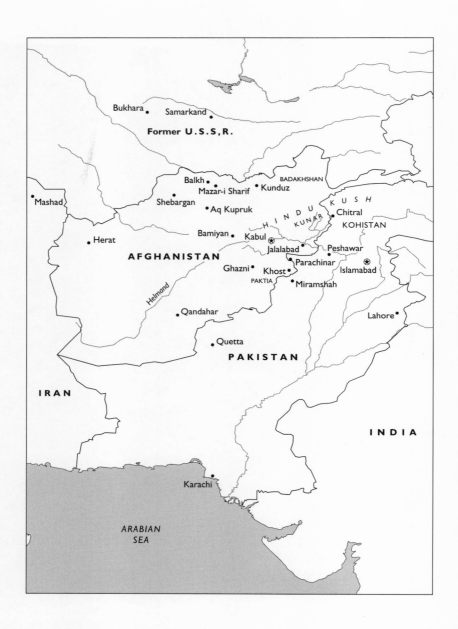

Bukhara

Samarkand

Former U.S.S.R.

Balkh

BADAKHSHAN

Mazar-i Sharif   Kunduz

Mashad

Shebargan

H I N D U   *K U S H*

Aq Kupruk

KUNAR   Chitral

KOHISTAN

Bamiyan   Kabul ✹

Herat

Jalalabad

Peshawar

AFGHANISTAN

Ghazni   Khost   Parachinar   Islamabad ✹

Helmand

PAKTIA   Miramshah

Qandahar   Lahore

Quetta

PAKISTAN

IRAN

INDIA

Karachi

ARABIAN
SEA

Before Taliban

Genealogies of the Afghan Jihad

DAVID B. EDWARDS

University of California Press

BERKELEY   LOS ANGELES   LONDON

University of California Press
Berkeley and Los Angeles, California

University of California Press, Ltd.
London, England

© 2002 by the Regents of the University of California

Library of Congress Cataloging-in-Publication Data
Edwards, David B.
    Before Taliban : genealogies of the Afghan jihad / David B. Edwards.
        p.   cm.
    Includes bibliographical references and index.
    ISBN 0–520-22859-6 (Cloth : alk. paper)
    ISBN 0–520-22861-8 (Paper : alk. paper)
    1. Safi, Samiullah.   2. Amin, Qazi Muhammad.   I. Title.
    DS371.2 .E38   2002
    958.104'5—dc21   2001006513

Manufactured in the United States of America
10   09   08   07   06   05   04   03   02
10   9   8   7   6   5   4   3   2   1

The paper used in this publication is both acid-free and totally chlorine-free (TCF). It meets the minimum requirements of ANSI/NISO Z39.48–1992 (R 1997) (*Permanence of Paper*). ⊗

for Majrooh

Lay down the burden of speaking that has left you so weary,
For now you have taken refuge with so loving a Friend.

Khamûsh bāsh tu az ranj-i goft-o gûy makhûsp,
ke dar panāh-i chenan yār-i mehrabān raftî.

—*Jalauddin Rumi*

Contents

Illustrations

Significant Persons and Parties

HUSSAIN, MAULAVI, a.k.a. JAMIL-UR-RAHMAN, early member of the Muslim Youth Organization, leader of the Wahhabi (also known as Panj Piri and Salafi) movement in Kunar

KHALES, MAULAVI YUNUS, leader of Hizb-i Islami Afghanistan

KHYBER, MIR AKBAR, leader of the Parcham wing of the (Marxist) People's Democratic Party of Afghanistan, assassinated in April 1978

MASSOUD, AHMAD SHAH, early member of the Muslim Youth Organization, commander in Panjshir Valley, minister of defense after the collapse of the Najibullah regime

MUJADDIDI, FAZL UMAR, known as Sher Agha, HAZRAT OF SHOR BAZAAR, leader in the movement to oust Amanullah

MUJADDIDI, MUHAMMAD IBRAHIM, eldest son of Sher Agha, Hazrat of Shor Bazaar

MUJADDIDI, SIBGHATULLAH, leader of Jabha-yi Nejat-i Milli Afghanistan

NABI MUHAMMADI, MAULAVI MUHAMMAD, leader of Harakat-i Inqilabi-yi Islami Afghanistan

NASRATYAR, SAIFUDDIN, founding member of the Muslim Youth Organization

NIAZI, ABDUR RAHIM, original leader of the Muslim Youth Organization

NIAZI, GHULAM MUHAMMAD, professor at Kabul University and advisor to Muslim Youth Organization leaders

RABBANI, BURHANUDDIN, professor at Kabul University and later head of Jamiat-i Islami Afghanistan

RAHMAN, ENGINEER HABIB-UR, founding member of the Muslim Youth Organization

RAHMAN, MAULAVI HABIB-UR, founding member of the Muslim Youth Organization

RIZWANI, GENERAL MIR AHMAD SHAH, follower of Faizani and leading Muslim activist in military during presidency of Daud

SAYYAF, ABDUR RASUL, later ABD AL-RAB RASUL SAYYAF, leader of the Ettehad-i Islami bara-yi Azadi-yi Afghanistan

WAQAD, QAZI MUHAMMAD AMIN, deputy leader of Hizb-i Islami Afghanistan under Gulbuddin Hekmatyar

MAJOR AFGHAN ISLAMIC POLITICAL PARTIES AND ALLIANCES

ETTEHAD-I ISLAMI BARA-YI AZADI-YI AFGHANISTAN (Islamic Union for the Freedom of Afghanistan), leader: Sayyaf

ETTEHAD-I ISLAMI MUJAHIDIN AFGHANISTAN (Islamic Union of
   Afghanistan Mujahidin), a.k.a. ETTEHAD-I HAFT GANA ("Seven Party
   Unity"), comprised both Hizb-i Islamis, Jamiat-i Islami, two splinter
   factions from Harakat (one led by Maulavi Nasrullah Mansur, the
   other by Maulavi Moazen), a minor splinter group from Jabha led by
   Maulavi Muhammad Mir, and Sayyaf's Ettehad; early 1980s
ETTEHAD-I ISLAMI MUJAHIDIN AFGHANISTAN (Islamic Union of
   Afghanistan Mujahidin), a.k.a. ETTEHAD-I SEH GANA ("Three Party
   Unity"), included Haroakat, Mahaz, and Jabha; early 1980s
ETTEHAD-I ISLAMI MUJAHIDIN AFGHANISTAN (Islamic Union of
   Afghanistan Mujahidin), comprised both Hizb-i Islamis, Jamiat-i
   Islami, Harakat, Jabha, Mahaz, and Sayyaf's Ettehad; late 1980s
HARAKAT-I INQILABI-YI ISLAMI AFGHANISTAN (Revolutionary Islamic
   Movement of Afghanistan), leader: Nabi
HIZB-I ISLAMI AFGHANISTAN (Islamic Party of Afghanistan), leader:
   Hekmatyar
HIZB-I ISLAMI AFGHANISTAN (Islamic Party of Afghanistan), leader:
   Khales
HIZB-I TAUHID (Monotheism Party), associated with Faizani and Rizwani
JABHA-YI NEJAT-I MILLI AFGHANISTAN (Front for the National
   Salvation of Afghanistan), leader: Sibghatullah Mujaddidi
JAMIAT-I ISLAMI AFGHANISTAN (Islamic Society of Afghanistan), leader:
   Rabbani
JAMIAT-I ULAMA MUHAMMADI (Society of Muhammadan Clerics),
   founded by Sibghatullah Mujaddidi during the 1970s
KHODAM UL-FORQAN (Servants of the Qur'an), founded by Ismail
   Mujaddidi in the 1970s
MAHAZ-I MILLI ISLAMI AFGHANISTAN (National Islamic Front of
   Afghanistan), founded by Gailani in 1978
SAZMAN-I JAWANAN-I MUSULMAN (Muslim Youth Organization),
   founded in 1969 by Muslim students at Kabul University

Author's Note

When terrorists attacked the World Trade Center in New York City and the Pentagon in Washington, D.C., this book was already in the hands of its publisher. Faced with the choice of revising the manuscript in light of these events or moving forward with publication, I have decided on the latter course of action. I have done so both because of the immediate need for informed material on Afghanistan and because it would be disingenuous to pretend to have known the direction events would take during the writing of this book. Naturally, there are things about the book I now wish I could change—sections I would add, emphases I would alter, tenses I would fiddle with, foreshadowings I would include. I've resisted the temptation to make these adjustments, however, and will let the book stand on its own merits, as a summary statement by one student of Afghanistan of the state of understanding as it existed before September 11, 2001.

David B. Edwards
WILLIAMSTOWN, MASSACHUSETTS
OCTOBER 15, 2001

Preface

The bootlickers of the old and new imperialism are treacherously
struggling to nip our popular government in the bud. They think
that since we took over power in ten hours, they would, perhaps,
capture it in fifteen hours. But they must know that we are the
children of history, and history has brought us here.

—Nur Muhammad Taraki, President of the
Democratic Republic of Afghanistan, August 2, 1978

Woe to the children of history. Still exultant four months after the coup
d'état that brought his Marxist party to power in Afghanistan, Nur
Muhammad Taraki could boast to an assembly of army officers that he and
his comrades had been raised to their position by transcendental historical
forces. Fifteen months later, Taraki was dead—assassinated by his own protégé, Hafizullah Amin—and a month after that the Soviet Union landed an
invasion force in Kabul in a vain effort to try to resuscitate Taraki's falter-
ing revolution with an infusion of troops and military hardware. History, it
would seem, was a harsh and capricious parent. Or perhaps it was Taraki's
Marxist vision of history that was defective. With every passing year, it is
more difficult to recall or comprehend that as late as 1978 many people still
believed that history had a motive force, that it moved inexorably forward
in progressive, dialectical, even sentient fashion. Though many of his comrades, Hafizullah Amin included, may have had a more cynical take on the
Marxist vision of history, there is good reason to think that Taraki at least
believed this much to be true: that history was moving toward a resolution
and that he was part of the vanguard of that process.

Like all parents, history, in fact, did have lessons to teach, but they were
of a local nature and not the sort of universal lessons that Taraki had in mind
when he spoke in August 1978. There were many such lessons, including
one about how Afghans treat outsiders who try to control their homeland
and another about how they feel when people in authority interfere in their
domestic affairs. And Taraki himself would have benefited, if he had only
listened, from the many tellings and retellings of the stories of rulers who
trusted too much in those around them. Afghan history is replete with
moral tales from which value can be gained. But Afghan children, like all
children, often do not want to listen, and this was certainly the case with the

People's Democratic Party of Afghanistan; but so too was it true of its enemies—the tribes and ethnic coalitions that rose up in the first months
against the new regime and the Islamic militants who eventually succeeded
in taking control of the anticommunist resistance until they too lost out to
the Taliban militia, which controls Kabul and much of Afghanistan today.
This book is about the Marxists and their enemies and about how they all
came to ruin in part at least because of their failure to heed the lessons of the
past. As different as they were, the factions that fought for supremacy in the
first, pivotal years of the Afghan conflict shared this in common: in their
eagerness to seize the present and shape the future they all forgot both
about the past and what it might teach them and about their own society—
its contours, its potential, its limits.

My objective here is to place the history of the present against the history of the past in order to gauge what happened in Afghanistan and why
the forces that in the first years of the war seemed between them to control
the destiny of the country have all been destroyed. The originative form of
history for Afghans is the genealogy, and I have framed my own exercise in
historical understanding in genealogical terms. Through genealogies Afghans
figure not only relatedness but, more important, their moral responsibilities
in the world. Through scores of generations, people have learned how to
comport themselves on the basis of genealogies. Genealogies are the blueprint, the map, the skeleton of relationships. Friendship, authority, love,
even enmity are volatile until they have been transmuted into genealogical
form, which traditionally and in the first instance is what Afghans—particularly tribal Afghans—"think with" and act on. Likewise, in the world of
Islam and the world of governance, genealogies have long played the same
central role. In mystical and clerical circles, genealogies are kept that indicate
the passing on of knowledge and the relationships of spiritual and scholarly
succession. In the calculations of rulers, would be and real, claims to authority have historically had to have a genealogical basis to be given credence,
and pretenders without such credentials have tended to be short-lived.

My own claim to credence is also based on a genealogical approach to
Afghan history. This approach is premised on the belief that we can learn
much that would otherwise be obscure by looking at individual lives and
trying to understand their connection to larger historical and cultural
processes. In all that has been written about the war in Afghanistan, there
has been little of note about individuals or about how the war was seen from
ground level. The lives that I look at are not those of "ordinary people."
Though attention to the experiences of noncombatants, women in particular, is needed, I was not in a position to conduct the necessary research to

produce such a work. I was able to examine the war from the vantage of men who participated in it and who sought to achieve through political and armed engagement goals that they viewed at the time as transcendent.

As in my first book, *Heroes of the Age: Moral Fault Lines on the Afghan Frontier,* which looked at three legendary figures from the turn of the previous century, I am concerned with men in positions of authority to whom other men looked for leadership. But few of the men involved in this war could be viewed as "heroes" in the sense I used the term previously. This was a war of attrition, a war in which relations of loyalty and enmity repeatedly shifted. It was also a war of changing purposes and principles that were confusing and alienating to those viewing the war from a distance, as they were for those directly affected. Even in Afghanistan, on the edge of the global, this is an overexposed age of hype and bombast, of exaggerated promises and deflated expectations. It is not a time conducive to the perpetuation of myth or the growth of new legends. But the men of today have still had to contend with the myths and legends of the past, and this book focuses on how three leaders who came to prominence in the first years of the war sought to square with the past as they endeavored to shape the future.

Genealogies are also about origins, about how things got to be the way they are based on the way they "originally" were. In this book, I use a genealogical method to try to uncover the origins of the *jihad.* The war in Afghanistan went through a number of phases, and to understand those phases one must also understand what came before. The starting point for this book is the *inqilab-i saur,* the Saur Revolution of 1978, which brought Taraki and his allies to power. But in order to understand the significance of this event and the demise of its revolutionary promise, it is important to consider prior understandings of the role of rulers in Afghan society and their relationship to those they ruled. The second phase involved the first tribal and regional insurrections (*qiyyam*) against the Marxist state, from late 1978 through early 1980, which were precipitated by a variety of factors and organized on different social bases in different areas. This period was brief, as Islamic political parties took control of the local rebellions and provided their organizational and ideological stamp to the scattered purposes of insurrection. This period of party control is the phase of jihad, of "struggle in the path of Islam." But, far from the implication of that term, there was little unanimity as to what the struggle was about or how it should be directed. To the contrary, this period was characterized by internecine struggle as much as it was by conflict with the government in Kabul, and the final objective of this book is to make sense of how and why jihad proved as inad-

equate a conceptual framework for unifying the Afghan people as "revolution" and "insurrection" had previously shown themselves to be.

— *||* —

Before Taliban is in many respects a sequel to my first book, and so it is only
natural that the people I thanked in the acknowledgments of that book
deserve thanks here as well. Rather than list all these names a second time,
I will simply express my gratitude to those people again for their various
and sundry acts of kindness and assistance, while singling out several whose
names have come up before but who had a special impact on this book.
These include Nancy Hatch Dupree, who has been a friend and inspiration
for more than twenty-five years and who generously made available to me
photographs from the Khalilullah Enayat Seraj collection. Nasim Stanazai
introduced me to Qazi Muhammad Amin, the party leader whose life forms
the principal focus of Chapter Six, and made it possible for the interviews
with Qazi Amin to take place. I also want to thank once again Sayyid Shahmahmood Miakhel, my longtime friend and collaborator, who has assisted
me from the start of my Afghan research in 1982 to the present and who
helped arrange a trip through eastern Afghanistan in 1995, which is
described in the first note in Chapter Eight.

In addition to those people I acknowledged before, additional friends and
relations have provided help more recently, and I would like to take the
opportunity to mention them. In particular, I want to thank Samiullah Safi,
who shared with me the stories from his youth and war years that are the
foundation of Chapters Four and Five, and the aforementioned Qazi
Muhammad Amin. Neither of these men had to take time to talk with me,
and I believe that each did so because he honestly wanted the story of the
war in Afghanistan told with some sensitivity and accuracy. In trusting in
me, an American whose personal agenda and political orientation they could
only guess at, these two men took a leap of faith. I cannot guarantee that I
have told the story the way they would have wanted it told, but I can say
that I have done my best to minimize my personal biases and have tried to
relate their histories faithfully.

In addition to these men, without whom this book would not have been
possible, I also want to acknowledge other Afghans who agreed to shorter
interviews and whose testimony has helped flesh out historical aspects of this
work. These include, for their help on the situation in Pech and Kunar, Aman
ul-Mulk, Dr. Delawar Sahre, Commander Abdur Rauf Khan, Commander
Abdul Wahhab, Yusuf Nuristani, Ghazi Chopan, and Hashim Zamani; for

their assistance on various aspects of Islamic belief and practice in Afghanistan, Agha Jan Senator, Hazrat Abdul Shokur, Muhammad 'Ali and Sayyid Muhammad Sahibzadgan, Maulavi Abdul Hakim Zhobul, Dr. Abdul Qader Suleimankhel, Wasil Nur, Mirajan Saheqi, Maulavi Fazel Hadi Shinwari, Sayyid Hakim Kamal Shinwari, Maulavi Abdul Ahad Yaqubi, Maulavi Muhammad Gul Rohani and Maulavi Ahmad Gul Rohani, Shams-ul Haq Pirzada, Sayyid Hissam, Muhammad Qayem Agha, Maulavi Amirzada, Fazel 'Ali Mujadiddi, Engineer Ahmad Shah, Abdul Sabur Azizi, Sayyid Isaq Gailani, Nur Agha Gailani, Sayyid Mahmud Gailani, Rohullah, Qari Taj Muhammad, Sayyid Abdullah Tora, Maulavi Abdul Aziz, Maulana Qiyammuddin Qashaf, Sayyid Mahmud Hasrat, Maulavi Habibullah from Logar, Abdul Bari Ghairat, Maulavi Wula Jan Wasseq, Maulavi Jalaluddin Haqqani, and Dr. Inayatullah Eblagh; and, for their assistance on Afghan matters generally, Dr. Zahir Ghazi Alam, Qasim Baz Mangal, Sayyid Shamsuddin Majrooh, Sayyid Bahauddin Majrooh, Ustad Khalilullah Khalili, Abdul Jabar Sabet, Rasul Amin, Hakim Taniwal, and Haji Zaman. I also want to thank the party leaders who granted interviews to me, including Hazrat Sibghatullah Mujadiddi, Maulavi Muhammad Nabi Muhammadi, Engineer Gulbuddin Hekmatyar, and Maulavi Yunus Khales. I apologize to anyone whom I have left out and for any errors of omission or commission that might be present in this work.

During the writing of this book, I have benefited from being able to spend a year in Santa Fe, New Mexico, at the School of American Research. Doug Schwartz and his staff provided a wonderful setting to complete this work, and I offer my thanks to them and to my fellow scholars who shared the year in Santa Fe with me: Alan Goodman, Roberta Haines, Nathan Sayer, Frank Salomon, and Ana Celia Zentella. In the final stage of manuscript preparations, I was able to incorporate useful comments and advice from various anonymous reviewers and especially from Margaret Mills, whom I met in Kabul while searching for a used bicycle to buy and who has remained a friend and valued colleague ever since. My first exposure to Afghan oral history was at a talk given by Margaret in Kabul in 1976 on Herati versions of the Cupid and Psyche myth. Ever since that time, Margaret has provided inspiration through her own work and her insightful editorial comments.

I also want to acknowledge the financial assistance of the National Endowment for the Humanities, which provided the fellowship that allowed me to spend the year at the School of American Research; Williams College, for its sabbatical support; and the Williams Class of 1945, whose World

Fellowship enabled me to take an additional semester of leave to complete the writing of this book. Finally, I want again to thank my wife, Holly, and my children, Nick and Melody, who put up with frequent office detours so that I could jot down an idea or write a paragraph. Their tolerance and love are acknowledged with much gratitude.

1 Introduction
Into Forbidden Afghanistan

Lowell Thomas needed another adventure. At age twenty-eight, the ambitious showman from Cripple Creek, Colorado, had become an international celebrity through his immensely popular lecture tour "With Allenby in Palestine and Lawrence in Arabia." Charming appreciative audiences and collecting handsome receipts, Thomas had spent most of 1920 and 1921 traveling the length and breadth of the British Commonwealth—from Scotland to India to Malaya to Australia—and his show had been seen by several million people. Two years into it, however, he was feeling the need for an encore, and Edmund Allenby and T. E. Lawrence were a hard act to follow—Lawrence in particular. Before Thomas had transformed him into a household name, Lawrence had been a somewhat reclusive figure whose story was well known to only a small number of military and diplomatic insiders. Thomas had changed that picture with his richly embroidered tales of the handsome archaeologist, garbed in the robes of "a prince of Mecca," who blew up Turkish trains and inspired a fierce devotion among the Bedouin tribesmen who followed him.[1]

In casting about for his encore, Thomas had originally traveled to India but quickly realized that while yogis and snake charmers could generate some interest in their exoticism, they were unlikely to produce the kind of palpable excitement his earlier show had achieved. For Thomas's tastes, India was altogether too tame; however, adventure beckoned just over the border to the west in "forbidden Afghanistan." Remote ("In fact, their country is still as isolated as Japan was at the time when . . . Commodore Perry went over there and convinced the people of the Land of the Rising Sun that they ought to be more neighborly"), rugged ("If there is a wilder country anywhere on earth today than Afghanistan, I know not of it"), and inhabited by tribesmen reputed to be as ferocious as any on earth ("So deep

1

is their love of fighting that when they can't pick a quarrel with outsiders, they snipe back and forth across their hills and carve each other, just to keep in practice"), Afghanistan was the perfect location for Thomas's brand of derring-do, and he could see that its frontier tribes were every bit the equal of the North Arabian Bedouin who had provided such a handsome supporting cast for Major Lawrence. Like the Arab Bedouin, the Afghan tribesmen possessed a hawklike grace that would make their violent customs all the more thrilling for a Western audience, and this bunch reportedly possessed one attribute in even greater abundance than their Arab cousins: religious fanaticism. Thus, as Thomas journeyed along the north-west frontier, his British hosts regaled him with stories of tribesmen who had "gone ghazi," colonial parlance for what happened when a tribesman suddenly and without warning struck off on his own private path of jihad, knifing or shooting the Christian closest to hand.

Afghanistan might be just the thing for his second act, but in order for this Thomas travelogue (and accompanying books and magazine articles) to live up to the success of its predecessor, it would need one last ingredient. Other showmen featured breathtaking landscapes, strange rituals, and local amusements—all of which Thomas deployed in his shows—but he had catapulted to the top of his profession by featuring a compelling narrative built around a galvanizing central presence. In "With Allenby in Palestine," Thomas had portrayed the gruff, no-nonsense General Allenby as a modern-day Richard Coeur de Lion, capturing the Holy Land from the dark eminence Kaiser Wilhelm. In "With Lawrence in Arabia," Thomas had cast the now-famous Major Lawrence as an eccentric scholar caught up in the mysteries of the past until compelled by circumstance and his Anglo know-how and nobility to mold a ragtag mass of native irregulars into a disciplined army. For this Afghanistan show, he needed something comparable: a story line and a leading man that could give his travelogue a deeper resonance and meaning. This time, however, there was no war going on and no European who was a logical candidate for the starring role.[2] This time, Thomas would have to look elsewhere for his leading man, and in short order he set his sights on a native character who, despite the handicap of not being European, just might serve his purposes.

The character he had in mind was the Afghan ruler Amir Amanullah Khan. A young man of thirty, Amanullah was in fact the same age as Lawrence had been during his adventures in Arabia. Photographs showed him to be handsome in a swarthy Rudolph Valentino sort of way, and he had the right pedigree. As the grandson and successor of the notorious Afghan ruler Abdur Rahman, Amanullah had the distinction of being "one of the few absolute monarchs left on this earth of ours." All reports indicated that he was "a capable young ruler indeed" and something of a visionary who was trying to bring his kingdom into the modern world. But the most interesting thing about him from Thomas's point of view was how he had come to sit on the throne of this turbulent kingdom, "for Amanullah Khan was not one of those who as heir to a throne, peacefully succeed their fathers. Far from it." His rise to power had been a violent one, with many still unexplained twists and turns. It was, in fact, the stuff of legend, the kind of story Lowell Thomas loved to tell, particularly when it could be put into the mouth of an "old Afghan" storyteller:

> It all began with the mysterious death of the King Habibullah, but there is also another mystery. The present Ameer [Amanullah] forgave his two elder brothers and merely made them renounce their rights to the throne. But nobody knows what became of the uncle. He was made a prisoner, and that was the last that any of us ever heard of him. Perhaps he may be deep in one of our prisons. Perhaps he is dead. Only Allah knows.

The prospect of meeting Amanullah at the end of the journey was just the narrative gambit that Thomas needed for his travelogue, and with that goal in mind he assembled his party for the journey to Kabul. "Soon, if Allah willed it, and if Amir Amanullah Khan, Light of the World, did not change his mind, and if his zesty subjects did not shoot holes in our car, and if none of the disasters that usually overtake travelers east of Suez befell us—why, then we would pass out of the old Bajauri Gate at Peshawar and journey to mysterious Afghanistan, where so few Westerners had preceded us."[3] Strangely, however, the events that followed this invocation turned out rather flat. There were, of course, the requisite heat, dust, and flat tires, but the trip itself proved anticlimactic—so much so, in fact, that Thomas was forced to stage and photograph the tribal ambush of a motorcar to illustrate the dangers of the Khyber Pass. The ensuing days on the road to Kabul proved no more noteworthy, up to the time that they were finally to meet the amir, an encounter that Thomas hoped would be "the high spot of our Afghan adventure."

Following the wont of monarchs, Amanullah made his visitors bide their time for several days, but finally the summons arrived, brought to them by horsemen "shining with cloth of gold turbans and scarlet and gold uniforms." They were to go to the summer palace outside Kabul and there meet "His Majesty Amanullah Khan, Ameer of Afghanistan, King of Kabul and Light of the World." The road to the palace took Thomas and his companions first across an open plain and then up a steep mountain road until they entered a long avenue of graceful chinar trees that opened onto "a scene that made us gasp." At the end of their journey into forbidden Afghanistan, at the gateway to the palace of the absolute amir, the sight that greeted them was far from the one they had been expecting, for it was not the Orient of their imaginings they saw before them but something more familiar still:

> "Why we're home," shouted [Harry] Chase [Thomas's cameraman]. "We've never left the old U.S.A. Why this looks like the outskirts of East Orange."
>
> And it did look like it. We were all amazed.
>
> The gateway through which we passed had an exceedingly familiar appearance. There was nothing Oriental about it. It looked like the entrance to a brand-new real-estate development on the outskirts of Kansas City or Detroit. And once we had entered we were among typical suburban bungalows, frame houses with sleeping porches and breakfast nooks.

To this shock was added another as the party of travelers was joined by one "Tewfik Bey, of Constantinople, Los Angeles, and Afghanistan," who introduced himself in American patois as the designer of the amir's new palace. Tewfik Bey, it turned out, had been an attaché in the Turkish Embassy in Washington when the First World War began, and rather than return to his home country he had decided to stay on in the States, where he eventually found work in Hollywood as an extra in "mob scenes." Thereafter, he made his way to Kansas, where he took classes for a time at an agricultural school on the assumption that knowledge of scientific farming techniques might some day land him a job back home. The investment paid immediate dividends, for when he arrived in Constantinople, he learned that the amir of Afghanistan was offering employment to Turks who would come and help him modernize his country. Availing himself of the opportunity, Tewfik Bey went to Kabul, first taking a position as an agricultural advisor and eventually helping to design the palace complex at Paghman. It was perhaps an odd career move for an "agricultural specialist," but he explained it this way to Thomas:

> His Majesty intended this to be his summer capital, and he said he wanted it done in the latest style. He thought some Western architectural ideas might go well. That's right where I shine. I told him just to leave it to me. Hadn't I been in Hollywood? So I've been making a new Hollywood out of this place, a Hollywood without movie stars, bathing beauties, movie lots, or cameras! It's been up-hill going. You see I'm the only one in Central Asia who knows anything about Hollywood architecture.

Following their meeting with Tewfik Bey, Thomas's party was left to stroll about, waiting for the appearance of Amanullah himself. With time on his hands, Thomas's ever-fretful cameraman worried aloud about the impending meeting. What, he asked in a whisper, was the proper way to address an amir? A third member of their group replied ominously that it was best "not to say anything at all. . . . If you start talking out of turn to an absolute monarch, you are liable to be turned over to the mad elephants or blown from the mouth of a cannon." No sooner were these dour comments uttered, however, then the amir himself appeared before them, "a stocky man of middle height, with a short mustache and protruding dark brown eyes. You could see that he was a man of jolly and yet strong personality. He also looked as though he enjoyed the good things of life."

Not only was Amanullah's appearance rather unexceptional, but "the Ameer was not dressed nearly so magnificently as you expect a king to be." In fact, his garb was "rather shapeless and clumsy," for it turned out that, as an encouragement to home industry, he was sporting English-style clothing made in a local factory. And if this attire were not enough to dissipate any illusions that the travelers might have retained about the absolute amir, there was also the evident ease and casualness with which he interacted with his companions and they with him. This group included the two older brothers whom Amanullah had displaced to become king. Thomas remembered the "many dark legends of the Orient, where it has been the custom for ages for a king to kill off all his near relatives for fear that they might try to dethrone him." However, such speculations were soon dispelled; the amir donned sporting attire to play a set of tennis with a group of these same relatives and later, while being photographed by Chase, relinquished his seat on a noble charger so that various of his companions could have their pictures taken on the same steed.

All these episodes diffused the air of mystery surrounding the Afghan amir, but perhaps the most telling moment from Thomas's point of view was their first handshake, which was "firm and decisive." As Thomas noted, there was "nothing languid and Oriental about it," a comment that signaled the demise of the Arabian Nights fantasy Thomas had been constructing in his mind. American to the bone, Thomas couldn't help but like a man with a firm handshake. Likewise, for Chase, Amanullah's status as a regular Joe was sealed in an equally convincing manner when he displayed his skill at tennis. Chase noted that he had played some formidable tennis himself in his day, but he was sufficiently impressed by the amir's "cannonball service" to offer the singular compliment that "this Oriental potentate is a regular Oriental wizard at this Occidental pastime" (Fig. 1). The amir further endeared himself to Chase when he willingly assumed whatever pose the cameraman demanded of him. Despite the evident discomfort of his

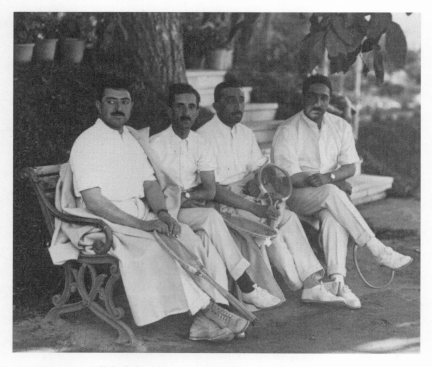

1.   Amir Amanullah (left) with courtiers, Paghman, 1922 (Lowell Thomas Archives).

courtiers, who wrung their hands at the sight of a bumptious American ordering their monarch to turn this way and that, Amanullah himself remained unperturbed by Chase's liberties and even suggested that a man who issued commands as forcefully as Chase could find useful employment in his army.

In the face of such down-to-earth good cheer, whatever suspicions and preconceptions Thomas and his party had been harboring soon disappeared, but so too did the story line that Thomas had been building for his travelogue. For all his affability, Amanullah would not make quite the leading man Thomas had hoped for. The air of mystery and intrigue had been dispelled, and the show that Thomas would end up producing would be less like the adventure epic he had achieved with Lawrence and more like the generic, narratively unfocused travelogues that Thomas hoped to avoid. Thus, when Thomas returned to London in the fall of 1922 and opened "Through Romantic India and into Forbidden Afghanistan" at Covent Garden, the show drew respectable audiences, but nothing like the acclaim and success of his earlier production. Ultimately, it seems, Western audiences of the day proved to be more intrigued by the tale of a Westerner who donned Bedouin robes than of an Easterner in tennis garb, and the story of a distant king trying gradually and peacefully to modernize his country did not have the same resonance as that of a European going in and doing the same job by brute force of will. What no one could know at the time was how either story would end. It was only just becoming apparent in 1922 that the cause of Arab independence that Lawrence had championed had been betrayed by the European powers. And in another seven years Amanullah would be overthrown by his own people, who resented and distrusted the Western-style reforms he was urging on them rather more forcefully than Thomas had realized during his brief visit.

Despite the different outcomes of Thomas's theatrical productions, it is possible to discern a greater affinity between Amanullah and Lawrence than either Thomas or his audience seem to have been able to recognize at the time—an affinity that is perhaps suggested in the unhappy outcome of both men's careers. In an odd way, Thomas's two leading men were mirror images of one another, each being seen in his dress, manner, and action as a variant of the "Oriental" of Western imagining. In Lawrence's case, the fantasy centered on the notion of the Westerner becoming more Oriental than the Oriental himself in order to tame the savage and to bring order to a far corner of the world. In Amanullah's case, the fantasy had to do with the Oriental himself recognizing the superiority of Western ways and voluntarily submitting himself to the discipline and enlightened attitude of the West in order to raise his people up out of their degraded condition.

In both instances, dress was useful to understanding the larger significance of the main character's progress in the world—Lawrence's borrowed robes and Amanullah's Norfolk coat being symbols of the process by which the fundamental dichotomy between Barbarian and Civilized that defined the world in the 1920s could be mediated. The issue of Lawrence's "cross-dressing" has come under intensive scrutiny ever since David Lean's 1962 film portrayed Lawrence as a politically and sexually ambivalent hero, motivated as much by masochistic impulses as heroic ones. Seen through the contemporary lens, Lawrence has been transformed from "the uncrowned king of Arabia" (as Thomas portrayed him) to the "prince" of our postcolonial discontents and psychosocial neuroses (as Thomas Mack and others have more recently characterized him).[4]

Though he has not received the same sort of fervent attention as Lawrence, Amanullah has himself been the focus of considerable attention, with Western writers tending to view him as a tragic hero whose noble attempt to modernize his country was ultimately undone by the forces of bigotry and backwardness. My own view, shared by many Afghans, is that Amanullah was a man blinded by his own egotism and fascination with the West into launching an ill-advised and overambitious set of reforms that his people were not prepared or ready to accept. Amanullah was the archetypal reform ruler so much in evidence in the colonies and colonial borderlands in the post–World War I period. Some of these native reformers were successful, but most left behind an unhappy legacy. Amanullah was among the unsuccessful; in this sense he can be seen, as much as Lawrence, as a Knight Templar of our disorders, and for him as well "cross-dressing" can be seen as a symbol of the ambiguous legacy he left behind.

As Thomas discovered during his brief stay in Afghanistan, Amanullah was immensely fond of wearing different styles of clothing. His most common dress appears to have been a spartan military uniform, but among the photographs that have survived of the king are a number showing him in costumes associated with the different ethnic and tribal groups in Afghanistan. He is also seen in royal regalia in a handful of photographs—sometimes dressed in the music-hall uniform of a pre–World War I military officer, complete with plumed helmet, sometimes in the improvised costume of a Eurasian monarch. One especially revealing photograph comes from a costume ball held in a villa in Paghman in 1925 (Fig. 2). The guests included Amanullah himself and most of the prominent members of his entourage. Typical of the progressive culture of the court, men and women bedecked in exotic finery intermingle as they line up to have their picture taken. Most of the guests have adopted ethnic dress from Afghanistan and its border lands. Others have found costumes from farther afield, including Burma, Japan, Africa, Europe, and Arabia. A few, including Amanullah himself, have chosen vintage outfits—Amanullah (second from the left in the second row) having donned a costume from the reign nearly one hundred years earlier of Amir Dost Muhammad (1828–1863), while his elder brother Inayatullah (at the right end of the second row) has chosen for the occasion an outfit of the sort his grandfather, Amir Abdur Rahman, typically wore (if, indeed, they are not the dead amir's very own clothes).

One gets from this photograph the sense of an insular world wrenched open, a world in which people have recently become aware of the larger universe of cultures outside their own and have rushed to embrace them. In court photographs taken five to fifteen years earlier, one can see the impact of European (specifically, English) goods—Victorian wallpapers, gowns, and the like—but here we see people dressing themselves not just in the European style but also in a way that is self-consciously cosmopolitan. In

2.   Costume ball, Paghman, 1925 (Khalilullah Enayat Seraj Collection).

earlier pictures, those posing in Western garb appear stiff and uncomfortable: they are adopting a foreign style in a purely imitative manner. Here, the attitude seemingly has changed. The evident playfulness and irony seem novel. At the same time, there is also a sense of unreality. This costume ball was held shortly after the government had suppressed the first serious popular uprising against Amanullah, an uprising that had gained momentum in large part because of discontent over Amanullah's reform program. In response to this challenge, Amanullah briefly curtailed some of his more controversial plans for modernizing Afghanistan, but the evidence of this photograph is that he was still living in a hermetic cultural space closed off from the reality of his society, a reminder of which can be seen in the lower right of the picture. There sits Adeko, one of the wives of Amanullah's father, the late Amir Habibullah. Alone among the partygoers, Adeko is dressed in the clothes appropriate to her background and station. While all about her others fashion themselves in identities other than their own, the not-so-merry widow stares forlornly into the camera, a grim reminder in the midst of gaiety of the old ways and the grimmer world outside the villa's gates.

The photograph illustrates the central paradox represented by Amanullah and all reformers of his era, the paradox of whether a person is who he was born to be or whether he is who he chooses to become. Traditionally, in both England and Afghanistan, birth had determined social position and action, but in the case of both Lawrence and Amanullah the idea became flesh that identity could be fashioned, that a man could become something other than what he had been born to be, something that he created for himself. Thus, just as Lawrence sought to fabricate an identity different from the one he had been assigned by the circumstances of his birth, so Amanullah also chose to create a persona and role for himself that was fundamentally different from the one that he had inherited from his father and grandfather.

Amanullah intended to be a more populist ruler, and it was his conceit that just as he would move closer to his people, so would he raise them closer to him through mass education, the elimination of stultifying social customs, and the reduction of religion's grip on people's values, practices, and concerns. Amanullah became famous for this project; it has been viewed as the substance of his failed reign. Less often remarked on was the extent to which Amanullah was also attempting to change the rules by which identity was formulated for himself and his people. In his dress, in his manners, in his actions, he was trying to become not just a different person but an entirely new sort of person, and in the process of constructing this person he was also attempting to construct a new sort of nation and a novel understanding of what exactly a king should be, what was properly in his scope of action, and how he should relate to the people he ruled. Like Lawrence's, Amanullah's transformation wasn't just a matter of putting on different clothes and appropriating manners other than his own. These changes were indeed one element in the equation, and their symbolic importance cannot be underestimated; but it must also be recognized that style and substance were intertwined. In fashioning his oddly amalgamated identity, Amanullah was trying fundamentally to reconstitute the moral foundations of Afghan society.

COMING INTO THE COUNTRY, 1975

I arrived in Afghanistan from the west, traveling by bus through Turkey and Iran, entering first the city of Herat in the west, then journeying by bus to Qandahar and finally to Kabul. It was late in June 1975, and I had graduated from college just a month or so earlier and was now prepared to teach English at the U.S.-government–sponsored language center. Like Thomas, I had been drawn to Afghanistan by exotic tales of camel caravans, turbaned tribesmen, and women in veils. All of this I discovered, to be sure, but Afghanistan in the mid-seventies was a very different place from the one

Thomas had encountered fifty years earlier. For one thing, where there once had been few foreigners to speak of in the country, there were now swarms, some tourists of the accustomed sort, but even more hippies or, as they called themselves, world travelers—WTs. The center of activity for the WTs was Shahr-i Nau, the New City, and the hotels and restaurants catering to them on and near Chicken Street, named for the area's poultry market, which had been displaced by the foreign invasion. WTs manifested little discernible interest in Afghanistan or Afghans. Foremost in most of their minds was hashish (which was plentiful in Kabul), inexpensive ratatouilles and omelets to assuage their drug-fueled appetites, and the pleasure of their own spaced-out, casually licentious company.

With the exception of those who served and benefited from the WT economy, most Kabulis with whom I came in contact ignored the young Westerners, not so much it seemed because they were shocked by them but rather because they were involved in their own intense love affair with modernity. The American Center, where I worked, was the largest of a number of English-language schools in the New City, and all were packed with students. Everyone from shopkeepers to businessmen to schoolgirls wanted to perfect their English, and they all crammed together in our classrooms—the girls sitting in clusters and the older men keeping to themselves, but otherwise all joined together in the shared communion of getting ahead. Most of my students also came to class in Western clothes, which they bought at the second-hand clothes bazaar. In and around the school, I rarely saw a turban or the all-enveloping *burqa* veil that traditional Afghan women wore. To the contrary, my nearest exposure to the exotic Afghanistan of my imagining anywhere close to the school was in neighboring antique shops, which sold rusting scimitars, helmets, flintlocks, and the like—most of which, one would assume, had been pieces of someone's patrimony, cherished artifacts of past battles before they'd been sold off for cash.

At the time, I had little grasp of what any of this meant or where it was headed, but a hint was given to me in the form of an ethnographic documentary that was previewed in the auditorium of the cultural center shortly after my arrival in Afghanistan. The film was titled *Naim and Jabar*, and it was the account of two boys who lived in the village of Aq Kupruk in northern Afghanistan. The older of the two boys was back in his village for summer vacation. His lifelong friend was a year younger and hoped to follow in his footsteps by gaining admission to the provincial high school. To that end, the two boys traveled to Mazar-i Sharif so that the younger boy could meet with school officials and complete the entrance exam. The documentary fol-

lowed the boys as they traveled by truck to the city and wandered through
the bazaar. It was the younger boy's first trip away from his village, and his
more experienced friend immediately took him to the used-clothes market
to buy a second-hand suit. If he was going to go to school, he had to look the
part. As they left the shop and were walking down the sidewalk, the camera
trailed close behind. The two boys looked the same except that the older one
had a more confident stride and the younger one was wearing a turban, the
loose end of which hung down the back of his newly purchased coat. The
camera watched from behind as they strolled along, and then it appeared
that the older, bareheaded boy said something to his friend, for the next
thing we saw was the younger boy removing the turban from his head,
wadding it into a ball, and stuffing it into his pocket.

It was a tiny gesture that took only a few seconds on screen, but I have
since come to believe that it represented a profound transformation not just
for one boy but also for a whole society. On one level, the boy's removing
his turban reflected the self-conscious rejection of one world based on the
sudden recognition of its difference from some imagined, other world. As
long as the younger boy had been caught up in the traditional world of the
village, the turban reflected his immersion in and commitment to the village
and its culture. For a sixteen-year-old, which is about the age of the younger
boy, the turban would have symbolized the essence of his identity and his
acceptance into the ranks of adult men. If someone back in the village had
knocked it off his head in an argument, the boy would probably have taken
it as a serious insult that had to be avenged. On the streets of Mazar-i Sharif,
however, the turban suddenly represented something else—something in
his present condition that he would have jettisoned if he could.

In his imagination, or so I presume, the boy stood on the threshold of a
new and inviting world that he had come to perceive as embodying his own
future existence. But this new world was as yet dimly perceived and could
only stir in him—besides a fierce desire to be part of it—an equally intense
consciousness of his own inadequacy. In and of itself, the gesture of publicly
removing a turban would seem to reflect a consciousness that imagined itself
as something other than what it was, only a moment before, and something
other than what it had always reckoned itself to be. It was, in some sense, a
hopeful gesture of faith in, or submission to, a possible future; but it was also,
and more tellingly, a condemnation—or at least a diminution or relativiza-
tion—of society as it had been known and what it represented.

When I first saw *Naim and Jabar,* I remember being more impressed by
the exotic beauty of the Afghan mountain landscape of the boys' village
than by the situation of the two boys themselves. At the time, I didn't know

the political controversies that seethed below the surface in Kabul, much less the maelstrom toward which Afghanistan was headed. Nor had I read Thomas's account of his trip to Afghanistan, and so I couldn't have recognized the possibility that the scene in *Naim and Jabar* completed an arc begun in Kabul fifty-some years earlier—from a king remaking his summer palace in the image of a Hollywood film to a poor boy pocketing his turban in order to fit into his own humble version of the modern imaginary. For Amir Amanullah, clothing was a symbolic manifestation of a nation's progress. For the young boy in *Naim and Jabar*, it would seem to have the related significance of "fitting in" and "looking the part" for which he too was auditioning. Looking back, I imagine that the Afghan students who sat in my classroom in their second-hand Western clothes must have felt a similar concern, but at the time I didn't make the connection between the boys in the film and the students I encountered every day at the school.

Only much later, when I rented the film to show a classroom of American college students what Afghanistan was like before the revolution, did I focus on the scene with the turban and come to reflect on the fact that many of those Afghan students I taught a long time ago must have experienced moments like the one in the film when they too had to make a decision between one world and another. Nor did I fully grasp until seeing the film a decade later that it was boys like Naim and Jabar, as well as my own English-language students, who provided the bulk of the membership of both the Marxist and radical Islamic parties that plunged Afghanistan into its quarter century of crisis. During my first stay in Afghanistan, in the 1970s, there were political rumblings to be sure, but I and most of the Westerners of my acquaintance were blissfully unaware of how deep the discontent was.

Everywhere one went in Kabul in the mid-seventies, one saw photographs of the bald and seemingly benign countenance of the Afghan ruler, President Muhammad Daud, who appeared very much in charge. Few of the people I spoke with doubted the country's basic stability, and only much later did we discover that beneath the apparent calm, leftist and Islamic political parties were both feverishly making plans to overthrow the government. As a newcomer to Afghanistan, I had no way to know the extent of the discord in the country, although two events might have provided clues if only I had been able to see them clearly. The first occurred shortly after my arrival in Kabul; Islamic militants belonging to the Muslim Youth Organization (Sazman-i Jawanan-i Musulman) staged armed uprisings in a number of provinces. The government had little trouble suppressing these attacks, and press reports indicated only that there had been local disturbances. They did not advertise the organized and political nature of these

attacks. I don't recall whether I read any press accounts or spoke with anyone about the incidents; however, I do remember that I had been planning
to take a trip to the north of the country but was prevented from doing so
when the main road crossing the Hindu Kush was closed.

My second hint as to the scope of dissatisfaction in the country came the
following October, when I finally made it to the north during an extended
school vacation commemorating the end of the month of fasting. I traveled
by bus to Mazar-i Sharif, then caught another local public van to the nearby
town of Balkh, where I arrived close to dark. I found a hotel and was able to
rouse the manager, but he soon made it clear to me that he didn't want me
to stay and indicated that I should return to Mazar immediately, that there
were thieves around who would steal my possessions and possibly slit my
throat. I couldn't tell whether the threats were real. They might have been,
but I suspected that he just didn't want to be bothered having to deal with a
visitor during the upcoming holiday. I was the only guest at the hotel and,
as far as I could tell when walking around, the only foreigner in the city.
That night at dinner in a local restaurant a young man a few years older
than myself, with a scrawny beard and thinning hair, sat down at my table
and started a conversation. I was initially suspicious of the man's friendli-
ness, particularly when he asked me to accompany him back to his residence.
The hotel manager's warnings were still with me, but I was lonely and
decided to go anyway. He lived by himself in a small rented room, amid a
clutter of books and papers. He split open a melon, which we savored
between cigarettes and cups of tea. He called himself "Aqcha Poor," the son
of Aqcha, which was the town a few hours west of Balkh where he was
raised, and I learned that he was working as an agricultural extension agent,
although it was clear that what he really enjoyed doing was reading in his
room, which he referred to as his "library." I spent most of the next two
days with Aqcha Poor, visiting friends of his in villages outside Balkh, eating sumptuous meals of rice pilau, kebabs, and dumplings, and all the while
hearing about his life as a young man.

Coming from a village family without wealth or influence, Aqcha Poor
had little money and poor prospects for the future. Like most high school
and university graduates of that era, he was among the first in his family to
go to a nonreligious school, and he had high hopes not only for himself and
his own career but also for what he might do for his country. Afghanistan
in the mid-seventies was awash in development assistance coming from the
West and the Soviet bloc. But few of those funds were making their way to
the local level, and most educated Afghans were finding their life prospects
little improved by the presence of foreign agencies. Corruption was ram-

pant. Most of those who were lucky enough to secure positions in the government found both that their jobs paid so poorly they still had to live at home or in small apartments and that their salaries were so insufficient they could not even consider getting married until they were well into their thirties. This was Aqcha Poor's situation, which he ended up trying to explain to me through a Persian song that was then popular:

> On the high mountain, a stalk of wheat
> *sar-i koh-i beland, yak dana gandom.*
> I am a poor laborer in a foreign land.
> *gharibi mekonom ba mulki mardom.*
> Working, working, I have grown tired.
> *gharibi karda karda khwar gashtam.*
> To both friends and enemies, I have become poison.
> *ba pesh-i dost o dushman zar gashtom.*

The song was one of several that Aqcha Poor taught me, and all conveyed the same despondence. In some respects, they were like the songs of another man from Balkh who sang of dispossession—Jalaluddin Rumi, or, as he is known to Afghans, Jalaluddin Balkhi. Rumi's recurring lament centers on his separation from the Beloved, and Westerners sometimes imagine that he is writing about a human lover. But it is God and the promise of eventual reunification with the Divine that give the poet the strength to continue his labors on earth. Aqcha Poor's lamentations, while they conveyed the same sadness, were more earthbound, and it did not appear to me at the time that he saw any end to or mystical significance in his present circumstances. Perhaps that too was one of the unintended legacies of schooling. Perhaps education not only promised more than it could deliver but also took away things that could never be recaptured.

As I look back on him now, it strikes me that Aqcha Poor had more in common with Naim and Jabar than I recognized at the time. Naim and Jabar, after all, stood on the threshold of a new life they imagined for themselves and for which they were willing to leave behind all that they had previously known. Aqcha Poor was on the other side of the divide. He had been accepted to schools and completed his education and found a job with the government, accomplishing what the younger boys were hoping for themselves. But instead of giving him the sort of responsibility and prestige he had imagined, the job only made him feel poorer than ever and less appreciated. Underpaid, with few resources to draw on and limited professional and personal prospects, Aqcha Poor found himself identifying with itinerant laborers who journeyed to Pakistan and other foreign countries to earn a living wage. This is not what he had envisioned would happen when he started school, and he was not alone in his disappointment. Some expressed their sadness and disillusionment the way Aqcha Poor did—through poetry. But others chose different means, the most important of which was joining political parties that promised to transform the system and make those presently powerless the new masters of the nation's destiny.

I don't know what happened to Aqcha Poor after our meeting. I don't know whether he became involved on one side or another of the conflict that was about to embroil Afghanistan, and I also don't know whether the song Aqcha Poor sang so passionately for me foretold his own fate of becoming a refugee in a foreign land like millions of Afghans in the coming years. Nor, finally, do I have any idea whether he has so far survived the conflagration and is alive today. I knew Aqcha Poor for only a few days, but, looking back on this man who was for a brief time my friend, I see him as representative of a generation of Afghans who, even before the war had started, despaired for their country and themselves, even as they continued to hope that modernity would lift them up.

Once during my short visit, Aqcha Poor asked me what I hoped to do with my life, and I told him that I wanted to be a writer. He replied, "Then you should write a book about me." And I faithlessly promised him that I would. But in a sense I honor that promise here, for if this book is not about Aqcha Poor himself, it is about his kindred, particularly those who decided that they would shape Afghanistan's promise to their own purpose. Aqcha Poor, I suspect, did not become actively involved in political activities. His temperament seemed more that of a poet than a politician, but many others of a more active nature were determined to convert their unhappiness with Afghanistan's situation into political change. These were the ones who were caught up in the ideological currents that came rushing through Afghanistan from abroad in the 1970s. Like Aqcha Poor, they felt the pull of the new, as well as the disillusionment that accompanied the realization that modernity meant mostly more corruption and a soul-dissolving break with the past. This book is about a few of the people who shaped the response to the place that Afghanistan had become—people who tried to implement their own visions of progress. At the same time, the book is also about the failure of these men and of the visions they had for their country, a failure that would lead to the total eclipse of the modernist dream of change.

LIFE HISTORIES OF REVOLUTION

Western attempts to understand Afghans and Afghanistan since the onset of the war in 1978 have centered largely on stereotypes and personifications.

Just as Thomas tried to fit the country into the preconceptions of his day, Western writers—Americans in particular—have resorted to modes of representation that make the complexity of the people and place simpler to comprehend. In the early days of the conflict, Afghans were widely portrayed as "freedom fighters"—twentieth-century throwbacks to Ethan Allen and the Green Mountain Boys, transplanted to the Hindu Kush. This was especially the case after the Soviet invasion in 1979, when Afghans were perceived as standing up single-handedly to a superpower. Vietnam still rankled in the United States, and the Afghans seemed to want nothing from that superpower other than the barest military necessities. Democrats and Republicans alike could support this cause, as theatrically illustrated first by Zbigniew Brezhinski, President Jimmy Carter's national security advisor, firing an AK-47 into Afghanistan from the Khyber Pass and later by President Ronald Reagan parleying in the White House with a group of bearded mujahidin leaders.

All of this cozying up to men in turbans ended abruptly after the Soviet withdrawal from Afghanistan in 1989. The first U.S. response to this event was massive indifference—Afghanistan ceased to matter, at least to non-Afghans. It simply fell off the radar screen of international attention. Indifference eventually gave way to another round of intense interest, this time precipitated by the World Trade Center bombing in New York City and the news that several of those arrested for the attack had fought with the resistance forces in Afghanistan. Investigative reports into the bombing hinted at vast conspiracies involving mosques in the outer boroughs of New York City, immigrant taxi drivers, and a blind cleric named Abdur Rahman, who appeared to have incited the bombers to declare jihad against the United States itself. The effect of this second wave of attention was to change people's minds about who it was the United States had been supporting and what those bearded men really wanted. Now, instead of being viewed as "freedom fighters," Afghans came to be thought of as terrorists, and Afghanistan took its place beside Syria, Libya, and Iran as a pariah state beyond the pale of President George H. W. Bush's much heralded "new world order."

Afghanistan's association with terrorism was not entirely unwarranted. And it was not simply a Western concern, for many of the Islamic militants who committed acts of terror in Algeria, Egypt, and other Middle Eastern nations received their basic training in Afghanistan and were often referred to in these countries as "Afghanis." Then, too, there was Osama bin Laden, who maintained a base in Afghanistan and who may or may not have financed the embassy bombings in East Africa in 1998 and the attack on the

U.S. Navy destroyer *Cole* in 2000. But one nuance that was generally ignored was that while an Afghan connection was often referred to in press accounts, few Afghans were implicated in these acts of violence. Those responsible, for the most part, were Arabs, and while many of these Arabs fought in Afghanistan, they were by and large uninvited guests. Afghans didn't ask these people to join their battle. They came for their own reasons, mostly kept to themselves while they were there, and went about their own projects after they left. Afghanistan's role was principally to provide a space beyond governmental control where ideologues could transform themselves into battle-hardened Muslim warriors.

Unbidden or not, Afghanistan's helpmates fixed the public's perception of Afghans, a perception that was amplified by news reports about the Taliban government, which installed itself in power in 1996. Many accounts in the media described how the regime forced women to leave schools and jobs to return to the veil and domestic seclusion, and frequent stories related how the government invited the citizenry, for their moral edification, to witness the surgical removal of the hands of thieves, the stoning of adulterers, and the toppling of brick walls onto the backs of sodomites. While international terrorism and the Taliban excesses were the focus of news and commentary on Afghanistan, more scarce were attempts to understand what life was like in Afghanistan in this protracted period of conflict and how the situation evolved. In their focus on the sensational and grotesque, the media led the public to assume, in essence, that "since all we ever hear about is violence, this must just be the way Afghans really are, the way they have always been, and the way they will continue to be."

The goal of this book is to provide a nuanced understanding of the war in Afghanistan by presenting the life stories of three Afghan leaders who played important roles at key junctures in the Afghan conflict. Because the impression of Afghanistan in the West has centered around a series of sensationalized stereotypes, my objective is to provide an alternative set of biographical representations that provide a sense of how leaders viewed themselves and the conflict they were involved in at different stages and how they attempted to mediate the longstanding problem of realizing present opportunities without abandoning the past.

The biographical framework employed here follows a model developed in my earlier book, *Heroes of the Age: Moral Fault Lines on the Afghan Frontier*, which was also focused on three approximately contemporary men from the turn of the century—Sultan Muhammad Khan, a tribal chief; the Mulla of Hadda, an Islamic mystic, scholar, and political leader; and Amir Abdur Rahman Khan, the grandfather of Amanullah and the ruler of

the Kingdom of Afghanistan from 1880 to 1901. I used the
to personify the traditional moral imperatives of honor, I
governance, and I argued that the development of a cohe
political culture was impeded throughout the century just pa
istence of these three competitive and contentious spheres of belief and
practice. Here again, I look at the lives of three men—this time individuals
who played important roles in the present conflict and who personify contemporary transformations in Afghan understandings of honor, Islam, and
state rule as they developed in and through the critical first years after the
revolution of 1978.

Contemporary understandings of honor, Islam, and rule bear similarities
to the forms that prevailed at the turn of the previous century, but they have
also changed in many ways, largely as a result of the ideological currents that
have swept into Afghanistan from abroad periodically since the time of King
Amanullah. One of the leaders whose life is examined in this book—Nur
Muhammad Taraki, the founder of the Marxist People's Democratic Party of
Afghanistan—played a pivotal role in initiating the revolutionary political
culture. The other two—Samiullah Safi, who was a leader of one of the first
tribal uprisings against the Marxist regime, and Qazi Muhammad Amin, the
deputy amir of the Hizb-i Islami party, which, along with several other
Islamic political parties, took control of the antigovernment uprisings and
effectively "Islamicized" the resistance—both came of age during the tumul-
tuous period of the late 1960s and early 1970s.

As befits the present age, the figures at the center of this book cannot be
called heroes—at least not in the sense that I used the term to describe the
men whose lives I examined in my earlier book. These men all played pivotal roles at crucial stages of the current conflict, but they are not larger-
than-life figures the way Sultan Muhammad Khan, Amir Abdur Rahman,
and the Mulla of Hadda were. They are instead men in-between who, as
much as they helped shape the events of their time, also got caught up in
and eventually pulled down in the backwash of those events. The men
whose lives are described and interpreted in this book failed in their purposes. The revolution, uprising, and jihad that they separately supported all
ultimately collapsed. But it is because of this failure that I find their stories
useful to tell, for ultimately the story of the war in Afghanistan is not the
story of success, despite the momentous achievement of defeating and helping to topple a global superpower. It is rather the story of a series of ill-con-
ceived, though fateful, attempts to define what Afghanistan stood for and to
make Afghanistan cohere as a nation in ways different from the ways it had
cohered in the past.

One reason I am particularly interested in the stories of Safi and Qazi Amin is that they both have a connection to the "heroes" of my previous book: Safi is the youngest son of the tribal chief Sultan Muhammad Khan, and Qazi Amin's father was a cleric and disciple of one of the Mulla of Hadda's principal deputies. These connections are significant because they help contextualize changes that occurred in tribal culture and in the social universe of Islam both prior to and since the Marxist revolution. As university students during the period of political turmoil in the 1960s and 1970s, Safi and Qazi Amin became involved in radical reform movements, but both also kept a foot in the world of their fathers, which for Safi was his tribal homeland in the Pech Valley and for Qazi Amin was the universe of religious schools. For these two men, the political controversies they became enmeshed in had to do partly with how to bring about the proper sort of reform and partly with how to salvage aspects of tradition. Safi and Qazi Amin would have disagreed on what beliefs and practices were worth saving, but they shared the quality of respecting features of their patrimony that many of their more radical peers would have happily destroyed.

For his part, Taraki does not have any direct connection to Abdur Rahman Khan, other than the distinction of being responsible for eradicating the last links to the old amir's lineage. However, his position as head of state forced another connection on him—that of having, in the words of Lord Curzon, "to ride the wild Afghan steed."[5] Which is to say, Taraki had not only to dominate; he had also to persuade, framing his leadership in ways that would be meaningful to the people he ruled, just as Abdur Rahman and all successful rulers have had to do. The future of the Marxist revolution thus hinged largely on the ability of Taraki and his comrades to convince the Afghan people that his socialism meshed with their cultural and religious values. As with Safi and Qazi Amin, the key to success lay in balancing reform with tradition, and his ambitions, like theirs, ultimately foundered on his inability to effect this balance.

Just as one of the lenses I employ for looking at the Afghan conflict is the agency of these particular men and how it differed from that of those who preceded them, I am also concerned with the events—more particularly the underlying structure of events—that they participated in and that they were finally unable to control. In the case of Taraki, those events principally were the conflicts within his own ruling party that led to his removal from power (discussed in Chapter Three). For Safi, they were internal failings within the tribal group and external subversion by Islamic leaders within his home area, which undermined his leadership and the viability of his tribe as a political force in the resistance (discussed in Chapter Five). With

Qazi Amin, the events were driven by the incompatibility between the radical Islamic vision of his group and the views of the other party leaders, which eventually opened the way for an alternative, and far more conservative, Islamic movement to come into being (discussed in Chapter Eight). This movement culminated in the transformation of the Taliban student militia, which took control of most of Afghanistan, including the capital of Kabul, in 1996, into the Islamic Emirate of Afghanistan.

Retrospectively, it is evident that ruptures in the resistance (between tribes and parties and among the parties) that developed in the immediate aftermath of the Marxist revolution and Soviet invasion created the conditions for the later triumph of the Taliban. These ruptures are the focus of this book and of the lives that are documented here. In many ways, the cruelest irony of the conflict is that the struggles of the early years should have resulted in the ascendance of the conservative Taliban government, for the three men whose lives I examine in this book were all committed in different ways to the ideal of progress—the opposite of what the Taliban have come to represent. All three were products of the Afghan educational system and were offended by what they saw as the backwardness of traditional society and committed to the ideal of bringing economic and social justice to the people of Afghanistan. At the same time, however, these men were cut off from those they sought to lead and had a limited or distorted conception of what the people wanted and how best to enlist their support.

This was especially true of two of these men—Taraki and Qazi Amin—who were leaders of political organizations that insisted that people's first loyalties should be to the party itself, which held the authentic hope for the future. Acquiring power for the party became for both sides more important than the ideals the parties stood for, and this focus, over time, became an obsession that ultimately cost them the trust of the people. This sadly has been the legacy of social reform in Afghanistan—a legacy that began with the social experiments of Amanullah in the 1920s and that finally resulted seventy years later in the advent of the Taliban regime, whose overriding ambition is to return the country to an imagined state of original grace before the coming of secular education and other imported evils from beyond Islam's borders.

Part I

THE SAUR REVOLUTION

2 Lives of the Party

Between April 1978, when the government of Nur Muhammad Taraki took office, and December 1979, when the Soviet Union took control of the Afghan government, a bold attempt was made to transform the Afghan nation into a different kind of social and political entity. Those responsible for this transformation envisioned the establishment of a socialist nation in which class oppression would be wiped out and the productive energies of the poor mobilized. Spearheading the new Afghan state would be the People's Democratic Party of Afghanistan (PDPA), which was envisioned as a vehicle for incorporating into the governing structure those previously excluded from power: low-ranking military officers and bureaucrats, students, and women.[1] After proper training and indoctrination in the principles of scientific socialism, cadres would go to the countryside to bring literacy to the people and, with literacy, an awareness of the economic and social conditions that consigned the poor to lives of brutal poverty and limited the economic and social development of the nation. There is little doubt that Taraki, Hafizullah Amin, and other leaders of the PDPA saw April 27, 1978, as the dawning of a new era, but the era that began was one of violence and discord rather than of revolutionary promise. Those who flocked to the party standard were far fewer in number than the tens of thousands who took up arms against the regime and the millions who chose exile in Pakistan and Iran over life in the new socialist paradise.

During the early 1980s, many observers came forward to offer their explanations as to why the Marxist revolution failed in Afghanistan. Opponents of the regime—especially the exile resistance parties headquartered in Peshawar—argued that the people saw through the regime's propaganda and raised the banner of *jihad* (struggle in the path of Allah) to preserve Islam and dislodge the infidel usurpers from power. Supporters of the regime blamed the popular backlash on the machinations of the traditional elite—members of the royal family, landowners, and religious clerics—who played on the "superstitions and prejudices" of the people in order to misrepresent the party's real intentions.[2] After the Soviet invasion in December 1979, which installed Babrak Karmal in power, Soviet analysts refocused their criticisms on the deposed leadership, especially former Prime Minister Hafizullah Amin, who was depicted as being an opportunistic despot willing to pervert the principles of scientific socialism in order to preserve his own power.

My examination of the Marxist revolution focuses on the first eighteen months—between the revolution of April 27, 1978, and the assassination of Taraki by his former disciple and successor, Hafizullah Amin, in October 1979. This first eighteen months constituted the crucial historical moment during which the revolution was still winnable. Taraki was the "father" of the revolution and its most visible symbol, and his death marked the demise of its promise, a demise that was fully signaled two months later when the Soviet Union invaded and transformed Afghanistan into an occupied country. The approach I take in understanding the failure of the Marxist revolution is different from that of other commentators on this period; it has two components, the first of which has to do with how I depict the regime. Thus, rather than trying to characterize the regime in generalities and from a distance, I use the government's own statements, published in newspapers and broadcast over Radio Afghanistan, to establish how its leaders viewed themselves, their relation to the people, their enemies, and their place in Afghan history. In keeping with this approach, the organization of the two chapters in this section is not chronological but thematic; they focus on such matters as the characterization of the revolution, the persona of the leader, the depiction of the party and of the people, and the portrayal of the regime's enemies.

The second feature of my analysis is my concern with understanding the regime in relation to traditional ideas of governance that held sway in Afghanistan. To date, most examinations of the revolutionary period have been undertaken through the lens of one or another imported ideology (and I view the declarations of the exile Islamic political parties as only slightly less "foreign" than any of the others). In this chapter, I use as my point of reference the principles of governance set forth by Amir Abdur Rahman Khan in the last part of the nineteenth century and subsequent reworkings of those principles, especially during an earlier period of revolutionary upheaval under Amir Amanullah Khan in the 1920s. Hated by many as a tyrant, Abdur Rahman nevertheless forged the basis of governance in

Afghanistan and the understandings that people have ret[
ral and proper duties, role, and comportment of its leaders
vides an illuminating secondary point of reference for this
he anticipated many of the reforms that the Marxists woul[
in place, though he did so from his position as a member o[
ily. The transformations that he sought to bring about before his overthrow
in 1929 were in many respects forerunners of those of the Marxists and
were particularly revealing of the problems they later encountered.

FROM COUP D'ÉTAT TO REVOLUTION

> Dream Comes True—Thousands Throng Arg
>
> KABUL, May 2 (Bakhtar).—Tens of thousands of our compatriots, old,
> young, women, men and children yesterday and today visited the Arg
> and Delkusha Palace and other edifices there which have been partly
> damaged due to ambitious resistance of the last link of despotic Naderi
> family, Mohammad Daoud. . . .
>
> The patriotic citizens of the country while looking at the majestic
> palaces and establishments inside the Arg talked to each other about
> tyranny, revelry and ambition of corrupt Naderi family who were using
> glamorous palaces for their treacherous deeds, and expressed apprecia-
> tion to the valiants who victoriously brought down the tower of
> tyranny and despotism.[3]

The events of the 7th of Saur, 1357 (April 27, 1978), soon came to be
referred to by the Marxist regime as "The Glorious Saur Revolution." In
truth, these events are more accurately described as a military coup d'état in
that the overthrow of the government of President Muhammad Daud was
engineered by a few thousand military officers under the instructions of the
outlawed People's Democratic Party of Afghanistan. President Daud had
once been allied with the PDPA, and with the party's help he had succeeded
in orchestrating his own coup d'état against his cousin, King Zahir Shah, in
1973. But, after taking power, Daud had gradually moved away from his
former Marxist allies and two days before the April 27th coup had struck
against them, ordering that both Taraki and his deputy, Hafizullah Amin, be
thrown in prison.

The officers in charge of the arrest had not done their job however. They
had allowed Amin to remain under house arrest for a number of hours prior
to taking him into custody, and during this time Amin had used his son as
a messenger to contact military officers and to set in motion the operation

at they had been preparing for and fantasizing about for years. The following morning, tanks moved into position at strategic installations and intersections throughout the capital, while jet fighters strafed the presidential palace where Daud, his family, and principal advisors were holed up. Daud's republican regime, which had ruled with an authoritarian severity for the preceding five years, collapsed with surprising swiftness. Other military units that might have come to the president's aid hesitated in their confusion or were delayed by officers sympathetic to or bullied by the coup organizers. Precious time was lost, and Daud and his entourage were killed in a bloody shootout that effectively beheaded the government and left it unable to respond to the crisis.

At first, the identity of the new regime was masked. Military officers made the first announcements, and the Marxist orientation of the coup plotters was concealed. This caution continued for several days until it was finally revealed that the man in charge of the newly instituted Revolutionary Council was Taraki. Educated Afghans at least knew of Taraki from his years as a publisher and writer for various leftist newspapers, most notably the *Khalq* (Masses), which was the organ of the Soviet-leaning PDPA during the late 1960s, when political parties were briefly allowed to operate in the open. The first and most crucial task of this new regime was to make good on its "revolution" by rallying people to the cause. Taraki and his party supporters (known as "Khalqis") knew full well that they had a negligible base of support outside the military. From the time that Daud had begun to turn against them, their principal strategy—the strategy that provided such ample and unexpected rewards—was to follow a "shortcut" to power, as Taraki himself admitted in a press conference on August 16:

> There were many ways for the deliverance of the people of Afghanistan among which was the classic one based on the ideology of the workers and peasant class. This classic path was a long one. . . . This is the scientific way and we have struggled on the basis of this ideology and this is the basic principle. But we thought to find a short way which could change the destiny of the people of Afghanistan. Fortunately we found this short way in the fact that first of all a party should be founded and through this party work should be done to this effect. . . . We were able to penetrate in the army and give political and class consciousness to the sons of the people and get them organized on party basis.[4]

The success of the coup d'état of April 27, 1978, brought with it the need for the PDPA government to justify its actions, especially its violent killing of President Daud and his family. The basis of this justification was "the historic crimes of the Naderi dynasty," which had ruled Afghanistan since

1930, when Nadir Khan, a distant cousin of the former king Amanullah Khan, seized power from the former bandit known as Bacha-i Saqao, who had forced Amanullah's abdication. Nadir qualified for PDPA scorn because of his opposition to the reform program of Amanullah and for having received British assistance in mounting his campaign to overthrow Bacha-i Saqao.[5] In Khalqi parlance,

> [Nadir,] with the help of blackguards of colonialism and under their leadership, . . . gathered around himself all traitors and intrigued against independence seekers and true and alert sons of the people of Afghanistan with the assistance of the very same masters, and as he assumed the throne, he indulged in creation of division among the people. He wrenched from the people their freedom, their rights and their bread, and put the men of the valleys and forces of the motherland in stifling chains.[6]

The most effective rallying cry in Afghanistan since the mid-nineteenth century had been the threat of British imperialism, and the Khalqis mined that vein by associating Nadir with the British. In their vision of history, Nadir was the British lackey who ousted Amanullah (the fact that it was Bacha-i Saqao whom Nadir overthrew rather than Amanullah is elided in the Khalqi account), thereby "undoing the good he had done and throwing dear Afghanistan into the dark labyrinth of oppression and misery."[7] One of the consistent themes that the Khalqis returned to was the use of religion by agents of imperialism—"Muslim-looking *farangis*" (foreigners) as they were often called—who veiled themselves "under the guise of Islam." In their interpretation of history, religion had consistently been used as a disguise that allowed outsiders to interfere in Afghan affairs.

Given his commitment to opening up the political process and introducing social reform, Amanullah would seem a natural ancestral figure for the PDPA to hold up for veneration, but because of his failure to implement these reforms, his having been a member of the royal family, and the general hostility to his memory still felt by many Afghans, Amanullah was not much commemorated by the new regime, and connections between his past and their present were not widely commented on. Rather, the government focused its attention on the Naderi dynasty, which replaced Amanullah, especially the last surviving member of that dynasty, whom they had deposed—Muhammad Daud. Daud had long been despised by many Afghans, particularly tribal Pakhtuns, for his harsh suppression of groups that had protested against government policy. Daud's anti-insurgency activities had been carried out during his younger days as a military officer and provincial governor, but Afghans have long memories for such offenses, and the regime tried to play on this animosity as a basis for pop-

ular support. "Now the Naderi dynasty and its last hangman representative
is no more, history is on the path of wishes and will of the noble nation of
Afghanistan. We shall tell constantly stories of high handedness and decay
of the Naderi dynasty to the brave people and the whole humanity. Long
live the great nation of Afghanistan and 'Long live the heroic army of the
country.'"[8]

When it first took power, the PDPA had soft-pedaled its Marxist orientation, but by the end of its first summer, the regime began to be more outspoken in its pronouncements, gradually dropping hints of its leftist orientation in its written declarations and providing even more visible indications
in the symbols of power it adopted. The most dramatic of these indications
was undoubtedly the display on October 19 of an all-red flag that resembled
the flags of the Soviet Central Asian republics. As the majority of Afghans
are illiterate, this symbol was more revealing of the government's direction
than anything published in the press, but at this stage the government
seemed confident that it could weather any adverse consequences of admitting its alignment with the Soviet Union and its adherence to Soviet-style
Marxism. Thus, on November 7, in honor of the anniversary of the October
Revolution, the *Kabul Times* published photographs of Lenin and Leonid
Brezhnev, and the next day a front-page headline quoted Hafizullah Amin
to the effect that the "Saur Revolution is continuation of Great October
Revolution."

Afghan leaders were in fact eager to draw connections to the Bolshevik
revolution because they saw their own revolution as the direct lineal
descendant of that earlier event, while also believing that the social exigencies of the Afghan situation made their own Saur Revolution uniquely valuable as a model for the rest of the world. This sentiment is evidenced in a
long speech by then–Deputy Prime Minister Amin delivered in 1978 at the
opening ceremonies of the Afghan Academy of Science.[9] The speech is
mostly a long-winded description of elementary Marxist theory, with myriad references to "infrastructures" and "superstructures" and "scientific
sociology," but it also contains a lengthy exegesis of how the PDPA envisioned Afghan society and why the Afghan experience could be considered
both the proud successor to the October Revolution and a unique event in
the annals of Marxist revolutionary struggles.

Thus, alone among all the world proletarian revolutions, "it was the great
Saur Revolution which transferred, like the great October Revolution, the
political power directly from the exploiters to the working class." What
made the Saur Revolution unique and gave it a distinction greater even than
that of the October Revolution was that "the great Saur Revolution for the

first time in the world triumphed under the feudal conditions when the feudal lords and peasants constituted its basic classes":

> In the great Saur Revolution, in spite of the fact that it triumphed according to the general and particular laws of the epoch-making working class ideology, the army played a major proletarian role that is the powerful center of the victorious revolution. The army, as a result of the regular work of PDPA, had been transformed into Khalqi forces equipped with the scientific working class ideology and organised through the People's Democratic Party of Afghanistan, the vanguard of the working class of the country.

Marx had predicted that a true proletarian revolution could occur only in a society where capitalism had triumphed and the working class had been thoroughly beaten down, and Lenin himself had despaired of mobilizing a revolutionary movement among the Central Asian peasant peoples. But, where Marx and Lenin had failed, the PDPA had triumphed by using the military as a "shortcut" to revolution.

On one level, Amin's speech can be seen as a glorification of what was in reality a necessity. Rather than being a stroke of strategic brilliance, the choice of the military as the avenue by which to seize power was an all-too-conventional one in the Middle East and South Asia, and one mandated in this instance by the fact that the other segments of the society with a proven capacity for military adventure—namely, the tribes—were generally opposed to parties of all ideological persuasions. Therefore, the PDPA's employment of the military was somewhat unusual merely because it had been able to mobilize this group as effectively as it had through ideological means. Since the recruitment of military officers had been Amin's responsibility, his glorification of this aspect of PDPA history can also be seen as an act of self-congratulation. Still in the thrall of his unexpected success, Amin glorified the military option as a stroke of genius that qualified the Saur Revolution—and he himself—for a special place in the Marxist pantheon.

In seeking reasons for the eventual failure of the Saur Revolution, one should keep the attitude exemplified in Amin's speech in mind, for it demonstrates the kind of hubris that led the party to believe in the historical inevitability of the process of revolutionary transformation it had set in motion. The word Afghans use (in both Dari Persian and Pakhtu) for hubris is *kibr*. A man who acts beyond his station or who behaves in a way that indicates that he seeks merely to benefit himself while ignoring the precepts of society will be accused of "doing kibr," or being excessively proud (*gharur*). Taraki and Amin are thought by many Afghans to have committed precisely this sin of acting beyond their rank and claiming a greatness for themselves that others were not prepared to bestow. The fate of such overweening men, Afghans will tell you, is usually disastrous for themselves and others, for their arrogance not only creates resentment in those around them but also makes them incautious. More than anyone else, the man who risks all on a bold gamble, as Taraki and Amin undoubtedly had done, must be most prudent and circumspect. The PDPA leadership, however, had forgotten or never learned this folk wisdom, and their self-absorption caused them to become ultimately more concerned with theoretically defined class relations than with the actual social relations that existed on the ground.[10]

A TRUE SON OF THE SOIL

> One may be able to introduce a certain person with a few words or phrases. But the fact is that one should deal with each person with as much details as his characteristics and qualities call for.
>
> The reason is there exist in human societies such personalities that a few words or phrases don't do any justice to introduce. They may need thick volumes to deal only with their thoughts.
>
> The True Son of the People, the Chief Commander of the Great Saur Revolution, the General Secretary of the Central Committee of the People's Democratic Party of Afghanistan, the President of the Revolutionary Council and Prime Minister, Comrade Noor Mohammad Taraki, is one of those prominent world figures who needs a few words or phrases for his descriptive title only. One has to compile volumes to introduce his formidable personality in due details.[11]

On October 30, 1978, the Political Department of the People's Armed Forces published the first extensive biography of Taraki. The biography is an interesting document that provides an insight into not only who Taraki was but also how he and the party thought their leader should be depicted. Many educated Afghans living in Kabul in the 1960s and 1970s knew who Taraki was, at least by reputation, but even in Kabul few knew much about the man. The name "Taraki" told them that his ancestors were from the Taraki tribe, a branch of the Ghilzai confederacy, which meant that he was in all likelihood a native Pakhtu speaker and that his family was probably originally from Ghazni Province, south of Kabul. But this was all most people knew or could infer since Taraki was unknown outside a small circle of educated Afghans in the capital; the fact that so little was known about the man who would be the ruler was a significant matter in a society where family background mattered a great deal.

Americans may look to the myth of the self-made man as justification for forgetting the past and starting afresh, and they have shown themselves willing to vote into office men like Bill Clinton who come from dysfunctional families of little means and less inherited prestige. However, in Afghanistan, especially among Afghan Pakhtuns, who make up the majority of the population, kinship is inescapable and vitally important in reckoning who a man is and where he properly belongs. The most profound innovation introduced by the PDPA was not in the area of land reform or women's rights. Amir Amanullah, President Daud, and other leaders had begun chipping away at these impediments to change, and the PDPA's plan—had it succeeded—would have sped up a process that other regimes had initiated. Far more radical for Afghan society was the notion that kinship didn't matter, that literally anyone could lead the nation.

One sees this idea made flesh in the person of Taraki, who—according to his official biography—was born in the aptly named Sur Kelaye (Red Village) in Ghazni Province in July 1917 to "a poor semi-peasant, semi-shepherd family." At the age of five, Taraki was hired by a widow to run her errands and look after her house; however, he did not stay in this position long, as his father wanted his son to become literate so that one day he might earn his living as a scribe. Life was never easy in this household. Securing sufficient food for the family was an uncertain proposition because of both poverty and the chicanery of others: "Comrade Taraki's father was always bothered by problems arising in connection with his precarious mode of living. The great and back-breaking difficulties that he had confronted as a peasant cum shepherd and destitute childhood in relation to the oppressing feudal lords and crafty tribal chieftains were indeed highly taxing to him." However, Taraki's father "suffered silently and consoled himself with the signs of brilliance he had traced in his prodigious son. The thought that one day he would see his son in such a movement triumphantly marching among the hard-working intelligentsia, serving the country, raised high hopes in his heart."

As the story progresses, we discover that there was no noble ancestor dispossessed of his rightful inheritance, no hint that the boy who would be president had any prior claim to that title. The only nobility here is the nobility of poverty and toil, which Afghans had never before seen exalted and treated as worthy of praise. In Afghan culture, nobility is inherited and can only rarely be forged through experience. As Shahmund, an elder of the Mohmand tribe described it to me, " 'The sword of real iron cuts [*tura pa asil ghutsa kawi*].' For example, Faiz Gul is the brother of Haji Reza Khan. Since Faiz Gul is a good-for-nothing, his son is just like him. His grandson is also nothing. Since Haji Reza Khan is a good man, his sons are also like him. His grandsons are also like him, and maybe his grandsons' sons will be even better than him."[12] Belief in the inherited nature of nobility is also the traditional pillar of Afghan political culture. With the lone exception of Bacha-i Saqao, who ruled forlornly for a year in 1929–1930, all the rulers of Afghanistan from 1747 until 1978 had come from the Durrani tribe. Within that tribe, there were vicious battles for the throne, but no one effectively challenged the right of this tribe to rule until the Saur Revolution.

Justification for the tribe's status was succinctly expressed by Abdur Rahman in a proclamation to his people; at the beginning he notes that "everyone's share [nasib] is determined by God on the basis of his merit, circumstances, and capabilities. . . . Each one stands in his own place and position, and hence you people should be grateful to God and to the king." The proper attitude of every subject should be gratitude, for it is God who has determined one's position in life:

> In whatever rank and position you are and wherever you stand look downward to know how many people are lower than you. When you look downward and see your high rank and position you will receive three blessings [ni'mat]. First is the consent and contentment of God, for it is written, "If you express your gratitude to God for the blessings He has given you, He will increase them for you." Second is the approbation and good will of your ruler for you. The third is that you can keep that rank or position that you have, and you can be hopeful for more progress and promotion in the future. God has said that "if you are grateful for His blessings, He will increase them for you." The increase of blessings, in fact, is progress in rank [daraja].[13]

Abdur Rahman's proclamation was written in 1898, eighty years before the Saur Revolution, but Afghans would still concur with the principles contained in it because they are based on transcendent values associated with Islam. Thus, at the center of traditional Afghan political understanding is the belief in the supremacy of God as creator of the universe and ultimate judge of human affairs and in the related tenet that the ruler is bound in a covenantal relationship with God to ensure the safety and prosperity of the community. The ruler's responsibility, above all else, is to enable the people to practice their faith and to keep them from *fitna*, a term that can be translated as sedition, disorder, or discord but that carries the larger metaphysical notion of being in a state of anarchy presaging a total collapse of the community.

Far from affirming the notion that "anyone can be president" or that "right ultimately wins out over might," Taraki's biography—read through the lens of traditional Afghan political principles—proposes the altogether novel and heretical notion that God erred in allocating his blessings and that human action can correct that mistake. In Afghan culture, people believed that the poor were poor because that is the way God made them; it was their duty to make the best of their situation and to be grateful and obedient to God as well as to those higher than themselves in return for the favors they were given. While this attitude didn't preclude people from trying to advance their fortunes and to make a better life for themselves than their parents had experienced, it was an altogether different matter who could claim to rule the country. To seek personal prosperity was one thing. To establish oneself as the ruler of all the people was something else entirely— something beyond what any ordinary person could aspire to. Taraki's life history, however, reverses these basic assumptions; it proclaims that the poor were that way not because of God but because of systematic oppression by "feudal lords and crafty tribal chieftains" and that anyone—even a lowly shepherd's son—could claim what had been until then the hereditary throne of the Durrani tribe.

Equally revolutionary in light of traditional culture is the implicit notion presented in Taraki's biography that the means to get ahead in the world is by deserting one's home and taking up with strangers. Thus, we read that, while still in his teens, Taraki left his native village and sought employment in Qandahar as an office boy at an overseas trading company that sent him to work in its Bombay branch. By dint of his intelligence and hard work, Taraki rose to the position of clerk and used his spare time to read, learn English, and become acquainted with a larger world of affairs otherwise unavailable to Afghans at that time. We don't find out as much in the biography as we might like about what happened in Bombay. There is the suspicion that Taraki may have been exposed there for the first time to works of socialist philosophy, and some have also speculated that he may have had his first contact there with a Soviet agent who cultivated him for future service.

However that may be, Taraki returned to Afghanistan in 1937, settling in Kabul and using his newly acquired education to begin a career in journalism, which was still in its infancy in Afghanistan at that time. According to the biography, during this period Taraki first "realized with a profound political and class consciousness the pathetic conditions under which the people lived in Afghanistan and became keenly interested in political activities." Allowing his emerging political sensibilities to influence his writing, Taraki was "harassed" for articles he wrote, but he persevered and began for the first time to meet with other like-minded members of the educated class who shared his convictions. He also started writing short stories and novels of a realist nature with strong political themes that reflected his experiences growing up in poverty.

Most important, from 1943 to 1948, Taraki began to lay the groundwork for the establishment of a political party by "preparing a large number of the intelligentsia to fight against absolute monarchy, aristocracy and despotism of the descendants of Yahya, Nader's grandfather." Ultimately, these "long years of struggle led to the founding of Weesh Zalmayan" (Awakened Youth), one of the nascent leftist political parties in Afghanistan that briefly flourished during a period of government liberalization. During the five years of the party's existence (1948–1953), Taraki, who was then in his early thirties, apparently played an active role but was not so central to its activities as other, older men were or as latter accounts produced by the party portrayed him to be. Thus, one PDPA report had it that Taraki wrote the statement of principles of the party, and the biography itself indicates that Taraki was so significant in the activities of the party that he was "exiled" for his activities to the Afghan embassy in Washington, D.C., where he was appointed press attaché.

Being handed a job in the foreign service in a desirable Western capital is admittedly a strange kind of exile, but, given the later pattern developed by Taraki and Amin of sending disgraced former colleagues off to serve as ambassadors in various distant locales, it is not improbable that the government, in sending Taraki away, was trying to rid itself of someone who was becoming if not dangerous at least a nuisance. Whatever the reality here, Taraki's moment of truth came when Daud—the same man he would later overthrow—was appointed prime minister by Zahir Shah. In protest at this appointment, Taraki publicly resigned his post in Washington and held a press conference, "explaining the conditions prevailing in Afghanistan, exposing the bankruptcy of the absolute monarchy under the Nader Family with a bunch of feudal lords ruling Afghanistan." In response, Daud is said to have recalled the former press attaché, at which point Taraki had to decide whether to stay in exile abroad or to return to Afghanistan to face the consequences of his protest. The biography tells us that he went back to Afghanistan, and, "upon his return to Kabul, he telephoned the despotic Daoud from the Kabul Cinema, telling him 'I am Noor Mohammad Taraki. I have just arrived. Shall I go home or to the prison?' " For reasons that are not guessed at in the biography, Daud allowed him to go home but kept him under police surveillance throughout his tenure as prime minister.

We can see in Taraki's several journeys abroad the reinvention of a common theme in Afghan life histories. In *Heroes of the Age*, one of the common threads I noted in the lives of a tribal chief, a would-be king, and a Sufi mystic was the protagonist's exile—sometimes voluntary, sometimes not—from his home. For the tribal chief, Sultan Muhammad Khan, that exile came at an early age, after the murder of his father, when it was no longer safe for him to remain at home. Exile for Sultan Muhammad brought the decisive moment in his life, when he had to resolve whether to stay in the court of his patron, the nawab of Dir, where he had manufactured a comfortable life for himself as a scribe, or to return home to face the dangerous challenge of confronting his enemies and thereby regain his honor. For the king-in-waiting, Abdur Rahman, exile came in his twenties, after seeing his father and uncle both lose the throne of Kabul. He too found a safe refuge and comfortable position with a foreign ruler; however, ultimately, like Sultan Muhammad, Abdur Rahman became dissatisfied with the subservient life of a courtier and set off to recover the throne that was rightfully his. For the Mulla of Hadda, exile meant leaving an impoverished home at a young age to gain religious knowledge and spiritual advancement in India. There, he not only gained the training he needed to become a religious authority but also encountered and fulfilled his preordained destiny by meeting the Akhund of Swat, who would guide him in the path of Sufi enlightenment.

In Taraki's life history, the journey motif was redeployed and reinvented in interesting ways, with the first journey to Qandahar and Bombay resembling that of the Mulla of Hadda in particular. Thus, Taraki at a young age also decided to leave the poverty, oppression, and limited horizons at home to seek refuge and possible advancement abroad. His search exposed him to other worlds and provided him with the tools needed to open up new fields of knowledge, tools that he then took back to others in his native land. The second trip abroad, to Washington, followed the pattern of the exile journeys of Sultan Muhammad and Abdur Rahman. In Taraki's case, it was not a family feud or dynastic upheaval that led to his exile but the early struggles of the radical movement to free Afghanistan from the chains of despotism and oppression. Both Abdur Rahman and Sultan Muhammad faced their moments of truth when they had to decide whether to chance a return that would lead them to their death or to their destiny. The biography tells us that Taraki also had to face the same sort of crisis; he had to decide whether to stay abroad in safety or to face the uncertain consequences of a return to the wrath of Prime Minister Daud.

His decision to return home and openly confront Daud is the most heroic act ascribed to Taraki in the biography. While his involvement in covert party organizing was certainly risky, this is the only time Taraki is portrayed facing off against an adversary (albeit over the telephone). Reading between the lines, one might speculate that Daud didn't take Taraki seriously enough to bother putting him in prison and felt that surveillance was perfectly adequate for so humble an adversary. Daud during this period was sympathetic to most of the ideological positions of the leftists, and the educated elite with whom both men associated constituted such a small circle in those days that some of Taraki's old friends might also have exerted their influence on Daud to keep him out of trouble. Or maybe none of this happened at all, and this story masks a more ignominious period during which Taraki accepted a government position for the money and then later had to explain it away by making up the story of his confrontation with the prime minister. Whatever the reality, the biographical depiction of these events provides Taraki with a narrative moment of reckoning that would have been typologically comprehensible to Afghans. Whether successfully or not, the biography tries to make of the new leader a recognizably Afghan, though also thoroughly modern, "hero" for a revolutionary age.

The next stage of this would-be heroic life features suffering ("Comrade Taraki . . . did odd jobs to eke out a living. However, as soon as he would land a good job, he was suspended through the intelligence service"); the production of a string of "revolutionary and class-conscious" novels;[14] and the founding of the PDPA ("Comrade Taraki with a high revolutionary spirit almost openly took the initiative to launch his political party. To achieve this end, he began his meetings with a number of youths whom he had already groomed as young revolutionaries so that he could establish the workers' party equipped with the working class scientific ideology"). The context of the party's founding was the advent of a period of democratic liberalization in which Zahir Shah promised to open up the political process. This era began with the drafting of a new constitution in 1964 and the election of a representative parliamentary assembly in 1965.

Taraki himself ran for the lower house (*wolesi jirga*) of parliament from his native district in Ghazni, but he was defeated, as the biography explains, "through Government machinations and shameless intervention in the election." Other Marxists, however, including Babrak Karmal and Dr. Anahita Ratebzad, were elected and immediately set about making their presence felt in the assembly. The elections had produced a lower house split between conservative and Marxist factions, with a relatively weak and ineffectual center, represented by Prime Minister Muhammad Yusuf, who had been appointed by the king to replace Prime Minister Daud. Immediately after the opening of parliament, the Marxists began accusing the new government of corruption and forced a vote of confidence; it was held on

October 24, 1965, before a gallery packed with shouting, chanting Karmal supporters, who managed to disrupt the vote. The next day, the police locked the demonstrators out of the parliamentary chambers, so they took their protest to the streets and were eventually fired on by overwhelmed Afghan troops. This event led to more demonstrations and finally forced the resignation of Yusuf.[15]

Although no direct role in the parliamentary crisis is ascribed to Taraki, the biography does tell us that he was working in this period to organize the PDPA and to found "the glorious historic and brilliant *Khalq* newspaper." Although the paper was allowed to run for only six weeks and six issues, it managed in that short time to further divide the already factionalized political climate, especially through its open declaration that "the main issue of contemporary times and the center of class struggle on a worldwide basis, which began with the Great October Socialist Revolution, is the struggle between international socialism and international imperialism."[16] Religious leaders in the upper house of the parliament (*meshrano jirga*) demanded an investigation, and the government decided to ban the paper outright on May 23, 1966.

Despite the banning of *Khalq*, other leftist newspapers were started, including *Parcham* (Flag) and the Maoist *Shu'la-yi Jawed* (Eternal Flame). These publications played a cat-and-mouse game with conservative opponents and government censors, taunting with cartoons and editorials, creating minor provocations that went right up to the line that would get them noticed but not banned. One incident in particular stands out during this period, the publication of a poem in *Parcham* written by Bariq Shafi, the former editor of *Khalq*, titled "The Bugle of Revolution." In this poem, the writer intentionally used forms of eulogistic praise (*dorud*) traditionally reserved for the Prophet Muhammad to celebrate Lenin. Where earlier provocations had resulted in scattered protests, impassioned mosque sermons, and delegations demanding an audience with the king, "The Bugle of Revolution" created a nationwide furor, as news of the outrage spread throughout the country. Inspired by the increasing immorality of the left, mullas from throughout the country traveled to Kabul, where they gathered in the Pul-i Khishti mosque near the central marketplace to protest the poem and give vent to their larger concern over the expansion of leftist influence.[17]

In the parliament, leftist deputies employed the same practice, provoking their clerical opponents while trying not to directly offend the government. Karmal, in particular, was famous for offering public praise of the king while getting into symbolic tiffs with religious deputies, as evidenced in the following story told by Samiullah Safi, a fellow deputy of Karmal's, whose story is the centerpiece of Chapter Four:

> One time Karmal started a speech without the usual invocation of *bismillah* [in the name of God]. One of the deputies announced, "I have a legal objection." The president of the assembly, who was Umar Wardak, stopped [Karmal] from talking and asked what his objection was. I don't remember which deputy it was, but he said that "whenever Karmal makes a speech, he doesn't say 'bismillah.' He must say '*bismillah ul-rahman ul-rahim.*'" If other people would forget to say the "bismillah," he presumably wouldn't have minded, but since it involved Karmal, who was a communist and a servant of Russia, . . . people were sensitive to his manner of speaking. So he said, "He must say the 'bismillah' before he begins his speeches."
>
> They put this objection to a vote—whether or not he should say "bismillah." When the voting took place, even Hafizullah Amin, who was present, raised his hand to show that he thought that "bismillah" should be spoken. The only person in the parliament who didn't raise his hand was Karmal. After that, Umar Wardak hit the desk with his gavel and said, "It has been unanimously decided that Mr. Karmal must say 'bismillah ul-rahman ul-rahim' before starting his speeches." Then they gave him permission [to speak], and the light went on the microphone; but he started speaking from where he left off and didn't say "bismillah." Immediately the assembly broke out in a great hubbub. There was lots of shouting. Karmal didn't say "bismillah," so he pushed the mic away and leaned to one side, giving up on his speech.[18]

Another, similar confrontation between Karmal and Maulavi Muhammad Nabi Muhammadi, a Muslim cleric who later became the leader of one of the exile Islamic resistance parties, resulted in a skirmish on the floor of the parliament in which Karmal received a cut on his head. According to Louis Dupree, "When his followers demonstrated outside the hospital, [Karmal] grabbed additional bandages and energetically tied them around his head before appearing to wave feebly to the spirited crowd."[19] The ultimate effect of this sort of incitement was the paralysis of the government, as a succession of prime ministers tried and failed to exert some modicum of influence over a dysfunctional parliament and incendiary press. Ultimately, this failure led to the mobilization of a coup d'état by Muhammad Daud, a cousin of Zahir Shah and the last prime minister prior to the advent of the democratic era in 1964. Among Daud's early supporters were members of the PDPA, but they soon became disillusioned with Daud as he reverted to the autocratic style of governing that he had relied on during his earlier decade of rule.

At this moment, according to Taraki's biography, Taraki struck on his plan to take "a shortcut" to revolution via the armed forces: "Previously, the army was considered as the tool of dictatorship and despotism of the ruling class and it was not imaginable to use it before toppling its employer. However, Comrade Taraki suggested this tool ought to be wrested in order to topple the ruling class thereby and this end could be achieved through extensively doing party work in the army and diffusing the epoch-making working class ideology among the armed forces." Taraki entrusted the job of mobilizing a military base to the man who was becoming his closest confidant and protégé, Hafizullah Amin.

> Comrade Amin who was responsible for the party affairs among the armed forces and enjoyed the trust of the young officers respecting his orders with extreme faith and loyalty soon realized that now the young officers in the armed forces on the one hand adored their great leader Noor Mohammad Taraki and on the other hand were ready to proceed with any revolutionary action with utmost discipline to place themselves in his command with deep loyalty and devotion. The Khalqi officers in the armed forces believed that Comrade Amin as the most faithful follower and disciple of Comrade Taraki was sincerely following his beloved leader's instructions and faithfully and loyally reported to him on behalf of the Khalqi officers.

Throughout the mid-1970s, President Daud, who earlier in his career had been known as the "red prince" for his leftist views, became steadily more suspicious of his former allies on the left and of the intentions of his Soviet patrons. Many believe that in the months before the Saur Revolution, Daud was sufficiently concerned for his position that he was making plans to renounce or severely restrict aid from the Soviet Union while increasing his reliance on assistance from Saudi Arabia and Iran, both of which he visited in early 1978. Daud's suspicions of the left were galvanized on April 17, 1978, when unknown assassins shot down Mir Akbar Khyber, one of the best-known Marxists and a close ally of Karmal. Khyber's funeral attracted a large and vociferous crowd, and a new wave of leftist protests appeared likely in the days ahead. To forestall that eventuality, Daud dispatched police officers in the early morning hours of April 26 to arrest Taraki, Karmal, Amin, and other leading Marxists at their homes. Taraki appears not to have anticipated this move:

> Holding his shot gun and on the verge of firing on the police, Comrade Taraki thought it was the thieves or the reactionaries who had raided into his house but soon realized that they were police officers of the inhuman Daoud Regime. When Mrs. Taraki confronted these officers,

one threatened her with his weapon and wounded her arm with his bay-
onet: Sprinkling her blood on the faces of the police officers, Mrs. Taraki
exclaimed "this blood would not remain unavenged."

Showing a political dexterity that would ultimately be his undoing,
Amin took advantage of the arresting officer's leniency in allowing him to
remain in his house for several hours to send a message to Marxist officers
instructing them to begin their coup d'état on the following day—April 27.
Thus, the long planned coup d'état got under way while Taraki, Amin, and
other party leaders were in prison. Not until the afternoon, several hours
after the beginning of the operation, were military officers able to "release
great heroic leader, Comrade Noor Muhammad Taraki and others from their
dark cells" and convey them by armored car to Radio Afghanistan, where
military officers announced to the Afghan people that a new revolutionary
government was now in control of the homeland. After the announcement
and as the battle for Kabul continued to rage, the officers took Taraki and
other leaders to an air force base outside the capital where they would be
safe until the outcome of the coup could be assured.

Thus ends the narrative portion of the biography, the last paragraphs
being taken up with fulsome praise for Taraki's personal attributes. What is
striking about the presentation of these attributes is the same thing that one
notes about the biography as a whole—that is, how atypical Taraki is as an
Afghan leader. Throughout, the story hardly mentions any acts of personal
bravery or heroism, beyond the possibly made-up instance of standing up to
then-Prime Minister Daud over the telephone. Where Amin (the likely
author of the biography) is singled out for praise for his coolheadedness at
the time of his arrest, Taraki in the same circumstances appears to have been
confused, thinking that he was under threat from burglars rather than from
the police, and the only real defiance comes from his wife.

According to one man with whom I have spoken, whose brother led the
detail assigned to arrest Taraki, the soldiers could not find him right away
because he was hiding in the bathroom. "A soldier opened the door of the
bathroom and found Taraki in there with his wife's chadar [veil] over his
head. Then the soldier took off the chadar and called out that he [Taraki] was
in the bathroom."[20] Whether this story is true or not, the hagiographic biography provides few details that augment the image of Taraki as a great leader
in any usual Afghan sense. To the contrary, we find out that in the moment
of battle, when the revolution could still have collapsed, Taraki had no hand
in coordinating operations but was instead whisked out of harm's way to the
relative safety of a military base already in the hands of coup leaders.

In addition to the absence of any singular deeds, Taraki's life is also notable for other missing elements, most importantly children. In Afghanistan, having children is not only a symbol of a man's potency, it is also his claim to immortality. In Taraki's native Pakhtun culture in particular, men without children are soon forgotten, and their names—having no more significance—are quickly elided from tribal genealogies. The absence of a family is also thought to make one vulnerable to the designs of others. Family members, and especially sons, are the ultimate insurance policy, for a man with many sons, along with brothers and nephews, has *mlatar*—male relatives who will "tie their waists" (something like "girding one's loins") for battle to defend their kin and avenge attacks on them. The only individuals who are exempt from needing kinsmen for self-protection are mullas, whose poverty and devotion to religion protect them from assault, and a few celibate saints like the Mulla of Hadda; these saints acquire a surrogate progeny through their disciples, whose names are linked to theirs through lines of spiritual transmission (*silsila*), which functions as a kind of genealogy in giving status and position to those included in them.

Taraki's childlessness is noted in the biography, along with the notation that "all members of the People's Democratic Party of Afghanistan revere him as their father and he reciprocally treats them as his own children."[21] The implication here is that the party for Taraki displaced the family. This equates in a way with a tenet of Leninist ideology—that the party should be more important to its members than the sentimental attachments of birth, kin, and nation—but this is a notion that only the most alienated and deracinated Afghans would willingly accept. And it would anyway appear that rather than the party's eliminating such attachments as bourgeois and antirevolutionary, for Taraki the party was a substitute family in which he invested the same sentimental attachments that others placed in their families. That Taraki had this need to treat his younger colleagues as children makes him in some ways a more sympathetic character, but it also made him in Afghan eyes somewhat pathetic and all the more unworthy as a national leader.

Another lack in Taraki's life prior to the revolution is property. As the biography notes, "Comrade Taraki does not own any personal property with the exception of a one story mud house in Sher Shah Mina, Kabul." This feature of the life history is again laudable from the point of view of Marxist doctrine and shows Taraki neither to have been corrupted by inherited wealth nor to have bent his principles to acquire property. But even if Taraki's relative poverty was a mark of his commitment rather than his incompetence, the valorization of being propertyless at age sixty-one is still incomprehensible in Afghan culture, which views property as both a sign of ni'mat and an indication of a man's success in life. A man of property is thought of as being "heavy," or *drund*, which implies that he is in a position to provide hospitality and benefit to others. Conversely, a man without property is considered "naked" (*luchak*) and unable to fulfill the requirements of honor, which dictate that a man must be able to provide for himself and for others. Such a man is also vulnerable to the assaults of the world, for he lacks the means with which to defend himself. If a man without property cannot meet the basic demands of honor, how much less prepared is he to handle the far greater obligations of rule? One might even say that having such a man as ruler would be a sign of God's displeasure with his subjects since the benefits that God allows to the people emanate in the first instance from the ruler.[22]

A final lack that can be noted in the biography is what might be called a kingly persona. Abdur Rahman, the so-called Iron Amir, was the archetype of the battle-hardened warrior who was quick to avenge any slight or suggestion that he was not in charge. Many considered him the cruelest of Afghan monarchs, but as Lord Curzon noted at the time, "None had given so large a measure of unity to the kingdom."[23] Abdur Rahman's son, Habibullah, was gargantuan in girth but a shadow of his father as ruler; however, he at least possessed the hauteur that Afghans expect of their rulers. So, too, did Amanullah. For all his plans for reform and his willingness to recast his subjects as citizens, Amanullah carried himself as a king and left no one wondering who was in charge. Zahir Shah was a less prepossessing man, and many Afghans believe that his apparent weakness and unwillingness to rule with a strong hand started in motion the disastrous decline that culminated in the Saur Revolution.

Given the respect accorded strong political personalities in Afghan society, one of the more curious features of recent history is that a man of Taraki's modest character and talents should have managed to topple Afghanistan's two-hundred-year-old dynasty. In the modest language of the biography, "Comrade Noor Mohammad Taraki is a dear friend to all hardworking, honest and patriotic compatriots. He is a just leader and teacher. He is highly cultured, modest and compassionate." What he was not was the "great leader" of government propaganda, at least not in any sense that Afghans traditionally recognized. As already noted, there was no evidence of physical stamina or bravery, no signs of any brilliance as a warrior or orator; and despite the exalted claims made by Amin for the strategic brilliance of Taraki's revolutionary "shortcut," he made no notable contributions to revolutionary ideology. Above all else, he was a dreamer and a conversationalist who was apparently most persuasive when speaking with a small group of younger men, and perhaps his single greatest talent was for bringing together more powerful and repellent personalities who, in his absence, could never have worked or even remained in the same room together.

In this sense, one could argue that Taraki's rise to the top of the Afghan political hierarchy was comparable to the rise of another previously unknown figure—Ahmad Shah Abdali—who was a second-tier tribal leader when a deadlock between more powerful khans led to his being chosen to lead the Durrani confederation of tribes in 1747. The difference is that Ahmad Shah proved to be a true leader; he seized his opportunity and led his tribe to foreign conquests and two centuries of unchallenged hegemony over the Kingdom of Afghanistan. Taraki's ascendance, by contrast, was short-lived, and his ultimate failure to consolidate his rule reveals a more telling relationship, that between the leader of the PDPA and his own tribal people—the Taraki Ghilzai.

Like most other Ghilzai tribes, the Taraki were opportunistic nomads. Some were sheep and goat herders who migrated with their flocks each summer to high pastures. Some were long-range camel nomads who hired out their animals to carry goods from one market to another. Some were itinerant workers who traveled to India in the winter months to engage in casual labor, while other, more ambitious and adventurous types journeyed as far as Calcutta, where they "hawk[ed] clothing on credit or carr[ied] on usury."[24] Taraki's own early career as a clerk for the Pushtun Trading Company in Bombay mirrored his tribe's age-old association with South Asian trade, and, in that tradition, Taraki remained throughout his life a middleman, a broker in foreign goods who operated on the margins between different social worlds, never fully committing himself to anyone, never being fully accepted any place. This is not the most generous but it may be the most realistic assessment of an itinerant and interstitial career that brought a most unsuitable figure to the pinnacle of power and precipitated a conflict that would consume his people long after his death.

THE PEOPLE'S PARTY IN CULTURAL CONTEXT

> Comrade Taraki was tirelessly in touch with those who were equipped with the working class ideology, struggling individually or in separate circles, linking them up with a view to creating the working class party. As a result of his creative work and on the basis of his ardent love for the people, about 30 young men representing all patriotic, progressive and

revolutionary youth gathered at Comrade Noor Mohammad Taraki's humble residence at Sher Shah Maina, Kabul on January 1st, 1965, establishing the first Founding Congress of the People's Democratic Party of Afghanistan.[25]

Hidden behind the rhetoric of fraternal feeling contained in this passage is the reality that the party that got its start on January 1, 1965, was in crisis almost from the start. The first outward sign of that crisis occurred in 1966 and involved a dispute over whether Amin should be made an alternate member of the central committee of the party. Taraki supported the proposal, but it was resisted by Karmal and a number of his allies on the central committee who would leave the PDPA in 1967 and form their own Parcham (Banner) party. There were a number of reasons for the split. Taraki and others in the Khalq branch of the party were mostly rural Pakhtuns and Pakhtu speakers, while Karmal and his supporters were predominantly Persian speakers from Kabul and other Tajik-majority regions. Karmal was also suspected by Amin and other Khalqis because of his supposed ties to the royal family, though the nature and extent of these ties have long been in dispute.[26] Some have contended that there was a close personal link between Karmal and Daud through Karmal's father, an Afghan general, who was appointed by Daud during his tenure as prime minister as governor of Herat and Paktia provinces. According to these sources, Daud is even suspected of providing financial assistance to Parcham after its split with the Khalq faction.[27]

While the extent of Karmal's personal association with the royal family is uncertain, there were philosophical and strategic differences between the Parchamis and Khalqis, with Karmal advocating a more conciliatory line toward the monarchy of Zahir Shah and a gradual approach to political change.[28] In apparent gratitude, the government allowed Karmal's faction to continue publishing its newspaper, *Parcham,* well after the *Khalq* newspaper had been shut down, a fact that further antagonized Taraki, Amin, and other staunch Khalqis. Later, when Daud overthrew the monarchy, Karmal and other Parchamis were initially welcomed into Daud's circle. Expectations that this embrace would lead to real power were quickly dashed, however, as many Parchami activists were dispatched to low-level government positions in out-of-the-way areas. Even then, the Parchamis continued to advocate a more cautious approach to political change while the Khalqis, led by Amin, were making secret plans for a military coup d'état.

Irrespective of ethnic and linguistic factors, possible royal connections, and policy disagreements, the source of the division between Khalq and Parcham arose more than anything else from the profound personal animosity between Karmal and Amin. In his role as mediator and benevolent friend to all the world, Taraki succeeded from time to time in overcoming the rift—Khalq and Parcham unified again in 1977—but the antipathy between Amin and Karmal was too deep to mend permanently. Some sense of the personality differences and the dislike that Amin and Karmal shared for one another can be gleaned from another story told to me by Safi:

> When Hafizullah Amin would come in [to the parliamentary chamber], he would go and sit down with some mulla, and talk and joke. Then he would sit with some elder or some khan or some other deputy or with some educated person. He'd joke, sometimes he'd sit in this chair, sometimes he'd sit in that chair, although everyone knew his seat was on the left [where the leftist deputies tended to sit]. He would talk and joke with everyone, and the deputies would say to him, "Hey, infidel [*kafir*]! Hey, devil [*la'in*]." They'd say that sort of thing, and he would laugh. Everyone rejected his political connections, but all of the deputies had social and personal relations with him—everyone, even this Muhammad Nabi Muhammadi.[29] So many times, Amin would sit at a table and talk and debate with them, even Muhammad Nabi Muhammadi. . . . Karmal [however] would act like a *sardar* [prince]. He would enter in the manner of a Muhammadzai [member of the extended royal family]. He wouldn't socialize with the deputies. He would come in, looking very serious. He would always go to the left and sit down in a chair in his customary and permanent place. That wretched man would just sit there, quietly, not saying anything. This was his character. . . .
>
> Karmal and Hafizullah Amin were not only opposed to the government, . . . [but] also opposed to each other—violently opposed. It was the most serious opposition that I saw in the four years I was in the parliament. Not once did I see Hafizullah Amin and Karmal shaking hands. By way of example, I tell you that we deputies would be standing around outside before the beginning of a session or during breaks. If Hafizullah Amin was standing in the circle and Karmal went by, he wouldn't be able to enter the circle—out of fear. He was scared of Hafizullah Amin, just like a mouse, and he wouldn't come into the circle. He would go far away and wouldn't shake hands with anyone, but when Karmal was standing in the circle and Hafizullah Amin arrived, Amin would stick out his hand like this to each one and look angrily in [Karmal's] direction, not offering his hand, but instead offering it to someone else. And in these circles he would dominate the whole conversation, and Karmal would eventually slink away like a mouse, as though he wasn't included in the group. He couldn't speak in front of him. That's the truth.

Amin's great gift was for persuasion. Where Karmal was an effective orator but aloof in person, Amin was personable and easy in interaction. A rural Pakhtun from Paghman, close to Kabul, Amin was unusually well educated for someone of his background, having gained the opportunity, after graduating from Kabul University in the late 1950s, to study at Columbia University in New York City, where he received a master's degree in education. On his return to Afghanistan, Amin worked as a teacher and principal at Ibn-i Sina High School and the national teacher-training college (*dar ul-ulum*). After the founding of the PDPA, Amin used his position and access to young people to recruit members to the party. Because of these early efforts, the Khalq had a considerable edge over Parcham and every other party in gaining support among young educated men, especially among primary and secondary schoolteachers who had been inspired by Amin and who went out into the provinces to spread the message. This support would initially give Khalq an advantage, but it would also ultimately prove to be part of the government's undoing after the revolution as zealous young teachers became a focus of popular resentment.

After the 1973 coup d'état against Zahir Shah and the decision by the Khalqis to begin implementing their "shortcut" to revolution, it was natural for Amin to play the role of organizer. In the case of military officers, he had an additional recruiting advantage in that many officers were already being sent by the Afghan government to the Soviet Union and Czechoslovakia for military training. By 1970, an estimated 7,000 junior officers were trained in those two states, compared to 600 who went to the United States and lesser numbers to Turkey, India, and Great Britain.[30] As Hasan Kakar has noted, the ideological training of these young men was well along even before Amin got to them.[31] Whether the majority of these officers became communists as a result of their indoctrination is doubtful, but the experience of studying abroad in a more advanced country does seem to have turned many against their own government. So too did the situation they found on their return, for as Anthony Hyman has pointed out, returning junior officers found it difficult "to reconcile their own lowly positions and poor pay with the prestige of army officers in Afghan society as a whole—or their own merits (as they saw them) against the superannuated and inefficient senior officers."[32]

Likewise, young officers saw firsthand the failure of parliamentary democracy and then experienced the disappointment of seeing Daud's left-leaning "revolution" become mired in corruption and turn increasingly defensive and conservative. With the collapse of emergent institutions, there was the additional failure of political leaders to come up with development programs for the country at large. Junior officers trained in the Soviet bloc may not have converted to Marxism as a result of their experiences in the Soviet Union. However, most of them did come back more radicalized than when they left, and the failure of the parliament and then of Daud's regime to make good on the promise of reform certainly made many officers sympathetic to the possibilities of a homegrown Marxist movement. At the same time that junior officers were feeling increasingly alienated from the military establishment and the government, they were also feeling increasingly cut off from their rural roots. In this context, Amin offered not only ideological comfort but also a sense of belonging. The party with its coded language of fraternal fellowship and its secret meetings became for many an alternative family and tribe, replacing the ones they had left behind and from which they had become increasingly estranged by education and distance. The vast majority of those whom Amin recruited were, like himself, deracinated Pakhtuns, and they appear to have felt considerable loyalty to him.

Amin was a strong personality and tended to create as many enemies as converts, but among those whom Amin clearly seduced was Taraki himself. As the biography makes clear, Taraki acted as Amin's protector when others on the central committee wanted to see his authority diminished. As the biography explained it, "Comrade Taraki used to pay much attention to the cultivation of Comrade Amin's tactical and strategic talents . . . [and] defended him against all sorts of intrigues and propagandas, . . . safeguarding his loyal disciple against all intrigues resorted [to] by some colleagues consciously or sub-consciously which eventually proved to be in the interests of the enemy." When the party reunified in July 1977, the Khalqi wing refused to let the Parchamis in on their plan to mount a coup d'état, both because of Parcham's cautiousness and because of the Khalqis' suspicion that Parchamis might tip off the government to their plans. According to Taraki's biography, Khalq suspicion of Parchami loyalty to the revolution proved well founded at the time of the April 27th coup d'état—first, when Karmal "argued that the revolution was doomed to failure and hence members of Central Committee should be dispersed in villages and hide there" and, then, when he urged that Daud only be arrested and not killed.

Rapprochement between the two wings of the PDPA proved short-lived after the revolution. Though Karmal was initially given the post of vice chairman of the Revolutionary Council and deputy prime minister (a title he shared with Amin), he was ousted, along with various of his Parchami allies, in July 1978 and dispatched as ambassador to Czechoslovakia. In reporting on Karmal's ouster, the government-run *Kabul Times* was respectful of Karmal and treated his new assignment as a considerable honor. However, with the news of the diplomatic posting of other Parchamis—Nur Ahmad Nur to Washington, Anahita Ratebzad to Belgrade, Dr. Najibullah to Teheran, and Mahmud Barylay to Pakistan—it became clear that this was nothing less than a purge, a fact the government made clear in August with the announcement of the arrest or ouster of various Parchami-aligned "traitors," whom the government accused of subverting the revolution. These announcements were followed on September 23 by published confessions of various Parchami conspirators who admitted to participating in plans for a counterrevolution that was being orchestrated by Karmal and his allies. The Khalq wing was in a position to execute this purge of its former allies because of its stronger position among military officers.

Following the purges of July, the government set about the task of revolutionizing Afghan society. The main thrust of this effort involved winning over the people, an effort that is discussed in the next chapter. But, particularly after the divisive Parcham purge, Taraki and Amin had also to ensure the loyalty of their own comrades, most important, those in the military who had brought them to power and who could just as easily remove them. On August 1, Taraki addressed the ranking officers of the Fourth and Fifteenth Armored Divisions of the People's Armed Forces of Afghanistan at the People's House (the renamed presidential palace) in Kabul. This was one of many speeches given by Taraki during this period, and it is representative in its focus and style.[33]

Taraki began the speech by indicating that he was addressing the officers "in a party capacity as comrades and members of the party cadres." He waxed nostalgic about "how we used to meet at night and how our comrades used to exert great caution and travel to our home under cover in order to meet us occasionally." Then, he reminded his audience that it was through these early efforts that "we were able to eliminate the class of exploiters, the era of pharaonic despotism, aristocracy, the ruling classes and those who traveled with them and bring a people's government in their place." After more preamble about the importance of "progressive ideology," Taraki turned to his main subject, which was the role of the military itself, and advised his audience "to once again carefully study the workers' and farmers' ideology," as well as "to closely observe party order, discipline and ideology and not only to observe them but to act on them." A productive party member, Taraki asserted, was "a philosopher, a dialectician, an historian. . . . Such prominent party members will be able to build our society in accordance with the needs and wishes of the people and can rescue them from the present social and economic ailments." After digressions into foreign policy and other matters, Taraki concluded his address with this counsel:

> Couple your studies and knowledge with action; find good, clean and pious comrades. You should not only be an example of political, social and moral piety in the army but throughout the country so that everyone will say that the Khalqis are truly honorable and trustworthy people to be proud of. Our comrades set such an example even before the revolution. I always used to advise them: Always observe your piety, whether you are a teacher, a director or whatever job you may have. . . . We are capable of attracting even greater trust in our society and of introducing changes for the benefit of the people thus implementing our slogan, which was bread, clothes and shelter. From then on the people can realize their happiness, prosperity and progress.

In examining this speech, I have been struck by certain parallels to the proclamation of Abdur Rahman's that I analyzed in *Heroes of the Age*.[34] That document was also addressed principally to members of the military, and the amir—like Taraki—had the same intention: reinforcing the loyalty of the army to the state. Likewise, the earlier text demonstrated some of the same rhetorical techniques as those evinced in Taraki's address—for example, when Abdur Rahman indicated his personal association with his audience ("During the time of my reign, I have always been sympathetic and benevolent to you people of Afghanistan"), which mirrors in its way Taraki's nostalgic remembrances of early party meetings. Like Taraki as well, Abdur Rahman offered benevolent advice ("Listen, obey, and weigh well what I am saying to you, for no use can come from lamenting later if you do something wrong now") and urged a sense of responsibility for those less fortunate than themselves ("You should sympathize with the subjects, who are your own tribesmen and who are continually employed in cultivating their lands, in cutting their crops, in thrashing their corn, in gathering in the harvests, and in winnowing the wheat from the chaff").

However, as obvious as the similarities are between Taraki's address and Abdur Rahman's proclamation, more striking and ultimately more significant for explaining the revolution's failure are the ways in which Taraki's speech differs from Abdur Rahman's proclamation. Thus, where loyalty to the party was Taraki's principal message, Abdur Rahman emphasized that loyalty to the ruler was an expression of obedience to God, who determines the ranks and positions of mankind ("Obeying the order of the king with complete devotion and loyalty is just like obeying the commands of God"). Taraki's address included no reference to God, as one would expect given his ideological orientation, but in leaving aside such references, he also left himself vulnerable to attack. In Abdur Rahman's stern pronouncements, it was sinful to feel envy for another's good fortune, and he warned of divine punishment for those who were bitter about their lot in life. Taraki, for his part, could only counsel caution and offer the lesser threat of earthly retribution against those who would try to subvert the revolution.

To further strengthen his message, Abdur Rahman also had the rhetoric of honor at his disposal. ("When you lose your position, you will be walking down a street in a state of disgrace [*be abru*] and dishonor [*be ghairat*]. No one will even mention your name. You will be forgotten.") And he had as well recourse to family and kinship. ("The most important thing for you to know is that the kindness and mercy of the king for his subjects is like the kindness and mercy of a father for his son.") This language is deeply rooted in Afghan culture, and Abdur Rahman appropriated that language for his own ends by portraying himself simultaneously as God's regent, honor's arbiter, and father of the nation. The language of class struggle, however, has no ground in Afghan culture. While the rhetoric of segmentary opposition (Ghilzai versus Durrani, Pakhtun versus Hazara, tribes versus state) is well entrenched in Afghanistan, the rhetoric of socialist opposition (the party of "workers, farmers and toilers" versus "the stinking, rotten, feudalist society")—which is at the center of Taraki's appeal—had little purchase beyond the circle of socialist true believers. This was particularly true given traditional Afghan suspicions of factionalism (*gundi*) as a phenomenon antithetical to and disruptive of the intrinsic and natural unity of the kinship group.[35]

The dangers of factionalism are, in fact, nowhere more clearly demonstrated than in Taraki's life story, which can be seen as a cultural allegory of the impermanence and flawed nature of factions, especially those that emulate or pretend to replace the kinship group. Reduced to its basics, Taraki's story is that of a childless father who adopts a number of sons, one of whom in particular stands out for his apparent loyalty and gratitude to the older man who has protected him and taken him under his wing. The favored son is, of course, Amin, who worms his way into the father's good graces through offering the father ever more flamboyant encomiums that delude the father into believing that he is something extraordinary and unique— virtually godlike in his powers and importance. Hubris blinds the father to the true intentions of the favored son and so too do the son's warnings that the real threat lies with another, evil son, who is not like them. The bad son is Karmal, who comes from the world of the court, and whatever his intentions, whether he is in reality loyal or simply less adroitly duplicitous, the effect of the warnings is to push the father ever deeper into the favored son's trap.[36] With the father rendered both paranoid and deluded, the favored son is able gradually to take away the father's power, reducing him ultimately to the status of a pathetic old man who trusts too much and pays too little heed to the dangers around him.

This allegorical approach to understanding the dynamics of Khalqi rulership accord with Abdur Rahman's account of his life's travails. As Abdur Rahman told it in his autobiography, most of the problems he encountered prior to securing the throne were the fault of courtiers and supposed allies, men who tried to appear to him as kinlike in their loyalties but who invariably betrayed his trust when given the chance.[37] In a tribal society, one trusts nonkin at one's peril, for only kin have a vested interest in protecting each other. One must assume that other relationships are contracted through self-interest and that expressions of loyalty—however sincerely uttered—can be contravened by circumstance. Kinship alone endures, and Abdur Rahman's life history showed that even kinship can be corrupted when an incautious ruler allows his courtiers and would-be allies to spread suspicion and feed their appetite for power and conspiracy. Not having children, Taraki was especially vulnerable, for in the end he had no one to trust, no one whose interests were coterminous with his own. There were only the putative "sons" he had recruited to the party, and the best of them proved only too willing to sacrifice the old man's trust for the sake of his own ambition.

CONCLUSION

While it failed in its ostensible goal of creating a Marxist state in Afghanistan, the Saur Revolution is nevertheless the single most important event in recent Afghan history. Some of the effects of the revolution are obvious, for it laid the groundwork for the popular rebellion that swept over the country in 1978–1979, the subsequent rise to power of the Islamic resistance organizations, and later the development of the Taliban movement. Beyond this, however, are other important, though less obvious, effects, which I have considered in this chapter. One of these is the transformation of the idea of what a leader should and could be. The unlikely ascension of Nur Muhammad Taraki to the pinnacle of Afghan politics proved to be an important stage in the evolution of political authority. In the preceding two hundred years, Afghanistan had experienced numerous dynastic feuds, assassinations, tribal insurrections, and a coup d'état; but in every instance but one (the brief reign of Bacha-i Saqao), a member of the Durrani tribe had come out on top.

Taraki changed that, and, in the act of murdering Daud and his entire family, his party virtually ensured that the Durrani dynasty would never return. While it has been noted that Taraki was a Ghilzai—the traditional enemies of the Durranis—and that his ascension could be seen as a revival of that centuries-old rivalry, the most significant fact about Taraki was not that he was from the Taraki Ghilzai tribe, which had little in the way of a corporate identity, but that he was from a poor and insignificant family. In the past, a pretender to the throne would have tried to mask this reality, as in the case of Bacha-i Saqao, whose humble background was improved on and ultimately glorified by his supporters.[38] Taraki, however, made no attempt to hide the poverty of his upbringing; indeed, he flaunted it, in the unrealized hope that other Afghans of similar means would identify with him and see him as their champion. Even though his strategy didn't work the way he had planned, the very fact that Taraki was able to secure the top position—while also ensuring that virtually all the remaining members of the royal family in a position to make a claim of their own were eliminated—forever changed the nature of leadership in Afghanistan. Taraki may not have succeeded in bringing about a revolution, but he did effectively destroy the mystique of royalty and the notion that only certain men from certain families could rule.

Another significant transformation brought about by the Saur Revolution was the use of the party as a vehicle of political struggle and popular mobilization. The PDPA was not the first political party in Afghanistan. In the early part of the century, during the reign of Amir Habibullah, courtiers and government officials had established the National Secret Party to press for political and social reform, and from the 1940s on political parties of various orientations had been in existence, some covertly, some with government sanction. But the Saur Revolution was the first time that a political party had actually come to power and the first time a party had attempted in any serious way to extend its reach beyond the capital to the population at large. That the effort was ultimately unsuccessful should not obscure how radical a transformation this was. Tribal Afghans in particular have long maintained a wariness with regard to political parties since they are based— in their view—not on enduring and trustworthy links such as kinship but on ephemeral ideas, temporary alliances, and opportunistic individuals. Party loyalties are seen as transitory and artificial and cannot be counted on, and they tend to divide people and create ruptures within kinship units and communities. This being the case, it is not surprising that the PDPA achieved its greatest success not in the countryside but in the two institutions—the military and the public schools—that long served as the principal pipelines through which deracinated tribal Afghans entered into the apparatus of the state.

If one looks at the history of these two institutions, one notices that the military and the schools were both at the center of a number of contests of authority between the state and the tribes. Throughout its history, the state required a strong military to defend itself from external and internal threats, and one of the best recruiting grounds was the tribal areas because of the Pakhtuns' valorization of warfare and the paucity of economic opportunities available to them. The point of friction was always the terms of tribal participation—the tribes traditionally wanting to set the number of conscripts and to stay as tribal units within the army rather than have their men dispersed to different groups. For its part, the government long resisted these terms, wanting to conscript tribesmen according to its own calculations and to assign them to mixed units whose loyalty would be primarily to the government, not to a tribe or area. On a number of occasions, most recently during what has become known as the Safi War (*safi jang*) in 1945–1946, individual tribes took up arms against the government over this issue. However, in the years prior to the Saur Revolution, the government was able to maintain the rules of military service, and it was through this institution that the greatest number of Pakhtun tribesmen were exposed to and incorporated within state culture.

Educational institutions were the other great pipeline of tribal Afghans into government service, and here as well there have been numerous contests between tribes and the government over how education would be offered in tribal areas and for tribal students. During Amanullah's reign, one of the sources of conflict that led to his ouster was the amir's insistence on making education universally available, including education for girls. Tensions continued to surround education after Amanullah's overthrow, but subsequent regimes reduced animosity by making coeducation voluntary and limiting it to the primary level, while offering incentives to male students who wished to continue their education beyond the primary level. Through these incremental measures, the government succeeded in establishing primary schools in most of the tribal areas, along with secondary schools in most provincial capitals and two boarding schools specifically set aside for tribal boys in Kabul (Khushhal Khan and Rahman Baba lycées).

In assessing the legacy of the Saur Revolution, it is important to take into account the history of party recruitment within the military and the schools and to recognize that the PDPA was able to come to power because it recognized and exploited the interstitial nature of these institutions, which lay between the governmental and tribal realms. Past actions against the government had relied on the twin engines of Islam and tribalism. Islam generally came in the person of a charismatic Sufi leader and his coterie of followers, who provided communications and logistical support, along with firebrand rhetoric; the tribes were represented by whichever combination of people had been swayed by the leader's preaching or the prospect of booty (or both) to join in the cause of the moment. While guaranteed to inspire fear and trepidation in far-off Kabul, these insurrections were unreliable affairs that were generally over in a short period of time; they were also relatively easy to defend against if the ruler was sufficiently astute to recognize the threat before it was too late and had enough political capital with other groups to mount a credible defense. Occasionally, such efforts succeeded in threatening the state, but even then there was no guarantee that the new rulers would institute any substantial change of policy. More often than not, as in the case of Amanullah's overthrow, the religious/tribal insurrection led to a different member of the royal family taking charge and exercising a more prudent, but not fundamentally different type of rule.

While ultimately unsuccessful, the PDPA takeover changed the formula or at least proved that the formula could be changed. Instead of the usual combination of religious and tribal leaders overseeing an unwieldy and undisciplined mass intent on plunder, Taraki and Amin oversaw a network of highly disciplined, tightly organized, and ideologically motivated cadres ready to risk their lives at their leaders' prompting. The availability of these cohorts was made possible by the prior existence of the military and educational institutions that established the liminal space within which Pakhtuns (who provided the backbone of the Khalqi movement) could leave one world and worldview behind and adopt another. Recall the scene described before from the film *Naim and Jabar* in which the boy slipped his turban into his pocket. Many young men during this period felt the seduction of the modern world as it appeared before them, moving past, seeming to promise so much if only they knew how to get on board. Schools and the officer corps were full of such people, hung out between the old and the new, caught up in the day-to-day routine of learning (most of which was still conducted on something approximating the traditional rote model), while longing for something bigger and better and, above all else, different. The triumph of the PDPA was that it harnessed this youthful desire, gave it energy and purpose, and set it in motion. As is discussed in the next chapter, the tragedy of the PDPA was that the path it took was not one the vast majority of Afghans were prepared to follow.

3 The Armature of Khalqi Power

Having considered Taraki's life history and his relation to the party, I now consider how the Khalqi government attempted to reinvent the relationship between ruler and ruled. I have already noted various ways in which Taraki and the PDPA leadership deviated from established notions of who rulers could be and whom they should rely on. In this chapter, I consider the manner in which the government presented itself to the people it ruled, how it sought to enlist their support, and how those attempts to mobilize the population diverged in significant ways from long-established understandings of how the government should operate in its dealings with the people. Style is substance, no less in Afghan politics than in our own, and successful politicians learn to negotiate the protocols and practices of their society. The Khalqis, however, in their mode of self-presentation misjudged the needs and wishes of the Afghan people at every stage. Before examining the Khalqi case, I discuss the manner in which some preceding rulers related to their subjects in order to contextualize the strategy chosen by the revolutionary regime.

The first point to note in this analysis is an obvious one: the PDPA government saw its role differently from the way earlier Afghan rulers saw theirs. To take Abdur Rahman again as a point of departure, in his view the sovereign's primary responsibilities were ensuring the security of the kingdom and providing an orderly and peaceful atmosphere in which his subjects could be free to fulfill their divinely appointed duties as God-fearing Muslims. There was nothing in this social contract about ensuring happiness or prosperity or equality of opportunity, and indeed it was not a social contract at all that bound ruler and ruled but rather divine injunction: "Everyone's share is determined by God on the basis of his merit, circumstances, and capabilities. Your king also pays attention to these ranks among the people. He has appointed each one of you in one of these ranks from the commander-in-chief to the common soldier. Each one stands in his own place and position, and hence you people should be grateful to God and to the king."[1]

A graphic representation of the traditional relationship of ruler and ruled is seen in a photograph (Fig. 3), probably taken in 1903, that shows Amir Habibullah, son and successor of Abdur Rahman, at an official *darbar* (court reception) in Kabul. Standing next to the amir is his son, Amanullah, and arrayed to each side are various court officials and advisors to the amir. A row of soldiers and lesser officials fill the rear of the photograph, while notables in line in the foreground wait to pay their respects to the king. Everyone in the picture is dressed in Western-influenced clothing, but the elements of style are still traditional—the amir alone is seated, the raised platform and carpet indicate the exalted position of the king and his court, the canopy overhead protects the royal party from sun or rain, and the presence on the amir's right of his young son signals the continuity of the royal line. Also instructive is the fact that the ruler looks neither at the camera nor at any individual in the picture. The assembly is turned toward the ruler, but the ruler heeds his own counsel.

Habibullah was a modernist in one sense—he liked Western inventions, be they automobiles, photography, or golf; but he had little time for the political and social agendas that modernists brought with them and that began to sweep through his kingdom in the first two decades of the century. His son and successor, Amanullah, however, took a different tack. Heavily influenced by his intellectual mentor and father-in-law, Mahmud Beg Tarzi, Amanullah wanted to transform Afghanistan into a modern nation, and he set about that task shortly after he took power in 1919. As noted in the previous chapter, Amanullah was much given to trying on new ideas, as well as different styles of clothing. The most significant of these ideas was that government had a role to play in improving people's lives. This idea was not original to him; Ottoman and Indian intellectuals, among others, had been formulating the outline for a new Asian and Islamic renaissance in which the non-Western peoples would combine Western advances in science, technology, and political democracy with Asian spiritual and social values. Amanullah intended to be at the forefront of this renaissance, and he demonstrated this commitment through the promulgation of economic and social reform programs meant to improve the social conditions of ordinary people and through the adoption of a more informal and democratic manner of dealing with his subjects.

Though most of Amanullah's economic reforms were directed toward

3.   Amir Habibullah darbar, c. 1903 (Khalilullah Enayat Seraj Collection).

rationalizing the government's financial infrastructure and developing new industries, he outstripped the Khalqis in the area of social reform, especially with regard to women's rights and education. In keeping with his commitment to change, Amanullah adopted a relatively nonhierarchical manner of interacting with subordinates, as indicated in the following assessment by the British diplomat Sir Henry Dobbs, who met Amanullah in 1921 during treaty negotiations:

> His Majesty Amir Amanullah Khan is himself probably the most interesting and complex character in his dominions. His manners are popular, jocular and easy to such a degree that even in his public appearances he sometimes lays himself open to a charge of want of proper dignity. In private he loves to indulge in sheer horseplay, changing hats with his courtiers, throwing bits of bread at them or sprinkling them with soda-water, and making most intimate and daring jokes about their wives, families and personal appearance. He eschews all ceremony except in the most formal durbars, dislikes elaborate uniforms and affects a spartan simplicity in his clothes, usually not even wearing a shirt beneath his rough military jacket. Collars, ties and cuffs, which were de rigueur in his father's time, are now forbidden at his Court. . . . When transacting business he is extremely polite and gentle in manner to his Ministers and courtiers and bears himself among them merely as primus inter pares, encouraging them to argue with him freely and appearing to trust to his superior agility of mind for the gaining of his ends.[2]

4. Amir Amanullah meeting with tribal leaders, Jalalabad, 1925(?) (Khalilullah Enayat Seraj Collection).

One can get a sense of Amanullah's manner of relating to his subjects in a photograph (Fig. 4), taken in about 1925 in the winter palace at Jalalabad, that shows the amir meeting with tribal leaders. In the photograph, Amanullah is seated on the same level as his tribal subjects and appears to be looking them squarely in the eye. He has eschewed ceremonial garb in favor of a rough military jacket of the sort Dobbs noted, and he seems intent on pressing closer to the leaders, even as they appear intent on maintaining a wary distance. In this meeting, we see no sign of the usual entourage of retainers and officials of the sort that Habibullah usually surrounded himself with; a single secretary with pen and paper is seated to his right, and a spare number of trappings of office are nearby: a fly whisk behind him, a clock across the way, and a telephone set close at hand.

Coming from a more populist tradition, Americans tend to admire this sort of behavior, but Afghans had a good deal more trouble with it, especially with Amanullah's egalitarian treatment of women. For Amanullah, women's rights may have begun as a political issue, but they became personal for him after his marriage to the daughter of his mentor, Mahmud Beg Tarzi. Soraya was well educated herself, and Amanullah appears to have been devoted to her, as evidenced by his unwillingness to follow the usual royal practice of contracting numerous marriages for alliance, convenience,

5. Meeting of parliamentary deputies, Paghman, 1928 (Khalilullah Enayat Seraj Collection).

and pleasure. Amanullah's commitment to monogamy was strange enough, but his concerted efforts to reform other customary restrictions on women and girls, as well as his willingness to have Soraya appear in public without a veil, outraged many of his subjects. So too did other mostly symbolic but no less unorthodox gestures, such as his requirement that all delegates to the national assembly (*loya jirga*) in 1928 wear Western suits.[3] Figure 5 commemorates this occasion, which followed on the heels of Amanullah's grand tour of Europe, during which he had developed new ideas for the social and economic development of his country. The setting of the photograph was the bleachers of the Paghman race track. Amanullah had spent five days telling the delegates about his trip and his plans for the future. At the moment the photograph was shot, the amir is standing at the top of the aisle, saluting the photographer. Over to the side, his wife, Soraya, wearing the thinnest of veils, stands out as the only women in a sea of male faces— all of whom are dressed in the requisite suit and tie.

Following Amanullah's abdication and the short-lived reign of Bacha-i Saqao, and with the brief exception of the chaotic period of democratic liberalization in the late 1960s, rulers returned to the more autocratic style that Afghans knew and understood. The first of these rulers was Nadir Khan, a former general who governed in a martial fashion. He was assassinated in

6. President Muhammad Daud, Persepolis, n.d. (courtesy of Qasim Baz Mangal).

1933, apparently as part of a long-standing family feud, and was nominally succeeded by his teenage son, Zahir Shah, though for the next thirty years power resided principally with his uncles (Muhammad Hashim and Shah Mahmud) and cousin (Muhammad Daud), who ruled sequentially as prime ministers until 1963.[4] During this period, social reforms were gradually introduced, but in a nonconfrontational, nonthreatening way; for example, in 1959 the wives of the prime minister and other important government officials appeared unveiled on the viewing stand at the independence-day ceremonies. Afghans saw that this sort of behavior was once again condoned by the government, but no one was forced to go along, and, in fact, most people outside the upper and middle classes in Kabul chose to ignore the example. The archetype of the mid-twentieth century ruler was, in many respects, Muhammad Daud, who served as prime minister from 1953 to 1963 and as president of his short-lived republic from 1973, when he overthrew his cousin Zahir Shah, until the Saur Revolution in 1978.

Seen in a photograph taken at Persepolis during an official trip to Iran (Fig. 6), Daud was a forbidding but also perplexing figure. During his tenure as president, portraits of the baldheaded Daud glowering at passersby through half-tinted glasses were omnipresent in teahouses and offices. But it was never quite clear what Daud stood for. Was he a leftist—the so-called red prince of his early years—or a Pakhtun nationalist? During Daud's term as prime minister confrontations with Pakistan regarding the status of the border tribes reached their peak, but he also actively sought Soviet patronage. No one knew where Daud stood for sure, and one might read his vaguely menacing stare as masking a deep uncertainty as to what he wanted to accomplish with his power. Certainly, people didn't know what to make of him, and while some feared his anger, they also finally didn't find him that significant in their lives.

RULER AND RULED

> The people recognize me by the name of Taraki which is the well-known name of my tribe and clan. But I say openly that I do not belong to any particular tribe or clan. I belong to . . . the Pushtuns, Hazarah, Uzbek, Tajik and all the country's nationalities, noble tribes and clans, and I live in the hope of serving the hard-working peoples of this country.[5]

Taraki made the preceding statement in a meeting with elders from various provinces a little more than a month after coming to power, and one can only wonder how it was taken by those assembled to meet the new leader. They, after all, had been called to Kabul precisely because they were representatives of particular tribes and clans, and their status as Pakhtuns, Hazaras, Uzbeks, and Tajiks was evident to anyone who saw them in their ceremonial clothing or heard them speak in their native languages and dialects. In the midst of these representative types, Taraki claimed to be no type at all. Perhaps he hoped to appropriate the interstitial status that the Durrani dynasties had developed for themselves over two centuries of rule. People, after all, had not generally thought of the royal family as being associated with a particular tribe, despite their Pushtun roots. Most of the royal family members spoke Dari Persian among themselves, and some spoke Pushtu only haltingly.[6] More important, many Afghans viewed the royal family as having its own interests but not as favoring any particular ethnic group or tribe among those constituting the Afghan people, loyalty to the royal family itself being more significant than ethnicity. Taraki was not from the royal Muhammadzai lineage, however, and his assertion that he belonged to no group must certainly have rung false to those who heard it, as it would have if anyone among them had stood up and made a similar declaration. Religious leaders—particularly Sufi mystics—could profess their nonattachment to worldly allegiances, but a secular politician could not, and one must assume that those who listened to Taraki's address and many more like it did not gain a great deal of confidence from what he had to say.

That Taraki should try to engage his audience in this way is not surprising. The truth was that his regime desperately needed popular support. Despite initial claims in the government press that the PDPA had fifty thousand "members and close sympathizers" or the assertion made in July that the government was run by "millions of honest, courageous and patriotic people of Afghanistan . . . from every tribe and region in the country,"[7] the new regime probably had only a few thousand committed members at the time of the revolution, and its ethnic base of support narrowed considerably after the Parchami purges of mid-July took out most of the non-Pakhtun leadership. In certain respects, the situation faced by the PDPA was similar to that of Amanullah when he took power after the assassination of his father in 1919. On that occasion, many people suspected that Amanullah himself might have had a hand in the assassination, a suspicion that appeared to be substantiated when he imprisoned his uncle and older brother, both of whom had a better claim to the throne than he did. Amanullah succeeded in stifling any move against him, however, by redirecting popular discontent into a short-lived border jihad against the British in India. Since religious leaders (who had been his uncle's primary supporters) had been calling for a jihad for years, Amanullah defused any immediate attack against him and thereby bought the time he needed to consolidate his authority.[8]

The PDPA did not have a recognized foreign bogeyman to turn to, and the action that it had to defend was not a dynastic upheaval, which Afghans understood, but a revolution, an *inqilab*, which was an entirely unprecedented occurrence. Choosing the cautious path, the regime initially attempted to conciliate rather than upset the people it hoped to lead, soothing suspicions by inviting rural elites to meet the new ruler in darbar in Kabul. This was the traditional custom: bring the elders to the palace, present them with ceremonial robes and turbans, and assure them that the new rulers would treat them well and respect their autonomy. Taraki was new to the role, but he did his best; all through May and June, government newspapers published photographs and stories of the new leader meeting with groups of religious leaders and provincial elders. The vast majority of elders came from the Pakhtun frontier areas, including areas under Pakistani control, and it was not difficult to ascertain why the government sought out leaders from these areas.[9] This is where most acts of antistate violence over the preceding hundred years or so had originated, and, even more than Bacha-i Saqao, it was the border tribes that had been responsible for sealing Amanullah's unhappy fate. The Durranis of Qandahar may have been the erstwhile tribe of kings, but the Pakhtuns of the frontier were the kingmakers and breakers, a fact that Taraki alluded to when he told a group of Pakhtun elders, "You brother tribes be aware and consider the bitter experience of the Amani movement [those who supported the reforms of Amir Amanullah]. . . . The state is yours. It is not your master. It is your servant."[10]

The parade of elders continued through May and early June but then abruptly stopped in July, about the same time as the Parchami purges.[11] At this point Amin's ascendance began in earnest, and the first sign of his new power was the adoption of a more aggressive plan of reform. From this time forward, the policy of conciliating traditional elites appears to have been abandoned in favor of a more radical and reckless plan to mobilize the rural poor, who had never before been treated as politically significant by the government in Kabul. Under Amin's leadership, the regime staked its future on an alliance with small landholders, tenant farmers, agricultural laborers, and women—politically dormant segments of the population that no previous regime had ever taken seriously. While they represented the largest percentage of the people of Afghanistan, the rural poor had been too preoccupied with making ends meet and too oppressed by rural landowners and creditors to have ever taken much interest in politics or to have speculated on the potential of government for making their lives better. Henceforth, however, the nontribal peasantry was to become the bulwark of the regime, while the tribal elders and other rural elites, whom the regime had initially tried so hard to impress, were labeled "feudals" and "exploiters," the enemies of the people and the state.

The first stage in Amin's campaign to politicize and mobilize this population came in mid-July with the promulgation of Decree #6, whose objective was to ensure "the wellbeing and tranquility of the peasants [by] relieving them from the heavy burden of mortgage and backbreaking interests collected by the landlords and the usurers."[12] In an attempt to rally the rural poor to its banner, the regime used Decree #6 to excuse landless peasants from paying back all mortgages and debts, while allowing those who owned modest amounts of land to pay back only the original sum on debts and mortgages.[13]

The second phase of the PDPA campaign to mobilize previously unpoliticized segments of the population was launched on October 18, with the publication of Decree #7, "for ensuring the equal rights of women . . . and for removing the unjust patriarchal feudalistic relations between husband and wife and for consolidation of further sincere family ties." Among other provisions, this decree forbad the exchange of bride-price as part of marriage arrangements, limited dowries to a token amount, stipulated that both parties had to agree to a marriage for it to be legal, and outlawed the practice by which the widow of a man could be compelled to marry one of her husband's relatives.[14]

Finally, the third major piece of the PDPA plan was a comprehensive program of land reform, which was first discussed in depth in the *Kabul Times* in an article on July 19. This article claimed that 95 percent of the population subsisted on half of all the arable land, while the other 5 percent of the population controlled the other half. Seventy-one percent of landowners, according to the *Kabul Times*, owned from one to ten *jeribs* (one jerib is two thousand square meters), and most of these small landowners were also required to lease additional land from wealthier landowners in order to make ends meet. "Hence the vast majority of the villagers lease land under feudal conditions, i.e., in most cases inputs such as water, seeds, farm tools and implements, chemical fertilizer, means of transportation and the like have to be provided by the owner of the land, and the one who works on the land receives a small portion of the crop, as little as one sixth, in compensation for his hard work."[15] Although Taraki indicated shortly after taking power that it would take at least two years for the government to prepare the necessary surveys and otherwise lay the groundwork for land reform, the regime decided to push ahead with this program, presumably in response to the first signs of popular dissatisfaction, which appeared over the summer. Consequently, on December 2, the government published its Decree #8, the most important stipulation of which was that no family could own more than thirty jeribs of first-quality land and that no person could mortgage, rent, or sell land in excess of that amount.

Although the government promulgated many decrees in addition to these and promised still more, Decrees #6, #7, and #8 were the base on which the regime made its appeal for popular support, and press organs went to extreme lengths to inflate the success of the programs and demonstrate the general acclaim with which they were greeted. Thus, on October 3, Taraki reported to the Central Committee that 11.5 million landless peasants had been released from "the backbreaking burden of usury and mortgage"; and on October 18 it was announced that, after five months of the revolutionary regime, "millions of peasants were freed from the clutches of money-lenders and at least Afs. [Afghanis] 30 billion was gained by landless peasants or petty landlords."[16] According to government statistics, eight hundred agricultural co-ops with two hundred thousand participants had also been established. The lands of forty thousand farmers had been surveyed for redistribution. Two hundred houses had been built for agricultural-extension officials, with 136 more under construction. Fifteen hundred kilograms of seed had been distributed. Eleven hundred seventy new orchards and vineyards had been organized. Thirty-seven threshing machines, 380 ploughs, 300 wheelbarrows, one thousand sickles, and two hundred pitchforks had been distributed. Four million animals had been immunized or treated for disease. Twenty-three veterinary clinics had been opened. Two hundred sixty thousand boxes of silk cocoons had been handed out; and two hundred thousand acres of land, thirteen orchards, and seventy-six houses belonging to the Yahya dynasty had been "bequeathed" to people.[17]

The declarations of popular support were equally extreme. Thus, in July, banner headlines announced that "Peasants Hailed Decree No. 6," and articles throughout that month told how the decree was releasing "landless and petty land holders from the yoke of exploiters and feudals." In August, it was announced that a Muhammad Wazir of Faryab Province was so impressed with the new regime that he donated all his property to the government, including 150 jeribs of land, 480 sheep, 220 lambs, forty-two large and thirty-seven small goats, fourteen cows and calves, three donkeys, and one horse.[18]

In November, the reception for Decree #7 in Kunar Province was similarly enthusiastic, as "students and local people of Sarkanai staged a march in the streets of that *woleswali* [district administrative center] carrying the photographs of our beloved and revolutionary leader, shouting revolutionary slogans, hurrah and prolonged clappings." Government-sponsored rallies on behalf of the first two decrees proved to be mere rehearsals for the launching of the land-reform program in the winter of 1979. Throughout January and February, the *Kabul Times* published articles on the jubilation of peasants who were receiving their new land deeds and celebrating "chain-breaking" Decree #8. In these articles, in among descriptions of peasants chanting "death to feudalism," "death to imperialism," "long live and healthy be Noor Mohammad Taraki," a now-dispossessed former landlord is quoted as welcoming land reform "because if I lost my lands on the one hand I got rid of all the psychological pressures and torturing engagements on the other hand."[19]

One typical article with the headline "Now No One Will Flog Me to Work on His Land without Wage, Says Peasant" contained the following description of a grateful recipient of government largesse:

Haji Nasruddin, a peasant from Balla Bagh village of Surkhrod [in Ningrahar Province] said smilingly, "God is with those who are helpless. Consequently the decree number eight has come to our rescue. Hereafter whatever we reap belongs to us. Hereafter no feudal lords or middlemen will be able to cheat us. This all has happened with the attention of the Khalqi state. We the toiling peasants have been delivered forever. Today the government is headed by those who work solely for the benefit, for the welfare of the poor and downtrodden. It is a happy occasion that we the peasants have achieved our cherished desire.

"Now with the six jeribs land given to me I am sure I will become the owner of a decent living and will not die of hunger. Before the Saur Revolution the feudal lords used to loot all our products. The rulers at that time sided with the oppressive landlords. Fortunately the Saur Revolution has destroyed their dreams and they can no longer achieve their ominous goals."

Juma Gul another peasant from the same village said that ["]all my age has passed in poverty but today I have become the owner of land and I hope to continue the rest of my life with the peace of mind. Hereafter no one will dare flog me to work on his land without wages and I will be the master of my own destiny."[20]

Throughout the winter and spring of 1979, the government pushed land reform forward and announced on June 30 that the program had been completed, with 2,917,671 jeribs having been turned over to 248,114 households. An additional 151,266 jeribs had been allocated to state farms, and 125,000 jeribs had been assigned to local municipalities and provincial departments. All told, the government claimed to have redistributed a total of 3,193,937 jeribs.[21]

It is difficult to guess where all of these figures came from, or, to be more precise, it is unclear whether the land-redistribution figures published by the government represented actual transactions that took place, if only on paper, or were simply invented. We do know that by the spring of 1979, the government had lost its campaign to mobilize popular support, and it was already fighting just to maintain its bases in some areas of the country. The best explanations for this failure are those that take into consideration the local conditions and the situation in which the regime tried to interpose itself. In Part Two, I provide an in-depth explanation for one area of eastern Afghanistan, but here I want to examine some general matters relating specifically to how the Khalqis formulated the relationship of ruler and ruled and how that formulation was popularly perceived.

When the PDPA came to power, it tried to convince the people of their shared values and common concerns, as well as the fact that the government was the "servant" of the people, but the language used to convey these sentiments was an alien one. It was derived from a Marxist lexicon that had no roots in Afghan culture and that struck no resonant chord in the hearts and minds of the Afghan people. The government premised its appeal on two assumptions: first, that material concerns were foremost in people's minds and, second, that abstract principles of recent vintage could carry moral force. The failure of these premises, as well as the antipathy widely felt toward the people empowered by Khalqi rule, is illustrated in the following account by a village elder from the region of Khas Kunar on the east bank of the Kunar River, close to the border with Pakistan:

> In the beginning, the common people of Afghanistan didn't recognize the true identity and face of the Khalqis and Parchamis as infidels [*kafir*] and communists. And in their own slogans they said, "We respect Islam, and this is a government of the working people. Everyone has equal rights. And we will save all the people from poverty and hunger." The slogans that they used were things like "Justice" ['*adalat*], "Equality" [*masawat*], "Security" [*masuniyat*], "Home" [*kor*], "Food" [*dodai*], and "Clothing" [*kali*]. . . .
>
> After Decree #7, Decree #8 concerning land reform was announced. Since the population of Khas Kunar is very high and the land is very little, few people had more than thirty-six jeribs of land. Their number reached ten or fifteen. By the most shameful kind of action, they took these people's land and gave it to others. On the land of each one of these people, they organized a march, and they invited all the uneducated people, as well as the students, clerks, etc., to take part. When the land was dispensed and the deeds signed by Nur Muhammad Taraki were given out, they shouted "hurrah!" and slogans like "Death to the feudals!" "Death to the Ikhwan [Muslim Brotherhood]!" "Death to American Imperialism!" "Death to Reactionaries!" and that kind of thing.
>
> Since the slogans of the people of Afghanistan during happier times were "Allah-o Akbar!" [God is great] and "Ya Char Yar!" [Hail, Four Companions of the Prophet Muhammad], they became very unhappy and said that, in addition to the other deeds of the Khalqis and Parchamis, the fact that they had changed "Allah-o Akbar" and "Ya Char Yar" to "hurrah" was a sign of their infidelity.[22]

For Pakhtuns, the slogans chosen by the Khalqis conveyed little of a positive nature. Justice, equality, and security are loan words that make abstract what Pakhtuns typically feel they already have, and, in their experience, when justice, equality, and security are absent, it is precisely because of government interference in their lives of the sort that the new regime was promising. Similarly, *home, food,* and *clothing,* which were generally chanted in rallies as a single phrase ("kor, dodai, kali!"), are words that glorify material things that are morally inconsequential and properly kept within the domain of family and kin.

Likewise, when recalling marches at which people were encouraged to shout such phrases as "Death to the Feudals" and "Death to American Imperialism," one should keep in mind the difference between the rhetoric of Marxist opposition and the dynamics of tribal opposition that heretofore had held sway through much of Afghanistan. In tribal culture, to boast that you intend to kill someone places you under the burden of that claim. Utterances have consequences, and for one to publicly promise to do that which one does not intend ultimately to do or which cannot be done makes one appear foolish and dishonorable. That is to say, if people do not realize that words have weight and use them carelessly, then they cannot be trusted, for they are clearly unaware of the implications of honor and, as such, are a danger to themselves and others.

Beyond the morally contradictory nature of the slogans themselves, government-sponsored rallies failed to achieve their intended effect for several other reasons. Given the defensive orientation of Pakhtun groups and their longstanding suspicion of government interference in their affairs, the arrival in their community of government representatives promising to help them by taking the possessions of one group and giving them to another was hardly welcomed. Even those who directly benefited from the land redistributions were unprepared to receive government largesse. The problem here was not only that the language used by the PDPA was novel but also that people had not tended to look to the government for benefits and, when they had, they petitioned the government; the government did not petition them.

The approach taken by the regime was unprecedented, and in Pakhtun society the assumption is that unprecedented actions should be treated with circumspection until such time as they can be rendered familiar and unthreatening. Thus, when strangers came and encouraged all the poor people in a community to come together as a united body shouting slogans, the need for circumspection and a unified front against the outsiders increased— regardless of the offers and promises being made. In this way, public rallies and marches backfired, especially in rural areas and small towns, and they created the opposite effect from what was intended. Instead of loosening the ties that bound wealthy and poor, government attacks on the "feudal class" encouraged a defensive solidarity among the group as a whole and evoked sympathy for the wealthy, who came to be seen as victims of a more immediate oppression than the abstract oppression invoked by the government.[23]

Another issue to consider is the government rallies themselves as a form of public performance. These events usually involved the presentation by provincial and sometimes national officials of newly printed land deeds to tenant farmers and formerly landless agricultural laborers who were brought to the center of the town or village and handed placards praising the government and damning its enemies. Most newspaper photographs of these events show groups of newly enfranchised farmers carrying shiny shovels and slogan-covered placards while standing or marching in parade-ground formation. However the government intended these performances to be perceived, local people generally viewed them as an embarrassment and a disgrace. Nothing in their experience had prepared them for such events, the symbolic construction of which was interpreted as contradictory to modes of self-presentation esteemed in Pakhtun culture. Thus, for example, such stock performance devices as the unison shouting of praise for the revolutionary party while marching in formation were viewed by people as acts of public humiliation that violated their sense of individual initiative and control. For generations, many Pakhtuns had resisted service in the Afghan army (except when they were allowed to retain their tribal character by serving as militia units) because the discipline demanded by the army ran counter to the cultural valorization of individual autonomy. Wearing a uniform, marching in formation, and obeying the commands of officers were demeaning to Pakhtun sensibilities. However, at least such parade-ground displays were performed at a distance from home, and while it entailed a sacrifice of personal control, military discipline did have the saving virtue of being oriented toward success on the field of battle, an objective Pakhtuns understood and valued.

Government rallies, however, were events staged in the presence of the local community and required individuals to comport themselves in front of their peers in order to glorify an alien institution—the Khalq party. In tribal culture, the only kind of public chanting one traditionally heard was of a religious nature, and the only occasion when individuals lined up in formation and collectively performed orchestrated ritual actions was when they submitted to Allah in public prayer. That people were forced to perform other sorts of collective gestures and utter novel phrases in order to glorify an entity other than Allah made apparent a contradiction that doomed the party's efforts to enlist popular support. Whatever views people might have had about the inequalities of wealth and power in their communities, their belief in Islam was sacrosanct, and once it had been demonstrated to them that the government authorities wanted them to perform in a manner that placed secular principles above religion, their loyalty could not be reclaimed.

Another example of how the Khalqis lost the confidence and respect of the people was their construction of a cult of personality around President Taraki that transformed him from a "true son of the soil" into a grotesque socialist icon. The first signs of this cult appeared in the early summer after the coup, when headlines began referring to Taraki as "Great Leader." (For example, the June 27th headline of the *Kabul Times* announced, "Great Leader Says, We Wish to Ensure Our People a Happy and Prosperous Life.") The published biography examined in the preceding chapter was another milestone in the cult's development, as was the announcement on December 9 that Taraki's birthplace would be converted into a national museum with a special road, three large bridges, and twenty-five smaller bridges constructed to provide public access at a cost of 2.5 million Afghanis. Later, in April, the newspapers proclaimed that, for the first anniversary of the Saur Revolution, Taraki's birthplace "will be illuminated and decorated with photos of Great Leader of Khalq, national red flags, revolutionary slogans and coloured bulbs."[24]

One of the more bizarre manifestations of the Taraki cult was the publication in the government press on June 17 of doctored photographs in which the larger-than-life image of Taraki appeared, seated at his desk. In front of him, arrayed around a table, government functionaries, dwarfed by Taraki, are clapping and smiling in the presence of the benevolent "Great Leader" (Fig. 7).[25] On June 18, the same sort of photo was published, this time crudely depicting a giant Taraki with representatives from the Achikzai and Noorzai tribes, Baluchis from Qandahar, and elders from Badghis Province. The retrospective irony here is that as the manifestations of the cult of personality became increasingly outlandish and bizarre, Taraki's actual authority was steadily being sheared away by his erstwhile disciple Amin, who in all likelihood was the principal author of the Taraki cult and most certainly the agent of Great Leader's demise. It is interesting to examine this photograph next to those of earlier leaders. Taraki was the one leader who actually rose up from the masses to lead his country. The other leaders whose photographs I have included—Habibullah, Amanullah, Daud—all inherited their right to rule. Taraki pinned his right to rule on the people, the "people's party," and his own humble origins. Yet he was the one who ultimately—whether because of insecurity or secret vanity or the manipulations of others—attempted to inflate his stature, thereby only accentuating his limitations and inappropriateness as a ruler.

The same could be said as well of those who flocked to the party banner and were taken on as mid- and low-level government officials. Time and again, Afghans have commented to me about the quality of the people who

KABUL TIMES

Great Leader receives DRA's five year plan course participants

7. President Nur Muhammad Taraki (*Kabul Times,* June 18, 1979).

came to power with the revolution in the local, district, and provincial branches of administration. When the Khalqis came to power, they brought with them a new style of rule, what they called "a people's government [that] doesn't belong to anybody." The new regime, they declared, was "not a hereditary government run by a number of traitorous Sardars (princes); rather those who run your people's government at present are millions of honest, courageous and patriotic people of Afghanistan . . . your best patriotic sons from every tribe and region in the country."[26] What this meant in practice was that considerable power was exerted by local officials, many of whom had been students before the revolution and some of whom had been recruited and trained by Amin himself when he was a teacher and principal at the teacher-training college in Kabul.

As in many developing countries, teachers in prerevolutionary Afghanistan were poorly paid and had little clout in the communities in which they served. Even if they were respected for their learning, they were often outsiders, and, like mullas, they tended to be viewed in a patronizing light because of their dependent status and the fact that their jobs required that they spend most of their time in the company of children rather than adults.

One of the accusations most commonly leveled at these teachers once they ascended to positions of authority under the new regime was that they were more concerned with Marxist ideology than with the realities of the social milieus in which they found themselves. Perhaps because of the patronizing treatment and limited respect they had received before the revolution, they did not tend to make much effort to modulate directives coming out of Kabul to local sensibilities and sensitivities, and people came to resent what they considered their high-handed attitude.

Likewise, many informants claimed that after the revolution the party attracted opportunists who exploited the power given them. In the words of one man from Paktia Province, those who first joined the party after the revolution were the kind who "had begun school but not finished, who had wanted to become bus drivers but only managed to become ticket collectors. They started off to work in the Emirates but only made it as far as Iran." One oft-heard claim is that the party was so short of members when it took power that it would take anyone willing and able to spout back party doctrine and sport the droopy mustaches then in favor among Khalqi supporters. Men from good families and with established reputations would never humiliate themselves in this way, but individuals from the lower strata of society had no family or personal reputation to disgrace and much potentially to gain by association with the party. In the words of Shahmund, the Mohmand elder quoted in the previous chapter, "the sword of real iron cuts." Men from poor families were unlikely to manifest nobility or to show abilities that had previously gone unnoticed just because they had been elevated to positions of power. In the view of most Afghans with whom I have talked, this type of individual—no-accounts from ignoble families—flocked to the government when the PDPA took power, and not surprisingly they were only too happy to carry out the regime's campaign against "feudal exploiters" by debasing the old elites who had previously held pride of place over them.

If these elites had been genuinely resented by the less-wealthy and less-prominent strata of society, then the treatment meted out to them by government officials might have been appreciated or at least tolerated. However, in most parts of Afghanistan in the late 1970s, differentials of wealth, while present, were not extreme, the economy was not heavily monetized, and investment opportunities were scarce, all of which meant that more prosperous landowners were generally not taking their profits out of the area. To the contrary, it was still most common for the wealthy to reinvest their profits within their communities through guesthouses (*hujra*) where they fed their allies, friends, kinsmen, tenant farmers, and potential political supporters.[27] The continuing involvement and investment of the wealthy in their communities, coupled with local beliefs about the sanctity of private property and the generally poor opinion people had of Khalqi officials, meant that in most locales people rejected out-of-hand government efforts to enlist their support.

ENEMIES OF THE PEOPLE

When the PDPA regime first took power in April 1978, the principal threat with which it was concerned was subversion from abroad. Thus, in the first issue of the *Kabul Times* published after the coup d'état, the regime lashed out at "the mass media of foreign reaction," which was spreading false propaganda against the "triumphant revolution of Saur Seven." The false foreign-press reports blasted by the regime labeled the revolution a coup d'état "launched under the leadership of the communist party of Afghanistan with the help of this or that foreign country." The government's position was that "the revolutionary stand of Seventh Saur is the beginning of a truly democratic and national revolution of the people of Afghanistan and not a coup d'état." In similar fashion, the regime railed at "international reactionary circles" that "shamelessly lie that thousands of our patriots were either killed or executed in the course of the revolution and that one of the great religious figures has been executed or that the revolutionaries had acted in contravention of the principles of human rights, the Islamic religion and our national traditions." At the same time the government was focusing primarily on the threat of subversion by reactionary forces abroad, the Interior Ministry also warned citizens that "in such a revolutionary situation a number of profiteering, wicked, intriguing, subversive and anti-revolutionary elements [might] appear on the scene posing themselves as revolutionaries and consequently cause inconvenience and indulge in threatening and provoking of compatriots and social disruption."[28]

In the beginning, no one in the PDPA leadership knew precisely where the greatest "antirevolutionary" threat might lie. Perhaps surviving members of the Daud regime would rise up to challenge the legitimacy of the Taraki government. Perhaps the former king, Zahir Shah, or those close to him, would mount an attack from abroad, as Zahir Shah's father had done when Bacha-i Saqao had taken the throne in 1929. Then again, there was the threat of subversion from within the party itself; this threat was dealt with summarily in July, when the leadership of the Parcham wing was sent abroad. Despite these uncertainties, however, both historical precedent and personal experience suggested to the leadership that their greatest threat would come from forces representing or claiming to represent Islam.

Amir Abdur Rahman, after all, had had to deal with hostile religious leaders, the Mulla of Hadda prominent among them, throughout his reign; and his grandson, Amanullah, had finally been undermined by a religious/tribal coalition centered around various religious figures, principally the Hazrat of Shor Bazaar.[29] Since Amanullah's downfall, religious leaders had generally been quiescent, but a new generation of secularly educated Muslim activists had risen up in Kabul at roughly the same time that the Marxist parties had begun their activities. Amin, in particular, would have been wary of this threat, for the students he recruited in the late 1960s and early 1970s had regularly faced off against the Muslim student activists in classrooms, in cafeterias, and on the street during sometimes bloody political demonstrations. For much of his tenure in office, President Daud—to his ultimate misfortune—had been more afraid of Muslim activists than of Marxist ones, and he had been responsible for imprisoning many Muslim student leaders. However, some had escaped his dragnet and had taken up residence in Pakistan, where they had been receiving assistance from the Pakistan government of Prime Minister Zulfiqar 'Ali Bhutto and were preparing themselves for battle against the new regime.

Given his leftist sympathies, Bhutto might have been willing to work with the PDPA and revoke his support for Islamic opposition leaders who had found a safe haven in Pakistan, but by the time of the Saur Revolution, Bhutto was out of power, and the more devout President Zia ul-Haq had taken his place. Whatever slim chance the PDPA regime might have had of reaching an accord with Pakistan over the removal of the still small and ineffectual Islamic parties on their soil was eliminated when the Kabul government began inviting Pakhtun tribes from the Pakistan border areas to meet Taraki. At various times since the founding of Pakistan, the Afghan government had contested Pakistan's authority over the border areas, most memorably in the late 1950s, when the two countries broke off relations and closed their borders. Consequently, the Khalqi government's decision to court the cross-border tribes must have been taken as an insult and threat, particularly after it announced its support for an independent Pakhtun state along the frontier.[30] Bhutto had first given refuge and assistance to the Muslim student leaders because of President Daud's backing of "Pakhtunistan." Daud had recognized the risk involved in continuing this policy over Pakistani objections and had backed off, but the PDPA made the decision to again embrace Pakhtunistan, presumably to help defuse tribal opposition to the regime. In so doing, however, it guaranteed the survival of the ultimately more dangerous Islamic movement, without in any appreciable way bolstering tribal support.

The regime tried to counter the still labile Islamic threat by reiterating its respect for Islam and equating the Islamic principles of "equality, brotherhood and social justice" with the guiding principles of the regime.[31] Likewise, at the beginning of Ramazan, which fell in early August in the year of the revolution, the regime arranged for the traditional recitation of the Qur'an and prayers to be held at the People's House. An article in the *Kabul Times* about this event noted that while in the past Ramazan prayers had been held in only 164 mosques in Kabul, this year they would be performed in 182.[32] However, at the same time that the regime was trying to affirm its Islamic beliefs, it also had to acknowledge the developing threat represented by Muslim extremists based in Pakistan. One example of the regime's manner of dealing with this threat can be seen in Taraki's address of August 2 to military officers, which was discussed in the previous chapter. In this speech, Taraki provided his first extensive commentary on the rising threat posed by the Islamic resistance movement:

> When our party took over political power, the exploiting classes and reactionary forces went into action. The only rusty and antiquated tool that they use against us is preaching in the name of faith and religion against the progressive movement of our homeland. The bootlickers of the old and new imperialism are treacherously struggling to nip our popular government in the bud. They think that since we took over power in 10 hours, they would, perhaps, capture it in 15 hours. But they must know that we are the children of history and history has brought us here. These agents of international reaction ought to know that by acting in this way they are banging their heads against a brick wall. These agents of imperialism who plot under the mask of faith and religion have not begun this task recently. They have been busy conspiring against progressive movements in this fashion for many long years. You will remember the crimes they committed in various forms in Egypt and other Arab countries. Now their remnants and pupils existing in Afghanistan are acting under the mask of creed and religion in a different fashion. They ought to be uprooted as a cancerous tumor is from the body of a patient in a surgical operation.[33]

While promising that the government and party were "so fully in control that they will not give them a chance . . . to carry out their evil deeds," Taraki's statements demonstrate that already at this early date the resistance was making an impact that the government couldn't ignore or pretend was insignificant. Taraki's approach to this threat though was predictable. He emphasized that those working against the regime were—like Nadir before them—"agents of imperialism" out to undermine Afghan independence. Echoing the propaganda of earlier regimes against Muslim opponents, Taraki claimed in this speech that the regime's enemies were not truly inspired by Islamic principles but simply "plot under the mask of faith and religion." In later speeches, he embroidered this allegation by referring to the Islamic forces arrayed against him as "made-in London *maulanas* [religious scholars]"[34] and as "the spies of the farangis" who "have spread fire in Afghanistan several times but this time the people of Afghanistan have spread fire against them."[35] Taraki was referring here to the overthrow of Amanullah, which many Afghans (including some who took up arms against the amir) suspected was secretly instigated and supported by the British government in India. The fact that the British had been absent from the scene for more than thirty years when the regime made its accusations against "made-in London maulanas" would seem to be evidence either of the enduring power of British imperialism as a symbol of evil in Afghan politics or of the inability of the regime to come up with more effective rhetorical ammunition to counter the growing threat.

By the fall of 1978, antigovernment violence had risen dramatically, and the regime announced that it was "declaring jihad" against "the *ikhwanush shayateen*"—the brotherhood of Satan. Drawing attention to the philosophical connection between the Muslim activists who had gotten their start at Kabul University and the Ikhwan ul-Muslimin (the Muslim Brotherhood) in Egypt, articles in the state-run press condemned Egyptian radicals for hollowing out copies of the Qur'an in order to conceal guns inside and accused Afghan "Ikhwanis" at Kabul University in the early 1970s of having torn up copies of the Qur'an and then blaming leftist students as a way of defaming their opponents. Anti-Ikhwan articles appeared throughout the fall and winter, climaxing in an article on April 1, which stated that "these 'Brothers of Satan,' these Muslim-looking 'farangis' clad in white but not able to cover their black faces, these false clergymen who have been inspired by London and Paris . . . they are actually ignorant of Islam as they have only learned espionage techniques in London. They wish our people to abandon their religion and be marked with a seal from London."[36]

The PDPA's decision to declare jihad against its enemies can be taken as a measure of its desperation after only half a year of rule, especially given the mixed success of state-sponsored jihads in Afghanistan. In 1896, as the Mulla of Hadda and other religious leaders were stirring up trouble against British posts along the frontier, Abdur Rahman had published and distributed among the border tribes a pamphlet in which he asserted—with appropriate Qur'anic citations—that only a lawful Islamic ruler could declare jihad.[37] With his unerring eye for subversion, Abdur Rahman recognized that the activities of the mullas, though directed against his neighbors and not his own regime, could nevertheless embolden the more fractious among them to redirect their efforts against the Afghan state and to claim religious justification for doing so. The anticolonial uprisings of 1896–1897 ultimately failed to achieve their objective of forcing the British out of Peshawar and the frontier, but they did set the stage for a continuing dispute between the state and Afghan religious leaders over who had the right to raise the banner of jihad.

This dispute bubbled up again in 1914–1915, during the reign of Amir Habibullah, when disciples of the now-deceased Mulla of Hadda again agitated for holy war against Great Britain. Habibullah resisted these efforts, on the same grounds set forth by his father, but shortly after his ascension to the throne in 1919, Amir Amanullah allied his government with the religious forces that had long been urging an attack against British bases along the border. Though he disagreed with religious clerics on almost every other matter, Amanullah had long shared their desire to curtail British dominance in the region and had futilely urged his father to declare war to achieve this end, undoubtedly also recognizing the opportunity provided by such a war to consolidate his own rule in the wake of his father's assassination. The hoped-for war began on May 15, 1919, with an address by Amanullah at the central Id Gah mosque in Kabul; these are some of the words that he is purported to have spoken on that day:

> The treacherous and deceitful English government . . . twice shamelessly attacked our beloved country and plunged their filthy claws into the region of the vital parts of our dear country which is the burial ground of our ancestors and the abode of the chastity of our mothers and sisters, and intended to deprive us of our very existence, of the safety of our honor and virtue, of our liberty and happiness, and of our national dignity and nobility. . . . It became incumbent upon your King to proclaim jehad in the path of God against the perfidious English Government. God is great. God is great. God is great.[38]

In this declaration of war, Amanullah hit all the notes guaranteed to arouse Afghan indignation. The British were not depicted as an honorable adversary but as bestial, dirty, and animal-like in their method of assault. They were the attackers, and in their attack they violated the inviolable: the sanctity of the community, defined here in culturally coded terms as "the burial ground of our ancestors" and "the abode of the chastity of our mothers and sisters." At stake here was more than land; it was honor, liberty, and dignity—values that Afghans esteem above all other virtues. Finally,

Amanullah framed his response in religious terms as a jihad, a struggle on behalf of Islam, and he concluded with the traditional rallying cry of *allah-o akbar* (God is great). Though in later years the war became known in more nationalistic terms as the *jang-i istiqlal* (the war of independence), it was framed at the time as a religious jihad, and Amanullah relied heavily on religious leaders to extend his message into the tribal areas. At his urging, the Hazrat of Shor Bazaar and several family members, who were well-known Sufi *pirs* (masters), accompanied the troops to Paktia, where many of their disciples lived, and convinced the local tribes to join the fighting. Similarly, in the eastern (*mashreqi*) border areas of Ningrahar and Kunar, disciples of the Mulla of Hadda served as Amanullah's messengers and preached to their followers the virtue of fighting against the infidel British.

The war was ultimately short-lived and inconclusive in its results, but the Afghans managed to achieve one significant military victory, and the British, still depleted after the First World War, agreed to a cessation of hostilities and diplomatic terms that the Afghans viewed as favorable to their status as an independent nation. More important to the discussion at hand, the war showed the potential advantage to a ruler of using the terminology and apparatus of religious jihad for his own ends. Amanullah's ultimate downfall, however, also demonstrated the risks of this strategy, for in lending his support to religious leaders like the Hazrat of Shor Bazaar, he gave them a stage that helped to energize and strengthen their own standing with the people. Consequently, when he began his controversial reform program, the Hazrat was well positioned to oppose him and rally the same tribesmen against Amanullah whom he had earlier mobilized against the British.

Taraki's use of jihad to check the Muslim opponents of his regime proved ineffectual by comparison with Amanullah's use of the same rhetoric to oppose Great Britain, in part because Taraki was directing his rhetoric not at a foreign enemy but at other Afghans. At the same time, given that he had come to power not through any recognized set of procedures but by the violent overthrow of the previous regime, Taraki was not in a strong position to argue, as Abdur Rahman had been able to do, that he alone had the right to declare jihad. His situation was even further compromised by his prior rejection of the title of *amir* (they being the ones who are named in the Qur'an as entitled to declare jihad) in favor of such Soviet-flavored titles as general secretary (*umumi munshi*) of the party and president (*ra'is*) of the Revolutionary Council. Of the various honorifics attached to his name, none made any reference to Islam or put him in a position to wield religious authority, which he had anyway eschewed in his oft-repeated assertion that he owed his power to the party, not to God.

Likewise, there had never been a religiously sanctioned installation cer-emony when Taraki had come to power. No religious figure had ever fol-lowed the time-honored practice of tying a turban around or placing a crown on Taraki's head or otherwise symbolizing religious ratification of his rule. The only support the PDPA regime had managed to secure was from a group of unrepresentative and much-maligned government-employed clerics. The better-known religious leaders had been conspicu-ously absent from official ceremonies and news accounts, and rumors had quickly spread that a number of well-known religious figures had been arrested after the revolution. Among these rumors was one concerning Muhammad Ibrahim Mujaddidi, the son of the same Hazrat of Shor Bazaar, who had played a major role in overthrowing Amanullah. Although not conspicuously political like his father, Ibrahim Mujaddidi was said to have been arrested, along with most of his family, on orders from the Khalqi leadership. No one knew for certain what happened to the Hazrat and his family, but after his disappearance people came to believe that they had all been executed on the orders of Taraki or Amin (or both). In time, those rumors would be verified, though no one has ever been able to prove—as rumors have indicated—that the family was bound and gagged and placed in tin shipping trunks, that targets were affixed to these trunks, and that soldiers who were ignorant of who or what was inside were ordered to use the trunks for firing practice.

In their efforts to check the spread of popular opposition, the regime was hobbled more than anything by its own terminology. From the beginning, it claimed to be different. It was a party of workers and toilers who had come to power not through dynastic succession or even dynastic strife, both of which had precedents in Afghan history, but through a revolution (inqi-lab)—a "turning around" from what was normal to something altogether out of the ordinary. For people who felt themselves to be oppressed by and alienated from their society's institutions, who took no solace in what the culture offered them, and who saw no hope in the present or the future, the language of revolution, of overturning the existing order for something unknown and untried, might prove attractive. But most Afghans—what-ever their economic circumstances—were not so radically estranged from their social institutions and their universe of cultural signs and signifiers that they found the language of revolution compelling. If anything, it smelled of trouble, of sanctioned disorder, which in the universe of Islamic belief amounted to fitna—sedition, nuisance, trouble, mischief. In the Qur'an, believers are warned against the dangers of fitna in a passage that urges the followers of Muhammad to expel their disbelieving kinsmen from Mecca because "fitna is worse than killing. Fight them until there is no more fitna and the religion of God prevails."[39]

In the winter and spring of 1979, the Khalqi regime went more and more on the defensive, attempting to counter charges by the "farangis and their puppets" that they were burning mosques ("We have never burnt the mosques but we have constructed them. We have painted them and decorated them well.") and confiscating sheep and arresting women ("We will neither take anybody's sheep nor anybody's woman—who is our sister. She is our honour, and we make efforts to defend them every moment.").[40] In the summer of 1979, the government tried to substantiate its claim that the resistance parties were the enemies of Islam by holding a press conference at which four residents from a village in the Zurmat district of Paktia Province recounted separate attacks on their villages by "Ikhwanis" who "were burning the Holy Koran and bombing and destroying the mosques. Those who were trapped in their criminal onslaught begged them, Holy Koran in hand, but Ikhwanis ignoring the sacred religious book of Islam, continued their ominous actions."[41]

During this same period, in a further effort to shore up its support, the regime began a second series of daily meetings with elders from the Pakhtun border zone and other areas with a history of antistate activity, such as Kalakan and Mir Bachakot north of Kabul. The government-sponsored religious organization, the Jamiat ul-Ulama Afghanistan (Society of Afghan Clerics), also trumpeted its support for the regime, declaring that it was lawful according to Islamic law for the government and its supporters to "kill Ikhwanis" in the prosecution of its jihad against enemies of the revolution.[42] Regardless of these efforts, however, the battle against the resistance was going more and more badly. Some reports indicate that Amin even tried to negotiate a power-sharing agreement with Gulbuddin Hekmatyar, the leader of Hizb-i Islami Afghanistan (Islamic Party of Afghanistan), one of the earliest and best-organized resistance parties. But a deal never emerged, and the regime's reputation continued to plummet amid rumors of arrests and nighttime executions and stories of civilian massacres.

Other rulers before Taraki had also been known for their ruthless suppression of enemies, notably Abdur Rahman, who blew enemies of the state from the mouth of the noon cannon in Kabul and locked up robbers in iron cages suspended on tall poles and allowed them to starve to death in public view so that passersby could reflect on the fate of those who stole on the king's highway. Nothing the Khalqis did ever approached Abdur Rahman's punishments in terms of conspicuous excess, but they nevertheless inspired revulsion: first, because general understandings of the acceptable limits of behavior had changed; second, because of their secretiveness; and, third, because many of their victims were known to be innocent of any offense against the regime. For the residents of Kabul and other cities, the regime's practice of arresting people under cover of dark and not allowing any communication between those accused and their relatives was the source of the most resentment and fear.[43] For those in the countryside, the source of fear was the possibility of being held responsible for antigovernment violence. The most notorious of such retributions was the massacre at the village of Kerala in the Kunar Valley, which occurred in April 1979 and resulted in the deaths of more than one thousand unarmed males.[44]

If the people needed evidence that the Saur Revolution had introduced not needed reform but an era of irreligious disorder, then mass arrests and incidents like the massacre at Kerala provided it and eroded the little store of credibility the regime had built up with the people. And while Taraki and Amin might have been oblivious to this fact or at least still hopeful that their fortunes might change, their Soviet patrons were less sanguine. They viewed the progressive disablement of the Khalqi regime with mounting dismay and horror, particularly the fact that the popular movement gaining the upper hand against their clients in Kabul was becoming increasingly identified with Islam, a force they knew very well could be revived in their own Central Asian republics. The Soviets were not about to let a sympathetic government fall to a popular insurrection. Better to give the lie to the rhetoric of peasant revolution against feudal oppression—a rhetoric that had been on shaky ideological ground to begin with in Afghanistan—than allow a well-meaning, if incompetent, government to fall to a minimally organized and undersupplied insurgency.

CONCLUSION

From an orthodox Marxist point of view, the PDPA was ahead of its time, trying to create a socialist revolution in a society that was still solidly feudal and a generation or more from achieving a full-blown capitalist economy. While it is doubtless the case that the party got ahead of itself, paying more attention to the ideological blueprint than to the complex realities of the society that blueprint was designed to transform, it is also true that the regime had an opportunity to stay in power and implement incremental change had they had the strategic sense to do so. Many of the mistakes the Khalqis made were avoidable; indeed, many were repetitions of the errors made by Amanullah fifty years earlier and should have been apparent to them as such. Of these, several stand out, such as the decision to highlight women's rights as a banner issue immediately after coming to power. The education, empowerment, and politicization of women promised to be a multigenerational struggle. It would not be accomplished in six months, and from a strictly pragmatic perspective the enlistment of women into the coalition—even if it could have been carried off—offered little practical political advantage to the regime. Contrary to what the Khalqis seem to have believed possible, women were not likely to become a "surrogate proletariat" any time soon, and if Amanullah's experience offered no other lesson, it should have been that interference in domestic affairs was a tripwire issue for conservative elements in the country.[45]

Similarly, one wonders at the decision by the regime to embrace the red regalia of Soviet rule, especially after its leaders had wisely distanced themselves from the Soviets in their first few weeks in office. Foreign interference is the other hair-trigger issue for Afghans, whose history is punctuated and defined by its wars with Great Britain. Adoption of red flags and other Soviet-inspired emblems was doubly troubling for Afghans in that it brought to mind their own history and mythology of foreign intervention, while also invoking the dismal specter of the Bolshevik conquest of Bukhara and other Central Asian polities. In the same vein, the use of Soviet-style rhetoric was another crucial mistake, for rural Afghans, who never read newspapers and rarely saw government insignia, did listen to the radio and recognized the resemblance between the rhetoric coming from Kabul and that from the local-language radio stations broadcasting from Soviet Central Asia. A final error on the part of the Khalqi regime—as discussed in this chapter—was the symbolic mismanagement of its reform platform, which succeeded only in alienating those it intended to win over. Viewed in this light, the Khalqis failed not just because of bad policies, inept leaders, or dreadful timing; of at least equal importance was the regime's rejection of the symbolic codes of Afghan society and the wholesale importation of an extraneous set of codes borrowed from Soviet Marxism. Given Taraki's career as a social-realist writer steeped in the minutiae of daily life and the regime's identification with peasants and workers, it is surprising that he and his partisans would be so disdainful of the sensibilities and sensitivities of the people they hoped to lead.

The only viable explanation for this blindness is perhaps that they were so seduced by the promises of ideology that they lost sight of the social realities around them. Taraki, Amin, and the lesser lights of the party were in the grip of a belief system that led them to believe in the inevitability of what they were doing, and their early experiences only confirmed that message. Thus, when the revolution came, it all fell into place so easily. The once terrifying, glowering Daud and his all-powerful ship of state slipped beneath the waves with barely a groan or a shudder. Few mourned their passing, and none of those left from the royal lineage had the stomach or talent to challenge the usurpers. As for the people, they had experienced a coup d'état before. Daud himself had conditioned them to this reality of modern life, and no one seemed to bother much when it happened again. In the eyes of the Khalqi leadership, the revolution had gone as planned. Really, it had gone better than they ever could have hoped, and their Soviet mentors were right over the border, eager to lend their support. What need then was there for caution? Taraki had been proven a prophet when the first phase of his "short cut" to revolution had gone off without a hitch. All that remained was to complete the process by incorporating the people. What the Khalqis forgot was that the people were still by and large very much in the grip of the old ways; among other things, they were willing to abide changes in Kabul only as long as the new rulers kept their distance and didn't try to alter the time-honored rules of relationship. Taxes were a recognized part of that relationship, as were schools, conscription, and the punishment of crimes; interference in domestic arrangements and other cultural practices was not.

In violating this basic tenet of governance, the Khalqis unleashed a firestorm of popular protest. That much we know; but less commonly remarked on is the role of the regime in helping to ensure that the popular insurgency took on a religious cast. This was the final and in some ways most lasting mistake of Taraki and Amin, for in focusing as they did on the threat of the Islamic elements of the insurgency they helped to define the ensuing conflict in Islamic terms. In retrospect, this seems almost inevitable, but at the time of the coup d'état, Islam appeared to be moving in the direction of many Western religions: it was becoming a matter of personal belief rather than of social or political consequence.[46] We know now what we didn't know then—namely, political Islam, marching in competitive lockstep with Marxism, had been gaining a constituency in the schools and military, and radical Muslim parties had been making their own plans to take power for some time before the Marxist revolution. However, these efforts, like those of the Marxist parties, were confined to interstitial institutions such as schools and the military and were not widespread in the society at large.

As discussed in Chapter Six, efforts by the proto–Hizb-i Islami party to spread its message of radical Islam to the general population had been conspicuously unsuccessful. People were not interested in supporting radical Islam any more than they were interested in radical Marxism. When the Marxists defied the odds and took power, however, they immediately assumed that their greatest threat would come from their old rivals, the Islamists, with whom they had often butted heads on campuses and in army units. They failed to recognize that their rivals had the same problem they did of mobilizing ordinary people to their cause. In April 1978, the Islamic parties were economically impoverished and politically marginalized, and, as will be seen, they played a relatively minor role when insurrections broke out that first summer. But that wasn't the way the Khalqis saw it. In their myopia—their vision still obscured by the covert campus and cadre struggles of the late 1960s and early 1970s—the hand of the Ikhwanis was behind all their troubles. Or maybe they knew that the opposition to their efforts was more broadly based than they were willing to admit publicly, and they hoped to limit and ultimately defame the popular insurgency by associating it with the heretofore unpopular Islamic student movement. If that was their strategy, however, it backfired, for in highlighting the role of the Ikhwanis and demonizing them as "brothers of Satan," they were putting a national spotlight on a movement that at the time was little known outside Kabul and giving it a prominence that would eventually translate into greater public visibility and material support from foreign governments eager to aid the anti-Marxist cause. Thus, just as the Khalqis mishandled the symbolic apparatus of power, thereby alienating those they sought to woo, so their maladroit rhetoric also helped to empower enemies who were as estranged from any significant base of popular support as the regime itself.

Coda The Death of a President

KABUL, Oct. 10 (Bakhtar).—Noor Mohammad Taraki, former
president of the Revolutionary Council died yesterday morning
of serious illness, which he had been suffering for some time.
   The body of the deceased was buried in his family graveyard
yesterday.[1]

Most observers date the end of the Saur Revolution to December 29,
1979, when the Soviet Union began its invasion and decade-long occupation
of Afghanistan. In a symbolic sense, however, the revolution came to an end
in late September of that year, when President Nur Muhammad Taraki was
put to death on the orders of his erstwhile protégé, Hafizullah Amin. Since
that time, there has been considerable speculation as to why Amin decided
to assassinate Taraki. The most widely accepted theory is probably that
Amin was afraid for his own position, afraid that the Soviet Union was conspiring with Taraki to eliminate him from power. A week or so before his
death, Taraki had completed a trip that took him to Cuba and the Soviet
Union. While in Moscow, he had met with Brezhnev, and it was later
reported that Sayyid Daud Tarun, an aide-de-camp to Taraki secretly in
league with Amin, had sent back word to Amin that the Soviets were planning on establishing a new coalition between Taraki and Karmal that would
mean Amin's ouster from power.
   According to Hasan Kakar, who has written the best and most unbiased
account of these events, the rift between Taraki and Amin had begun back in
March of 1979, after Amin was promoted to first minister. One point of difference between the two leaders concerned relations with the Soviet Union,
with Taraki advocating Afghanistan's incorporation within the Soviet bloc
and Amin wanting to maintain greater neutrality. Equally important was
Amin's increasing monopolization of power, which alienated him from

87

Taraki and other former Khalqi allies who, "being more or less of the same age as Amin, felt a sense of rivalry with him. They rallied behind Taraki, who, as a cofounder of the party and as an elder, was like a father to them." Thus began a complicated chess game, involving various Khalqi leaders and Soviet advisors, each working for himself and most deciding eventually that Amin was a danger to them all. Despite the growing animosity between them, Amin continued to build up Taraki's cult of personality, by calling him "genius of the East," "the powerful master," and "the body and soul of the party," all the time continuing to refer to himself as "his loyal disciple." In Kakar's analysis, however much Taraki enjoyed the attention lavished on him, he was not willing to serve "as a figurehead under 'his loyal disciple,'" and he resisted Amin's efforts to marginalize him.[2]

The first open demonstration of a rift came in July at a politburo meeting at which Amin blamed Taraki for the government's failures. Taraki retaliated the next month, accusing Amin of nepotism. The climax came on September 14, following Taraki's return from Moscow, when Amin was called to a meeting at the presidential palace. Despite assurances from Soviet advisors as to his safety, the meeting was a trap, during which Amin was to be captured or killed. However, Amin managed to escape from the ensuing gun battle, and, with his greater political strength in the armed forces and the military units of the Interior Ministry, he succeeded in having Taraki secretly arrested. On September 16, Amin was "elected" general secretary of both the Central Committee of the People's Democratic Party of Afghanistan and the Revolutionary Council, as well as president and first minister of the Democratic Republic of Afghanistan. At the same time, newspapers announced that Amin had appointed a new cabinet, ousting Taraki loyalists. They also published a report that Amin's ally, Tarun, had been buried without indicating that he had been killed protecting Amin during the skirmish in the presidential palace. People were also not told why the eastern city of Jalalabad was officially renamed Tarun shortly after Amin's takeover or why the newspapers were declaring that "one-man rule will be no more in Afghanistan."

Most important, no one yet knew the fate of Taraki, the once ubiquitous presence who without warning had disappeared from the news. This situation was untenable, and in early October Amin informed the press that the former president was gravely ill, without specifying the nature of the illness or appearing in any way saddened by the surprising and sudden decline of the man he had once so publicly worshiped. Kabul was inevitably awash in rumors about Taraki's whereabouts, and they were only partially allayed by a two-sentence article that appeared in the press on October 10; it confirmed

Taraki's death and indicated that he had been buried in a family plot. Amin thereafter attempted to consolidate his own authority, but the Soviets had been committed to Taraki and his planned coalition with Karmal and the Parchamis. Although Taraki was now dead, the coalition was still a possibility, if only Amin could be removed from the scene. To accomplish this end, the Soviets set in motion their plan to topple Amin and return Karmal to Kabul aboard a Soviet aircraft, a move that would effectively place Afghanistan under Soviet control but at the price of alienating the people once and for all from the government.

Karmal's return on December 27, 1979, effectively signaled the end of the Saur Revolution, but what of Taraki himself—the architect and most visible icon of revolution? Amin announced the death of his former mentor after a grave illness, but the truth of course was different and is worth recounting. And it can be recounted because one of the first official acts of the Soviet-installed Karmal regime was to publish an article on the "martyrdom" of Taraki at the hands of "Hangman Amin." The focus of this article is a "confession" by Lieutenant Muhammad Iqbal, former head of the patrol group of the People's House Guards, who, along with two other lower-ranking officers, was assigned the task of murdering the former president. Iqbal's statement begins with a description of how he was coerced into participation in the murder by his commanding officer. Next comes a long account of trying to find the grave of Taraki's brother, securing a shroud from a local shop, and finally getting the grave dug. Then comes the encounter with Taraki himself:

> Rozi drove the car to the entrance of Koti Bagcha. After he entered, I followed him. We saw Wodood there standing to the west of a building standing on the steps. At this time, Rozi asked him where was "he"? He said "he" was here inside the room. Now the three of us went in. Rozi took out the key from his pocket. The down stair room was locked. He opened the door and entered. When he climbed the steps, he was followed by Wodood and me. We went upstairs. He knocked [on] the door. It did not open. He entered the room through another door. . . . We also entered as he called us to come in. Taraki was standing, wearing a cloak. Rozi told him he was being taken by us to another place. Taraki asked us to carry his bags. Rozi told him he should come down. The bags would be taken care of later on. Then Taraki went back and brought a small bag which he opened, saying it contained Afs. 45,000 and some ornaments. If his wife was still alive, we ought to deliver it to her. Rozi told him to leave the bag there as it would be taken there later on. Taraki led the way followed by Rozi. Wodood had taken one blanket from there. When we came downstairs, he told Taraki to go to a certain room.

... [Taraki] gave Rozi his wristwatch to be handed to Amin. Rozi left this on the table. Then he took [out] from his shirt pocket his party membership card and gave it to Rozi which he also placed beside the watch.

It was Rozi now that issued the commands. He took off the bed sheet and asked me to tie up his hands. Rozi tied one of his hands. I tied his other with the help of Wodood. Rozi asked us to stand there while [he] closed the door. We stood there. Taraki asked Wodood to give him a glass of water, Wodood ordered me to do so. When I took the glass Rozi told me it was too late. When I came back, Wodood asked me why I had not brought the water. I told him I was not allowed by Rozi. When Wodood took the glass, he was equally dissuaded. The next day, I asked Rozi why he did not permit us to serve Taraki some water? He said he did not want him to be in trouble after drinking water.

Afterwards, Rozi brought a bed and asked Taraki to lie down on it. After he lied down, I began to tremble. I could not move. Rozi closed his mouth. However, his legs began to kick. He hollered at Wodood to hold his legs. So he seized them but still they kicked notwithstanding. He asked me to hold his knees. After that, he pushed the cushion into his mouth. And when he released him, Taraki was dead.

There follows Iqbal's account of how the three men took Taraki's body to the Abchakan cemetery and buried it in the hole that had previously been dug. The confession concludes with a series of questions:

QUESTION: When Taraki was being martyred, did he not ask you to desist?

ANSWER: Taraki said nothing of the sort. He only gave us his watch and party membership card. And when Rozi ordered that his hands be tied, he even helped us in this. He said nothing at all.

QUESTION: When he was told to lie down, he said nothing. He just carried out the orders?

ANSWER: He said nothing to us. But with your permission, we can inform the people of Afghanistan the working people of the whole world that we as sons of the people were forced to do this. Whatever we are ordered by the party, we will carry it out. In order to hide his sins, from the people of Afghanistan, Amin resorted to this action. So he imposed this on us.

QUESTION: And Amin also forged a news item as if Taraki had died a natural death.

ANSWER: Please forgive me because I forgot to tell you about this beforehand. The guard commander told us that the news would be announced over the radio but in a different way. When we heard the

announcement the next day, he told us that we were unduly upset. He
had told us it would be announced over the radio in a different way.
Then he telephoned our detachment that it must wait for contingency.[3]

Not surprisingly, Iqbal, Rozi, and Wodood, along with others associated
with Taraki's murder, soon met their own deaths, as Karmal tried to put as
much distance as possible between himself and what the renamed *Kabul
New Times* referred to as the "sanguinary Amin band."[4] In an effort to salvage some credibility with the Afghan people, the new president, who had
once refused to recite the bismillah before his parliamentary speeches, now
not only regularly employed that phrase in his addresses to the people but
even adopted a new emblem for the state consisting of a pulpit under an
arch. The pulpit was included, according to Karmal, because "it is from the
pulpit that thousands of the faithful are led to the right path." Likewise, the
new regime decided to abandon the all-red flag adopted by Taraki and
return to a tricolored black, green, and red flag. The symbolism of this color
scheme, according to the government press, was that black was the color of
the great Central Asian mujahid Abu Muslim's banner; green represented
the "victory of our people over the British"; and red was the color of the
standards under which the Ghaznivid armies converted the inhabitants of
present-day Pakistan to Islam.[5]

Thus, along with Taraki were buried all pretensions to "jump start" a
communist revolution in Afghanistan. Karmal inherited a government that
had the full force of the Soviet Union behind it but that was devoid of moral
authority. This more than anything else was the legacy of Taraki, a well-
meaning but fatally misguided man who sought to help his people but
brought only disaster on their heads. From Iqbal's confession, it would
appear that the visionary who wrote with passionate intensity of impoverished peasants struggling against ruthless oppressors went to his own death
like the proverbial sheep to slaughter. Did he recognize that these men were
his designated assassins? Did he know what was coming? The fact that he
asked the guards to deliver money to his wife would indicate that perhaps he
did. But why did he also give them his wristwatch and ask them to give it to
his betrayer, Amin?

In reading this account, my mind turns to the story that was told of
Abdur Rahman's final days—how people from the countryside, hearing
rumors of the amir's illness, descended on the capital like vultures to a kill.
Fearing that a mob might take hold of the body and rend it to bits should
they try to carry it to the place where Abdur Rahman had chosen to be
buried, the frightened courtiers who surrounded the dying amir decided to

bury him in the palace grounds. So it happened, and fitting it was that the man who had so often fulminated against the falsity of courtiers had his final orders betrayed by those closest to him—while outside on the streets, the people he had ruled with an iron hand, sensing at last a weakness in their dying master, snarled and snapped like whipped dogs finally let off their leash.

How different Taraki's death, though there are elements in common, most obviously the treachery of courtiers. Did Taraki's dispatching of his wristwatch to Amin signal that he had forgiven him, or was it an ironic gesture perhaps, the return of a gift? There is another point in common with Abdur Rahman's death, namely the secret burial, which was likewise undertaken to protect the courtiers who had sworn to protect their leader but who in the end chose the path of expediency. Missing from Iqbal's story though is a sense of the main character. Abdur Rahman fought to the end against the disease that was killing him as well as against his enemies. Taraki, for his part, went quietly to his death, suffocated by his own guards. But this too was perhaps in keeping with the man and his life. Taraki was a storyteller, after all, a producer and consumer of myths, and it is thus especially fitting that the last thing to leave the hand of this "true son of the people" was his party membership card.

Part II

THE PECH UPRISING

4 A Son of Safi

I will tell you the story of the Khalqis. It's interesting. When the Khalqi coup d'état occurred, [I was with] a guy by the name of Habib who worked with me at the journal *Erfan*. He was a Khalqi of the first degree, but he didn't know what was happening. A person would think that they had just captured some thief or something. There were some gunshots coming from in front of the presidential palace [*arg-i jumhuri*], but not a lot. It didn't seem important. We were close by, so we went to see what the firing was all about. Then we realized that it must be a coup d'état or some other matter.

We went from there, and finally we discovered that it was a coup d'état. While the coup d'état was going on, everyone left work, and I climbed up the shoulder of Asmai Mountain and saw that the presidential palace was under bombardment. It all really happened while I was sitting there. The airplanes weren't using explosive bombs. They were engaged in tactical maneuvers over the palace, not destructive bombing. It was late afternoon, Thursday.

I was happy about this, that the airplanes were maneuvering over the palace and attacking. I was happy. I don't know if it was conscious or unconscious, but I was happy. I went from there to the house. When I came in the house, I was still happy, and I told my wife, "Something very good has happened." I told her how I had seen the bombardment of the palace with my own eyes. I wasn't able to see the people who would flee, the oppression that would come upon them, and everything else. I didn't see all of this when I was looking at the palace, but when I saw all of [the airplanes] overhead, I became happy. I was happy.

The radio went, "Dong, dong, dong, dong." It's the late afternoon, and all of a sudden, for the first time, [Aslam] Watanjar is speaking. I didn't recognize his voice. There's a shop nearby, and occasionally, in the late afternoon, Watanjar and I would sit and chat, but I knew him only as "Jaghlan Saheb," not as Watanjar. He would sit and wrap a turban on his head. He would rarely come dressed in his military clothes. It was a shop on the biggest street in Kabul. It was a pharmacy. The owner of the shop, who was named Wali, was martyred later on in the uprising in Chandawal. He was a very manly person. I would never have foreseen that. He fought well and was martyred.

This man, his voice came on, but I didn't recognize it. Right after that came the voice of Hafizullah Amin. Since I had known him from long ago, I was acquainted with his voice, and earlier I had heard that they [the Khalq party leadership] had been arrested and were in prison. Therefore, I realized that since it was he, this coup d'état must be a Marxist coup d'état.

I had a cigarette in my hand. I threw the cigarette in the ashtray like this. I let out a sigh and stretched back in the chair.

My wife said to me, "Up until now, you've been happy. What's wrong?"

I told my wife, "Until today, I was the father to my children, and you were their mother. After today, from this minute, you are both their father and their mother."

"Why?"

I said, "The Russians have taken our homeland. The Marxists have come to power."

My wife said to me—she was trying to understand what I meant— "It's Hafizullah Amin's voice?"

I said, "Yes."

She said, "He's your professor and also the friend of your father and your personal friend. So why?"

I said, "This isn't a personal matter or a question of friendship. He's the servant of Russia, and as far as our friendship is concerned, how was I to know he'd take power? Our relationship was personal, but no one would approve of his taking power into his own hands. By whatever name they call themselves, the people of Afghanistan don't want foreigners, and these are the servants of Russia."[1]

The success of the Marxist coup on April 27, 1978, initiated a struggle in Afghanistan that continues to this day. For Samiullah Safi, the struggle was not simply about ideology and political control. It was also intimately tied up with his personal and family histories. Like other educated Afghans of his age and status, Samiullah, who is known to all as "Wakil" (representative) for his years spent as a parliamentary deputy,[2] was acquainted with many of the principals in Afghanistan's political struggle, from the former king, Zahir Shah, to leaders of dissident political parties, including the Marxist Khalq party, which succeeded in taking power in the Saur Revolution of April 1978. The single figure whose story was most intimately bound up with Wakil's own, however, was probably President Muhammad Daud himself, who was engaged in an ultimately futile gunfight with rebel officers in the inner chambers of the presidential palace at the very moment that Wakil was watching the aerial maneuvers of rebel air force officers from the heights of Asmai Mountain. Daud's involvement with the family had begun thirty years earlier, when the Safi tribe had risen up against the government and then General Muhammad Daud had been dispatched to end the hostilities. When Wakil saw the palace of Daud under siege, he had reason to rejoice since this same man had been responsible for exiling his entire family far from their home in the Pech Valley in eastern Kunar Province to the western part of Afghanistan.

Wakil himself was a child of four or five when these events occurred, but he remembered some of them well. They were the formative events of his youth, and so when he talked of his initial happiness while watching the bombing of the presidential palace, he was speaking indirectly of this enmity and his family's troubles, and his happiness was directly connected to the grief then being inflicted on his family's old adversary. But Wakil's euphoria was short-lived. He had only to hear the voice of Hafizullah Amin, the chief planner of the coup d'état and number two man in the Khalq party, announcing the destruction of Daud's government over the radio to know that he could not remain inactive.

As Wakil's wife indicates, Amin was a close acquaintance of Wakil's. Amin had been his teacher in secondary school and then the principal of the teachers' college he attended as a young man. They had stayed in touch over the years, and Wakil certainly knew about Amin's involvement in Marxist politics. In Afghanistan, however, the only politics that mattered much in the half century prior to the Marxist coup were the politics internal to the royal family and the retinue of ministers and retainers that surrounded that family. But all of this had begun to change in 1973, when Daud had overthrown the king and dismissed the parliament. The Khalqis, along with their bitter Islamic rivals, had gone underground, and their activities had become more secretive and ambitious. The openly incendiary politics of parliamentary debate had been replaced by a covert politics of recruitment, organization, and plotting. Behind the scenes, as Afghans were well aware, was the specter of the Soviet Union, waiting its opportunity to place its own puppet rulers in power and make Afghanistan an extension of its own domain.

That was the common perception, and Wakil's reported response to the radio announcement reflects this perception. But Wakil's dramatic pronouncement to his wife that henceforth she must be both mother and father to their children has a deeper resonance as well that relates specifically to Wakil's family history, part of which I recounted in *Heroes of the*

Age. In that book, I transcribed verbatim a story told to me by Wakil concerning his father's coming of age. Wakil's father, Sultan Muhammad Khan, was a well-known tribal chieftain (*khan*) from the Safi tribe of Pech Valley, and part of his renown stems from this story—which begins with the murder of Sultan Muhammad's father by political rivals whose lands adjoined his own. At the time of the murder, Sultan Muhammad was a young boy and had few paternal kinsmen to support him in the conflict, which was driven by the family's considerable wealth but relative lack of male kinsmen who could help in defending the family's lands and properties. In this situation, Sultan Muhammad was forced to leave his home and take refuge with a local potentate, the Nawab of Dir in present-day Pakistan, in whose court he became a respected scribe. But Sultan Muhammad knew that a day of reckoning would have to come. To accept the diminished status of a court scribe meant also turning his back on his tribal inheritance. So he returned and bided his time, waiting for his rivals to strike at him but knowing that he would have to strike first. The opportunity came when his rivals had become so brazen and sure of their own power that they accepted an invitation to meet in his guesthouse to discuss the terms by which Sultan Muhammad would turn over a portion of his family's disputed lands to them. Sultan Muhammad, in league with a handful of kinsmen and tenant farmers, ambushed his rivals while they sat in his guesthouse, killing all seven of the brothers who had been responsible for his father's death.

The story of Sultan Muhammad's revenge told in its entirety is complex and primordial, and it was an important part of Wakil's legacy. Even more than Taraki, he was a "child of history," the son of a legendary figure whose life was dedicated to the unrelenting pursuit of honor. Sultan Muhammad's life story demonstrates that the pursuit of honor, once embarked on, can never be abandoned; nor can the goal ever be achieved. Wakil inherited not only his father's legacy, which would serve throughout his life as a goad and rebuke, but also the recognition that the pursuit of honor entailed costs and consequences for the individual and those around him. Wakil also grew up in a more complicated world than his father's, a world where honor's value was not so self-evident. Sultan Muhammad faced the choice between remaining in the relatively secure but socially debased position of a servant in the court of Dir or returning to the insecure, but more highly esteemed, role of a Safi tribesman—the son of a Safi father and the father of Safi sons. Wakil's choices, as this chapter illustrates, were more varied. He could be many things, earn other laurels, and live in a variety of places inside Afghanistan and abroad. But always there was the specter of his father and his father's commitment to honor and the recognition that in the land of his birth a man's first obligation was to live up to the obligations that being a son of a renowned father entailed.

Wakil's reported response to his wife on hearing the voice of Amin over the radio—whether it accurately reflects what happened or not—shows us the way that the past casts its shadow on the present and how some people at least gauged their response to the Marxist revolution in relation to traditional cultural understandings and modes of conduct. But also striking here is the extent to which traditional cultural understandings and modes of conduct didn't apply. Afghans had never before faced a situation like this one, and their society was a good deal more heterogeneous than the one in which Sultan Muhammad and other remembered ancestors had made their fateful choices. The most straightforward of the changes impinging on Wakil's life had to do with the division of the world into realms of tribe and state. In the past, tribes and states had interacted with and relied in various ways on one another, but the domains of tribe and state were governed by different moral understandings, and these differences were sustained by the continued existence of spatial separation and political autonomy. By the time Wakil came of age, however, such practical distinctions had blurred, as had many of the cultural underpinnings that someone like Sultan Muhammad could take for granted; the choices Wakil had to make were far more ambiguous in significance than any that had confronted his father. In the pages that follow, I chart the course of Wakil's life history as revealed in his own words and stories and focus on what I take to be the pivotal moments when the moral logic of honor clashed with the exigencies of living in an increasingly modern and hybridized society.

In my discussion of Sultan Muhammad in *Heroes of the Age*, I was concerned with the distant past, and the vehicle by which I sought access to this realm was a family's legends of an ancestor's youthful deeds. In this discussion of Wakil's life, I move into a more proximate realm of history and rely on another resource—the personal memory of the person whose life is thus narratively shaped and fashioned. The stories that he told me, while they aspire to consistency and completeness, are still fragmentary in places, inconsistent in others. The voice I listened to was by turns vainglorious and uncertain, abject and self-serving. As history goes, Wakil's account is probably badly flawed, and I don't doubt that if it were shown to others who were present at the events recounted, his version might be challenged at various points. All this is to be expected and goes with the territory of oral history. But Wakil's tale has a complicating element beyond that of most oral histories because of the looming presence in the background of the heroic father, Sultan Muhammad Khan.

A great man casts a long shadow, and we can see in the stories that follow Wakil's attempts to come to terms with his father's legacy—in particular, to make his own deeds live up to his father's, even though the opportunities that life afforded him were not congruent with those his father encountered and despite his having values that diverged in important respects from those of his father. Wakil spent most of his life outside the insular world of the tribe and the valley; he lived in various provinces far from the frontier and in the capital of Kabul, and he attended secondary school and university. His horizons were thus a good deal broader than his father. But still there was that shadow, and the glories, the travails, and the ironies of Wakil's life history are all finally bound up in the difficulties of finding a place for honor in the modern world.

FIRST MEMORIES OF WAR AND EXILE

> I think the Safi War [*safi jang*] was in 1945. It continued for a year and stopped in the winter of 1946. The government secretly planted some paid spies among the people. Approximately five hundred families were exiled after the war. I remember. They brought lorries. I was still small, and I was very happy that I would see a new world. The adult men and some of the women were crying. This exile suddenly came upon our family. I was just small, and I heard that my father had come. He had been in prison along with my uncle. Just one of my uncles was at home. One of my brothers was at the military high school. People arrived—all of a sudden. We heard. One or two people said, "Look!" They were all wearing normal country clothes—not uniforms. I thought that people were coming, and it was announced that my father had been released from prison. My father would be back home with us the next day. I was happy. [It was as though] the Jeshen (Independence Day) celebrations had begun. I was very happy. They were all armed, and as soon as they had come, they suddenly captured my family. Two or three hundred people, all dressed in civilian clothes, all are with the government, they captured us and said, "In the morning, you will be leaving."[3]

This is one of only two stories (fragments is perhaps a better term) that Wakil told me about his life in Kunar as a young boy, stories that are from his own memory (see Map 1). There are probably others, but not ones that he considered appropriate or significant enough to share. The impression I received when I talked with him, an impression that has been reinforced by hours of listening to the recordings of our interviews, is that Wakil's remembered life begins on the day the troops came to take away his family. Stories told about earlier episodes, including those involving the Safi War

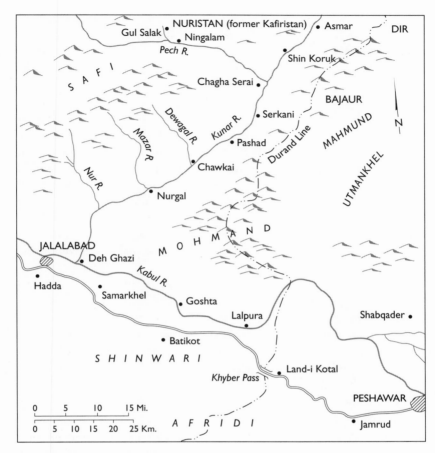

MAP 1.   Eastern Afghanistan

itself, were all impersonal. They are not part of his story. They belong to others, and it was clear even when he did not say so that these were events he had heard about and did not witness himself. All of this changes, however, from this point on. From the time the troops arrive at his family's home through ten more hours of interview, it is Wakil's story that is being told, and that story often has a harrowing quality.

In telling the story of the coming of troops to his village, Wakil's voice became that of the small boy who witnessed the events described, and the story manages to convey the sense of enthusiasm that he must have experienced at the time as he watched the strangers arrive in his village. Were theirs the first motorized vehicles he had ever seen? There were many of these strangers, but since they were wearing the same sort of clothes as everyone else, he was not frightened by their appearance. To the contrary, it was all a great holiday for the young boy, what with all the activity and the news that his father might be coming back.

Along with the enthusiasm, one also senses the boy's confusion, which is reflected in what appear to be inconsistencies in the narrative itself. When he saw the lorries, did he know that he would soon be leaving the valley? If it was such a happy occasion, why were "the adult men and some of the women" crying, particularly if his father would soon be home? Also, if he knew and was excited that they would soon be seeing "a new world," why did he believe that his father would be returning, and why was it such a shock when the soldiers suddenly arrested his family? These elements in the story are unclear and cannot be easily resolved, but, instead of being instances of bad storytelling, perhaps they signify the bewilderment of the five-year-old child who has never before seen so many strangers in his village.

The story's inconsistencies cannot be reduced to this however. They are not simply the product of childish distraction, for there are also indications in this shred of memory of deeper confusions in a society that was in the midst of conflict and change. The relatively cohesive and integrated world within which Sultan Muhammad came of age was not the world that Wakil was coming to experience. The pole star of honor by which Sultan Muhammad was able to chart his life choices would not shine so brightly for the son, and this first memory gives preliminary signs of the atmospheric disturbances that will cloud the boy's course.

Thus, for example, we see soldiers wearing civilian clothes, and we hear of tribesmen (Wakil's older brother among them) who are not present because they have already been sent off to boarding schools where, the government must have assumed, their interests would come into alignment with those of the state. The old divisions were breaking down. The worlds of the tribe and of the state had always been linked by the binary logic of their contrastive moral codes (tribes defining themselves by what they were not—the state—and vice versa). However, in this slight, but revealing vignette, the lines of distinction seem to have blurred. People were not who they appeared to be, and one sort of thing was easily mistaken for another, as when the young boy compares his (soon-to-be disabused) happiness at the excitement around him to the happiness he had previously felt during celebrations of Independence Day.

The event that led to Wakil's exile from Pech, the so-called Safi Jang, followed almost two decades of relatively calm relations between the Pakhtun tribes and the Afghan state, the last major conflagration having been in 1929, when the Shinwari tribe of Ningrahar Province and various of the tribes of Paktia Province had spearheaded the insurrection that toppled the regime of King Amanullah. The single most significant factor in inciting the Safi tribe to battle was a government plan to change the rules by which it conscripted tribesmen into the army.[4] For many years prior to the uprising, the accepted procedure for enlisting military recruits—referred to by the tribe as the *qaumi*, or "tribal," method—had been for individual tribes to supply a certain number of men of their own choosing; these men would always serve together and generally in locations that were not far removed from their homes.[5] For several years prior to the uprising, however, the government had insisted on employing a system referred to as *nufus*, or "population," in which the army conscripted its recruits directly from the population without consultation with any tribal body. The previous system of conscription was clearly beneficial to the tribe—especially the tribal elders, who decided who would serve. Under this system, the government recognized the tribes as part of the institutional apparatus of governance, and it also implicitly allowed the tribes to share in the exercise of force in the kingdom.

Underlying this arrangement was the practical reality of tribal power, dramatically demonstrated in the overthrow of Amanullah, who had switched to the nufus system; his successor, Nadir Shah, reverted to the traditional qaumi procedures. By the late 1940s, however, the government apparently felt itself to be in a stronger position in relation to the tribes and able to consolidate its position by eliminating the intermediate role of tribal elders in the recruitment process. A group of Safi leaders in the Mazar Valley resisted this initiative, however, and precipitated hostilities by capturing a detachment of troops that had been sent to collect conscripts. Following this incident, fighting quickly spread to the neighboring Waigal and Pech valleys, and before long all four of the Safi valleys (Pech, Mazar, Nur, Waigal) were involved in the insurrection, which continued for the better part of a year.

Wakil's father, probably in his late fifties or early sixties when the Safi uprising broke out, was prosperous by local standards. According to Wakil, few people had as much land as Sultan Muhammad or such a big family: he had nine wives (although never more than four at a time, as allowed under Islamic law), along with eleven sons and thirteen daughters. However, as fortunate as his life had turned out to be, Sultan Muhammad's prosperity could not be considered an unmitigated blessing. The more a man has, the more he has to lose, and never more so than in a time of strife such as the Safi War. Younger men could fight their battles, then flee to the mountains until it was safe to come down. For the man of property though—a "heavy man" (drund salai) in Pakhtun parlance—fighting the good fight was not as easy or straightforward, and consequently Sultan Muhammad, according to Wakil, demurred initially when others asked him to lend his support to the cause: "Listen Brother, you're alone. You have a cart. You can put a bed in it. Your wife is stronger than our men. She can travel easily in the mountains. She can endure hunger. My wives are like invalids. Where could I take them? Even if we tried very hard, it would be impossible for us to move all our property. I can't do these things. I can't, but you can."[6]

Sultan Muhammad resisted the commencement of hostilities and offered little encouragement to those among his tribe who first took up arms, but by the end of the rebellion he was considered one of the insurrection's leaders. The primary event responsible for propelling Sultan Muhammad into the ranks of the rebels appears to have been an encounter with General Daud following the looting of the government treasury at the provincial capital of Chaga Serai. Until this meeting, Sultan Muhammad's had been a voice of moderation in the tribe, but the confrontation with Daud changed all that, pushing him openly into the dissident camp and creating an enmity between the two men that continued until Sultan Muhammad's death twenty years later.

The story that Safi told me of the confrontation between his father and Daud pivoted around an act of arrogance (kibr) on the part of the general. At one point during the meeting in the capital, he told the tribal elders, "If I give the order to my brave and courageous soldiers, you of the Safi tribe will surrender your rifles as though they were canes; you will turn them over like wooden walking sticks." In response to Daud's insult and threat to disarm them, Sultan Muhammad stood up and challenged the general, telling him, "These soldiers whom you call brave and courageous are the brothers and children that we have given you to protect the soil, the homeland, honor, Islam, and they must be used for this. You should not set brother against brother. How is it that my brother, who happens to be a soldier, is courageous but I am not? You should regret all that you have said and not say it again."[7]

Sultan Muhammad was inspired to challenge Daud because of the nature of his threat. As Daud understood, taking away a tribesman's rifle was morally equivalent to raping the women of his family.[8] A man's rifle was categorized along with his land and his wife as his namus, which can be translated as both the substance of a man's honor and that which is subject to violation and must be defended. The threat to have soldiers take away rifles as though they were the canes of old men was an attack on the elders as individuals and tantamount to a declaration that they and their tribe were impotent and incapable of protecting themselves against the basest sort of assault. In defending himself and his tribe against Daud's insult, Sultan Muhammad took the moral ground away from Daud and humiliated him in front of the elders. According to Wakil, Daud never forgave Sultan Muhammad for the rebuke and used the pretext of the Safi uprising to sentence him to death, along with the rebel leaders more directly responsible for the insurrection.

Honor and Revenge

Following the defeat of the Safis, Wakil's family, along with hundreds of others from their tribe, were exiled to the western city of Herat. During the first part of their exile, Sultan Muhammad was awaiting execution until Zahir Shah granted him a reprieve on the day of his scheduled hanging. Thereafter, he remained in prison, first in Herat, then in Mazar-i Sharif and other northern provinces until he was finally released during the period of democratic liberalization in the late 1960s. Sultan Muhammad's family was free during his imprisonment, but they remained nearby, providing food and other resources.

In many ways, the most vivid of Wakil's stories are those that date from his first years in Herat. This period of exile was not a time of isolation for the boy. A number of other Safi families accompanied them to Herat, and his own family included not only the several wives and numerous offspring of Sultan Muhammad but also various uncles and their families. The first story Safi told me of his time in Herat comes from the first days after their arrival, when the older members of his family believed that Sultan Muhammad would soon be executed by the government. For the family, this period was clearly a time of anguish and uncertainty, for not only was the family patriarch languishing in prison awaiting his death, but most of the other senior males of the family were also locked up in the Herat prison, where they were serving shorter sentences for their part in the recent hostilities. The first story that Wakil told of this period of exile has a feeling similar to that of his story of the soldiers coming to take his family from Pech. It is the quality of a fragmentary childhood memory, sharply focused in some places, but blurred in others:

> One time—this happened when we were in Herat—my uncle told me to stay out. I was small, but the adults—my older brothers and uncles and cousins—met together in a room in the compound. One of my uncles was in prison. It was the other [uncle], but he had undoubtedly been in touch with [his brothers] in prison. They had gotten [his father's and other brother's] consent, and they were talking it over here.

Now I recall a letter that was written in green ink. I was watching from the doorway and listening to hear what they were saying. I was small, and they wouldn't let me [be present]. They decided that since my father was under a sentence of death, they had to do something. "Since there is no way we can enable the women and children to escape, we will have to leave all of them in the house and then set it on fire. After that, the rest of us will escape. We will escape and go to the border. If we have the power, we will avenge our father. If we don't, then we will move from place to place like madmen, like Majnun we will wander in the mountains. But, for us it would be very shameful if they killed our father while we remained in prison or continued living here."[9]

As the narrator remembered the scene, he was a boy standing outside a room, straining to hear what was going on behind the closed door. Too young to be among the adults, he was old enough to sense the importance of the meeting. The memory was fuzzy, but a distinct image came to mind of a letter written in green ink. The adult Wakil could piece together what undoubtedly eluded him as a child: that the letter was probably written by the uncle who was then incarcerated in the Herat prison. That uncle would probably have been Abdul Qudus, Sultan Muhammad's brother and the senior member of the family after Sultan Muhammad. The fact that the letter was etched in the adult's memory indicates that the boy somehow knew it to be significant, but at the time Wakil did not fully realize that the letter was effectively a writ of execution for the boy and much of his family.

The voice coming from behind the closed door was unidentified, but the passage seems too well composed and complete to have been overheard and remembered almost forty years later. One senses that the boy must have later on pieced together snippets of overheard speech into a single coherent speech. Or maybe he did hear all these words, and maybe he was just old enough to understand what they meant, and this understanding permanently seared the words in his memory. We cannot know and perhaps cannot even guess unless we have been afflicted ourselves with such memories. For the men talking among themselves behind closed doors, it was a question of honor. The sons and kinsmen of Sultan Muhammad could not remain inactive while the great man himself was executed by the government. Revenge had to be taken; if it was not, then they had to relinquish any pretense to being men of honor. The usual routines could not go on under such conditions. Just as Sultan Muhammad had once had to leave his child behind to avenge his father, so his sons and kinsmen had to abandon the pleasures of domesticity until their relative's death could be avenged. Since the enemy responsible for Sultan Muhammad's death was not other tribesmen but the government itself, vengeance would not be easy to obtain. How, after all, was a group of (presumably) weaponless tribesmen hundreds of miles from their homeland to wreak vengeance on their enemies, and just who was it they should target as the responsible party?

The logic of honor does not translate easily to the more impersonal realm of tribe/state relations, so it is not surprising that the kinsmen of Sultan Muhammad were forced to imagine the unimaginable: the physical annihilation of the dependent members of their family and their own assignment to the liminal realm of the dispossessed, where they would wander until their deaths in the wilder regions of place and mind. The kinsmen of Sultan Muhammad thus envisioned themselves as incarnations of Majnun, the classic figure of romantic tragedy in Afghan folklore, whose love for the beautiful Leila was forestalled when her father married her to another. Before his death from grief, Majnun (whose name has come to be synonymous with madness) wandered in the desert, heedless of who he was or where he was going. Majnun's love was so deep that, with the loss of the beloved, life itself became a trackless void. In similar fashion, the kinsmen of Sultan Muhammad recognized the impossibility of living a normal life in the absence of honor.

Majnun may be cited as the model for this sort of single-minded obsession, but we know that Sultan Muhammad himself was the model his kinsmen were emulating. Having such a man as the family patriarch imposed a special burden on his kinsmen, and the family elders responded in what must have seemed to them an appropriate manner to the prospect of Sultan Muhammad's execution. It was one thing, though, for the men of the family to choose their path of vengeance, but one wonders what effect this plan must have had on the boy who overheard it and who was among those condemned to die. He and the other dependents in the house were to be the lambs on this sacrificial altar. If the plan succeeded, they were destined to become—quite literally—burnt offerings to honor, with no hope of some ultimate vindication or even of a future spent in heroic renunciation.

Since Wakil never informed me of his response to hearing the news of his impending death, I can only speculate what it might have been. Much later, he would have understood the cultural terms of his predicament, but, as a small child, he would have been old enough to understand only the words that were being said and their immediate import—not their larger significance or what was at stake for his family. The boy could not have made sense of or cared about these matters, and consequently I wonder in what ways this scene left its scars on him as he grew up. In particular, I wonder to what extent the adult Wakil's more self-conscious and ambivalent attitude toward the ethos of honor wasn't determined in part by his having witnessed this peculiar primal scene. Was Wakil's later ability to self-consciously deconstruct the imperatives of honor in any way connected to such early experiences?

Wakil was a man who, when I met him, had never spent any significant periods of time outside Afghanistan, yet he had an uncanny capacity for reflecting analytically and dispassionately on the cultural logic of past and present events. Unlike the vast majority of tribal men whom I have interviewed and gotten to know—including many who have been abroad—Wakil had a keen ability to analyze his own society and anticipate how I, as an outsider, would respond as I learned more and more about its idiosyncrasies. This ability to see and interpret his own culture from the outside indicated to me that he also understood on some level that his society's truths were constructed, not absolute, and I have wondered whether this sense wasn't first instilled when he overheard his own sentence of death. Be that as it may, the plan was never carried out since word arrived after this meeting that the king had commuted Sultan Muhammad's sentence of death.

Imprisonment and Relocation

I'll tell you of an incident that happened when I was a boy. This story happened in Mazar-i Sharif. . . . Since I was small, I would take some books and pens and papers and go to the prison, where I would study with my uncle. Every day in the morning, I would study with my uncle or my brother, who was also in prison, and then in the late afternoon I would return home with my cousin.

There is a room on the upper story of the prison. One day we were sitting there studying when we heard it announced that Muhammad Aref Khan, the minister of defense had arrived. All the soldiers there came to attention since the minister of defense was in the prison. Many members of the Safi tribe who were in prison had decided not to accept any land in Mazar-i Sharif: "Our land—whether it is good or bad—is in Kunar, and one stone, one seed on that land is adequate for us. It is our homeland. We grew up there. Even if we decide to move here, it will be under our own authority. We will not take this land that you are imposing on us. We will not give up this [land in Kunar] to take that [land in Mazar-i Sharif]. This would separate us from our tribe. We won't do this." They decided this.

I am witnessing this from above. I am watching to see what happens. The tribe is standing all around. The soldiers are also standing. Muhammad Aref Khan is still living. He was next to a very large canal that flowed through the courtyard of the prison in Mazar. Alongside of this, flowerbeds had been planted. [Muhammad Aref] was sitting there in a chair. My father—only my father—was sitting in a chair across from him. They were talking, and he told my father, "You must accept this land. It's so valuable, and this and that. However much land you want. I will give as much land as you want to whomever you want."

My father replied to him, "You have your authority, and I have mine. If we are talking about the authority of the government, the situation is clear. You have taken my land, and I am in prison. If you wanted to, you could kill my children. My hands and feet are tied. You can kill all of us if you want. You can do whatever you desire. It's up to you—what can I do? It is up to you. What is within my authority? I can refuse to give you one stone of Kunar for all of Mazar. If you were to give me the whole province of Mazar, I would not give you one stone from Morchel in Pech Valley. That is my right." He said this with great force.

They argued on and on about this, but nothing came of it until finally [Muhammad Aref] told him that "the government has the power to force you."

My father said to him, "Yes, that is your way. Standing behind you is the army, the armed forces, soldiers. It is your custom to capture some-one, push them around, and beat them. This is all through the force of soldiers and arms. But if I were to take this uniform of yours off your body, and I went in among the people, and you were also to go, you wouldn't find anyone who would flatter or pay any attention to you. Your power is the power of the government, but if the power of the government—these soldiers, the army—if these were not there and the political power was not in your hands, then you wouldn't even qualify as my servant! "

This was a form of insult [*paighur*]. If something was in my father's mind, it was also on his tongue. Truly, that's the kind of man my father was. He was not afraid of this kind of talk. He was only satisfied when he spoke his mind and let whatever was going to happen just happen.

Then this Muhammad Aref threw a punch at my father. He hit him with a punch, and my father grabbed him by the belt. It was the kind of belt that had a buckle attached to it. When he grabbed the belt in his hand, it came apart, and then Muhammad Aref Khan jumped over the canal and shouted behind him, "Soldiers, soldiers, soldiers, soldiers!" My father was left on this side, and he jumped to the other side. Then the soldiers picked my father up by his two hands and two feet. They picked him up and beat him severely. In the course of the beating, his hand was broken, and the bone came out through the skin. It was just hanging down, and [he] was holding onto it.

My father raised his head, and Muhammad Aref said, "Enough!" He was thinking that certainly he had been convinced and would take the land. But my father said to him, "You are infidels [*kufr*]! You're not

Muslims!" What he meant was that they didn't have compassion [*rahm*]. "Tell your men that they have injured my arm! The bone is broken!"

A strip of flesh was hanging down from his arm. Eight men lifted him up, and two men hit him with a stick from this side and two from the other. "At least take my hand." Then they held his arm [off to the side] and hit him some more. His clothes were white, but it looked as though they had hung them on a piece of meat and then beaten it with a club. It was all cut up and bloody.

I saw this situation from behind; [I saw how they] had picked him up and beaten him. My older brother . . . was also in prison with my father. The soldiers grabbed him, and he started yelling at them and picked up a brick to throw at them. The other prisoners in that prison were all from our tribe, they also picked up bricks. It was like a rain of bricks, but the soldiers—it was really a small army—they were on the other side, and some of them took [my father] in one direction, and others went toward the other prisoners, throwing four or five in each cell and locking them up.

All this was still going on when I left the prison and ran home. I was afraid. When I arrived at the house, I didn't say a word because—before I had left the prison—one of my brothers had said to me, "Be careful that you don't say anything when you get home. Be sure no one at home hears about this, that you don't tell the kids and the women and people we know."

I went and quietly sat down—silent and stunned. I thought that my father had surely died from this beating. Then I saw the brother who had spoken to me and who had been in the prison come in. He was free. He wasn't in prison. He had a little box in his hand when he came in. He went into his room. I realized that he had brought something. Maybe it was my father's clothes. I was looking through a crack, and saw that my brother—he was a young man at the time, about eighteen or nineteen years old—he had taken my father's clothes like this, and he was holding them over his eyes and crying. He had latched the door so that no one could come in. He was sitting in his own room with the clothes pressed against his face like this.

I saw this scene. I saw this scene and suddenly burst into tears, sobbing. Then my brother came out, aimed a stone at me, and I fled. He was angry because he didn't want anyone to find out.[10]

Sultan Muhammad and the other Safis had been in prison in Herat for about a year when the order arrived from Kabul that they were to be transferred to a prison in Mazar-i Sharif and that the exiled Safi families would also be given land in the north. Since the reign of Abdur Rahman, the government had used the northern plains of the country as a site for relocating dissident Pakhtun tribes. One such mass resettlement occurred after the Ghilzai Uprising in 1886–1888, and many other small outbreaks had ended with the perpetrators relocating in the north. Resettlement accomplished the double goal of removing troublemakers from the heartland of the kingdom and seeding the ethnically distinct northern areas, where Turkic and Tajik populations predominated, with Pakhtuns. As Abdur Rahman had guessed, Pakhtuns who created difficulties for the government in their home areas tended to become loyalists of the Pakhtun-dominated Kabul government once they were placed in areas where they were in the minority, especially when surrounded by Uzbeks, who had long been their enemies.[11]

In the case of the Safis, the government decided to provide generous tracts of land to the families while the prisoners continued to serve their sentences. The government's intention was to encourage the Safis to stay on in the north even after their prison terms had expired, and eventually that is what tended to happen: many families decided to settle in the north rather than return to their relatively impoverished native valleys in Kunar. In the short run, however, the government plan ran into considerable opposition as many Safi leaders recognized the government's intention to split off the dissident leaders from the rest of the tribe. Sultan Muhammad was one of those most steadfastly opposed to taking the land, and this refusal estranged him from some of his fellow Safis, as well as earning him the animosity of the officials who were trying to co-opt tribal support.[12]

In the story of Sultan Muhammad's beating, several narrative elements stand out. First one gets a sense of the illicit nature of the events depicted because of the observer's having witnessed these scenes from a place of hiding. It is the same sense that one gets from the tale of Wakil eavesdropping on his elder kinsmen in Herat. In that story, the boy was listening from outside a door to a conversation being carried on inside. Here, the boy was watching, unnoticed, from a balcony of the prison as his father was beaten, and then later we see him again looking through a crack at his brother weeping over the bloodstained clothing of their father. In each of these scenes, the boy has unintentionally become a witness to adult concerns that are beyond his ken. He has intruded into a realm of violence from which children are normally excluded, and this presence makes the actions described all the more startling.

A second feature of this story that is found in the others as well is the sense of helplessness it conveys. In every story that Wakil recounted from his childhood, he is seen as powerless to affect the outcome of events, and this quality is made all the more dramatic for being demonstrated in relation to the larger-than-life figure of Sultan Muhammad. The son was not the father however. He seems, in many respects, a more interesting and empathetic character because he is more human and introspective than his father appears to have been and because he seems capable in a way that his father never was of revealing parts of himself. The father kept his emotions tightly leashed. Wakil does not. He tells of his fear, and in his personal history he allows himself to be pitiable in a way that the father probably would not have. At the same time, however, Wakil is still the son of a great man, and the prevailing tension in his life—a tension that is first hinted at in these early memories—is how he will live up to his father's example.

A final element of the story is the brutality itself and the boy's response to it. In Afghan prisons during the time Sultan Muhammad was incarcerated, the wealthier and more influential prisoners received better treatment than the poorer men. Thus, if you had the money to buy food or other commodities, you could purchase them through the guards or have your family bring them to you on a regular basis. Those who had nothing had to work for other prisoners or do other services to receive anything beyond bread and gruel. This feature of the prison system meant that Wakil was frequently enlisted to carry supplies to his imprisoned relatives and consequently saw firsthand the degradation that went on behind the prison walls. On many occasions, he witnessed the poverty and debasement of the prison's lower classes and the brutality of the guards; these experiences left their mark on him and made him sympathetic to leftist calls for social and economic reform. Even as he rejected the way radical leaders wanted to transform the country and how they went about taking power, he still understood the need for social change.[13]

In the years to come, the government moved Sultan Muhammad to various prisons, sending him finally to Shebargan (in northwest Juzjan Province), which was about as far from Kunar as the government could send him and a place—to quote Wakil—"where people don't even understand Persian, much less Pakhtu." To increase the family's isolation, the government split it up so that only the wives and dependent children of Sultan Muhammad were allowed to accompany him while his brothers and grown sons remained in prison in Balkh. As a result, Wakil grew up far from his own society, in a family environment dominated by women and in an alien social milieu where the language and customs were unfamiliar to him. His was thus a hybrid upbringing, surrounded beyond the compound walls by Turkmen, Uzbeks, and Tajiks, but overshadowed within by the powerful but absent father.

Pech Valley itself was a distant memory, and while he certainly knew about the culture of honor that flourished there, his must have been a largely abstract familiarity since he did not have around him the society of close tribal kinsmen in relation to whom the principles of honor have traditionally been first assayed.[14] While his familiarity with the life of his people was in many ways deficient, one advantage that Wakil had beyond those of his Safi peers was a wider exposure to different cultures and a substantial education. As a result of his peripatetic upbringing, Wakil became conversant in several languages and fluent in Dari Persian, the Afghan lingua franca, and he also had the opportunity to continue his education through the secondary and then the university levels, opportunities relatively few Safi boys had.

THE FAILURE OF DEMOCRACY

All told, Sultan Muhammad spent over twenty years in prison and was among the last Safis to be allowed to return to Pech. But, even before receiving permission to return home, the family was able to move to Kabul, which enabled Wakil to continue his education and, in the process, receive his first exposure to the ideological struggles that were beginning to reshape the landscape of Afghan political culture. In 1964, the year of Wakil's arrival in Kabul and his enrollment at the university, Zahir Shah gave permission for the drafting of the nation's first truly democratic constitution, which was followed in 1965 by the passage of laws permitting the establishment of newspapers and political parties. The university was the site of the most radical and outspoken political activity in the capital, and while he was involved in the campus debates of the time and witnessed the first mass demonstrations, Wakil reports that he did not participate in or seek to join any of the political parties that were then beginning to actively recruit members among the student population. Wakil was living away from the campus in a small house that his family had rented rather than in a dormitory on campus, and this appears to have insulated him somewhat from the more extreme political movements, which were attracting many students. He also seems to have been put off by ideologues from both sides, and while he took an active interest in the political questions that were then dominating discussion, the influence he cites as critical to the development of his own political thinking was not Karl Marx or Mao Tse-tung, Sayyid Qutb or Maulana Maududi—the theorists who inspired the more radical students—but an unnamed American political scientist then teaching at the university, who "smoked a cigar and gave us the best lectures covering every nation in the world—East and West—and which ones had come closest to putting democracy into action."

Politics and Prestige

I graduated from the university in 1967. My father was in Kabul for that year. Then he returned to the homeland. There were many people there who greeted him. Prior to my father's return, some people who had been spies during the time of the Safi War were given our lands. They took these lands by force while we were in exile. The people who had taken our lands included some *maleks* [chiefs] and other influential people. Other Safis who had been exiled also had their land forcibly confiscated by the government. These people who had previously spied were opposed to our return and were saying, "If they come back to their homeland it is possible that some riot will occur again in Kunar. It isn't wise to let them come back." Their objective in this was the land that they had gotten hold of. They wanted to keep this land in their hands.

Before my father went back to Kunar, they were telling the government that if we were to come the people would be unhappy, but when my father returned to Kunar, the people gathered in Bar Kandi, the first village at the beginning of Pech Valley, and, based on tribal customs, they fired their rifles and took care of us. This tribal hospitality [*melma palinai*] continued for about a year. It wasn't over for a year, and during that year people would come to our house to greet my father and pay their respects.

It was at that time that I graduated from the university, and I wanted to finish up my period of military training and obligation, and I was accepted into the army for training. After one year of training, the people of Pech Valley told me that the election campaign for the thirteenth session of the lower house of parliament [*wolesi jirga*] was beginning and that I had to be a candidate. I went to talk to my father. One of my stepmothers, the mother of Matiullah, who is now a commander in the jihad, was sitting there. No one else was present, and I told my father that it was my desire to run as a candidate for parliament and he must give his permission since I was responding to the wish of the people.

My father said to me, "My boy, we have seen many difficulties. We have been thrown in prison, and all of this was solely for the prestige [*haysiat*] of our family. For the sake of this, I have sacrificed my property, my life, my children. I have sacrificed everything for my reputation [*naminek*], and you should look at this position the same way that you view the earth."

I said, "There's nothing wrong with being a representative."

He replied, "The governments of the present are not the type of government that represent the people. In this government, not even a hundred people could benefit from your service. It's all right for your own affairs. For your own interests, a seat in the parliament is very good. In this position, you will lose the reputation that I have among the people

of my own tribe. People expect something to be done, and you won't
have the power to do it if you want to continue eating the bread of your
position. I refuse to give you my permission."

This conversation with my father occurred when I was in [military]
training. On January 1, 1967, my father died at the age of between
eighty and eighty-five. After this, because of the expectations of the
people, I prepared myself to become a candidate. For the dignity of our
family, I participated in the forty-day ceremony that took place after the
burial of my father, and I was exempted for these forty days from military training. During this period, I began my candidacy.[15]

Wakil's willingness to run for office against his father's wishes indicates
that he had taken the class lessons on democracy to heart, but it reveals
other things as well. First, it reminds us that in Afghanistan prestige was
still largely an inherited asset. A man could certainly lose the status he
gained by descent from a famous father, but—as the example of Nur
Muhammad Taraki would later prove—it was not so easy to rise to a position of prominence without the proper background. Thus, Wakil, an army
conscript barely out of university and away from his home area for most of
his life, was nevertheless in a position to run for parliamentary deputy by
virtue of his being Sultan Muhammad's son. However, as Sultan
Muhammad reminds his son, he was also in a position to squander that status and, in the process, squander the reputation of his family.

A second feature of this story involves Wakil's act of disobedience to his
father, an act that mirrors a pivotal moment in Sultan Muhammad's life as
recounted in *Heroes of the Age*. Sultan Muhammad had rushed to the side
of his father, Talabuddin, when he had just been struck by the bullets of his
killers. In his desire to assure himself a martyr's reward, Talabuddin had
ordered his son not to seek revenge for his murder. Sultan Muhammad,
however, had denied his father's dying request, telling him that it was his
duty as a son and a Safi to avenge his murder. Sultan Muhammad's last
command to his son—that he not run for parliament—was likewise
premised on his desire to preserve what was most valuable to him—in his
case, his reputation as a man of honor. This story, like its predecessor,
occurred against a backdrop of conflict in which rivals are willing to use
underhanded means to steal the family's land and usurp its political position. The tribe as a whole, however, supported the beleaguered family,
although in both instances the son had to take a stand that violated his
father's determination of what was in his own and the family's best interest. For Sultan Muhammad, that stand involved making an oath to avenge
his father's death. For Wakil, the stand involved running for elective office,

which he believed would enhance the prestige of the family while also providing him an opportunity to participate in shaping Afghanistan's future.

For both Sultan Muhammad and his son, the events that ensued after their decisions to disobey their fathers were defining moments in their lives. In Sultan Muhammad's case, his vow to avenge his father led to his fashioning an elaborate and risky plan for destroying his enemies in a single, fell stroke. To accomplish his plan, he had to enlist the assistance of kinsmen and old family retainers who pledged their help to the boy not for himself but for the sake of the father and the family. A similar scenario played itself out in Wakil's case as well, as those who supported Wakil's candidacy conveyed to him the same message that his father had received as he prepared for his defining test:

> People were coming at that time for the elections. They were coming. It was in the course of the election, and some of the elders were saying into my ear, "We don't know you, if you are good or bad, if you will serve the people or not, since your life has been passed in Mazar-i Sharif and Kabul. You shouldn't think that we are giving our votes to you." This is what they said. "Don't think that we're giving our votes to you. We are giving them to the dead bones of your father."[16]

In response to this message, Wakil invited the people of his area to a great feast in Ningalam, the administrative center of Pech Valley. The feast was held following prayers on the Friday before the election, and it attracted a great crowd:

> We killed some cows, and gathered the whole tribe together. . . . I went onto a stage and told the people, "If you think that once I become your representative, then you'll be in a flower garden, or that I can bring down the sky for you, this isn't within my power." I explained to them that . . . my father had not given me his permission. My father's point was that these governments are not the kind that will allow you to serve the people—you can't [help] even one hundred people. But I persuaded the people that I had become a candidate in opposition to the advice of my father and that my only goal in doing so was to take a stand in the election, not to win it. [I told them,] "All of you have the right to be a candidate. It's only a question of struggle, and in reality it's a matter of making sure that this democracy that the king of Afghanistan claims to have implemented in the constitutional law must be brought into existence by you the people of Afghanistan. This will bring democracy into existence—not the king or any person. Through these struggles, the election becomes very honorable, not by being pessimistic or that kind of thing. Everyone has the right to be a candidate and everyone has the right to vote for whomever they choose."[17]

Wakil's speech sought to transect the divide between the morality of honor and the principles of democracy, and it also made it appear that the distance between them was not all that great. Both honor and democracy, after all, were premised on notions of equality and individual agency, both demanded a degree of independent thought and action for those who constituted the community, and both conspired in their own way against the rise of tyrants. On a practical level, as well, it would seem that democracy was on a sure footing in this milieu given the existence of the tradition of *jirga* (assembly), in which male elders sit together and reach collective decisions on all manner of problems, from guilt and punishment to water use and taxation, war and peace. Wakil played on the points of similarity between honor and democracy, and it would appear from what he said that democracy as a system of government had found a naturally fertile ground in which to grow.

Such was not the case however. The democratic tradition never took root in Afghanistan, and while many practical reasons could be cited—having to do with how democratic institutions were established—there were also ideological reasons, which can be seen at the grassroots in accounts such as this one. In particular, one can see some of the fundamental, if not immediately self-evident, differences between honor and democracy in Wakil's story of the opposition that his candidacy inspired. One source of opposition, which continued even after his father's death, was from within his own family. Wakil was the youngest of eleven sons, and some of his brothers were much older than he—old enough, in fact, to be his father. Unlike Wakil, these older brothers were adults when the family was exiled, and they had been more directly immersed in Pakhtun culture than their younger sibling and were also less educated. Some of Wakil's older siblings shared their father's view that Wakil's running for parliament would place the family's honor at risk, not because they didn't want him associating with the government but because they were fearful that he might lose. In the words of one of Wakil's kinsmen (quoted by Wakil), "If a man becomes a candidate and is unsuccessful, this would be a great defeat for him and would place him under threat from his rival. And if the government doesn't want him to be elected and succeeds in having him defeated, then this failure would actually be thought of by the people as a humiliating insult."

This conflation of personal shame and electoral defeat illustrates one of the obstacles that democracy faced in adapting to Afghan soil. In the view of many of his kinsmen, Wakil's loss would have been interpreted by the society at large as an insult directed at the father and the family, not just as the defeat of the individual himself or a rejection of his ideas. When the unnamed relative said that an electoral defeat would be an insult to the family, he implicitly foreshadowed what would have to happen if such a defeat were to occur. Insults must be avenged. A man who has suffered humiliation at the hands of another must redress that humiliation through action. But who exactly could be held responsible? The voters? The rival candidate? Government officials who might rig the election? In this context, an election was not just about candidates and their ideas. It was also about families and family honor, and those who entered the arena placed themselves in a situation in which they allowed others to determine their destiny—a position in tribal culture that is to be avoided at all costs.

In the election Wakil described, it was understood that if opposition arose, it would come from among those families that came to prominence after Sultan Muhammad and other Safi leaders had been exiled from the area. Any candidate who opposed Wakil would come from their ranks, and that meant that a defeat at the polls would have constituted solid evidence that the influence of Sultan Muhammad's family had slipped. Everyone would have been able to see that their rivals had gained strength at their expense, and the likelihood of a direct confrontation between them would have thereby increased immeasurably. Indeed, since defeat would have been interpreted as an insult to the family, a violent confrontation was all but assured.

As his relatives feared, such an opposition did materialize from among the rival families who had stayed in Pech, but a confrontation was avoided, first, because Wakil won handily and, second, because the opposition, perhaps recognizing their disadvantage, intentionally chose a second-tier surrogate to run against Wakil and in this way blunted the humiliation they would have suffered by defeat. Further, Wakil's rivals protected their position by invoking the general honor of the tribe, as well as Wakil's own defense of democratic principles, as their reason for running a candidate in the first place. As Wakil tells it, this was their response:

> If [Wakil] were to go to the parliament without any opposition, it would be as if we had sent a mulla. This isn't right. When a mulla turns up, he goes to the front and leads the prayers. No one tells him not to lead the prayers. But, this isn't the work of a mulla. This business involves the rights of the people of Afghanistan. Everyone has the right to be a candidate. This was Wakil's own challenge.[18]

The declaration is interesting, not least because it shows the lowly position of mullas in tribal society. Mullas were fine for leading prayers or for giving a religious imprimatur to the results of tribal negotiations. However, their power was largely symbolic, and from the tribal perspective any group that sent such a representative to a national assembly would be either admitting its weakness or declaring its disdain.[19] In any event, Wakil's rival was not able to muster sufficient votes to constitute a real challenge, and one reason for this failure was the relatively humble status of the challenger. Wakil had declared grandiloquently during his campaign that anyone had the right to run for office, "whether he is a shepherd, a peasant, whether he is poor or wealthy, the son of a khan or the son of a poor man."[20] However, the reality was that a candidate had to have the resources to play his role properly. If the representative to parliament were a mulla, well, that was one thing, and the statement the tribe would be making in sending such a representative was that the whole business was beneath their concern. But if the representative were to come from a prominent family like Wakil's, then a different set of expectations was invoked.

A man like Wakil could not just show up and give speeches; he had to play the expected part, which meant speaking eloquently, and—perhaps most important of all—feeding the people. That is to say, the parliamentary representative had to conduct himself in the same way that khans had always done. This was the only model available: if the tribe wasn't going to send a mulla, then it had to send a khan (or the khan's representative), and this meant among other things that the representative had to be able to offer largesse to those whose assistance he needed. Wakil was able to. Because of his ancestry, his relative wealth, and the many allies he could claim by virtue of his family ties, he was in a position to mobilize the resources needed to feed a great assembly of people, and his prestige within the tribe thereby increased accordingly.

King and Commoners

The secretary to the king telephoned and asked me to come and see the king. The secretary asked me what time would be convenient for me to come, and I told him that I am always ready to speak with the king of Afghanistan. The secretary then told me to come at nine, but I was about five minutes late. When I arrived at the palace, members of the cabinet, along with some generals, were sitting there in the antechamber. I was led past them directly to the king's salon. As I was shaking hands, I noticed that His Majesty had written my name at the top of a piece of paper.

I sat down, and right off he asked me a question. "Honorable representative [*wakil sahib*] of Pech Valley, what do you make of the government, which receives the vote of confidence and broadcasts its voice over Radio Afghanistan? What opinion do you have? A person might think that this government didn't have the confidence of the parliament since all of the representatives rise to speak against it, but when the vote is taken, then the hands go up, and the vast majority, with the exception of one or two or three people, all give their votes to it. What's the reason for this?

"That's one question. My second question has to do with these demonstrations that occur in Kabul. Behind the scenes, there are people who have their hands in orchestrating them, but my question isn't about them. It is about the children who run to participate in these demonstrations, the shopkeepers, and everyone else who innocently runs along and participates in the demonstrations. What's the reason for this, that little elementary school kids join in and shout "Long Live" and "Death to" without knowing what they are saying or what the demonstration is about? What's the reason for this?"

My response to the first question was this. "The parliament is composed of 216 representatives and 216 parties. Those who speak out against the government are under the pressure of public opinion from the whole country of Afghanistan since everyone believes that this government doesn't represent the people. They have to speak against it so that they can get reelected in the future and not become the object of hatred in their own communities. But then when they vote for the government, it is for their personal reasons. They have their own affairs. They have their own businesses. They vote for the government, [and] then in front of the ministers they can say to them, 'See, I gave you my vote.' That way they can do their personal business without losing the support of the people."

The King then asked, "What's the solution to this?"

I said, "The solution is that this parliament must be a party parliament. The [Political] Parties Law should be passed, and then one representative from each party can speak instead of all 216 deputies. Then the government can represent the people outside the parliament. Until the government is connected to the real representatives of the people, it won't feel its responsibility toward them. The kinds of government that nowadays are coming are only thinking about protecting their own positions. They think, 'For the year or two years or three years that I am here, I have to fool these deputies and the people.' They only pass their time. This situation will be corrected in this way."

On the other matter that he asked me about, I gave an example that I had seen with my own eyes one time when I was traveling in Pech Valley:

"Several elders and other people were with me. It was in the dark of night. A woman was sitting by the bank of the river. Something black could be seen, and we could hear the sound of water. Something was being washed.

"I said, 'Who's that?'

"Someone replied, 'It's a woman.'

"I asked, 'What's she doing?'

"He replied, 'She's washing clothes.'

"I asked, 'Why doesn't she wash during the day?' (This is what actually happened.)

"He replied, 'She has nothing else to change into. These are her only clothes, and she washes them at night. She's sitting there naked under that veil. She washes them, dries them, and puts them on in the morning. She doesn't have a change of clothes.'"

I told this story to His Majesty. I told him, "This is something that I myself saw."

Then I told him the story of another incident I had seen in the Badel Valley. I was the guest some place and was on my way there when I came upon a man with a load of barley. He was carrying a huge load of barley on his back. His clothes were torn, and his body was half-naked.

I asked him, "What's this?"

He replied, "Barley."

"Where did you buy it?" I asked.

He replied, "I bought it at such-and-such a place and I carried it over the mountains."

I asked him, "Isn't any barley grown [where you live]?"

He said, "No, I don't have anything." At that time, things weren't so good, and barley wasn't available that year.

Then he said, "A man gives me a note that [says], 'I will give so-and-so the money for the barley.' As the middle man, I carry the barley back to him. One day and night have passed since my children last ate. I carry this and have the barley made into flour at the mill. Then I leave it for them. Then I go after another job in some other place. Then I buy some more barley and come back."

I told these two stories to His Majesty. I told him that this was the condition and the economic life of the people. "There are also other people who have nothing to do. They don't work. They have nothing to worry about: everything is prepared for them, and they don't have any miseries."

The king of Afghanistan picked up his cigar and lit it. He placed his glasses on the table. He was sitting opposite me, looking very serious, and he said, "Wakil Sahib of Pech Valley"—this is a quote of King Zahir Shah—he said, "I am not a capitalist." These are the words of the king of Afghanistan. "But I also don't want socialism. I don't want socialism that would bring about the kind of situation [that exists] in Czechoslovakia. I don't want us to become the servants of Russia or China or the servant of any other place. Here is the government. Here is the people. My effort is to work together with this government and the people. These have been my sincere efforts as king of Afghanistan, and I don't lie to you." These were the words of Zahir Shah.[21]

In this account of a meeting with Zahir Shah, Samiullah Safi provides a
partial explanation for why democracy failed in Afghanistan. There are two
features of this analysis, the first having to do with the government in
Kabul and the second with the situation in the country as a whole. The
approximate date of this meeting is not indicated, but we can assume that it
was sometime after December 2, 1969, when the parliament of which Wakil
was a new member had ended an extended period of debate over the status
of the government of Prime Minister Nur Ahmad Etemadi. Etemadi had
come to power in November 1967 during the session of the twelfth parliament, and he had been reappointed by the king after the election of the thirteenth parliament in September 1969. The newly elected parliament, however, had chosen to exercise its legislative might by subjecting the king's
choice to a prolonged and rancorous debate. From November 13 to
December 2, the parliament considered whether to grant the prime minister and his cabinet a vote of confidence. In the course of the debate, the proceedings of which were carried live over Radio Afghanistan, 204 of the 216
parliamentary deputies rose to speak, and the great majority used their
moment before the microphone to lash out at government corruption, inep-
titude, and inaction. In the end, however, only 16 deputies chose to follow
through on their criticism by casting votes of no confidence against the
king's choice of prime minister.[22]

Zahir Shah's first question to Wakil concerned the apparent incongruity
between the vociferous rebuke offered by the parliamentary deputies in
their speeches and the tail-wagging compliance seen in the final tally itself.
The king's second question concerned another persistent feature of democratic politics during that era: the participation in antigovernment demonstrations of ordinary people who were not otherwise involved in political
affairs. Wakil's answer to the first question focused on one of the most
apparent failings of the democratic system instituted by the king—its pro-
hibition of political parties from involvement in the electoral system.

Political parties were not altogether absent. In 1965, the king had allowed
the free publication of newspapers, and the vast majority of papers that
came into existence following this decision were party-based organs espous-
ing particular, and for the most part extreme, points of view. Parties therefore existed, including the Soviet-allied Khalq and Parcham parties, and at
least briefly they were publicly airing their views in print. However, these
parties were not allowed to operate openly within the electoral system
because of the government's fear that they would become too popular if
they were legitimated and allowed into the chambers of power.

The decision to keep the parties out of the open political arena was fateful for several reasons. First, it forced the parties to operate outside established channels, and energies that might have been devoted to openly contesting elections were instead turned to the recruitment and organization of covert cells, especially within the government, military units, and schools. Second, as Wakil claims to have told Zahir Shah, the absence of parties in the parliament meant that the proceedings of that body were even more chaotic than they might otherwise have been. Without parties, the parliament consisted of "216 parties," one for each deputy. Agreements on legislative issues were virtually impossible to arrive at in this atmosphere. On such matters as the no-confidence votes against the prime minister, there were no parties to organize sides pro and con, and so every deputy availed himself of the opportunity to speak his mind. However, when it came time to work on more mundane legislative issues, the throng of deputies usually disappeared. Time and again, parliamentary officers were unable to convene a quorum, and enduring coalitions were all but impossible to arrange and keep together without the organizational apparatus and discipline that parties could provide.[23]

The second question posed by the king, regarding the demonstrations, produced a reply from Wakil that seems in many respects irrelevant. Wakil's stories of the poor woman doing her wash at night because she had only one set of clothes and of the man carrying barley across the mountains to earn enough to feed his family accurately depicted the conditions of a significant percentage of Afghanistan's rural population. And the insinuation at the heart of these stories—that the government in Kabul was out of touch with the rural population—was also correct. However, the king's question had more to do with why people in the city were attracted to radical movements. Why did those who were relatively well off and who benefited directly from the king's peace thoughtlessly lend their voices to the slogans of radical political parties?

The people that Wakil refers to—the rural poor—had rarely been the beneficiaries of government largesse, but, as noted in the discussion of the Khalqi government's misconceived program of reform, few would have indulged this expectation. Nor would most of them have been attracted to demonstrations or other radical political options. Never having benefited much from government programs, they had little reason to expect help from this source. Because of his exposure at university to the theories behind various governmental systems and his experience in Pech of some of the extremes of rural poverty, Wakil concluded that it was the government's job to take care of the poor, but the poor themselves did not necessarily share this conviction. Involvement with the government was as likely to create problems as to solve them, a fact that most rural people well knew and that the Marxists who took power nine years later proved beyond any doubt.

Many of those who joined in the urban demonstrations—the shopkeepers and children referred to by the king—had less to be dissatisfied with than the rural poor, who viewed the government as an entity that periodically showed up to extract resources and people for its own purposes. The residents of Kabul, however, even the urban poor, benefited from the king's rule if only because he provided them with conditions of peace, within which they could conduct their business, and with a modicum of justice when disputes arose between them. According to traditional principles of governance (as articulated in the proclamation promulgated by Amir Abdur Rahman and analyzed in *Heroes of the Age*), Zahir Shah had reason to expect gratitude from those whose security his government protected, and he was thus surprised and upset at the sight of Kabul citizens mindlessly shouting "Death to the monarchy" when it was the monarchy that ensured them their livelihoods.

Wakil's stories did not begin to answer the king's question, but then again the king wasn't looking in the right direction either, for the threat he needed to worry about was not shopkeepers and schoolchildren. Rather, his attention would have been better directed at his own family, especially his paternal cousin, Daud, who was also responsible for the arrest of Wakil's father. Daud had been forced to resign from his position as prime minister with the onset of democratic reforms, but he would stage a successful coup d'état against the king in July 1973. The other great source of danger, greater than the demonstrators in the street, were those who were inciting these demonstrations—namely the leaders of the leftist political parties that the king had banned and that were even then beginning to provide crucial assistance to Daud by organizing cadres within the army and air force that would rally to his assistance when the order to rise up was announced. What Daud didn't realize was that these leftist allies, who would come to his aid in 1973, would eventually seek power on their own and bring about his violent demise in 1978.

AFTER THE REVOLUTION

> I think it was Monday. It was the next week [after the April 1978 coup].
> It was Sunday or Monday. That evening the government announced
> itself—the ministers and others—it announced all of them. It an-
> nounced its new organization. The phone rang for me. I picked up
> the receiver and said, "Hello?"

He said, "Is Safi there?"

I said, "Oh, Amin Sahib, how are you, how are you doing? . . ." It was Hafizullah Amin. The call was from him. He had telephoned me.

He said, "There you are, and you haven't even congratulated me. Nothing! You haven't even picked up the phone to offer your best wishes." I didn't say anything, and after a moment, he said, "Are you still there?"

I said, "Where else would I be?"

He said, "You should have gone to the grave of your father and congratulated him. Daud Khan has been killed."

I said, "Amin Sahib . . ." My colleagues [in my office] were sitting there. I said, "If I go to my father's grave and stand there, it would be with whose eyes, through whose zeal [*ghairat*], with whose bravery [*shuja'at*]? The spirit of my father would say, 'You haven't even bloodied your nose. How do you know who killed Daud Khan? How do you know who did what?' "

For this reason, I told him, "Only if I had been included in your coup d'état (I didn't call it a revolution) and I myself had been up against Daud Khan in the fighting, would I have the right to go [to my father's grave]. But how can my conscience accept this when I don't even know for sure who killed Daud Khan? I was asleep. I had no direct knowledge. I was drinking tea in my office when Daud Khan was destroyed, and then I go and offer congratulations?" I told him, "My conscience won't allow it."

Then he hung up his receiver without saying a thing.[24]

Following Daud's coup d'état in July 1973, Wakil settled into a period of relative inactivity. Initially, he worked in editorial and journalistic positions connected to government ministries, but he stayed with none of these jobs very long and eventually resigned from the last one—a six-month stint as the director of the government press agency in Kunduz—"because of the conditions I saw there—the extreme corruption." For most of the remainder of Daud's tenure in office, Wakil was unemployed, though he eventually accepted another government posting in Kabul as the deputy editor of the journal *Erfan,* an organ of the Ministry of Education. He was in this position when military units loyal to the People's Democratic Party of Afghanistan (PDPA) stormed the presidential palace, killed Daud, and declared the advent of a new era in Afghan history.

As discussed in previous chapters, Amin, the man on the other end of this recounted telephone conversation, was the architect of the Khalqi coup d'état and had recently been appointed to the posts of deputy prime minister and minister of foreign affairs by President Taraki. Given the disparity in position between Wakil and Amin, one might wonder why Amin would take the trouble to make this call, but then one must remember the limited base of support enjoyed by the PDPA. Despite the insignificance of his position, Wakil would have proven a useful ally to Amin. He was after all a former parliamentary deputy, the son of famous father, and a prominent member of a notoriously fractious and disruptive tribe. There was also the history of enmity between Wakil's father and former President Daud, whom Amin had helped destroy, and the long-standing connection between his family and Wakil's, extending back to when Amin's father, Habibullah Khan, had been a helpful and relatively humane official in the Kabul prison where Sultan Muhammad had been incarcerated. This connection had been strengthened by personal familiarity going back to Wakil's days as a student, when Amin had been his teacher and principal at the Ibn Sina secondary school in Kabul and his principal again at the teacher-training college, and also by the time they had served together as parliamentary deputies.

Given the extent and generally amicable nature of their relationship, Wakil's resolve to reject Amin's overture might lead one to conclude that his claims to have decided on a course of resistance to the regime on first hearing Amin's voice over the radio after the coup d'état were trumped up after the fact, except that eight months after the April coup Wakil did indeed leave Kabul to join the nascent resistance movement in Pech Valley. In making sense of Wakil's opposition, we need first to take seriously his own statements. Amin's identification as a Marxist was one of Wakil's reasons for opposing him, but it is not the one that Wakil emphasized. In Wakil's mind, Amin was not so much concerned with justice and reform as with power, and he relied on a small band of family members and unprincipled allies willing to do his bidding:

> Hafizullah Amin counted on his personal relations and friends. He didn't have much to do with the party and that sort of thing. He wouldn't give it any importance. All of these people would gather around him. It was like some sort of band, like a band of thieves and highwaymen. It didn't matter who they were as long as they were his friends. It didn't matter whether they were Khalqis; he would find some position for them in the party.[25]

In many respects, Wakil's politics were not that different from Amin's. His experiences in exile—particularly, scenes he had witnessed of abject and starving prisoners—had inclined him to a more progressive orientation, and in 1978 he had even taken up with a well-known leftist organizer named Majid Kalakani. It is a mark perhaps of Wakil's relatively cosmopolitan upbringing that unlike the Khalqis, who recruited primarily among their fellow Pakhtuns, and the Parchamis, who drew mainly from Kabulis and other non-Pakhtuns, Wakil was drawn to a Tajik from the Kohistan region north of Kabul. Kalakani had a reputation for cleverness and daring not unlike a fellow Kohistani from an earlier era, Bacha-i Saqao. Unlike Amin, whose support came principally from a small band of cronies and acolytes, Kalakani had widespread support in Kohistan, which was the result not of the favors he could dispense but of his inborn charisma. That Kalakani was also viewed as a threat by the Khalqis and at the time of Amin's call to Wakil was being actively hunted down probably also was a reason for Wakil's rejection of Amin's entreaty.[26]

Another source of Wakil's contempt for Amin was his treatment of opponents and his branding of all those who criticized the regime as Muslim extremists, "Ikhwanis":

> At that point, if a person said prayers, then they thought he was an Ikhwani. Prayers are part of the beliefs of the people of Afghanistan. We have to say our prayers since we are Muslims, but it doesn't mean that I am an Ikhwani. Their idea was that if a person wasn't a Khalqi, then he must be an Ikhwani. . . . A Khalqi would see someone I had known since childhood saying his prayers [*namaz*] or fasting [*roza*] and would say that he was an Ikhwani. They wouldn't accept my opinion. They would accept some Khalqi's opinion just because he had been involved in the coup d'état.[27]

Though he was not especially devout himself, Wakil recognized and respected the importance of Islam in his society and knew that Khalqi paranoia about Islamic resistance made them see simple instances of personal piety as acts of treason.

Probably the most important factor in Wakil's opposition to Amin was his sense of responsibility to his father's legacy. Amin knew that Sultan Muhammad's specter weighed heavily on Wakil's mind, and, in his call to Wakil, he tried to invoke the father for his own ends. However, Wakil's story tells us that Amin's telephone call had the opposite effect, reinforcing in Wakil's mind his own passivity and the scorn that his father would undoubtedly have felt for Amin and his minions. Wakil knew not only that he had no right to take any satisfaction in Amin's achievement but also that Amin's call contained a not-so-hidden message. To have accepted the logic of what Amin was saying, Wakil would have had to admit to being in a dependent relationship to him. If Amin was responsible for avenging his father, then Wakil would have owed him a debt, a debt that would have required that he be willing to do something of equal importance for Amin. Amin was thus using the moral logic of honor to advance his own interests and those of an institution—the party—that was committed to destroying the social network of relationships on which honor depended; and while he was intent on enlisting Wakil to help him accomplish this end, Wakil showed that he was on to Amin's game and not about to admit any gratitude whatsoever.[28]

Wakil also indicated to me that his attitude toward the Khalqi regime had been affected by stories reaching him from Pech the summer after the coup. Toward the end of June 1978, three months after the Marxist coup d'état, the town of Ningalam, the administrative center of Pech Valley, became the site of one of the first acts of antigovernment violence against the PDPA regime. Although some have referred to it as a popular uprising, the incident was something less than that; it was based not so much on general displeasure with the government as on a specific episode: the arrest of two elders who, after questioning in the local government office, were transported to the provincial headquarters at Chagha Serai.

According to some accounts, one of the arrested men, a mulla named Muhammad Sadiq, was an enemy of the local administrator (*woleswal*) and had been involved in a land dispute with him for some time. Many local people believed that this dispute was one of the reasons for the arrest, and it helped to convince them that the charges against the men were illegitimate. When the jeep carrying the prisoners passed through the Ningalam bazaar, an old woman who had heard of the arrests reportedly cried out, "Is there no man among you? Two of our men are being taken away!" Some men in the crowd responded by firing at the jeep, killing an officer and two soldiers. The next day, June 23, 1978, soldiers, accompanied by tanks and artillery, entered Ningalam. Local residents fled the town, taking refuge in neighboring valleys as soldiers began looting their houses. The military was then ordered to open tank and artillery fire on the village, with support from the air force.

According to one report, the bombing lasted from dawn to dusk, while "communist elements poured gasoline on houses and burned them. They fired on the mosques and burned all the religious books and the Holy Qur'an."[29] One incident during the attack on Ningalam stood out and was much talked about in the following days. A widow who had refused to leave Ningalam when the other residents fled was burned alive in her house with her child. Government troops reportedly threw the bodies of the woman and her child out on the street, where they lay exposed for several days. Wakil was among those who had heard the story of the burning of Ningalam and the killing of the woman and her child, and he told me that the incident hardened his resolve to leave Kabul and return to Pech, which he did the following winter.

CONCLUSION

There is nothing ordinary about Samiullah Safi's early life. His story does not tell us why other, "average" Afghans decided to take up arms against the Marxist regime, but it does tell us something about the demands of honor that were felt more generally, if not in so distilled a form as Wakil experienced. The status of Wakil's father placed demands on his sons—in death as well as in life—that were beyond what other sons had to acknowledge in degree perhaps, but not in their basic nature. The utility of Wakil's story is that it brings into focus the perpetuation of the culture of honor in a time and context when it might have been thought that honor had ceased to matter as a relevant factor in matters of state politics. The legend of his father's life and deeds made the burden of honor inescapable for Wakil in a way that it was not for others, but even for the humblest and poorest of Pakhtuns, honor weighed on their minds, if more inchoately and less self-consciously than in Wakil's case.

The utility of his story, for my purposes, is that it reveals in a dramatic fashion how the past continued to haunt the present, how Afghan responses to the novelty of the Marxist revolution were conditioned by an understanding of what had gone on in the past. Taraki and his followers represented an entirely new circumstance, unlike any that Afghans had ever seen, but that meant that to an even greater degree people looked to past precedents to understand and respond to them. Wakil was unusual in several respects: he was well educated, and, although he had never traveled abroad to that point in his life, he had seen far more of his own nation than all but a few of his countrymen; and, of course, he had the father that he did. All these factors made Wakil an unusually astute and valuable guide for revealing the pressures that others also felt, though perhaps less profoundly or coherently.

Wakil's story hinges on his relationship to his father, but it is also important to remember how different they were and how different also the context in which they conducted the seminal events of their lives. Sultan Muhammad faced his greatest challenge after his father's murder, when he was in exile, leading a comfortable life in Dir. He had to decide whether to stay there or go back and face the likelihood of his own death in the effort to avenge his father. Wakil also had a secure position in Kabul, working, like his father, as a "scribe" on a government-sponsored journal of Pakhtun culture and literature. His function in this position was presumably to assist the government both in preserving "culture" and in consigning it to the confines of print. However, with the Khalqi coup d'état, the imperatives of culture leaped off the page for Wakil, and he too had to make a life-transforming decision that also involved a return to Pech.

Where the two men differed was in their character and the context in which their characters were shaped. From all accounts, Sultan Muhammad was a moral absolutist who lived by the dictates of honor. In Pakhtu terminology, he was a *qahraman,* a champion or hero "who molds passionate anger into exemplary violence."[30] However, as I note in *Heroes of the Age,* this role is full of hidden perils, for the qualities embodied in the hero are deeply antagonistic to the common cause, threatening the security and happiness of the many, even as they provide them with an avenue of transcendence.[31] Wakil was neither so single-minded nor so severe as his father. It is not surprising that he became a journalist and editor, for in many ways his sensibilities were those of an observer more than of an actor. Though events compelled him to action, a part of him—the part that made him a good storyteller—recalled the little boy observing the imagined and real violence of others from behind closed doors.

The worlds that Wakil and his father inhabited were also starkly different. Coming of age in the last decade of the nineteenth and first decade of the twentieth century, Sultan Muhammad lived in a less complex environment defined by the egalitarian, kinship-based universe of the tribe in Pech and the hierarchical, alliance-based universe of the court in Dir. Tribe and court were factors in Wakil's world, but there were also other choices as well: for example, whether to study overseas in order to learn a profession and whether to join a political party to pursue a particular political agenda—and, if so, which one. Ultimately, these choices too were variations on the theme of kinship versus alliance, but they were far more variegated and diversely presented than any faced by Sultan Muhammad, for whom the crucial life choice was essentially whether to abide by honor's demands within the confines of the tribe or to live elsewhere as a different sort of mortal.

Wakil had to come to terms with honor's demands too, but he encountered a more abstract situation than did Sultan Muhammad, whose father's death required vengeance and who literally had to fear for his life every time he went back to Pech. Despite years of hardship culminating in nearly two decades of imprisonment, Wakil's father ultimately died in his own bed in his village in Pech. Whatever grudges the family might have borne for the indignity of imprisonment, Wakil was sufficiently reconciled to the government to become a parliamentary representative and later a government employee. Many other tribal Pakhtuns made similar choices, rationalizing that the past was past and the world no longer operated according to the simple binary logic of tribe versus state. The moral order of the modern world was based on compromise, and most educated Afghans eschewed moral absolutism of one form or another to follow situational strategies for getting by and getting ahead.

Given the long history of animosity between his family and Daud, Wakil more than most of his peers surely could have found sufficient grounds for joining the Khalqi bandwagon and taking advantage of the opportunities offered by Amin and his allies. Doing so would certainly have been in keeping with the moral relativism that had helped erode the demands of honor to which Sultan Muhammad adhered throughout his life. But Wakil chose not to do so, and that decision makes his story compelling and his example instructive. To a greater or lesser degree and at about the same time, many Afghans from different strata, regions, and backgrounds were grappling with the choices that Wakil had before him. And though many—if not most—from his strata chose paths between the extremes, staying in Kabul, quietly going about their lives, and staying out of the line of fire, more than a few felt the pull of history and culture and shouldered arms against the state. Wakil was one such individual, and the story of his time in battle and the ultimate failure of his attempt to revive honor as an element of state politics is told in the following chapter.

5 Anatomy of a Tribal Uprising

It was on the eleventh of January 1979 that I left Kabul, and I reached my home on the third night. I spent one night in Narang, the second night I spent in the district center [*alaqadari*], and the third night I reached home. Before I reached home, I went to the house of a man who was originally from my village of Gul Salak. All the people were gathered there. They were worried. "How did he get here? What happened? What's it all about?" Some of them thought that I had become the governor since I knew all the ministers. They were thinking things like this. When they gathered, they wanted to find out my opinion. One asked, "How's everything in Kabul? How did you get here? How did you get permission? How did you come?" That sort of thing. I saw that there were probably forty or fifty people inside the room and there were some more sitting outside.

The owner of the house was there. All the people from his village were there, along with whomever happened to be there from other places. Opponents of the government had also come. I took a 500 Afghani note out of my pocket. I gave it to the owner of the house.

He said, "What am I supposed to do with this?"

I told him, "Brother, you are a poor man. You can't give all these people food."

He said, "To whom?"

I said, "To them. You can't feed all of them. Even if you can't give them anything else, you can give them sugarless tea."

He said, "To which people?"

I said, "To the mujahidin."

He said, "Really?" His mouth dropped when he said this, and then he turned to his relatives and said, "Replace the red flag with the white one."

I said, "Don't put up a white flag. If you've got a red one up, then take it down." Immediately, his sons and cousins went out and took

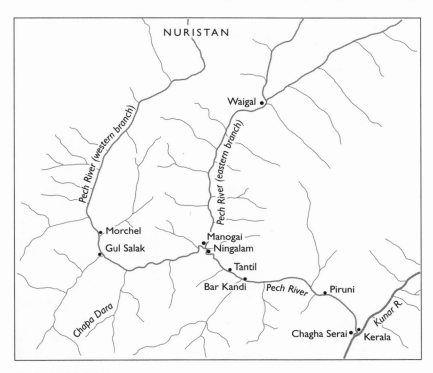

MAP 2. Pech Valley

down the flag—the red flag—while we were sitting there. The people there immediately realized what was going on.[1]

The mouth of the Pech Valley runs north and west from the provincial capital of Chagha Serai (also known as Asadabad), which sits at the confluence of the Pech and Kunar rivers (Map 2). The Pech River has two main branches that join at the village of Ningalam: the one entering Ningalam from the north flows from the Waigal Valley of Nuristan; the second descends through most of its length north to south from the Parun Valley of Nuristan before entering Ningalam from the west. The two branches of the Pech are of considerable strategic and commercial significance because they link the Kunar Valley and the Pakistan frontier with Badakhshan Province in the northeast, Panjshir to the west, and Laghman to the southwest. While vehicular traffic can traverse only the lower and middle reaches of the valley, Pech offers foot travelers access to the northern and central flanks of the Hindu Kush without having to go through any major cities, a fact that made the earlier opposition in Pech of considerable importance to the government.

The pre-1978 population of Pech has been estimated at around sixty thousand, divided principally between Safis in the lower and middle reaches of the valley and Nuristanis in the more inaccessible northern valleys. While relations between Safis and Nuristanis have improved in the last half century, they have been antagonistic historically. Until 1897, when Amir Abdur Rahman sent troops in to force the submission of the population, Nuristan was known as Kafiristan, and it was the last remaining region of Afghanistan to resist conversion to Islam. Prior to that time, Safis and Nuristanis raided one another, with young Kafir men wearing turbans taken from the Safis they killed as emblems of prestige.[2] Nuristanis speak several distinct languages unconnected to Pakhtu, the language of the Safis and the other Pakhtun tribes along the frontier. Despite these impediments, relations between Safis and Nuristanis improved after the conquest, with marriage alliances and trading partnerships becoming frequent occurrences. Language differences aside, Nuristanis and Safis share a number of other things in common: both traditionally organize themselves as nested patrilineal lineages and tribes; both adhere to a code of honorable conduct that exalts male bravery, female modesty, hospitality to guests, and the centrality of the tribal council in resolving disputes and making collective decisions. Here as elsewhere on the frontier, the dark side of this code of conduct is the proclivity for tribesmen to become enmeshed in rivalries and feuds with close agnatic kin and the frequent resort to violence in response to major grievances and minor insults.

In the summer of 1978, however, rivalries were held in check as more and more of the population of the area threw their support to those advocating armed insurrection against the government. The general reasons for this opposition, while similar to those expressed by Wakil, are also more extensive and, according to a report by Delawar Sahre, a Nuristani who was active in the uprising, revolve around several themes.

Disrespect for Islam: "They openly told people to give up the old Qur'an and study the new books of Marx and Lenin." "Muhammad was said to be a somewhat intelligent man who wrote the Qur'an himself." "There is no time for saying prayers, fasting during Ramazan, or paying *zakat* (religious tax). We should all just work and obey Taraki's decrees." "They arrested and killed many of the scholars and banned the prayers and preaching in the mosques." "Instead of 'Allah-o Akbar,' they shouted the slogans of 'hurrah.'"[3]

Immorality of government officials: "They illegally entered peoples' homes and robbed them. They also committed many cruel acts and killed people." "When talking to people, they were impudent and in-

sulted them and used abusive language." "They encouraged people to
do bad things, like drink alcohol, gamble, smoke hashish, use prostitutes,
and avoid their religious duties." "They worshiped the Kremlin as their
qibla (the direction toward which Muslims offer their prayers)."

Interference in domestic affairs: "They threatened and summoned
people to the sub-divisional headquarters and interrupted their work."
"They tried to aggravate tribal and personal differences." "They indoc-
trinated school children in communism and taught them to spy on their
parents." "They said that women were free and equal to men and that
dowry and bride-price, along with marriage itself, would gradually be
eliminated." "They decided disputes—even those involving marriage
and divorce—by decisions taken by the party provincial council." "The
Khalqis wanted to enlist women in organizations and send most of them
to Moscow."[4]

Disrespect for traditional elites and private property: "They dishonored,
insulted and killed the tribal leaders, and told us that landowners and
khans are the people's enemies and should be destroyed." "They told
us that land is not private property. It belongs to the farmers, and the
farmers are the government's hired workers." "They stole the farmers'
labor under the pretext of co-operatives."[5]

The grievances cited here are similar to those mentioned by residents of
other areas that took up arms against the Khalqis in 1978 and 1979. The
emphasis varies from region to region, so that sometimes abuses involving
women predominate, sometimes attacks on traditional elites, sometimes
land reform, sometimes the character and behavior of government officials.
In the case of Pech, the causes of discontent seem fairly evenly divided
among the above categories, although disrespect for religion and religious
leaders is probably cited more often than any other issue. Despite this fact,
however, the vast majority of the population in Pech, including many mullas initially, joined a tribal front in which religious figures played their traditional supporting role of helping to mediate between opposing sides and
between combatants and noncombatants without assuming positions of
outright leadership.

In their separate descriptions of the events of this period, both Samiullah
Safi and Delawar Sahre divide the Pech Uprising into three primary stages,
the first of which, when the insurrection remained limited in scope, lasted
roughly from the burning of Ningalam in June to December 1978. The second stage, through the winter and spring of 1979, was the period when tribal
leaders took control of the uprising, and the population as a whole joined
together to oust government representatives. The third stage, beginning in
the summer of 1979, was the period of Islamic party ascendance, which

essentially signaled the end of the tribal rebellion and the beginning of the Islamic jihad controlled by resistance organizations in Peshawar, Pakistan.

In the period following the government's destruction of Ningalam, the insurrection was not generalized, even though most people were outraged by the regime's actions. A small force did succeed in capturing the government base in the village of Manogai after the Ningalam incident, but it was quickly recaptured, and the rebels fell back, demoralized and aware that the ground had not yet been established for a popular uprising. Most government installations were still untouched, and government programs—including the establishment of a cooperative fund—were going forward. Khalqi officials moved freely from village to village, and many homes still had red flags fluttering above them. To rebel leaders, it was clear that the uprising would be hamstrung as long as Khalqi sympathizers were present in the villages and the government was able to co-opt village leaders, some of whom supported the government simply because their rivals were on the side of the rebels.

Shortly after the recapture of Manogai, the government organized a large delegation (jirga) to meet with the rebels. The jirga was composed of Safi elders from neighboring valleys (Mazar and Badel), prominent Safis living in Kabul, and elders from other parts of Nuristan not yet committed to the uprising. The official in charge promised to rebuild Ningalam, but leaders of the rebellion, including the commander, Abdul Jabar, who was himself from Ningalam, refused these entreaties, and the jirga ended in failure for the government, which quickly resumed air attacks against rebel positions and armed tribal militias in the lower part of the valley. Many of those who supported the resistance at this early stage did so covertly, in some cases even working for the government during the day and joining the rebels at night for mostly ineffectual hit-and-run attacks.

Wakil's departure from Kabul occurred in January 1979, after he announced to the editor of the journal *Erfan* that he intended to take his allotted twenty-day vacation and travel with his family back to Pech. Though the government tried to stop them en route, Wakil and his family were able to proceed to their village. From there, he sent out a message to the leaders of the nascent uprising, requesting that they attend a meeting in his home. Antigovernment activities were still scattered at this stage of the uprising. Although the rebels were being given food and shelter in neighboring valleys, few others had as yet shown any willingness to follow their example by taking up arms, and government officials were still going about their business. Wakil's appearance back in Pech seems to have been a significant factor in galvanizing popular sentiment against the government and

8.   Samiullah Safi ("Wakil"), Pech Valley, May 1985 (courtesy of Samiullah Safi).

setting in motion preparations for an expansion of the resistance. As a former parliamentary deputy and son of one of the tribe's most legendary khans, Wakil was an established leader who was considered more knowledgeable than other Safis of the ways of Kabul and the wider world. In addition, he was also known as an effective speaker, and his powers of persuasion were widely recognized (Fig. 8).

Wakil's oratory would prove most useful in the period to follow because the pressing need for the rebels was to enlist the support of the great number of people in the area who remained undecided in the conflict. This was to be Wakil's primary role, and most of the stories he told me from this time, including the story quoted here of his first meeting with a group of Safis on the day of his return, involve speeches he made to massed groups of his fellow tribesmen (Fig. 9). The most important of these meetings took place three days after his homecoming, on January 18, when he invited Abdul Jabar of Ningalam, who had been in command of the uprising to this point, and other Safi and Nuristani leaders to his house in Morchel. The decision was made at this meeting to destroy the district headquarters at Chapa Dara two days hence.

Of primary concern to Wakil in the days after his arrival was that the government not be given any inadvertent assistance in stifling the still tentative antigovernment agitation. Thus, for example, because the district

9. Samiullah Safi (center, facing left, bare-headed), Dewagal Valley, August 1989 (courtesy of Samiullah Safi).

administrator was from the Wadir lineage of the Safi tribe, it was decided that the first attack should be led by members of that branch so that the government could not later propagandize among the Wadirs that a Gurbuz or Mahsud Safi captured "your Wadir brother." Once the district administrator was captured, he would be kept not in Nuristan (even though it was more isolated and safer from government counterattack) but among his fellow Safis to prevent the government from driving a wedge between Safis and Nuristanis. Finally, the order was given that there should be no looting because this would also allow the government to announce that "they had attacked the government center to plunder the rifles and weapons, that this Wakil tells us to rise up and these khans tell us to rise up only because they want to digest these weapons. It was for this reason that even the smallest theft was forbidden [*haram*]."

JIRGA AND LASHKAR

The tribal army [*lashkar*] stretched all the way from Nuristan to the district headquarters [*alaqadari*]—this whole district. It was such a lashkar that I thought to myself, "It seemed like every bush had one hundred flowers and they were all human beings." Their enthusiasm was shared by the women and children who were also there, and they were all shouting slogans, very loud. Starting from Parun and Kantiwa [in Nuristan, at the top of the Pech Valley], all the way to Chapa Dara—all this was one district. All the people from this district were there. No one except the very elderly who couldn't walk remained at home. They all came armed and committed to fight. There were maybe fifteen or twenty thousand people. They had destroyed the district headquarters, and now it was the turn of the woleswali [regional administration center].

The capture of the district headquarters was the first major event in the second stage of the uprising—a period in which jirgas were held and a tribally organized uprising was begun. At this stage, the lower half of the valley was still solidly in government hands. A Khalqi militia was also in place, and the mouth of the valley was open, so the government was able to bring in troops and supplies from the provincial capital. The government tended to have greater support on the south side of the formidably wide and swift Pech River. The south side is where the main road lay, which meant that the government had greater contact with villages on this side and greater ability to exert its force. It also meant that villages within sight of one another were often on opposite sides of the political divide, which by this point had thoroughly split the region. The leaders of the uprising recognized that they had to accomplish two goals: to gain the support of villages that were still under government control and to cut off the lower part of the valley to prevent the government from sending in reinforcements.

Wakil, along with other tribal and religious leaders from Nuristan and all three branches of the Safi tribe, formed jirgas representing the upper half of the Pech Valley to visit villages in the lower part of the valley, the various side valleys, and parts of Nuristan. Accompanied by a small detachment of armed men, the jirgas would approach each village and ask to meet with the village elders to encourage them to support the uprising. If they agreed, they would take an oath on behalf of their village (*qaumi do'a*) and guarantee their oath by dispatching a contingent of young men—representing each branch and lineage of the tribe resident in that area—to join the lashkar, which was usually trailing a few villages behind. Then the jirga would set off for the next village, gradually moving closer and closer to the regional administration center. As the jirga moved down the valley, the lashkar followed in its wake. It was important at this stage for the first contact with a previously uncommitted village to be made by the jirga and not by the lashkar. The leaders were determined to preserve tribal unity, which necessitated that villages be given the opportunity to join the movement voluntarily. This was not always possible, however, as the jirga sometimes came under fire as it approached villages in which the government still had influence.

Wakil recalled for me one such confrontation near the village of Udai-gram. After the jirga approached the village "in a rain of bullets," the village elders sent out two old women carrying a copy of the Qur'an in their hands. This is a traditional way to initiate a cease-fire, and Wakil went forward to speak with the women:

> A woman came in front of us with a Holy Qur'an in her hand. The people of the village had sent two women to meet us. I said, "Mother, what is this?"
>
> "I swear by this Holy Qur'an that our houses are under their guns. They will kill our children and nothing will remain behind."
>
> I told these mothers, "You should be ashamed before this Qur'an. You are our mothers. In the village of Ningalam, they burned the homes of three or four thousand families. Did they have mothers there like you? Did they have children like your children? Did they have property or calves or goats, yes or no?"
>
> She said, "They had them."
>
> I told her, "You should go and tell those who are sitting peacefully, 'Shame on you! Rise up!' You've taken up the Holy Qur'an. You should be ashamed of yourselves. You come to us from the Khalqis, from their ranks. They don't believe in the Qur'an, but those who are rising up, they respect the Qur'an. You shame this book."
>
> She said, "What can I do? They made me do it." The old woman said this. "And we are also under their bombardment, and our houses are under their guns."
>
> I said, "We'll buy time for you. We'll transport your children and your property to the mountains or wherever. We'll do this. In one night, we'll do it. You shouldn't worry at all." I kissed the Holy Qur'an and placed 20 rupees on it. I said, "This is a matter of honor [nang] for you. It's shameful. You are Safi mothers. Your children, what sacrifices they are making, and you say this. It's bad."

Following this encounter, the jirga met with the elders of the village throughout that day, and that evening they took an oath to support the jihad and invited the jirga to stay with them as it was cold and they were "under the threat of the [government's] guns." There were twenty people in the jirga—ten to twelve representatives and mullas and a few members of the lashkar who were there to protect them—and they were sent off to differ-ent houses in the village so that "no one villager would have to go to too much trouble or supply too much food." That night, a group of Khalqi sympathizers who had not accepted the elders' oath to support the jihad conceived a plot to attack the members of the jirga:

> All of a sudden there was a hue and cry. It was raining—it was such
> heavy rain. It was evening. I put on my boots and got up. I asked
> someone, "What's happening?" One of our elders was shouting at
> the villagers. He said, "You are untrustworthy. Before you took an
> oath with us, and now your young men want to start some sort of a
> plot." He suddenly fled—he didn't flee exactly, he ran in the direction
> of the lashkar, which was two or three villages behind us in order to tell
> them to attack the village.
>
> As soon as he had left, the other elders quickly gave me the responsi-
> bility of intercepting the lashkar. "Go. You can never tell. The lashkar
> might became impassioned and arrive suddenly and enter the village,
> and the soldiers would fire at them from above, and this might become
> like Ningalam, all because they have been overcome with passion. Go
> ahead and tell them to wait. Don't send more than five hundred men,
> five hundred armed men and no more since any additional force would
> be dangerous."
>
> I agreed, and as I was going, up ahead of me, all of a sudden, I could
> hear [the lashkar] shouting, "Allah Akbar!" They almost killed me.
> Most of them were people from our own village. They were in the first
> group to arrive since the man who had gone before me—a *haji* [an hon-
> orific title for a man who has completed the pilgrimage to Mecca] whose
> name I have forgotten—he's from Ningalam—he let out a cry that
> they had captured the elders and they had even taken Wakil—he meant
> me. "They took him! The government took him! The government took
> our elders with the help of the villagers, and if we don't finish them off
> tonight, they will send all of the elders to Kabul tomorrow and execute
> them. [They will take them] in the helicopters!"
>
> Suddenly, that very night, it was all lit up, in the direction of the
> government forces. See the difference in sentiments on this side of the
> river and that side of the river. I immediately sent men to the other side
> of the river to tell them that the elders hadn't been taken and to be care-
> ful not to go or they'd capture all of us.
>
> Later, I scolded that haji—I mean those other elders scolded him—
> "You haven't done a good thing. The danger here was that the govern-
> ment has seen this, what the situation is." He had panicked when there
> wasn't even any firing going on. Who knows—if we had fired at [the
> villagers] and hurt them, they would have captured us. They wouldn't
> have let us live.
>
> After that, all of us stayed there in that village. Nearly five hundred
> from the different tribes—we divided the men into groups and stationed
> them in different places. There were 120 from two of the branches, and
> 100 each from the other two. We brought them to the village, and that

night we were in their houses, and we told them to cook us some chicken. And that night they cooked chicken for all of the four or five hundred mujahidin, the young men who had come. In every house, they ate well off them until the morning. This was a tribal punishment [*jaza*] that we inflicted on them—that one time you take an oath, then, some among you attack us. We didn't punish them anymore than having five or ten people going to every house and having them kill a chicken for them and show them good hospitality.

We told them, "Not even one of you can leave. If they bomb us, you will get killed along with us. We're in the same village, in the same predicament." They had to do it, and they vowed again—their elders vowed again—to support the jihad.

While the jirgas were moving down the valley, another group of mujahidin attacked a large government force at Tantil. The mujahidin managed to encircle the force, but the siege was broken when government militia fell on them from the rear. Both sides suffered heavy casualties, but the mujahidin captured a large quantity of weapons and ammunition and gained renewed confidence that, under the right conditions, they could take on and defeat the enemy. This battle—the bloodiest to date—was followed on March 10 by the conquest of Bar Kandi. Again, in an attempt to preserve tribal unity, the mujahidin followed their victory by not allowing anyone from the village to be punished and offering their opponents a full pardon if they agreed to join against the government. To prevent disputes over booty—which is one of the most pernicious sources of tribal rivalry—the jirga decided that individual mujahidin could keep only one light weapon each. All other captured weapons had to be turned over to the jirga, which would be responsible for their disposition.

The decisive battle of the uprising to that point in time occurred later in March, when the mujahidin attacked the Khalqi position at Utapur, near the base of the valley. The battle continued for several days before the mujahidin finally succeeded in taking the fort at Srah Morgah and then Utapur itself. After the capture of Srah Morgah, the battle turned into a rout, with Khalqi officials, soldiers, and sympathizers trying to flee in convoy to the provincial capital. Mujahidin hidden along the route of escape at Pirunai Dag succeeded in damaging several of the lead vehicles, effectively blocking the road and forcing the enemy to surrender. Within days of this victory, which isolated the remaining government forces within Pech, the remaining government outposts, including the base at Ningalam, were subdued, and the valley was liberated from Khalqi control.

FIRST SETBACKS

At that time, [a woman who] had come to my house told my wife that for thirty days her children had been eating boiled grass and no bread. In the house, I was told that this woman had come, and I was very moved by her situation. In the house we had some crops, and I asked one of my servants what we had. He told me that we had seventy ser of raw potatoes, which was equal to forty-five ser in Kabul—one Kabul ser is equal to seven kilos—and we had about a week before the wheat harvest. Although we had a big family and many guests and they said we wouldn't have enough, I told him to give the woman five ser. This was more important than our experiencing hunger because the woman had little children.

This was to be given to them, but before getting his portion the young husband of this women had taken his bag and gone about fifteen kilometers away to see whether he could find some corn to bring back. He also had a gun with him, the kind we call *baghalpur*, which has a very short effective range. It has very big bullets. It's very old, actually an antique, and is sold in antique stores. He had this kind of gun, and while he was off trying to find corn, he heard that there had been an attack—the Russians attacked again—and he left his things there and went to fight. He was missing for three days before he returned to the area, and we thought that he had been killed someplace.

I asked him, "You went to get corn. Your children are hungry. Why did you go to fight?"

He replied, "I heard that there was a battle. I had a gun with me. What else could I do? Food wasn't as important as fighting." He was young.

I asked him, "Were you able to fire?" He replied, "No. I didn't see anyone. It was a bombardment. There was nothing else." From there, he had gone to Bar Kandi, then to Waigal Valley. From Waigal Valley, he had come to his house in Tsarigal. This was the spirit of jihad among the people.

The capture of Utapur and Ningalam represented the high point of the uprising in Pech—militarily, organizationally, and culturally. During this second stage of the uprising, not only had individual tribes succeeded in working together, but also Safis had joined in common cause with non-Pakhtun Nuristanis and Kohistanis from neighboring valleys. A council of jihad had been established and had elected a Nuristani, Haji Abdul Ghafur Khan, as its chief (amir) and a Safi from Ningalam, Abdul Jabar, as commander-in-chief of the fighting forces. The lashkar itself was divided into four tribal fronts (one Nuristani and three from each of the branches of the

Safi tribe—one of which was led by Matiullah Khan, Wakil's younger brother). To this point, disputes had generally been kept in check, in large part because of the care taken by jihad leaders to respect the conventions of tribal culture. For example, during the battle of Utapur, Said Ahmad Khan and Matiullah had been responsible for killing a Safi who had joined the Khalqis. Although it was still winter and snow was on the ground, Said Ahmad Khan, who was from the same village as the dead man, insisted that they carry the body back to the man's family. They set out that night, reaching the man's home the next morning, and "because of this, he convinced many of the members of this man's family to become mujahidin." This story is one of a number Wakil told me in which personal and tribal enmities were avoided because actions that might have been taken as insults or attacks against individuals by rivals were shown to be collectively sanctioned by the jihad council and the tribe as a whole.

Throughout this period, the Khalqis fought back both militarily and through propaganda, which they hoped would win over the hearts and minds of the citizenry. In particular, the regime tried to convince the people that its programs were in the best interests of Islam, but few were inclined to trust government statements, no matter how hard the regime tried to make them convincing:

> One time, the Khalqis had failed to write "bismillah" on the top of leaflets dropped from a plane, and with one voice the people said that this was proof of their blasphemy. Another time, presumably to make up for their earlier mistake, they wrote not only "bismillah" but also "Allah Akbar" and the *kalama* ["There is no god but Allah, and Muhammad is His Prophet"]. This time, the people with one voice said, "They have thrown the blessed kalama on the ground, and in this way they pollute it under the feet of humans and animals."

One of the regime's aims in spreading propaganda was to try to aggravate long-standing differences and prejudices in the region. For example, it tried to incite Safis against Nuristanis by dropping leaflets on Safi villages that reminded the people how the Nuristanis had taken arms from the government and assisted them in defeating the Safis during the 1945–1946 conflict. Similarly, the regime also tried to take advantage of age-old disputes over grazing rights between Gujars, who traditionally brought their flocks to Nuristan in the summer months, and Nuristanis, who controlled the pastures, by promising the Gujars arms and title to disputed lands if they joined the government side. They also reportedly told the nontribal peasants (*dehqan*) in lower Pech and the area around the provincial capital that their time had finally come. "The peasants had supported the government during the first Safi War, and the Safis had looted their homes and businesses in retaliation. The Khalqis tried to fan this resentment but were unsuccessful, and again the houses of those people who supported the government were burned by the Safis and Nuristanis." Finally, the government tried to undermine tribal unity by bringing in militias from more distant tribes, principally Shinwaris from Ningrahar Province, to fight against the Safi rebels. According to Wakil, the fathers of these Shinwaris had previously helped defeat the Safis during the Safi War, but the Safis were careful not to aggravate the bad blood between the tribes any more than necessary.

In the spring of 1979, everything seemed to be going right for the resistance. The Khalqis had been removed from Pech, and other tribes and groups in Kunar were also beginning to organize themselves to join the uprising that the Safis and Nuristanis had started. Within Pech, the jihad council began to look beyond its own valley to the capture of the provincial capital of Chagha Serai, located at the confluence of the Pech and Kunar rivers. With their capture of the government bases at Chapa Dara, Utapur, and Ningalam, the mujahidin of Pech had the weapons and ammunition to mount such a campaign, and so in April they made their first attempt to capture Chagha Serai.

The assault was carried out at night, but from the first the mujahidin encountered more resistance than they had anticipated and were unable to penetrate the town itself. One group of mujahidin tried to enter Chagha Serai through the neighboring village of Kerala, but the army was able to circle the village with tanks and armored personnel carriers before the mujahidin could escape. The mujahidin held out until noon the next day but ultimately ran out of ammunition. Only three of the original fifty-two mujahidin survived the battle. The following day, Friday, April 20, 1979, the army, accompanied by Soviet advisors dressed in Afghan uniforms, returned to Kerala and gathered all the adult men and teenage boys into a field, where they were to participate in a "jirga." Women and children were forced into a neighboring mosque, where they watched as officers first accused the villagers of collaborating with the mujahidin and then unloaded their guns into the mass of men. In all, an estimated seventeen hundred men and boys were massacred, and the women and children were forced to flee to Pakistan, where they became some of the first of the 3.5 million Afghans who would take refuge in that country in the next two years.[6]

If one had to point to the key moments when the tribal uprising began its steady decline, the massacre at Kerala would be one, for this event forever changed the terms of engagement. The government, under the supervision of its Soviet advisors, decided that the only way to deal with an uprising of the sort they faced in Kunar was to terrorize civilian populations into withholding their support for the insurgency. For their part, the rebels were shocked by what happened in Kerala, especially the fact that the government had targeted noncombatants. According to tribal custom, fighting should be carried out between armed men who willingly court the risks of combat, while civilians are kept out of the line of fire. To target unarmed men was antithetical to the code of conduct expected of men who value honor. Clearly, however, honor was irrelevant to the government, and the realization of this fact demonstrated to the rebel forces that traditional rules no longer applied and that they would have to reconceive how they organized against and confronted such an enemy.

Honor is a total system of belief and action and requires commitment on both sides to work.[7] When one party to a conflict demonstrates its willingness to abrogate the rules of honor to gain an advantage, the relevance and viability of honor are put in question. Thus, one of the long-term effects of Kerala and of the government's general willingness to target civilians and to use impersonal means of destruction against its own population was to undermine the ways in which tribes interacted with the state. Honor was no longer a sufficient frame either to explain the conflict or to rationalize the death and destruction rained down on the tribes by government aircraft and artillery. Honor presupposes that those killed will be male combatants who willingly faced the risks that lead to their deaths. It cannot explain or justify the deaths of innocent civilians or of large numbers of combatants who die not in hand-to-hand combat but from machine-launched missiles, bombs, and artillery shells. In providing a framework for comprehending evil and valorizing the death of innocents, Islam proved much more effective than traditional tribal codes, and the eventual takeover of the uprising by Islamic parties is partly to be understood by this fact.

A second setback to the tribal jihad was suffered shortly after the Kerala massacre. In the wake of the defeat at Chagha Serai, the jihad council, realizing that its forces already surrounded the provincial capital on the west from Pech and on the north from the Nuristani valley of Kamdesh, decided that its chances would be improved if it could attack from a third side as well.[8] To achieve this end, Wakil and other Safi and Nuristani elders traveled to Bajaur to ask the Mahmund and Salarzai tribes on the other side of the border to join the mujahidin of Pech in clearing the Kunar Valley of government forces. While largely independent of Pakistani authority in most civil and judicial matters, Bajaur was still under the political jurisdiction of Pakistan, and the Pech jirga knew that the Pakistan government might oppose having its tribes directly participating in an Afghan conflict—even if it was against a government for which Pakistan felt no affection. Still, Wakil reasoned that Safis had repeatedly crossed the border to assist their Pakhtun brothers in jihads against the British, and so it was assumed that honor would oblige the Bajauri tribes to reciprocate the assistance they had received in the past.

The Pech jirga stayed for two months in Bajaur, trying to convince the Nawab of Khar, the paramount political figure in the area, and other tribal leaders to join the jihad. Wakil even tried to shame his counterparts in Bajaur into offering assistance ("Either you should come yourselves and fight, or we will fight and you should provide food for us"). The most he could extract, however, was a promise from the Nawab that the jirga could take four artillery pieces—an offer Wakil reports to have answered with disdain. ("I told him, 'If you need artillery pieces, I'll give you the ones we have taken from the Russians. The only assistance we require is that food and water and other necessities be dispatched to the mujahidin. Or you yourself take up the Mauser [rifle] and fight from this side so that we can completely surround [Chagha Serai] and free the province.'")

In retrospect, Wakil appears to have been naïve in expecting to receive assistance from beyond the border. To the best of my knowledge, the last contingent of Safis to join in a cross-border jihad did so in 1959, when Prime Minister Muhammad Daud convinced tribesmen from the border area to cross over into Bajaur to attack government positions in that area.[9] This skirmish was supposed to aid Daud's advocacy of an independent Pakhtuni-stan, but although several tribesmen were killed, the Pakhtunistan movement made little headway. Nevertheless, the governments of both Afghani-stan and Pakistan had continued to draw "their" tribes into their own national orbits through the enticements of education, employment, and commerce. Wakil also failed to recognize that the Khalqis would have their own partisans along the frontier, where such well-known Pakhtun leftists as Ajmal Khan Khattak, Abdul Ghafar Khan (the founder of the "red shirts movement"), and his son, Wali Khan, had all been active. At any rate, the failure of the Bajauri tribes to join the Safis and Nuristanis for an attack on Chagha Serai was a significant reversal and an indication that the ideal of a transborder tribal lashkar rising up to reclaim the Kunar Valley would remain a chimera. Significant as it was, however, the failure in Bajaur was a relatively minor setback compared with others that would befall the tribes during the spring and summer of 1979 and that would forever change the character and direction of the Afghan jihad.

THE ASCENDANCE OF ISLAM

Two months later, I think it was in April or May 1979, we went back to Kunar, and the mujahidin who were with us were saying, "[The Bajauris] won't be able to do anything. We should fight ourselves. They won't do anything." Then we returned, and I was in Nuristan. Hizb[-i Islami] and Jamiat[-i Islami] [political parties] had differences between themselves. They would both take the weapons from each other, but there wasn't any bloodshed. There were also other parties whose names I hadn't heard. Before that, we only knew of Hizb-i Islami and Jamiat-i Islami. We hadn't heard the names of the other parties that were established later. We didn't know about [Maulavi Yunis] Khales or any of the others, except that [Commander] Jabar would sometimes mention the name of [Hazrat Sibghatullah] Mujaddidi every once in a while. In the beginning, there was only Jamiat-i Islami. Not even the name of Hizb-i Islami existed. The only known organization was Jamiat.

To this point, I have not mentioned the role of Islamic leaders or parties in the Pech uprising because they had not been of major significance. The first assault on a government base—before the burning of Ningalam—was carried out in Shigal on May 23, 1978, by Islamic militants affiliated with the Hizb-i Islami party, but this was an isolated and unsuccessful incident in which one Khalqi schoolteacher was killed. For their part, most of the Safis and Nuristanis who had taken up arms did so in part because they viewed the Khalqi regime as a threat to Islam, but this conviction had little practical significance since the command structure and fighting were organized on a tribal basis. Beginning in the summer of 1979, however, Islam began to increase in importance relative to the tribe. To make sense of this change, it is necessary to consider the traditional place of religion in Pech.

Both the Safis and Nuristanis of Pech express devotion to Islam, but this devotion, in itself, does not differentiate them from the vast majority of other tribes on the Afghan frontier or in Afghanistan generally; the Islam practiced in this area is distinguished, however, by its more "fundamentalist" interpretation of proper Islamic devotion and practice. Thus, in contrast to many Pakhtun areas, this region—Nuristan in particular—has a paucity of shrines, and the veneration of Sufi saints—alive or dead—is much less common here than elsewhere and is even frowned on by many. Likewise, the use of amulets, the donation of alms to mullas (a'ena or chanda), and other acts not expressly permitted in the Qur'an or hadith (traditions attributed to the Prophet Muhammad) have long been viewed by some clerics in the area as unlawful innovations (bidat) that must be expunged from popular practice.

Many have speculated about why people in this region should have proven more receptive than most other Afghans to a fundamentalist interpretation of Islamic practice. One theory more relevant to Nuristan than to the Safi tribe is that because Nuristanis have more recently taken up Islam, they—like converts elsewhere—have embraced the faith more zealously and more rigorously than most other believers, who have generations of accumulated tradition behind them and who often take faith and practice for granted. If this theory is too pat, it can still be argued that those responsible for bringing Islam to Nuristan were principally madrasa-trained mullas in service to the government rather than the more entrepreneurial Sufi saints responsible for conversion in many other places. Popular traditions such as saint veneration and the use of amulets, which have developed in other regions over many centuries and which are rooted deeply in domestic practice, have also not had time to take hold in this area. If it is true, as many believe, that the Safis themselves were originally "kafir" in origin (via exile or emigration from Kafiristan) and thus relatively recent converts to Islam, then the same might also be the case for them.

Proximity to Pakistan also must be factored in, for a large percentage of Nuristanis and Safis who were interested in studying Islamic doctrine beyond what was available to them locally chose to study at madrasas on the other side of the border. The Pakistani madrasa most often mentioned as the destination of would-be Nuristani and Safi religious scholars is the Panj Pir madrasa, which is famous for its reliance on the Qur'an and hadith as sources and its vehement rejection of popular and scholastic beliefs that lack sanction in the original sources. Prior to 1978, most mullas who returned from studying at the Panj Pir madrasa focused their efforts on expunging from local practice the innovations in popular religious devotion that had been taken up in the area. A few younger Panj Piri mullas did stray onto more dangerous ground, criticizing King Zahir Shah and later President Daud for the religious shortcomings of their regimes, but these mullas did not find many supporters—even among those who supported their attempts to reform popular practice. After the revolution and first uprising, however, these same mullas became the conduits through which the Islamic resistance parties headquartered in Pakistan established themselves in the region, and later they became local liaisons for would-be mujahidin from Saudi Arabia and other Arab countries trying to gain a foothold for themselves in the Afghan jihad.

At the beginning of the uprising, though, Islam had not yet risen to the fore as the dominant idiom of government resistance, and mullas—while generally respected for their religious devotion and knowledge (minimal as it usually was)—were viewed as dependents (*hamsaya*) of the khans and maleks and not quite the equal of others in the tribe. Because independence is so highly esteemed in tribal society, the clientage of mullas ensured that respect for religious learning was interlaced with a measure of contempt, as seen in Safi's comment that "the innate characteristic of mullas is to expect to be given something from others. If you give them money, they will do anything." This is a common stereotype, and while people recognize that there are good and bad mullas, the general perception during the first months of the uprising was that the proper place for mullas was as functionaries in the jirgas, where they could help mediate disputes and provide religious validation for the decisions arrived at by the tribal elders. Mullas were not expected to participate in the fighting or to make command decisions; so when the Islamic parties first appeared, their determination to take a more active leadership role in the conflict was unexpected, unprecedented, and unsettling to many. According to Sahre, roughly 80 percent of the people of the region supported tribal unity against the government; 15 to 20 percent backed the government; and less than 5 percent supported one of the Islamic parties. Echoing comments made by Samiullah Safi, Sahre noted that few people in the first months of the uprising had ever heard of the parties, although Hizb-i Islami and Jamiat-i Islami had begun to make minimal inroads in the region.[10]

All of this began to change about the time that Wakil returned from Bajaur. At this point he became aware that Hizb and Jamiat were offering money and weapons to those willing to join and to accept identification cards. Everyone's major concern at that time was getting weapons, and this more than anything else became the prize over which tribe and party would fight for supremacy. The first instance of this sort of internal conflict occurred after the capture of Utapur and Ningalam, when the rebels came into possession of a vast quantity of weapons, including rifles, shoulder-held rocket-propelled grenade launchers (RPGs), Dshika anti-aircraft batteries, and 76-millimeter automatic guns. While individuals were allowed to keep one light weapon each, everything else was initially held by the jihad council. In the first flush of euphoria over their victories and in full expectation of an incipient national uprising and further acquisitions of arms, the council distributed many of the weapons to mujahidin in the neighboring valleys of Kunar, as well as in Badakhshan, Panjshir, and Laghman. The council also gave out heavy weapons to local people who had been in the military and knew how to use them, and these people became one of the first targets of Islamic-party recruitment:

Hizb-i Islami and Jamiat-i Islami—both of them were working among these mujahidin. They were working very hard, and they were working covertly. For example, you are from the Mahsud tribe. You have a rocket launcher. Someone over there . . . has come and has talked to you and given you a pistol. He has become your friend and given you money and other things. Secretly, he has brought you individually into the party. Here, there's the general organization of the tribe, but in actuality Hizb and Jamiat were working covertly among them. The Ikhwan was working in Kunar from way back. They had been here for a long time; whether within Hizb-i Islami or Jamiat-i Islami, they were working vigorously among the people. Those whom they had turned into Hizbis or Jamiatis were those who had been given their heavy weapons.

While the tribal council was giving away weapons, Hizb and Jamiat were hoarding theirs, realizing perhaps more clearly than others that the conflict would not be over any time soon. They also recognized that weapons were not only an important resource for battle but also a way to leverage support away from tribal unity. Thus, as inspiring as a story like the one about the young husband who went running off to battle with his antique rifle might be, the reality was that people needed reliable and effective weapons not only to fight the enemy but also to best their tribal rival (*sial*). A vital dynamic of tribal society—arguably the fuel that keeps honor alive as a moral code—is the understanding that a man will not willingly allow his paternal cousins and other peers to outdo him in any competitive endeavor, particularly combat. One gains renown by being the first into the fray, the most daring in the pursuit of glory, and the most successful in battle. Rivalry (*siali*) therefore required results, and when weapons were not available from tribal sources, individuals turned to the parties who were only too happy to give them some as long as they agreed to become members and to submit to party discipline.

In the early summer of 1979, after the failure of the jirga in Bajaur, relations between the tribes and the parties, which were already strained, deteriorated even further as the jihad council came to realize that Haji Ghafur, to that point the overall amir of the Safi and Nuristani lashkar, had been secretly working with Hizb-i Islami. In response to this news, the council took away its support from Haji Ghafur and elected Wakil to take over as amir. It also tried to improve communications and logistics within the region by appointing regional and district administrators in each of the old government centers and maleks in every village and voted to give the organization a formal name—the Front of Free Mujahidin (Junbesh-i

Mujahidin Azad). The idea behind the name was to contrast the tribal lashkar with those guerrillas who were tied to the exile political parties. However, in adopting some of the attributes of a formal organization, the tribe also acknowledged the increasing influence of the parties and the fact that to fight them the tribe had increasingly to become like them.

Despite efforts at better coordination, the organization Wakil took over was beset with problems, the most important of which was probably its susceptibility to subversion. The government still had many informers and spies in the valley and even within the council. According to both Sahre and Wakil, these government agents sowed disunity within the council and reported council plans back to the regime. The vulnerability of the council to infiltration reflected one of a number of inherent structural problems faced by the Front, in this case the necessity in a tribal coalition to include elders and commanders from every branch and village in all deliberations. Every group expected to be involved in decision making, and tribesmen do not readily accept the authority of others in the best circumstances and certainly not in situations in which they do not even have the opportunity to express their opinions. Consequently, council meetings tended to attract hundreds of people and to continue for days on end; meetings were so large and lengthy, in fact, that they were sometimes strafed and bombed after being noticed by government aircraft.

Another structural problem had to do with the nature of the lashkar, which is organized along tribal lines, with each lineage fighting as a group and accepting the authority of its own leaders (Fig. 10). Members of a lashkar do not readily accept the authority of outsiders, and so decisions are difficult to reach without exhaustive consultation. Further, as I noted in *Heroes of the Age* in a discussion of a tribal jihad against the British at the end of the nineteenth century, the ethos underlying the lashkar tends to impede the mounting of effective military campaigns, in part because tribesmen resist the idea of assigning specific roles to different individuals or groups, especially if such assignments mean that some men will be relegated to providing food for other tribesmen or otherwise being kept out of battle. According to the Pakhtun ethos, battle was "an opportunity for besting . . . personal rivals every bit as much as for gaining larger victories, and this ethos meant that few were willing to accept subordinate or specialized roles."[11] Problems such as these are compounded when a campaign stalls, as the Pech Uprising did after the capture of Ningalam and Utapur. Lashkars operate most effectively when they are moving and able to replenish their food, supplies, and morale through new conquests. But because the Pech lashkar had to rely on nearby villagers for food and shelter, it soon depleted

10. Safi lashkar, n.d. (courtesy of Samiullah Safi).

the supplies close to hand, while overwhelming local reserves of hospitality as well.

Wakil's problems were further complicated in July with the sudden appearance of a local religious leader named Maulavi Hussain, an event witnessed and recorded by Sahre:

> One day, the sound of guns and bombs was heard. Everybody ran towards the caves in the mountains, thinking the enemy was attacking Utapur. Eventually, some people were sent to see what was going on, and it was discovered that Maulavi Hussain had arrived in Utapur from the Hezb office in Peshawar and the firing was done by Hezbis to welcome him. The Maulavi opened the Hezb office in Utapur, and, to keep up with them, Jamiat opened an office as well.[12]

Maulavi Hussain, also known as Jamil-ur-Rahman, was a Safi from Ningalam who had studied in the Panj Pir madrasa in Pakistan. During the democratic period, he had gained some local notoriety when he ran for parliament, but, in keeping with popular sentiments about the proper role of religious scholars, he gained few votes and finished last among a dozen candidates. In the early 1970s, when the Muslim Youth Organization (Sazman-i Jawanan-i Musulman) first became active, Hussain began working with them and was briefly arrested in 1973. Most of the Muslim Youth leaders either were imprisoned or fled to Pakistan during President Daud's time in office. Hussain maintained his contacts with Gulbuddin Hekmatyar, Qazi Muhammad Amin, and other former student leaders in Peshawar, who at that time were in the process of transforming the Muslim Youth Organization into the Hizb-i Islami Afghanistan political party. Immediately following the Khalqi coup in 1978, Hussain returned to Kunar to organize against the new regime and was involved in the incident in which the Khalqi schoolteacher was killed. In the following months, he continued traveling between Pakistan and Shigal, where he established his primary base and from which he worked to extend his influence into the Pech Valley.

On arriving in Pech in the summer of 1979, Hussain wasted little time asserting his presence, as Wakil discovered when he traveled to Nuristan shortly after Hussain's triumphal arrival in Utapur. The reason for Wakil's trip to Wama was that he had heard that the Khalqis might be trying to create dissension in the area. He found, however, that the greater threat was coming from Hizb-i Islami:

> The Hizbis there were distributing identity cards, and they were telling [the people], "You can't do this or that, and the amir must also be a religious scholar. And he must have a beard, and he should be clean [*sutra*] and pure [*safa*], and wear white clothes, and his appearance should be the typical example of a mulla. Only such a person can be the amir—no one else." And at this time they put forward Maulavi Hussain as the amir. They had only been using Haji Ghafur. Since he wasn't a scholar and was illiterate, he couldn't be the amir. Instead Maulavi Hussain should be it. This was a plot against the people in the interests of Maulavi Hussain and Hizb-i Islami.

Instead of operating in unison with Wakil's Front, which still maintained the loyalty of the majority of Safis and Nuristanis, both Hizb and Jamiat worked separately, using their supply line to Pakistan to provide their supporters with food, clothing, weapons, and ammunition. Hussain also sought to undermine the legitimacy of the Front by disseminating a decree declaring that the collection of religious taxes (in the form of food) for the Front was against Islamic law because the free mujahidin did not have an amir who was a religious scholar. Further, and even more destructively, he announced that the campaign that had been conducted so far against the government could not be considered a lawful jihad because it had not been authorized and commanded by a legitimate Muslim leader operating according to religious principles. Consequently, all those who had died to this point could not be called martyrs (*shahidan*), and the religious reward promised to martyrs in Islam was not guaranteed to them. These decrees created confusion and demoralization within the Front, for neither Wakil nor any other tribesman could say definitively that Hussain was wrong. He, after all, was the most credible religious authority in Pech, and the mullas associated with the Front were generally village educated and unable to stand against Hussain in an argument involving religious sources.

THE MUTINY AT ASMAR

In the midst of the conflict with Hizb-i Islami, news arrived in Pech that the army base at Asmar had mutinied and was preparing to attack Chagha Serai. This was a milestone event, for it not only indicated the growing dissension within the regime, but also presented a signal opportunity to expand what was to that point a series of local uprisings into a major campaign to capture the Kunar Valley and even the city of Jalalabad, which is at the base of the Kunar Valley and the most important city in eastern Afghanistan. The mutiny at Asmar was a major coup for the resistance, not least because the mutineers brought with them forty-five artillery pieces, forty zigoyak anti-aircraft guns, and nearly four thousand AK-47s.[13] Equally important, the soldiers from Asmar had the training to use these weapons and were prepared to turn them against the regime. In preparation for an attack on Chagha Serai, Commander Abdur Rauf transported his men and weapons from Asmar to the villages of Shin Koruk and Shigal, which were close to Chagha Serai. Shigal, it will be recalled, was also the principal center of operations for Hussain, and his involvement in the ensuing events was most controversial and ambiguous.

What is known for certain is this. A plan of attack was drawn up by the Front, the Islamic parties, and Commander Rauf. According to this plan, the artillery brought out of Asmar by Commander Rauf would begin firing on Chagha Serai at dawn, and the combined forces of the various mujahidin groups would approach Chagha Serai under cover of the artillery fire. The attack began as planned with the commencement of the artillery barrage, but the assault never took place because of rumors spreading among the mujahidin that the operation had been called off. In the confusion that followed, the arms belonging to the Asmar garrison were stolen, and it is reported that the bulk of the readily moveable weapons—AK-47s, RPGs, and recoilless rifles—were eventually transported to Pakistan and sold in the Bajaur arms bazaar.

The failure of the assault on Chagha Serai and the looting of the Asmar garrison were crucial events in the war. Not only was the possibility of a regional tribal uprising foreclosed by the failure of this operation, but relations between groups, already strained, were also permanently poisoned. From this point on, the antigovernment resistance was permeated with suspicion. Never again would the Front give away weapons to groups from other regions. Weapons hereafter became the principal currency for economic and political survival, and they had to be jealously bargained for and controlled. After Asmar, distrust and dispute became the hallmarks of the Afghan jihad—not only in Kunar but in every province. Asmar also was a significant military setback. In the summer of 1979 the regime in Kabul was coming unglued. Amin had become first minister in March and had instituted an increasingly brutal campaign to cement his own power and destroy his rivals. Amin's reign of terror would culminate in his assassination of President Nur Muhammad Taraki, which in turn precipitated the Soviet invasion of Afghanistan in December 1979. Amin's unpopular leadership had made the regime particularly vulnerable. Military desertions were increasing, as more and more soldiers wanted out of a situation in which they were arresting and killing their own countrymen. Asmar could have served as a signal to other military units unhappy with the Khalqi regime that the regime could be overthrown, but it was not to be. Instead, after Asmar, military units came to realize that the resistance was deeply divided and that offering their support to either side could be their undoing.[14]

Not surprisingly, there are many different interpretations of what happened, most of them critical of Hussain and Hizb-i Islami. Wakil, for example, claimed that at the time of the Asmar incident a letter from a Hizb-i Islami mulla living in Nuristan came into his hands that declared that the operation against Chagha Serai had been called off. The distribution of such letters was enough, in his view, to sabotage the assault, for "someone would attack and get a foothold inside, and then someone else doesn't attack and leaves their flank exposed. . . . All of this was a conspiracy." Wakil also tells of a time shortly after Asmar when Hizb mujahidin tried to transport fifty-four zigoyaks, Dshikas, and Kalashnikovs looted from the Asmar garrison. The weapons were on their way to Kohistan via Pech and were stopped by the Front. For two months, a jirga met to consider the disposition of the weapons, and despite vigorous objections from Hizb leaders, including Hekmatyar himself, the jirga elected to keep the weapons on the grounds that they had been stolen from Asmar and the mujahidin and were not owned by any one party. In the jirga's view, even if these weapons were bound for another mujahidin group, it would be dishonorable to allow this theft to go unnoticed and unavenged. As Wakil explained, "If someone were to take away someone's gun, it would be an insult and a great shame. Even if a man doesn't have the power to defend himself [right away], he keeps the insult in his heart, and whenever he has the power, he will kill the person who takes his gun."[15]

In an interview in Peshawar in the spring of 1983, Abdur Rauf, the commander of the Asmar garrison and himself a member of the Safi tribe from

Kapisa Province, told me of his growing disenchantment with the regime prior to the mutiny, the laborious secret planning that had gone on, and the final execution of the plan, which involved killing Khalqi political officers and sympathizers within the garrison. After successfully eliminating the opposition and before news of the mutiny had leaked out, he met with Hussain and, "because he was from the same tribe," told him his plan to attack Chagha Serai. Commander Rauf believed that there was still time to launch an assault before a counterattack could be organized, but Hussain insisted that such an attack should be undertaken only by order of Hizb-i Islami, and he began to fulminate against the other Peshawar-based parties, which he described as representatives of former King Zahir Shah and full of communist sympathizers.

Commander Rauf said that Hussain informed him that these rival parties should be eliminated first and only then should the jihad against the communists begin. Hussain also insisted that the weapons from the Asmar garrison be turned over to him and later met with Rauf's troops, urging them to lay down their weapons and return to their home provinces. Despite his growing distrust of Hussain, Rauf claims to have accepted his demand to turn over his weapons because he did not have any personal familiarity with the organization of the resistance and Hussain appeared to be in charge of the area. He also told me that he was confused by all the talk of Zahir Shah and the treachery of the parties and, recognizing his own vulnerability, wanted to be accepted by his new allies—despite his own past service to the regime—as a true believer and faithful servant of Islam.[16]

Not surprisingly, Hussain's commentary on the Asmar incident differed markedly from the views of the others.[17] He claimed in an interview with me that Rauf was an opportunist who joined in the planning of the mutiny only after officers who were secretly aligned with Hizb-i Islami had laid the groundwork. Like Rauf, these officers were not all they appeared to be, and, in Hussain's account, they agreed to accept a bribe from rival political parties in Peshawar to sabotage Hizb-i Islami and the Chagha Serai operation. In his version of events, these officers, in conjunction with local tribesmen, seized on the confusion surrounding the Chagha Serai assault to loot the Asmar garrison. Although the bulk of the testimony is stacked against Hussain, it is still not improbable to suppose that Safi tribesmen might have jumped at the opportunity to obtain the Asmar weapons. A generation before, during the Safi War of 1945–1946, tribesmen had shown their passion for booty when they looted the government treasury at Chagha Serai, and by the summer of 1979 many were in desperate economic straits because they had not been able to work their land or to carry on the business and trade that sustained many residents of Pech. However, even if Safis did participate in the looting, Hizb still appears to have been at least indirectly responsible for establishing the climate of distrust and noncooperation within which the rumors that destroyed the assault on Chagha Serai could have taken hold and might have seemed believable. Three months earlier, when Ningalam and Utapur were taken, such rumors probably would not have been believed, and if they had been believed by some, the communication between leaders and troops was such that they could have been squelched. However, by the summer of 1979, with the biggest and most important military operation on the line, no one knew whom to believe, and the result was the effective collapse not only of the assault but also of the tribal uprising itself.

SECOND EXILE

On Saturday night, May 10–11, 1980, the Russians landed twelve helicopters behind our front lines in Bar Kandi, which is a Mahsud [Safi] area. About six MiG jets provided air support. A number of mujahidin immediately went in that direction—the mujahidin who had fronts in Utapur. The Russians initiated a fierce attack on the mujahidin headquarters at Utapur. Near this place, at the entrance of the mountain valley near Utapur, the Russians landed a second force, on this side of Qatar Qala. In this attack, the forces were in all likelihood Cubans. They had black uniforms. Through this tactic, the Russians managed to disperse the mujahidin forces and cut our communications. It became difficult for one mujahidin front to help another, and they were scattered in different valleys. But the next night, the powerful force of the heroic warriors of Pech Valley routed and inflicted heavy casualties on the Russian force that had landed behind the mujahidin lines at Bar Kandi. That night, the entire Russian force was destroyed and most of the enemy were killed and the rest fled.

Following that, on Tuesday, they landed more forces by helicopter, and that same day they landed other troops in Ningalam. They also dispatched soldiers to Tangi Rechalam, Chapa Dara, and toward Morchel. Really I myself had never seen such a huge force and such modern military equipment and such tactics for scattering the mujahidin. I couldn't have imagined it. I had taken a position high up on a mountain and saw through my binoculars that the majority of the enemy forces were Russians and Cubans and two-thirds of their force were armed with rocket launchers. When the infantry hit one of the huge trees [with a rocket], the whole trunk would collapse. They were all carrying rockets. I was trying to count the number of modern military helicopters, and I lost count after thirty or thirty-five. At this time, the wheat was ripe. The harvest would have started a week later, but we immediately began our great exile [*muhajirat*]. It was a great flight toward the inaccessible mountains inside the Nuristan part of Pech Valley.

Following the looting of the Asmar garrison and the failure of the assault on Chagha Serai, the formerly unified tribal alliance became factionalized. The Front of Free Mujahidin under Wakil's leadership continued to advocate fighting on the basis of tribal organization, but the parties were able to offer weapons to those who joined, and this proved a powerful incentive to many Safis. In an effort to reclaim the unity that had been lost at Asmar and Chagha Serai, Nuristani leaders met in October 1979 and then sent a delegation to Utapur to meet with the Safi leaders headquartered there, but continued disagreements with Hizb-i Islami prevented any progress from being made. Efforts to reunify the fighting forces remained stalled throughout the critical period between Taraki's assassination and the Soviet invasion in December. In March, a Soviet force attacked Asmar, Pech, and Dewagal, with helicopters and MiGs bombing and strafing mujahidin bases and a Soviet force entering Ningalam. Despite these setbacks, the mujahidin made a spirited defense of their homeland, and Wakil even noted that two women, around fifty years of age, appeared at the front with swords in their belts and participated in the fighting. The government base at Utapur was dislodged, and the mujahidin managed to inflict significant casualties as the invaders were forced to retreat down the main road to Chagha Serai.

The following month, the mujahidin staged a nighttime raid on the provincial capital, during which the government armory was looted and destroyed, but the euphoria from this victory was short-lived, as the Soviets responded by mounting a far larger and more effective assault on Pech. This time, the absence of a unified command along with the overwhelming superiority of Soviet arms took their toll, and the "great exile" Wakil refers to began in earnest. Hizb-i Islami leaders had been urging people to emigrate for some time, but the combination of disunity and the direct intervention of Soviet troops with their sophisticated weaponry finally convinced people that the situation had become hopeless. Initially, Safis headed for the relative safety of the high mountains of Nuristan. It was spring, however, and the Nuristanis, who lived on a minimal subsistence diet of milk, cheese, and barley in the best of times, could not support the additional population; the Safi refugees decided that they would have to continue on to Pakistan:

> After the people had offered prayers and decided to become refugees, my older brother, Sho'eb Khan, took me aside privately. He said to me, "My wife and children, we have never experienced anything like this,

going to an unknown place. We cannot accept charity [*khairat*]. Our conscience won't allow us. I can't do construction work, and we don't belong to those parties. Therefore, this is what we should do—these wives of ours"—he was very serious, he's still alive—"our wives and the children whom we can't take care of—we should kill them all. We should kill them so they won't fall into the hands of the Russians. We will gather them at the grave of our father, and then we ourselves will become martyrs. There's nothing else to do. Our death would be more honorable than if we were to expect some hand from above to come down and give us our daily bread. Our wives have never even walked along a road, and these are high mountains—very high! They are in purda [*satr*] and never even leave the house and can't walk two steps outside. Where could they go? The only way is to die, and the only honorable way is that we kill them with our own hands so that they don't fall into the hands of the Russians or anyone else. We kill them, and then we fight until we die."

Then I told him, "This is both against Islam and also cowardly [*najawani*] and dishonorable [*be ghairati*]. Our women are going to tell us, 'You can't fight against the Russians, so instead you kill us. What have we done wrong?'" After this, I managed to convinced him, but he is that kind of person and he would have done it. But I convinced him that doing this wouldn't be [according to] Islam or honor or magnanimity [*hemat*]. Whatever is ahead for this tribe and people is destined for us too. We had no other choice since it was a tribal decision.

Sho'eb Khan's inclination to kill all the women of the family rather than have them migrate to Pakistan is reminiscent of two earlier episodes referred to by Wakil in his life story. The first is the statement attributed to Sultan Muhammad Khan that he could not join in the Safi War in 1945 because his women were "like invalids" and would be unable to endure the rigors of war. The second is the meeting of Wakil's older kinsmen after Sultan Muhammad's arrest and their deliberation over killing their women and children rather than submitting to the humiliation of exile. Here, thirty-five years later, the same vehemence and zeal are manifest in the proposal of Wakil's older brother. Sho'eb Khan's motivation was his fear that his family would suffer humiliation and dishonor, but wealth was also an underlying factor in this situation. The family's material prosperity, which allowed the males of the family to confine the women to the house while tenant farmers tended the fields, had the unintended consequence of making the family more vulnerable. Having female dependents is a manifestation of a man's honor, but the obverse of that relationship is that one's dependents can also compromise honor. Seclusion is a partial response to that problem, but it is always incomplete and subject to disruption. In this instance, Wakil was able to convince his brother that killing the women of the family would be a false solution to the problem, but the problem nevertheless remained and continued to fester for Safi and other Pakhtun tribesmen as they experienced the reality of exile and their own incorporation as dependents within a bureaucratically organized refugee system.

Wakil and his family, accompanied by sheep and goats, journeyed for twenty-four days, camping at night and traveling furtively through the mountains, always fearful of being detected by helicopters. Adults carried one or two children on their backs, and each evening an animal would be slaughtered to provide food. In late June, they reached the pass overlooking Chitral. When they reached the border, Wakil recalled looking at his sister and seeing tears on her cheeks. He asked her why she was crying, and she replied, "When we were exiled from Kunar to Herat, we were crying and saying to ourselves that they were making us flee. But Afghanistan was our homeland. That was Herat. What difference did it make where it was? That was our feeling then. Now we are becoming refugees from our homeland; we are going into exile. Now we are leaving our homeland. See this side is the soil of Pakistan and that side is the soil of Afghanistan." Pakistani militia units were stationed at the border. Wakil asked one militiaman how long the exodus from Pech Valley had been going on. He replied that people had been arriving at the border for the last twenty days, with between five and seven hundred families passing through the check post every forty-eight hours.

Initially, the Safi families all congregated in Dir, the place that Sultan Muhammad had gone to when he was exiled after his father's murder. For a month, they fended for themselves in makeshift tents while waiting for the authorities to give them a site and resources for an official refugee tented village; but this permission was not forthcoming, and the elders sent Wakil to Peshawar to speak to higher-ups in the refugee administration about establishing a camp for the families of the Front of Free Mujahidin. The authorities in both Peshawar and Islamabad denied the request, however, on the grounds that they supported only those refugees who belonged to one of the authorized Afghan political parties. This was the final and in some ways greatest indignity—that in becoming refugees they had also to accept the leadership of the very groups that had helped to undermine the tribal uprising and forced them to become refugees. If the Safis wanted to receive rations and tents and be allowed to live legally in Pakistan, they had first to stand in line at the office of one of the parties to receive from them a party membership card.

CONCLUSION

There is a Mahsud Safi from Gul Salak named Haji Jalal Khan. He is
a very simple old man but also the best example of a white-bearded
mujahid that you could find. The young would not go to any battle if
he didn't accompany them. The young fighters would say to him, "If
you don't come with us, we won't go to battle." He would go to a battle
and would sit in a cave, or someplace, and watch over all the belongings
of the mujahidin and fix their food and do all of the work. He was con-
tinuously involved in the battles.

I will tell you one story about this Haji Jalal Khan, who was a very
simple man and illiterate. Someone had sent a cow to feed the free
mujahidin in our Front. We didn't kill the cow but instead sent it to
the fighting front for the mujahidin to eat. They took the cow up in
the mountains to Shahbazai, where the front was located, above Chagha
Serai. An artillery shell falls and explodes, and before it can be properly
butchered, the cow is wounded and falls down.

When the mujahidin see that it is wounded, they immediately
butcher it. Then the mujahidin divide up the meat among the mujahidin.
Haji Jalal Khan won't eat any of it, and they ask him, "Why aren't you
eating?"

He doesn't say anything to the mujahidin about why he isn't eating.
He says to them, "I have a stomach problem. If I eat anything, I will get
sick. I can't eat either its soup or its meat." But, after this, I asked Haji
Jalal Khan, "Why didn't you eat this?"

He said, "Well, this cow was a martyr."

I said, "If you wouldn't eat this cow because it was a martyr, why did
you let the other mujahidin eat it?"

"Because if they hadn't eaten, the poor guys, they were hungry. Not
even bread was available. They were hungry. They had to eat, and if I
had said anything, they wouldn't have eaten, and that would have been
a great cruelty against the rights of the mujahidin. But my conscience
wouldn't allow me to eat the meat of a cow that had been wounded by
the cannon of the enemy, the cannon of the Russians. In my opinion,
she was a martyr."

Samiullah Safi told me the story of Haji Jalal Khan as an example of the
spirit of the tribal uprising in its early days. Many people had that feeling
and commitment. Participation in the fighting against the government
became an extension of the Pakhtun ethos of individual zeal (ghairat) and
bravery (shuja'at). As Wakil noted to me, when a boy reaches adolescence,
his first thought is to get his father to buy him a gun since only through
fighting can a boy demonstrate his worth as a man. Safis, like other
Pakhtuns, idealize heroes, and one of the important sentiments that helped

ignite the uprising against the Khalqis was the desire of individual men to prove their ability as fighters. "Because they hear the legends about how so-and-so fought like this in this war or that, people know that so-and-so is a true war hero, has never been defeated in war, and has never caught a bullet in his back. If he has been wounded, it was always in the front. . . . This sentiment was one of the elements that inspired the rebellion."

As part of this ethos, every individual tried to show his bravery and skill in battle, and every tribal unit tried to outdo rival groups. Those who were slow to enter battle or who failed to demonstrate the proper attitude would be subject to the ridicule (paighur) of women in their group, which, as the following story illustrates, was a sanction that Pakhtun men took seriously:

> In Gul Salak, there was a family with four brothers. [The jirga] had decided that it should only be required for one member from every family to be continuously present at the front, but all four of these brothers went to the war front. Once I went back to the village from the front and saw that all four were gone, and I asked why. Then I learned that one of the brothers had been at home, and he had slapped one of his sisters-in-law because of some problem. When he slapped her, she said, "You're ready to hit me. Your brothers are at the front while you are sitting at home, and you only hit me." After this incident, he wouldn't sit at home but instead would go to the front. This was the mentality then.

The enthusiasm of this first period lasted little more than a year, and for a variety of reasons it then declined. Some of these reasons have to do with problems inherent in the tribal way of making war. Others have to do with government efforts at subverting the tribal uprising. But probably the most important involve the emergence of the Islamic resistance parties. With respect to the internal problems, some, having to do with the lashkar as a vehicle of military mobilization, have already been mentioned. The lashkar is a formation that does best when it is moving through enemy territory and is able to live off conquered booty in the villages it passes through. With minimal logistical support and division of responsibility, it does less well when stalled for a protracted period of time, as was the case in Pech in 1978–1979. The jirga as a decision-making body also has its problems in this context, privileging as it does maximal involvement over coherence, consensus over quickness. Furthermore, with so many participants, jirga deliberations were difficult to keep under wraps, and consequently government agents could easily infiltrate and disrupt the proceedings.

Among the government's agents were some of the better-off and more influential men in the tribe. As was the case in the Safi War of 1945–1946, the most enthusiastic fighters were generally younger men with less to lose and more to gain from taking on the government. Men of wealth, however, had a great deal to lose, and so the Marxist government, despite all its talk of enfranchising the masses, as often tried to buy off local elites as to destroy them. Some of these elites responded positively to government entreaties and bribes in a generally futile effort to preserve their influence, which was being taken over by rising leaders, who were, in some cases, younger tribesmen making reputations for themselves in the fighting and, in others, mullas brought to power by the Peshawar parties.

The martial ethos of the Pakhtuns and the desire of every male to be involved in the fighting also had a downside. In the beginning, people joined with whatever weapons were at hand, but over time they clamored for better weapons. The capture of government bases supplied this need initially, but this input of better weapons seemed only to stoke the greed of some tribesmen, who began to focus more on booty than on the battle itself: "There were even one or two people . . . who had ropes wrapped around their waists. This was so that they could carry all the booty and captured weapons on their backs with this rope and take it away." The larger problem with weapons was that the parties had more of them than anyone else, and, as a result, those who wanted them had to come knocking at party doors to get them. The parties took advantage of the demand for weapons to play rivals against one another. Since it was the prevailing ethos for each individual to want to outdo his peers in fighting prowess, it was in the individual's interest to have the best possible weapons, as much to outperform his rival as to defeat the government. Similarly, tribal leaders also wanted to demonstrate their continued power by supplying their followers with weapons and resources. The government was one source that these leaders could go to, but as it became clear that the tribe was overwhelmingly against the government, continued involvement with the government became overly risky. That left the parties as the only viable source of the resources tribal leaders needed to continue supplying their followers and thereby preventing a mass defection to other leaders.

More than anything else, weapons were the lever with which the parties dislodged tribal leadership, but there were other factors as well, including the use of Islamic ideology. As noted, Maulavi Hussain and other party leaders flummoxed tribal leaders with their announcements that Islamic doctrine required an Islamic scholar be in charge of the uprising, that taxes and donations collected for the benefit of the fighters were meritorious only if they were collected by and for the Islamic parties, and that only members of an Islamic party were guaranteed entrance to paradise if they should die in battle. With more and more people emigrating, the party control over the refugee camps also helped cement their power back home, as tribesmen came increasingly to realize that they could neither fight effectively nor leave their families in the safety of the camps without the support of one of the parties.

One of the overall effects of the parties was to deaden the enthusiasm of the first stage of fighting:

> In the beginning, when the movement was spontaneous, [people] would fight with sticks and clubs and axes, and now they have all the weapons they could want, but they don't fight like before. Before they would go to the mountains on empty stomachs and without proper clothing, but today what happens has no resemblance to that. Before, people had no fear of death because of the idea of *ghazi* [being a veteran of jihad] and martyrdom, but now before thinking of their own martyrdom they think about the martyrdom of their leaders and those close to them. They wait to see their leaders do it first before doing it themselves. This is the spirit that has entered the people. They think that what they have gotten in the name of Islam they won't give up to free their country.

Another effect of the parties was that people began to fear these new leaders, not only because of what they might do to them in the present but, more important, because they feared God and the divine sanctions that would come their way if the Muslim leaders condemned them:

> Parties deluded people into thinking that they had to become true Muslims. For example, there was a man from Pech named Qayyum who was about sixty years of age. . . . This man was studying a book, a book written by Maududi. [A friend of mine] asked him what book it was, and he said, "It's a very good book. It shows you what Islam is." After he had become knowledgeable about this book, he would sit out by the public path and study it. People had told him that he was under suspicion by Hizb-i Islami—that since he had a son who had a clerk's position in Kabul he couldn't be a good Muslim. Therefore, he was obliged without even thinking about it to go to Hizb-i Islami and work for them to prove his religiosity. He had to do the work of the Hizbis to show that he was a good Muslim.[18]

Over time, party domination became complete as the Front was forced to cease operations in Pech and was prevented by the Pakistani government from opening an office in Peshawar. In other border areas, the same pattern was followed with local variations, as independent fronts were squeezed out by the wealthier, better connected, and ideologically more resilient religious parties. As discussed in greater depth in Chapter Seven, those who did survive usually managed to do so by accepting the nominal authority of one of the more moderate parties run by Sufi leaders and traditional clerics. These parties were generally more poorly funded than the radical parties, but they were also not as ideologically extreme and were more tolerant of local leaders and the continuation of traditional patterns of association and action. Consequently, tribal fronts sometimes did continue to operate, although the context and content of their activities were different from those of the first year of fighting, when the spirit of unity was at a peak that was never again approximated in the subsequent two decades of fighting.

As for Wakil himself, he initially became one of the leaders of a Kunar provincial unity organization (Ettehad-i Wilayat-i Kunar) that was founded in 1980. Despite the involvement of many prominent Kunaris and leaders from the first stage of uprisings, the organization floundered for lack of funds and was shut down in 1981 by the Pakistan government when it decided to allow only the seven religious parties to operate and receive official support. Thereafter, Wakil worked intermittently with a group of other educated Afghans to run the Afghan Information Center, which provided objective, nonparty-based information on the war. However, he was never convinced of the utility of this work and frequently found himself in arguments with other members of the center. Eventually, he left the group and remained unattached and more or less unoccupied until January 1990, when he was attacked in Peshawar by an armed group of men. Because of this attack and other threats made against him, he was given travel documents by the United Nations and received a visa from the Norwegian government to resettle in that country. Though most of his brothers have returned to Pech, Wakil has gone back only for brief visits and has decided to remain with his immediate family in Norway, where he lives today.

Coda The Death of a Safi Daughter

One story that Wakil told me captures better than any other the tensions at the heart of the tribal uprising. This story had particular poignancy for Wakil, as I will explain. But first let me provide some background. The events described culminated during the month of Ramazan in 1980, when Wakil, along with other members of the tribal council, decided to go home for the feast marking the end of fasting. Wakil's home was fifty kilometers from the front, and while he was away, Haji Ghafur, the head of the tribal council, had a young Safi woman stoned to death. Here is the story of the woman's execution as Wakil told it to me.

> Regarding this girl—maybe it's important, maybe it's not. But in my view it's very important. I have forgotten her name, but I used to know it. She was from the village of Udaigram in Pech Valley, which is about three villages away from Ningalam, the center of the woleswali of Pech Valley. The area was completely free at that time, and the leaders of the fronts were all at Utapur, eight or nine kilometers from Chagha Serai. At that time, this girl had a husband but no children. She was pregnant though, and her husband had gone off to do his military service.
>
> When he returned to Pech Valley on leave from the military for a while, this girl whom I've been talking about said to him, "All of the people are doing jihad, and all of the young men from here have joined the jihad fronts against this Khalq and Parcham government. And now you are going to the military. I had thought that you had escaped from the military when you came here. Now you tell me that you're going back. If you go back, the women of the village are going to insult me— 'Your husband is a Khalqi. He's gone to the military.' Don't do this."
>
> But, the husband didn't agree. "Only two months remain, and I will have finished my service and come back. I'll take my chance."
>
> The girl told him, "If you go, you're not my husband. If I can't

167

convince you, I will flee from here with whomever wants to go. I'm
telling you this beforehand so you will know."

Her husband didn't pay any attention to his wife's words, and he
returned to the army. While the husband was away, . . . the girl spoke
with her paternal cousin, [who was] not from a distant place, [but] from
her own village, and one of her own relatives, a young boy who was
still immature, around twenty years old. [She said to him,] "Won't you
escape with me? I have made a vow that I will no longer accept him as
my husband since he has returned to the Khalqi government to serve in
the military, and the women in the village insult me and taunt me. Since
you are a mujahid and go to fight and also you are my relative, I am
ready to run away with you, wherever you want to go. If you don't take
me, then I'll go with someone else. So you can't say you didn't know."

This boy became obliged [to go with her]. She told all of this in her
confession. He traveled together with this girl. They headed for Pakistan
by way of Shigal, but they were captured by Hizb-i Islami. When they
captured them, they sent them back to Pech . . . and announced what
had happened; [they] sent them back to the amir of jihad, who was Haji
Ghafur. They considered this matter there in the tribal council.

I supported this girl in the meeting: "It's her right. She's a mujahid.
This girl is a man. She has done the right thing. Why should she be
stuck with the name of Khalqi? It is her right. She has done something
manly; she has acted bravely. She has done jihad."

They said, "What you say is right."

I said, "Fine, then release her."

They replied, "We will release her, but be patient. Who knows? If
she goes back to her home, her father or her brothers might kill her for
escaping. We have never had an incident like this in our tribe before.
Although she's in the right, she did flee, [and] her brothers, her father,
her family might kill her. . . ."

They convinced me that if we released this girl, if she had enemies,
there was a danger she would be killed. They said that they would
resolve the problem. I agreed. She remained in prison. Two, three, four
months passed after this. After this, [it became clear that] she was also
pregnant. This pregnancy was from when her husband had come back.
It was then that she became pregnant.

As I was saying, all of us left, including some of the elders and the members of the tribal council, all of us went back to our homes for the Ramazan
feast. This Haji Ghafur, along with some of the Hezbis, remained behind,
and I heard that they brought this boy—the girl's cousin—and lashed him.
They lashed him on the basis of religious law. They gave him one hundred
lashes and then released him, and he went away. But the girl, since the girl
had a husband—because the boy wasn't married, they lashed him—but
since the girl had a husband, they stoned her.

One of the mullas who made this decision, he was from Nuristan, but this bastard had lived all his life in Saudi Arabia and came back only at this point. Even his own people didn't know him. Some people say that he had been away for twenty-five or thirty years. He comes back, renders his judgment, and then escapes. Where is the judge [*qazi*] who made the decision? The amir [Haji Ghafur] is illiterate. He doesn't know how to sign his own name. Any judge who makes a decision—first of all, his residence should be recognized, his property should be recognized, so that people know that when he passes judgment he will be responsible to answer questions in the future. Instead, a judge comes down the road, comes and makes a decision, kills people, then goes away, maybe to Saudi or some other place. We wanted to question him, but when we looked for him, we couldn't find him. Even to this day, we don't know where he is.

Those who told me this story, those who were present there and who told me the story, they were full of hatred and very upset. They said, "The girl stood up. She was standing straight. She was very tall and very beautiful and strong. She was smiling, she . . . pointed toward the mullas and smiled. And they struck her. She smiled. After some time, she was buried under the stones. Then she moved, and they saw that she was still alive. So they pulled her out, and she stood up again. She had not lost any of her passion."

They say that up to her last breath, she was smiling and staring at the people. She was smiling. As the amir of Hizb-i Islami, Haji Ghafur threw the first [stone]. She told him, "It's all right." She understood that they were going to stone her. She only said this to them: "Bravo for your jihad! Bravo for your bravery!"

After that, she stared at the people and smiled. In fact, she was humiliating them, [asking them] "What kind of justice is this? What kind of fairness? What did I do to deserve this? This man was a Khalqi and my husband. He left to join the Russian trench. He took refuge there and serves in their army. He's fighting on their side against you. I did this for Islam, for the honor and respect of these people. It was for this that I became an enemy of my husband. Not because I liked this boy or to betray my husband. And you stone me for that." . . .

The whole village was sad about this girl. We consider her a hero. She was a sacrifice [*qurbani*] to the prejudice and foolishness of a group of corrupt leaders who just wanted to do politics. This had nothing to do with knowledge, understanding, ethics, nothing. And the mulla who made the decision, there is no trace of him.

But the people themselves haven't forgotten what happened. It's in their minds, and sometime someone will pay for this. We just don't know when. And the boy, the husband, who I understand has gone back to the army, he is still walking around.[1]

As Wakil went on to explain to me, determining the right and wrong of this execution from the tribal point of view was a complicated matter. If the

woman had been unmarried and had fled with some man against the wishes
of her parents, she could have taken refuge with an elder; a jirga would have
met, and in all likelihood the man would have been assessed a fine (*tawan*)
to pay to the woman's family to clear up her "bad name" (*bad nama*). Then
they would have been allowed to marry. Wakil told me that on a number of
occasions unmarried runaways had taken refuge with his father, and he had
always helped work out arrangements by which the couples were allowed to
marry. However, if the runaway couple were to leave the area and then were
subsequently captured in some other place and returned, it would become
much more difficult to take care of them: "If they don't kill the girl, they
will definitely kill the boy. And if they kill the boy and the girl isn't killed,
the family of the boy will ask the killers, 'If this is a "bad name," why didn't
you kill your daughter or your sister with him? Why did you kill only my
son?' Therefore, they are obliged to kill her with him."[2]

In affairs in which one or both individuals are married, the penalty is
straightforward: they are both put to death. Wakil told me a story involving
a runaway couple from another area who sought asylum with his father,
who subsequently discovered that the woman was married. In that instance,
he turned them over to the woman's husband, who intended to kill both his
wife and her lover, but the man managed to escape. The mitigating factor in
the previous case was that the woman left her husband not for romantic reasons but because of her husband's actions and the disrespect that his actions
brought to her. Given the fact that the entire tribe had sworn an oath to
fight the government and the husband had joined forces with the government, Wakil argued that the woman acted properly—in his terms, "like a
man." Unlike her husband, who reasoned that he had only a short time of
service remaining, the woman put honor above expediency and for that reason should not have been punished.

Another source of Wakil's anger over this affair was the decision of Haji
Ghafur to sentence her to public stoning. From the perspective of their customary tribal law (*safi qanun*), if a woman is found guilty of adultery, the
husband (or his male family members if he is not present) has the right to
kill her since she is his namus. Likewise, from the point of view of tribal law,
the husband is obliged to kill the man with whom she ran off:

> From the point of view of Pushtunwali and Safi qanun, since the girl is
> dead and the boy is still walking around, the husband is obliged to find
> the boy and kill him. . . . His wife has been ruined, she has lost her repu-
> tation and has been killed, and the boy is still alive. [The husband] is not
> relieved from dishonor yet. He is obliged to kill that boy. . . . In Safi law,
> this is an enmity. Whenever he has the power, he has to do it, but [until

then] this kind of person can't sit in any group. He would be ashamed to sit in a gathering.[3]

What galled Wakil the most, it appears, was that the tribe had allowed a group of mullas—including one man who was illiterate and another who was a virtual stranger to the area—to use religious law to contravene tribal law and to carry out an execution of one of their own people against the expressed orders of the tribal council. Mullas have traditionally held a subordinate position in tribal society. In judicial cases, they would always be consulted for precedents from religious law, but the final decision belonged to the jirga. Here, the jirga was ignored and then found itself powerless to redress the disrespect shown to it, first, because the man responsible for executing the woman was their own amir of jihad and, second, because the parties directly implicated in the affair (the families of the husband and the wife) failed to play their expected roles.

For Wakil, who brought up the affair a number of times in the course of our interview, the stoning of this Safi woman exemplified the degradation of honor and the deterioration of tribal unity that was happening in Pech at that time. Tribes that had long stood up against government interference now found themselves paralyzed in the face of interference by the Islamic parties that used the circumstances of jihad to subvert tribal structures and principles. Even though Haji Ghafur was displaced as amir of the tribal council and Wakil himself was chosen to replace him, the demoralization caused by this woman's death lived on after the event. Wakil could take little satisfaction in his own elevation to a position of authority and respect in his tribe, for the circumstances of his being chosen as amir demonstrated that the demise of the tribe as an effective fighting force was at hand.

In addition to what it tells us about the changing balance of power in the tribe, the story of the woman's death by stoning also crystallizes another set of themes running throughout Wakil's narrative, themes having to do with the ambivalent relations between men and women and what they signify. Consider in this regard the first story recounted in Chapter Four involving Wakil's response to the Khalqi takeover. When Wakil heard Hafizullah Amin's voice over the radio, he told his wife that henceforth she would be both father and mother to their children. By this statement Wakil indicated that, as long as the sanctity of the homeland was in question, men of honor could not go about their ordinary business nor assume their normal domestic responsibilities. More profoundly, Wakil indicated that his status as a father (and consequently as a man) was in jeopardy as long as the Marxists had control of his homeland—homeland here being a metaphorical extension of the homestead, with the Marxist rulers being equated to house-breakers who had violated the sanctity of the family quarters. The homeland, like the domestic quarters, is sacred space, and a man who cannot defend what is sacred to him is no man at all and is viewed as something like a cuckold (*dawus*).[4] Wakil does not say this about himself, but he does acknowledge his responsibility for setting things right through transmuted gender roles, the wife being father and mother to the children.

The themes of violation, emasculation, and gender reversal percolate throughout Wakil's narrative, but the first such example in the book comes not in his stories but in the biography of Taraki, where we found the account of government soldiers "violating" the Taraki home and Mrs. Taraki facing down the soldiers while her husband cowers beneath a woman's veil (burqa). Similar vignettes, where women take on male roles in the absence of male action, appear at various points in Wakil's narrative:

- In the story of the arrests in the Ningalam bazaar, prior to the beginning of the Safi insurrection, the nameless old woman, taking on a role somewhere between scold and sentinel, declares, "Is there no man among you?"
- In the story of the man in Gul Salak who slaps his sister-in-law, she berates him for hitting her while his brothers are all fighting at the front.
- In the story of the old women carrying Qur'ans who come out as emissaries from their village to meet Wakil's jirga after the commencement of the insurrection, the implication is that the men of the village have shamed themselves by hiding behind these women and the holy books they were carrying.[5]

In addition to these stories, there are the two instances in which the inability to defend honor causes Wakil's male relatives to contemplate the need to sacrifice their women and children on honor's altar. In related stories men have their guns taken away from them and are thereby emasculated. The first is the story of Sultan Muhammad Khan's confrontation with General Daud, and the second is about the looting of the Asmar garrison. These two stories relate to the theme of tyranny being a form of emasculation, with those in power (or, in the case of the Islamic parties, seeking to gain power) violating the sanctity of honor in their pursuit of their ambition.

These various stories, in sum, reveal that, at its most profound level, Afghan politics revolves around gendered ideals of personal integrity. When those in power overstep the bounds of their legitimate authority, it is often narrativized in terms of violation and emasculation. That is one reason why female education and veiling have perennially been such powerful and explosive issues in Afghanistan and why rejection of the Khalqi revolution was so often explained through stories of Khalqi violations of domestic space and male prerogatives of personal regulation over their own households. It is also, I believe, at the root of Wakil's story of the stoning of the Safi woman, where once again, but from a different and unexpected direction, tribal autonomy was contested by outsiders whose bid for power was expressed through control of women's lives.

Part III

THE ISLAMIC JIHAD

6 Muslim Youth

The development of an Islamic movement in a country depends on the mercy of God. When God wants to show mercy on a place, he orders the wind and clouds to gather and leads them to a specific point where he wants it to rain. There it rains, and immediately the land changes, and a movement is created in it. The soil breaks up, and life raises its head from that spot. The Holy Qur'an is like this, and the country and people of Afghanistan are like that fallow land.

Gulbuddin Hekmatyar made this statement in a speech to Afghan refugees in Peshawar, Pakistan, in the early 1980s.[1] As the leader (amir) of Hizb-i Islami Afghanistan (the Islamic Party of Afghanistan), one of the principal Islamic parties then fighting to overthrow the Marxist regime in Afghanistan, Hekmatyar was primarily concerned in his speech with condemning the leftist leadership in Kabul and its Soviet sponsors. However, the head of the most radical of the Afghan resistance parties also took time to inform his audience about the origins of his party as a student group at Kabul University in the late 1960s. This reminiscence of student days was not a digression or flight of fancy. To the contrary, Hekmatyar's historical reflections had considerable significance in the context of Afghan national politics, for it was through history that Hizb-i Islami staked its right to rule Afghanistan. Thus, because the Muslim student organization could claim to have been the first group to have warned the nation of the dangers of Soviet communism, Hizb-i Islami could declare its preeminence among the various resistance parties in Pakistan and assert its leadership of the Islamic government that it hoped to establish in the homeland. And because so many of the group's early leaders were arrested and martyred by the communists, Hizb-i Islami was able to justify its often controversial actions: its relentless control over party members, its summary execution of political opponents, its often ruthless attacks against rival resistance parties, and its sabotage of attempts at political compromise to end the interminable conflict in Afghanistan.

In Part Three, I am again concerned with history, specifically, the history of the Hizb-i Islami political party, and with how this organization, which began as a campus study group, was transformed into an authoritarian political party. Although Hizb-i Islami has faded in importance, it was the dominant Islamic political party in the period preceding and following the Soviet invasion, and more than any other group it was responsible for undermining independent regional efforts to overthrow the Marxist regime; it also created the organizational template adopted (more or less successfully) by other Afghan resistance parties, and it established the climate of distrust and division that has plagued the development of an Islamic governing structure in Afghanistan to this day.[2] Hizb-i Islami had an impact far beyond the number of its fronts, which were many, or the effectiveness of its military operations, which was considerable. Indeed, the party's principal legacy was political not military, and it is my contention that, along with the Khalq party, which it resembled in many respects, Hizb-i Islami was responsible for prolonging the conflict by consistently destroying grounds for common cause within the resistance and within Afghan society more generally.

My interest here is not only how this particular party forged a dominant place for itself in the Afghan resistance during the early 1980s but also how the party deviated from more traditional forms of Islamic political practice, especially the clerical and mystical traditions that had been at the center of earlier antigovernment political movements, and how it helped to keep the various Islamic political factions disunited in the face of the Soviet invasion, thereby laying the groundwork for the eventual takeover by the Taliban militia. In keeping with the general pattern of this book, this first chapter of Part Three has both a biographical and a historical focus. My main concern here is with the development of a political party and ideology, and my principal strategy for dealing with that topic is to consider one man's life in the context of the larger historical events shaping his personal career and the trajectory of the party during the last half of the twentieth century. The second chapter of Part Three examines the structural divisions within the Islamic political movement in the wake of the Marxist revolution and the role of Hizb-i Islami in exacerbating these divisions.

The life history at the center of this chapter belongs to a man known as Qazi Muhammad Amin Waqad, whom I met in Peshawar and interviewed once in 1984 and twice in 1986. "Qazi" means "judge" and is an honorific deriving from the fact that Muhammad Amin's father was an Islamic judge and Muhammad Amin himself completed his studies in Islamic law and was qualified to serve as a judge. Muhammad Amin's last name—"Waqad," or "enlightener" in Arabic—is also significant, for it is a name he gave himself. Afghans traditionally do not have family names, but this lack began to create problems for those living in urban centers and mixing with large numbers of unfamiliar people, most of whom had similar names. Tribal Pakhtuns frequently dealt with this problem by using their tribe's name as a family name, and the children of well-known fathers sometimes adopted their father's name as a family name (for example, the sons of the Paktia tribal chief Babrak Khan became known by the name "Babrakzai"; sons of Mir Zaman Khan came to be known as "Zamani"). Others, however, among them many of the students who streamed into Kabul to attend the newly opened university in the 1960s and 1970s, made up their own last names (*takhalus*). Qazi Muhammad Amin was one of those students, and he chose a name that symbolically denoted the role he hoped to assume in the revolutionary political matrix that was emerging in his student years.

Although he served as the amir of Hizb-i Islami at various times during the late 1970s and early 1980s, Qazi Amin's most familiar post was that of deputy amir (*mawen*), or number two man in the party. He held this position until resigning from the party in 1985 in protest over the acceptance of a Saudi-brokered political alignment that brought together the seven major political parties. Thereafter, he headed his own minor party but stayed mostly on the sidelines until a short-lived appointment as communications minister in the Islamic government that formed between the collapse of the Najibullah government in 1992 and the Taliban takeover in 1994. During the period of my interviews with Qazi Amin, the war inside Afghanistan was bogged down in what appeared to be a limitless stalemate; in Peshawar the resistance parties were engaged in their usual internecine disputes, and various outsiders—Pakistanis and Arabs in particular—were hovering around the edges of the action, trying to exert their authority. It was a time of corruption and of maneuvering for position—not a time of fervent conviction or inspired action.

Qazi Amin was very much in the middle of a scene that many people, outside observers and Afghans alike, were growing to loathe and resent. Ordinary mujahidin and civilians were getting killed, the refugees were sweltering in fetid camps, and—as far as I could discern—the party leaders were concerned primarily with their own interests and not with those of the people they supposedly represented. By the time I met Qazi Amin, I had already interviewed most of the party leaders and was convinced that the jihad would drag on endlessly and that the political situation would likely get more fragmented and corrupt before it got better. I was generally depressed with the whole situation and would not have been displeased had all the leaders been dispatched in a sudden accident.

Despite this attitude, I was able to muster some enthusiasm for meeting Qazi Amin, in part because I suspected that he might provide interesting links to historical figures like the Mulla of Hadda, whom I had already spent many months investigating (and whose story is told in *Heroes of the Age*). I had been informed that Qazi Amin was a Mohmand from eastern Afghanistan and that he was the son of a locally prominent judge who had also been a disciple of one of the Mulla of Hadda's principal deputies. I also knew that, in keeping with family tradition and in contrast to most of the Muslim student militants who came to Islamic politics from secular schools, he had attended religious schools and had originally set out to follow the same conservative religious career path trod by his father.

The biographical facts that I had been told indicated that Qazi Amin's life would provide a useful vehicle for looking at the transformations in Islamic political culture in recent years, but, given the general reticence I had encountered in other top leaders I had interviewed, I had no reason to think that this interview would prove any more enlightening. To my surprise, however, I found that Qazi Amin was quite welcoming in his attitude and sometimes even expansive in his answers. While I had a great deal of trouble getting detailed information from Hekmatyar and other radical leaders about their formative years, Qazi Amin allowed me to probe this area of his life and was not put off when I wandered into politically sensitive areas either. I didn't always get satisfactory answers to my questions, but I never felt any hostility for having asked them.

At the same time, however, throughout the time I was interviewing Qazi Amin, it never left my mind that he was a top-level politician in a resistance organization whose mission was to destroy the government in the country next to the one in which I was then residing and whose political philosophy was equally antagonistic to the government of my own country (even if that government was at the time the party's chief arms supplier). Kalashnikov-wielding guards were always present to remind me of Qazi Amin's position, lest I forget, and the sometimes bemused but always wary cast of eye in his thickly bearded countenance continually reminded me of the status of the squat man sitting on the floor mat across from me.

Since Samiullah Safi and Qazi Amin are approximate contemporaries of one another (Safi being five years older than Qazi Amin, who was born in 1947), the life history in this chapter covers much the same historical period as that discussed in the two previous chapters.[3] Both stories also share a common regional focus in the Afghan-Pakistani frontier and certain prevailing themes, such as the transformation of older moral principles and organizational forms in the rapidly changing milieu of Afghan society. Despite these similarities, however, the two life histories share little else in either content or style. When I conducted my interviews with Samiullah Safi, he had been in exile for nearly two years, and he saw little chance of his returning to Pech. Consequently, our conversations had a somewhat elegiac quality to them, and I had the distinct impression that I was being used to record the completed story of another man's life. My job, I perceived, was to get the story straight and to recognize in it the sense of moral coherence that the speaker intended to impart through his choice of words. During the course of the several hours of interviews—and I even hesitate to use the word "interviews" since it inaccurately represents the way he dominated our interaction and dictated the direction and flow of his reminiscences—I listened, nodded, and poured more tea.

The time I passed with Qazi Amin was invariably cordial, perhaps more so than that spent with Wakil, who was quite purposeful and at times even impersonal as he went about telling his story. But where I sometimes felt as though Wakil, despite his personally detached mode of presentation, was opening up chasms in his soul, my impression of Qazi Amin was that the more friendly he became in manner the more evasive he became in his answers. Thus, when Qazi Amin discussed his father's life or his own early memories, his reminiscence flowed along without substantial prodding. However, when we began to drift into more contentious matters, such as the conflicts among the resistance parties, he often balked, providing a clipped reply and waiting for me to ask my next question. At the time of our interview, Qazi Amin was more engaged in the flow of political events. While Wakil was an exile from his home and the center of his own political gravity in Pech, Qazi Amin was right at the heart of the things in Peshawar, where the Islamic political parties carried out their business. What I didn't realize completely then, however, was how at the time of our interviews Qazi Amin was also in decline. Like Wakil, Qazi Amin's greatest influence was behind him; he would never again enjoy the degree of power and authority he wielded in the early part of the jihad. Like Wakil as well, Qazi Amin declined in importance largely because he was a hybrid—neither fully one thing nor the other. In his case, hybridity had to do with his having one foot in the world of the traditional cleric and the other in the world of radical student politics. Initially, being able to negotiate and maneuver in both these worlds was his strength and great contribution to the jihad, but when the fissures in the jihad proved too deep to cross he became peripheral to the interests of men more single-minded and ruthless than himself.

To reflect the differences that I sensed in the two interviews, I have chosen to represent them in somewhat different ways. Since Wakil's interview consisted of a series of stories, I fashioned them that way, excising extraneous comments by others who might have been in the room (including myself) and, in some cases, taking out the noise, clutter, and repetitious filler that occasionally obscured the narrative contours of Wakil's material. For Qazi Amin, however, I have retained the interview framework within which the life history emerged because it was always within this context that our conversations proceeded, and the question-and-answer format was never left behind.

My primary concern in this chapter is with the evolution of the Hizb-i Islami party, but before turning to that subject I provide accounts of Qazi Amin's father's career, the transformation of Islamic politics in the first half of the twentieth century, and Qazi Amin's own early education. These sections of personal and political history help to contextualize developments while also providing a link between the earlier forms of religious dissent and those that were to emerge in the democratic period. Following these introductory sections, I use Qazi Amin's personal history to examine the development of Hizb-i Islami up through the Marxist revolution. As a way of organizing this discussion, I divide this history into two principal stages: an initial period of campus-focused activism and peer engagement lasting roughly from 1966 until the official founding of the Muslim Youth Organization in 1969 and a second period of increasing radicalization between 1969 and 1978, during which time the Muslim Youth launched an abortive coup d'état against the government; the failure of this coup almost destroyed the party, but it also set the stage for Hizb-i Islami's emergence as the most radical, secretive, and controlling of the Islamic resistance parties.

EARLY HISTORIES

INTERVIEWER (I): Would you please provide us with some information about your father, other family members, and your background?

QAZI AMIN (QA): My name is Muhammad Amin. My father's name is Muhammad Yusuf, and my grandfather's name is Maulavi Sayyid Muhammad. We are from Ningrahar Province in Afghanistan. In Ningrahar Province, our home is Batikot, and we belong to the Mohmand tribe. Within the Mohmand tribe, we belong to the Janikhel branch. My grandfather served as the prayer leader [*imam*] of the village and taught Islamic subjects in the mosque school. I never saw him. My father was only about fifteen or sixteen years old when his father died. . . .

My grandmother belonged to a *sayyid* family [those who claim descent from the Prophet Muhammad] that lived in a place near Inzari of Shinwar. They were very wise people, and my grandmother was also very wise and able and knew how to educate her sons; so she sent all four of her sons, including my father, to India to educate them in religious studies. After being in India for some time, the older brothers sent their younger brother, Amir Muhammad, back home to serve their mother while they stayed on [in India]. One of the brothers died during this time, and the other brother returned home without finishing his education. But my father, Muhammad Yusuf, spent twelve years in India and completed his education . . . at the Deoband madrasa, which was the greatest center of religious sciences at that time. Everyone who could finish his education wanted to go there. . . . He spent two years in Deoband and graduated first in his class.

My father returned from Deoband in 1937 or 1938. . . . At that time, there was a custom in Afghanistan that the religious scholars who had graduated from Deoband or from any other madrasa in India would be appointed as judges by the government. In 1938, Mia Sahib of Kailaghu asked my father to accept a position as a judge. Mia Sahib was a judge and a very high-ranking religious scholar in the Afghan government of the time, so my father accepted the offer. First, he went to Gardez and later to Khost. Then he moved to Katawaz, and for some time he was in Ghazni. In the beginning, he was a lower-court judge and later became a provincial judge.

My father was a very accomplished scholar and had an attractive appearance, and when part of his body became paralyzed, people said to each other that it was because of the evil eye. He also had the power of eloquence in his speaking, and he knew a great deal about the political and social affairs of his time, especially the different tribal traditions. Because of this, when the government accepted him as a judge, they sent him to Paktia, which is a border province of Pakhtuns, and he was able to work successfully there—first as a lower-court judge and later as a provincial judge. He was a judge for a total of six years. In 1945, the sixth year of my father's employment, I was born in Khost [Paktia Province]. So I am now forty years old. At that time, the Safis had started their war against the government in Kunar Province.

(I): What did your father do after he got sick?

(QA): After his sickness, my father spent the rest of his life in Kot. Even though the government asked him many times to go back to his job, he wouldn't agree. We lived on the income of our land. We had oxen for plowing and also a tenant farmer to work on our land. Besides that, our father was the preacher in the main mosque, and he also had some students. But unlike other mullas, he didn't accept any assistance from the people, and because of this, the people of the area called him "khan

mulla," the mulla who is like a khan. Our father was a mulla who had
his own guesthouse and fed every kind of visitor there. We didn't need
anyone's help. Our father always tried to help the people in our area
settle their disputes, so our living standard was equal to a khan's living
standard. We had land, we had a guesthouse, and we could solve the
problems of the people.

(I): Did your father have any kind of relation with pirs or Sufis like
Enzari Mulla Sahib?

(QA): My father was a disciple of Pachir Mulla Sahib, who lived in
Pachir, which is near Agam. I have seen him myself. He was alive until
recently. His sons were martyred in the jihad: Maulavi Abdul Baqi and
his other son. Pachir Mulla Sahib was a disciple of the Mulla of Hadda,
and my father was a disciple of Pachir Mulla Sahib, who was a very
prayerful and pious man. [Pachir Mulla] liked to lead the life of a simple
man of God [faqir].

(I): You said before that your father was both a good preacher and was
popular with the tribes. Did the government send him to work in the
tribal areas because he was better able to control the tribes than a secular person would have been?

(QA): Yes, that was the way the government kept control of the tribes.
In those days, the people were uneducated, and the military bases
weren't very strong, so the only way the government could keep its
control over the people was by using religious scholars and popular
tribal leaders. Military force was not enough. For example, the people
of Paktia were uneducated, and the military bases were not strong
enough to control the tribes. The government at that time was newly
formed and still quite weak. Consequently, they had to depend on religious scholars and popular tribal leaders to maintain their authority
over the people. On the one hand, religious scholars had spiritual influence and power, and as good orators and preachers of Islam they could
easily find an esteemed position among the people. On the other hand,
they had government authority, too.[4]

Qazi Amin's description of his father's life reveals some traditional patterns in Afghan religion. Following time-honored precedents, Muhammad
Yusuf, while a young man, journeyed far afield for scriptural knowledge
before returning to his homeland to assume the mantle of a respected cleric
in the government. Like the young Najmuddin Akhundzada, who later
became known as the Mulla of Hadda, Muhammad Yusuf had a religious
background. He was, in fact, more favored in this regard than Najmuddin,
for not only were his father and grandfather religious scholars, but his
mother had also inherited sanctity as the result of being a member of a fam-

ily claiming descent from the Prophet Muhammad. Muhammad Yusuf, however, also had the same disadvantage as Najmuddin—of being left fatherless at a young age—and like Najmuddin and many other boys in similar circumstances, he responded by going in search of religious knowledge and the credentials that would allow him to establish his own identity and social position as a scholar.

All of this is familiar, and so is the fact that on completing his education Muhammad Yusuf returned to his home area to marry and begin employment in a local mosque as a prayer leader and teacher. This was not the route that Najmuddin took, but few had the inner disposition to lead the life of a mystic and ascetic who could forego family, wealth, and position to single-mindedly serve God. While he had mystical leanings of his own and became a disciple of a well-known pir, Muhammad Yusuf's orientation was primarily scholarly, and his decision to return to his home to start his own madrasa reflects this fact. Traditionally, Afghan men of religion have combined elements of both the mystical and the scriptural in their lives. While in some settings Sufism and scripturalism tend to attract different sorts of adherents, who keep their distance from one another, most well-known Afghan mystics (including the Mulla of Hadda) have been respected scholars, and likewise most respected scholars have been themselves Sufi pirs or disciples of Sufi pirs. The decision whether to be primarily a mystic or a scholar is an individual one, but clear social incentives and disincentives come into play in each situation. In the case of Najmuddin, apparently very little pulled him back to his home area. He was from a poor family, and he would likely have ended his days as a poor village mulla if he had returned home. Muhammad Yusuf, however, was from a relatively prosperous family, which meant that, on his return from India, he had land and income waiting for him, along with the prospect of a socially beneficial marriage.

Another pattern that we see in the father's life history that is less familiar, at least if we take the Mulla of Hadda and his disciples as our point of reference, is the scholar accepting employment with the government. As I discussed in depth in *Heroes of the Age*, the reputation of the Mulla and his closest followers stemmed in large part from their separation from and periodic opposition to the government, but such opposition became increasingly rare through the early part of the twentieth century as the government expanded and offered an ever larger number of religious scholars employment in its service.[5] In this sense then, Qazi Amin's father's life exemplifies the increasingly common trend toward the routinization and bureaucratization of religious authority—and the increasing irrelevance of religion as a force of political dissent through the first half of the twentieth century.

The pattern of increasing cooperation between religious leaders and the states can be seen quite clearly by considering the case of the Mulla of Hadda's *tariqat* (Sufi order). Following the death of Amir Abdur Rahman in 1901, his successor, Amir Habibullah, persuaded the Mulla to return to Afghanistan and treated him with great respect and tolerance.[6] The Mulla had been a vociferous opponent of Habibullah's father, who had tried to arrest him. The Mulla escaped, but several of his disciples had not been so fortunate. Habibullah wanted to mend this break, and signaled this attitude in a number of ways, one of which was the exemption of religious leaders from paying taxes and, in some cases, the assignment to them of tax revenues. Because of the Mulla of Hadda's standing as the most renowned religious figure of his day, Amir Habibullah gave him valuable land in the fertile valley of Paghman, a few kilometers outside of Kabul, and later issued a decree that the government's tax receipts from the area around Hadda, which amounted to 3,500 rupees in cash and thirty-two *kharwar* of wheat, be given to the Mulla for the support of the *langar* where he fed his disciples and guests.[7] The state also allocated annual stipends to his principal deputies, including Sufi Sahib of Batikot, who received 2,500 "silver rupees," and Pacha Sahib of Islampur, whose allowance included 1,400 silver rupees and twenty-one kharwar each of wheat and straw to support and maintain his langar and mosque.[8] While many religious figures appreciated this more favorable treatment, a number, including the Mulla of Hadda himself, recognized the potential danger entailed in accepting government largesse. Hadda Sahib even went so far as to return to the amir the land he had received, saying that it was the property of the people (*bait ul-mal*) and therefore forbidden to him.

Though Amir Habibullah's efforts at placating traditional religious leaders appear at odds with his father's style of rule, the same impulse toward consolidating monarchical authority was at its root. Where Abdur Rahman had recognized the necessity of strengthening the power of the center at the expense of religious and tribal leaders, Habibullah apparently believed that the balance of power had now shifted in the government's favor and that the moment was auspicious for taking a more conciliatory approach focused on symbolic inclusion of dissident elements rather than forcible removal.[9] Whatever his motivation, one effect of his largesse to religious leaders was the decline of their popular authority. Acceptance of government funds for the upkeep of a langar was tolerable in most people's minds, but the perception became increasingly widespread that some of the mullas' deputies and their offspring were on the government dole and were more devoted to property than piety.[10] Given the unstable nature of charismatic authority, it is probably the case that the Mulla of Hadda's tariqat would have declined with or without Habibullah's assistance, but government interference certainly accelerated the process, as did the government's practice of implicating religious leaders in local administration.

This policy was played out during the Anglo-Afghan War in 1919. In the decade and a half between the Mulla of Hadda's death in 1903 and the outbreak of hostilities with Great Britain, various of the Mulla's deputies, including Mulla Sahib of Chaknawar and Sufi Sahib of Batikot, had appeared from time to time among the border tribes to try to provoke an uprising against the British government in India. None of these efforts had created the sort of widespread disturbance that the Mulla of Hadda had helped to instigate in 1897, but the labors of the mullas were sufficient to keep the frontier in a state of nervous alarm for much of this period.[11] They also succeeded in keeping alive their own reputations as men of political action, but this was to change when their independent efforts were harnessed to the government's cause in 1919.

Upon declaring jihad against the British, Amir Amanullah, Habibullah's son and successor, immediately sought the assistance of religious leaders, including the Mulla's deputies. By this time, many of those personally associated with the Mulla were getting on in years, but those who were still in a position to participate in this new jihad did so.[12] This time, however, they were not treated as independent leaders but rather were incorporated into the command structure as subordinates of Amanullah's own representative, Haji Abdur Razaq Khan, who recognized the value of these spiritual figures for organizing the tribes. Religious leaders were a key ingredient in Abdur Razaq's plan because of their ability to move across sometimes hostile tribal boundaries and coordinate activities among groups that might otherwise have only ill-will for one another. Razaq also understood that spiritual leaders had both the education and the trust needed to oversee the movement of weapons, ammunitions, and supplies to different locations and to keep rival tribes focused on the enemy rather than on each other.[13] The religious leaders went along with this plan because of their longstanding interest in combating British influence on the frontier, but their cooperation came at a cost. The Mulla of Hadda had been careful never to accept a subordinate position to the Afghan amir and in fact had contested the amir's right to declare a jihad on the grounds that he was not a proper Islamic ruler. In the 1919 war with Great Britain, however, the Mulla's deputies, who succeeded him after his death, not only conceded the right of announcing jihad to the state but also ceded their position as independent leaders of their tribal followers for the more circumscribed role of logistical coordinators charged with supervising operations at a middle rung in the chain of command.

While the organizational arrangements established during the 1919 war demonstrate the changing relationship of religious leaders to the state, the best illustration of the government's harnessing of religious leaders to its own ends came in the ceremony that the government held following the conclusion of hostilities to commemorate Afghanistan's "victory" over Great Britain.[14] The site of the ceremony was a field next to the Mulla of Hadda's tomb. When the delegates to the assembly had all gathered, General Nadir Khan (later King Nadir Shah), who was Amir Amanullah's representative, called on the members of the assembly to prove their readiness to renew the jihad against the British by signing their names on the inside cover of a Qur'an. As each leader signed his name, he was also asked to indicate the number of mujahidin he would provide and the area where he would fight. Nadir then presented them with engraved pistols and battle standards inscribed with Qur'anic verses. Playing the symbolic dimensions of the occasion to maximum effect, the government had decorated the meeting ground with black banners (a time-honored emblem of Islamic militancy) that had been consecrated at the shrine of Hazrat 'Ali in Mazar-i Sharif, the principal shrine and pilgrimage site in Afghanistan. These banners were embroidered with religious motifs, such as the outline of a hand (symbolic of the five principal members of the Prophet's house), the star and crescent, and the silhouette of a mosque.

The deployment of these symbols for the state's purposes demonstrates the way in which Afghanistan was moving from a nineteenth-century kingdom to a twentieth-century nation-state. The symbols that we see arrayed on this occasion were traditional ones that governments in the past had also found it in their interest to use. So, to a certain extent, nothing new is going on here. However, if seen in relation to more general patterns of government centralization and administrative rationalization, the political performance at Hadda, with its skillful management of tribal and religious leaders, can also be recognized as one part of an overall consolidation of political authority in the hands of the government. In 1920, when the assembly at Hadda occurred, this consolidation was by no means complete, and in the years to follow religious and tribal leaders would make renewed assertions of independence, but the overall direction was toward increased government control and a more institutionalized role for traditional religious leaders.[15]

The general trend toward compartmentalizing religious leaders in the apparatus of state rule would appear to have suffered a major setback with the overthrow of Amanullah, which is generally thought of as a victory for conservative Islamic leaders over the social reformers who wanted to modernize Afghanistan and the high-water mark of religious influence in the affairs of state.[16] The legacy of that event is more ambiguous and complex than it might appear however. One of the interesting features of the movement that succeeded in toppling Amanullah is that its principal religious leader, the Hazrat of Shor Bazaar, had his base not in the tribal areas (as was the case with the Mulla of Hadda and his deputies), but in Kabul itself. It is true that most of the Hazrat's disciples were Pakhtun tribesmen living in the tribal areas, but he himself chose as his base of operations the capital city. In the past, religious leaders tended to have regional power bases, but the Hazrats found that they could sustain a multiregional constituency from Kabul. This reflects the changing articulation of religious authority, as more and more of the Hazrat's disciples were doing business in Kabul, and it became easier to stay in contact with his scattered deputies from the capital than from a rural location. The Hazrat gave up the security of having tribesmen close at hand and mountains nearby to flee to in case of government attack; however, he discovered that his larger base of disciples gave him protection, even in Kabul, since the government feared the agitation that would result if it tried to arrest a leader of his stature. At the same time, having established himself in the capital, the Hazrat was loath to see the dismantling of the state, even if he had been more than willing to help unseat the head of state. Thus, even though the overthrow of Amanullah unquestionably represents the moment when the expanding authority of the Afghan state received its most crushing setback (at least until the upheaval of the 1980s), the two consequences that stand out after the sound and fury of the uprising itself are put aside are how quickly the central government reasserted its authority in a form much like that which had preceded it and how quickly religious leaders like the Hazrat of Shor Bazaar acquiesced to this development and accepted an administrative niche within the structure of state rule. Kabul may have been overrun and the various palaces and offices of the government ransacked and looted, but those who had attacked the city quickly returned to their places of origin and resumed their former lives. Government bureaucrats reoccupied their offices. The army was put back together. Students took their seats in class as they had before, tax collectors returned to their rounds, and the fiery Hazrat of Shor Bazaar accepted a post in the new government, becoming the head of a council of clerics (*jamiat ul-ulama*), which was appointed to advise the government on religious policy.

In fact, neither the Hazrat nor the council ever wielded as much influence as they seemed prepared to do at the beginning of Nadir's reign, when he reportedly availed himself of their counsel and accepted their authority in certain areas such as judicial sentencing and the oversight of government legislation. Likewise, in testament to the preeminence of the Hazrat, Nadir not only contracted marriage relations with his family but also gave the family a large tract of land for a new compound on the outskirts of Kabul. These privileges and perquisites, however, did not provide the ulama with the authority that they sought. Indeed, bringing them into the councils of power and even into the royal family itself seems to have gradually reduced their authority by diluting the importance of their relations with the people in the rural areas. Ultimately, once the throne was secure and the tribal areas were pacified, the king and his ministers gradually began to pay less attention to the advice and dictates of the council of clerics. While the state continued to pay stipends, build madrasas, hire judges, and otherwise ingratiate itself with religious leaders in material ways, it also came to pay less heed to their admonitions on social and legislative matters.

Since the government was not embarking on any radical reform programs that might have stirred the ire of religious leaders, they had little to protest; most clerics simply accepted the largesse offered them without complaint. The government's generosity was of the calculated variety, however, and its principal objective appears to have been to forestall the religious establishment from uniting against the government in the future. While it was impossible for the government to prevent the appearance of charismatic malcontents like the Mulla of Hadda, it could limit their effectiveness by maintaining a stable of compliant clerics who could be called on to denounce outsiders' charges and complaints. This strategy was in fact recognized by the very group that was implicated in the government's web of generosity, as is indicated by the following statement made to me by the descendant of one of the Mulla of Hadda's deputies who had served for many years as a judge in the Afghan court system:

> [Prime Minister] Hashim Khan [1933–1946] encouraged the children of pirs to move toward the government. He wanted to enroll them in madrasas to turn them away from Sufi orders [tariqat]. Hashim also offered them good government positions and did his best to provide them with everything possible. In this way, he also strengthened his own position and power. He could claim that that pir or his sons are working for us or they are our subordinates and we pay them. In this way, Hashim gradually broke the people's link [to the pirs].[17]

Returning to the case of Qazi Amin's father, we can see that while he was situated far lower on the ladder of prestige than the Hazrat of Shor Bazaar or the children of the Mulla of Hadda's deputies, he too was affected by the changing balance of power. Like these more exalted luminaries, he was consumed with affairs of government, and when a tribal uprising appeared on the horizon, he and his fellow scholars naturally tended to take the government's side and protect its interests. Thus, according to Qazi Amin's recollection, his father helped to mediate three tribal uprisings—one among the Zadran tribe in Paktia Province, the Safi uprising in 1945 (about which Qazi Amin had little information), and an uprising among the Shinwari, which he believed occurred in the late 1930s or early 1940s.[18] The one traditionally independent political role that Qazi Amin's father did perpetuate was in connection with the practice of *amr bil ma'ruf* (calling people to proper faith and action), a role that the Mulla of Hadda and many of his deputies also performed. In this tradition, groups of religious leaders traveled from village to village, urging people to renew and purify their faith. Sometimes they also tried to convince the people to abandon customary practices, such as taking interest on loans and money in exchange for giving their daughters or sisters in marriage. The continuation of this form of proselytizing at a time when other political activities were discontinued would seem to reflect an interiorization of religious politics—a movement toward local social reform as opposed to the more dangerous and uncertain area of antigovernment dissent.

THE MAKING OF A MUSLIM RADICAL, 1959–1964

(I): Tell me about your early education and how you got interested in Islam as a career.

(QA): We are two brothers. My elder brother is Muhammad Yunus. He is eight years older than I. After my elder brother, my sister was born, and I was the last one. . . . Our life was a typical rural life. It was an ordinary village life. We were away from the city. My elder brother started his primary education under his father's supervision, and he also attended the madrasas that were located close to our area. When I reached school age, I also started to study some elementary books of Islam. . . .

I was fifteen years old at that time. I didn't attend any official madrasa, and I thought that I couldn't finish my education at home. So, without my father's permission, I came to Pakistan. I was sixteen years old, and I made up a story that I wanted to visit my uncle's family in Kama. First, I went to Kama, and from there two other boys and four sons of my uncle joined me, and we all came together to Pakistan through Gandhab. Here, we stayed in an official [government] madrasa [*rasmi madrasa*]. My family found out where I was after six months of searching, and my brother came after me. He asked me, "Why did you come here?" I replied, "You know that there isn't any suitable place for higher education in our area, and I have the right to continue my studies. I knew that father wouldn't let me go to Pakistan, so I came without his permission."

I had spent nine months in the madrasa. Then I went home and tried to convince my father to let me stay. I told him that I had gone to get my education, and eventually he allowed me to go to Pakistan for a second time. Again, I spent nine months here, this time at the madrasa in the Mahabat Khan mosque in Peshawar, where I studied some advanced books and learned calligraphy. At that time in the madrasa, they didn't pay much attention to calligraphy. After that, the idea came to my mind that it would be difficult to continue my education in this foreign country. There was another problem also that if someone had graduated from [a school or madrasa in] Pakistan they would be criticized by the government. When I was a student [*taleb*] in the Mahabat Khan madrasa, the idea came into my mind that I had to go back to Afghanistan and register myself in one of the official madrasas of the government.

So in 1340, which is equivalent to 1961, I returned to Afghanistan after being in Pakistan for eighteen months. Then I applied to madrasa and took an examination. After successfully passing the examination, I went with my father and registered in the fifth class of Najm ul-Madares of Hadda. Although the usual period of study was seven years, I finished the program in six years. Since I was good at my lessons, I prepared myself for the examination of the eleventh class during vacation, and I passed and registered in the twelfth class.

(I): What were the rules for admission to the madrasa?

(QA): Generally, they admitted just those who had finished in the first, second, or third positions in their classes, and they also had to pass the examination. Recently, they have been accepting talebs from local mosques as well.

(I): Can you describe the program of study? Did you just attend classes in the morning, or did you have them in the afternoon as well?

(QA): Our lessons were conducted from eight in the morning until twelve noon. Since this was a religious school, the majority of the subjects were of a religious nature, but there were some other, nonreligious subjects like Pakhtu, Farsi, and Arabic. In the preliminary program up to class six, there were also mathematics, geography, geometry, and history. In the last year before my graduation, they added English to the preliminary program as well. There was also a little bit of modern science in the advanced program—courses like mathematics, geography, and social science—but the main subjects were religious.

(I): Did you take any interest in Sufism [*tasawuf*] at that time, and did you ever become the follower of a pir?

(QA): No, I didn't pledge obedience [*bayat*] to any pir.

(I): Was this because you didn't believe in it, or were there some other reasons?

(QA): I didn't have faith in what they were doing then. The other side of Sufism is its spiritual side—doing *zikr* for Allah.[19] I believe in this side. It has a positive effect on people's morale. I have some books about it. One of them gives directions for [making] amulets [*tawiz*] and [doing] zikr. I study [this book], but what the pirs are doing nowadays is simply deceiving people to get money, and this is condemned by Islam. They are using religion as a way of getting material benefits and power, which is a very bad use of religion. Because of this, I haven't taken an interest in that kind of master/disciple [*piri-muridi*] relationship.

(I): What did you do when you graduated from madrasa?

(QA): It was a rule of the government at that time that they would employ some of the graduates as madrasa teachers and they would choose others to be judges. It seemed like a crime to the majority of people if someone wanted to go to university after graduating from madrasa. The people considered it frivolous and maybe even deviant. Despite this, I thought that my education was insufficient. I had to study more, and for that reason I asked my father about going on for more education. He asked me what kind of position the government wanted to give me after graduation from the madrasa. I replied that I could be a teacher now or a judge after attending a special one-year judicial course. He told me that being a judge was an important job: "It is my advice to you that you don't need more education. You can attend the judicial course, and later you will be a judge, and it is enough for you."

I didn't accept his advice, however, and convinced him that I had to complete my education. I was the only graduate of the Hadda madrasa at that time who registered his name for the university examination. A total of twenty-four students graduated from the Hadda madrasa, and I was number two in my class. All my classmates rebuked me. Even our teachers criticized my action, especially Maulavi Fazl Hadi. He asked me, "Why are you going to go to the university? That is like a Western society there, and the people are decadent. So how can you—the graduate of a madrasa—go to such a place?"

(I): Why did you decide to go to university when no one else supported this decision?

(QA): I registered in the madrasa in 1961. Democracy came to Afghanistan in 1963, when Daud was deposed [as prime minister]. Afterward some of the political parties started their activities. For example, Khalq and Parcham began their work in 1964. The Afghan Millet party also began its activities at that time. So after democracy came to Afghanistan, we could get some information about political ideas, but the political awareness of our teachers was very low. I myself was not very aware when I was in madrasa, but, in spite of this lack of awareness, I and Maulavi Habib-ur Rahman [later a founding member of the Muslim Youth Organization], who was three years ahead of me, and some other close friends had a feeling of hatred toward the deviations and unjust activities of the government. . . .

There was a rule in the madrasa then that the students who had reached the tenth, eleventh, and twelfth classes had to preach twice a week in front of a big gathering. Our preaching was different from the others. Sometimes we discussed the current political problems that the other mullas never talked about. We had some teachers in the madrasa who were against that sort of political awareness. There were some other people who didn't know anything about political ideas and were unaware of that kind of political thinking or feeling. For instance, they didn't know what jihad is, what politics or the movement is, and what the significance of the leftist parties is, what democracy is. We were in a very backward environment, and since I had a feeling about these things, I decided to go to Kabul University for my higher education. So it was in the university environment that I became aware in a good way about the problems of my country.[20]

Qazi Amin's story begins much like his father's (and that of so many other scholars before him) with the mandatory pilgrimage in search of knowledge. In his case, the act of undertaking this pilgrimage also entailed an act of disobedience since he did not have his father's permission to make the trip to Pakistan. That such permission was not forthcoming is not surprising considering both the boy's tender age and his father's established position in society. Qazi Amin was not an orphan seeking social advancement as his father had been, and there were better career options close to home than there had been when Qazi Amin's father was a young man. At any rate, Qazi Amin's decision to leave his home shows early on his independent character, just as the later decision to return home shows his pragmatic bent.

At the time of his journey (roughly 1959–1961), Afghanistan and Pakistan were embroiled in a bitter dispute over the control of the tribal territories along the frontier. The status of the frontier tribes was an ancient source of acrimony, but the tensions had escalated further when Muhammad Daud became prime minister in 1953. As a result of this dispute, there had been occasional clashes between army units of the two nations, sporadic border closings, and much vituperative rhetoric flowing out of both Kabul and Rawalpindi. While it was still as easy as ever for local people to cross the border, it was not always expedient to do so, and Qazi Amin wisely decided to return home so as not to jeopardize his chances for either further schooling or future employment in Afghanistan. The fact that a young religious scholar from the border area would have government employment on his mind is one indication of the extent to which the balance of power had shifted in favor of the state.

In a few short years, Qazi Amin's life would take an unpredictable turn that would make considerations of employment irrelevant; but in 1961 he was preparing for a career as an Islamic judge, and that meant applying for entrance into one of the government madrasas, whose graduates were being awarded an ever larger percentage of the judgeships in the country as well as the most sought-after teaching posts in government secondary schools. All of this seems unremarkable, unless we compare the course of Qazi Amin's early education with that of an older scholar, like his father or, better yet, the Mulla of Hadda. Such a comparison makes clear the degree to which education was becoming both routinized and centralized. In the past, students had had to go far afield to gain the requisite training, but increasingly that was neither necessary nor, from a career standpoint, desirable. The government had always looked to religious scholars to meet many of its administrative needs, but from the time of Abdur Rahman on, and particularly in the middle decades of the twentieth century, it strove to exert control over the process by which religious scholars were produced.

As revealing as Qazi Amin's choice of career trajectories is for understanding the changing nature of relations between the state and Islam, an even more telling index of the government's control over religious affairs is the fact that he received his preliminary training for later government employment in a madrasa built next to the Mulla of Hadda's center. At the turn of the century, this very same center, whose grounds the government was now grooming, had been one of its primary sources of worry and irritation. In the Mulla's day, the center at Hadda had been a pilgrimage site for disciples and scholars. Following the Mulla's death, however, Hadda began a slow decline into ramshackle senescence. Given the renown achieved by the Mulla, it might have been expected that the center to which he had devoted a good portion of his life would have become a place of pilgrimage after his death, but Hadda, for reasons that are difficult to assess, failed to flourish as a shrine center.[21] During the 1930s and 1940s, the government, prompted by religious scholars, embarked on a program of underwriting the construction of madrasas in various regions of the country. In all, ten government-sponsored madrasas were established, and the graduates of these institutions went on to become judges, administrators in the Ministry of Justice, and high school teachers in the secular educational institutions that the government was then constructing with even greater avidity.[22] The madrasa at Hadda was not only established on the site of the Mulla's center but was also named after him (the *najm* in Najm ul-Madares comes from the Mulla's birth name, Najmuddin) and used his collection of books as the core of its library.

Although the Mulla was long dead by the time Qazi Amin arrived in 1961, the Mulla's spirit, it seems, was all around and was often invoked. Yet one wonders what he would have thought of the government taking so prominent a role in the maintenance of his legacy. On the one hand, it was precisely the sort of development he had always advocated. The state needed to be guided by religious precepts, and what better way to ensure that it was than by providing religious adepts in each generation with education and employment. On the other hand, religious leaders had the responsibility to ensure that the government was not corrupt, and it was not always easiest or most reliable to seek such assurances from within, particularly in the absence of men on the outside decrying lost virtues and rallying the opposition. One can imagine that Hadda Sahib would have had good reason to worry, and the reason can be seen in the career choices of the offspring of his own deputies, the majority of whom pursued the path of Islam on the government payroll.

However, Qazi Amin's generation was to prove different, for while its members were afforded the opportunities of a government-sponsored education, some were skeptical of the government's good will and were inclined to challenge authority generally. As Qazi Amin's testimony indicates, most of his classmates were not radically disposed. They viewed their education as the necessary means to the end of a decent government sinecure, and they were not inclined to talk back to those who were offering this largesse. But some, and Qazi Amin was among this number, were more aware of the political currents then beginning to circulate in the country and more cognizant of the limits of their own education.

In contrast to the situation at the time of Hadda Sahib, or even later during the movement against Amanullah, government opposition was no longer centered in the hinterlands but rather was focused in Kabul, within the narrow universe of the educated elite. During Qazi Amin's youth, in the 1950s and early 1960s, the most vociferous opposition came not from the conservative side of the political spectrum but from the left. Several newspapers published briefly in the early 1950s advocated social reforms of a type that had not been espoused since Amanullah's rule.[23] The most vocal of these publications demonstrated a willingness to attack not only the religious establishment but also popular religious practices, which many adherents of secular reform were ready to brand as superstitious and inimical to progressive ideals. This provocative attitude was dramatically demonstrated in a letter to the editor in which the government was criticized for spending money to refurbish the so-called *mou-i mobarak* (miraculous hair) shrine in eastern Afghanistan, which housed what was purported to be one of the beard hairs of the Prophet Muhammad. Clerical outrage over this letter led to public protests against the growing influence of secular reformers in Afghan public life, and the government responded in 1952 by banning *Watan* and other independent newspapers that were giving voice to these inflammatory challenges to traditional beliefs and practices.[24]

By the time Qazi Amin was finishing his education at the Hadda madrasa in 1968, leftist provocations were being revived through the efforts of leaders like Nur Muhammad Taraki and Babrak Karmal, both of whom had cut their political teeth working for progressive newspapers in the early 1950s. By and large, those living in the rural districts of the country were only dimly aware of leftist activities in Kabul, but news of a few episodes, like the mou-i mobarak incident, did reach the countryside and created a general though unfocused sense of alarm. Qazi Amin did not mention any incidents specifically, but he and his madrasa classmates were aware of the reputation of leftists in Kabul. They were equally aware that established Muslim leaders had proven ineffective in responding to these events, and in his own immediate context he could see the reluctance with which the ulama involved themselves in political matters. Older religious leaders had risen up to meet the challenges of colonial rule in India and of corruption and abuse in Kabul, but the current generation of religious leaders seemed more interested in maintaining their positions and their paychecks than in embracing their political responsibilities. Equally distressing, they appeared hardly to recognize the nature and extent of the challenge represented by leftist forces in Kabul, a challenge that would demand forms of redress unlike any that Muslims in Afghanistan had ever resorted to in the past.

While it is impossible to judge how politically aware Qazi Amin was during his madrasa days, it is interesting that he represented his resolve to meet the challenge presented to him as an act of defiance against his teachers and his father. Two paths were available to him. The first was the one for which he had been training all his life—the path of an Islamic judge, the path his father took before him and that he himself set out on when he followed his father's example of seeking religious education in the subcontinent. This path was the one expected of him and the one that the majority of his contemporaries chose, but he rejected it in favor of the second path, enrollment in the university. Like Samiullah Safi, who felt the pull of the city and the allure of participation in the emerging political debate over national development, Qazi Amin recalled this turning point in his life in relation to the national political debate of the time, and he too framed his decision to join that debate as an act of disobedience, which links him not only to his contemporary, Samiullah Safi, but also to Taraki, to Samiullah's father, Sultan Muhammad Khan, and to the Mulla of Hadda, all of whom likewise had to break from their fathers and the traditions of the past in order to become what they imagined themselves to be.

THE BIRTH OF THE MUSLIM YOUTH ORGANIZATION, 1966–1969

(I): What was the atmosphere like when you arrived at the university?

(QA): Our four years of university were the most important years of political involvement because democracy had just come into being and the parties were just starting their activities. The parties that were actively working at that time were Khalq, Parcham, Shula-yi Jawed, Afghan Millet, and Masawat; but among all of these the communists were the most active, especially in 1968, when I registered in the university. It was the time of political clashes and conflicts at the university. On that account, among some Muslim youth at the university the idea occurred to form a movement according to Islamic rules. I joined this movement in its first stages.

(I): Where were most of the students who attended the Faculty of Islamic Law [*shariat*] from and what kind of conditions did you find there?

(QA): I graduated from madrasa in 1968 and entered the School of Islamic Law at Kabul University in 1969. There was only one university in Afghanistan, and the students were from all parts of the country. Since the Faculty of Islamic Law admitted only graduates from religious schools, most of the students at the faculty came from Abu Hanifa Madrasa [in Kabul] and from [madrasas in] the northern parts of Afghanistan. There were only two students in the school from the Hadda madrasa, and there were very few students in general from other border-area madrasas. About 60 percent of the Islamic law students did speak Pakhtu however.

(I): What were conditions like in the university dormitory?

(QA): Kabul University had one dormitory, which could accommodate twenty-five hundred students. We were all living in the central dormi-

tory of the university. About six students could live in one room, and I
lived with students from different parts of the country. One was from
Kunduz. His name was Yusuf, and now he is an official with Jamiat-i
Islami. Two others were from Mazar-i Sharif. Some of the students in
our room went to the Faculty of Islamic Law, but others attended different schools. . . . There was a mosque on the fourth floor of our hostel.
The students who prayed there knew each other well. . . .

(I): In which faculty did the movement first begin, and later on how
were relations established with other faculties?

(QA): When the Islamic movement began at the university, it wasn't
started through the efforts of one faculty's students or teachers. It
depended on the feelings, thoughts, and social awareness of everyone
who joined the movement. The students who had deeply studied the
goals of the communist parties and had the desire to struggle against
the regime and the influence of the West and who could think clearly
about the future of the country, these people felt a kind of responsibility
to form an Islamic movement. It was a matter of feeling responsibility
toward Islam for the future of the country. Since the students and
teachers of the Islamic law school were studying Islam and knew a lot
about it, their feeling of responsibility was stronger than that of others
toward Islam and society. For that reason, a greater number of our
students and teachers joined the movement and had a more active
part than others. . . . Other members were from different schools like
engineering, agriculture, medicine, and so on, but still the number of
students in the movement from the Faculty of Islamic Law was more
than from any other school. At the second level were the students of
engineering, medicine, and agriculture. The students from other schools
like literature were very few and also dull-minded.

(I): Was there one leader at the beginning?

(QA): The most active student of all was [Abdur Rahim] Niazi. He was
among the senior students of the Faculty of Islamic Law, and in 1969 he
had the first position in his class. He had a very active role in the movement. He was a leader in all the meetings and demonstrations and all
the other activities of the Islamic movement. He was a good speaker, and
a spellbinding preacher. His speeches had a strong effect on people, and
he was able to attract people through his speaking. He always explained
the weak points and defects of communist ideology and their parties.
Because Niazi was from the Faculty of Islamic Law, people thought that
the movement was limited to there. Some people even called members
of the movement "mullas," so they started to be called by this name.
The Khalqis, for instance, always called them "mullas," but actually the
movement was spread throughout the university and involved students
and faculty members from different schools.

(I): How did Abdur Rahim Niazi first organize the group? Did he meet with people privately, or did he bring them all together?

(QA): In the beginning, when the demonstrations and meetings of Khalq and Parcham and Shula were first going on, students with Islamic ideas became familiar with each other because they would argue with the communist students. Because of these discussions, the Muslim students came to know which ones had an Islamic ideology and hated communism and other colonialist activities. For instance, I knew Maulavi Habib-ur Rahman because we had graduated from the same madrasa, and we were aware of each other's ideas and feelings. In the same way, Maulavi Habib-ur Rahman had also spent time with Niazi at Abu Hanifa madrasa—Habib-ur Rahman as a student, and Niazi as a teacher.

They knew very well what everyone's ideas were, and when Niazi started the movement, he invited the students, like Maulavi Habib-ur Rahman, whom he knew directly and in whom he had confidence. Then, in consultation with them, he chose other students from other schools who were also known to them, such as Engineer Hekmatyar and Saifuddin Nasratyar. They were known to have Islamic thoughts and feelings, and so were some others like Ghulam Rabbani Atesh, Professor [Abd al-Rab Rasul] Sayyaf, Ustad [Muhammad Jan] Ahmadzai, Sayyid Nurullah, and so many others. They were all known as Muslims and anticommunists, so Niazi brought them together and convened the first meeting in Shewaki.

(I): Do you know how many people attended that first meeting and when it was held?

(QA): We were about twenty to twenty-five people, and he discussed the issues and problems that we were facing. He said, "We are working individually everywhere; let's come together and establish a regular way of working." All the invited people agreed with him, and then we talked about the plan of how to work.

(I): Do you know the date of that first meeting?

(QA): It was toward the end of 1347 or at the beginning of 1348 [winter/ spring 1969], but I don't remember the exact day and month. . . . When these people came together, they organized groups of five persons each, and they were directed to make that kind of circle [*halqa*] wherever they found others in whom they had confidence. And they were told to give regular reports of their work to the head [*sar halqa*] of their circle. . . . Niazi always met with the heads of each of the circles privately, and sometimes they would bring new members to introduce them to Niazi or to have him answer their questions or explain the goals of the movement. He gave answers to their questions about different aspects of Islam, especially economic matters. . . . In private meetings, they trained the members how to discuss and explain their goals. There wasn't enough time to write brief notes for them, but the members could use the books of famous writers. . . .

Unfortunately, Niazi was alive for just one year after starting the movement. He died in June 1970, so he lived just fourteen months after the beginning of the Muslim Youth Organization (Sazman-i Jawanan-i Musulman). He delivered a total of six speeches during that time—one was at Ningrahar University and another was in Qandahar. He had studied very deeply and was a very eloquent speaker. He had a full command of Pakhtu and Persian and could deliver speeches in both languages. There is no doubt that he was a very knowledgeable and extraordinary man. Every one of his speeches explained some aspect of the movement, like our goals, foreign and domestic policy, the quality and conditions of Islamic ideology. The speeches of other elder brothers of the movement like Maulavi Habib-ur Rahman or Hekmatyar were not equal to his speeches. Every time he spoke, it was like a lesson in theory for the members of the movement.[25]

The most important fact to keep in mind when considering the development of radical Muslim politics in Afghanistan is the place where it all began—the campus of Kabul University. Although originally established in 1946, the university was a small, scattered, and insignificant institution until the mid-1960s, when a major expansion was undertaken that included the consolidation of the formerly dispersed faculties onto a single campus. Bankrolled by large grants from the United States Agency for International Development and other foreign-assistance programs, the university added new classrooms and laboratories, as well as dormitories for the ever-increasing student body, whose numbers rose from eight hundred in 1957, to two thousand in 1963, to thirty-three hundred in 1966. Along with the infusion of money, students, and facilities came foreign instructors from the United States, Europe, and the Soviet Union.

The most significant feature of the university, however, was not that it brought Afghans together with foreigners but that it brought Afghans face-to-face with each other. Never before had there been an opportunity for so many young Afghans to interact over an extended period of time with other young Afghans from different regions of the country. Despite efforts by rulers like Abdur Rahman to convince citizens that their primary identity was as subjects of the state, Afghanistan had remained a patchwork of disparate tribes, regions, sects, and language groups that was held together, at times rather flimsily, by strong men at its center and foreign enemies along its borders. The one institution that consistently worked to mitigate and blur the boundaries between groups was the army, but since many of the army units retained a tribal and ethnic cast and most soldiers were illiterate and poor, the influence of this institution was limited.

The university, however, brought together students from all over the country. Entrance to the university was difficult. A large number of students were from the elite—not all of whom deserved or desired to be in university—but many others made their way to the campus by dint of their own achievements in provincial secondary schools. And those who did make it were rewarded not just with an education and the prospect of a life lived outside the village but also with the prospect of being an instrumental part of the nation's development. Never before had Kabul been so flush with funds. Never before had so much building been undertaken for the benefit of ordinary people. This munificence helped to inculcate in the students a sense of their own importance. So too did the fact that they had been dropped down in this exciting new place at a moment in the nation's history—the period of the "new democracy"—when it appeared that just about anything was possible. These were exciting times, and it seemed to the students that they themselves were one of the things that was most exciting about it. That, anyway, was the perception. The reality, not surprisingly, was different.

In *Heroes of the Age*, I discussed the importance of location in the success of Sufi orders in the late nineteenth century. The Mulla of Hadda, as well as most of his principal deputies, situated their centers in areas interstitial to tribes and the state. Hadda itself was a barren area between the provincial capital of Jalalabad and the mountain fastness where the Shinwari, Khogiani, and other tribes made their homes. Most of the Mulla's deputies set themselves up in villages in the Kunar Valley, where they were accessible to but not dependent on their tribal disciples, who were living in the mountains lining both sides of the valley. Interstitiality was equally important for the development of radical politics in the contemporary era, but in this case that interstitiality was located at the university campus.

Students from rural areas, who were accustomed to hearing only their native language spoken and to dealing primarily with kinsmen and others they had known their whole lives, were suddenly placed in tight quarters with people from different ethnic and linguistic groups. Most of the students were serious and valued the opportunity to be at the university, but a number had gotten into the university through family connections, and they had no interest in studying. Some of these students spent their time gambling and smoking hashish—which was less expensive and more readily available than alcohol—and in extreme cases students who didn't want to attend a course on a given day coerced others into staying away, so the professor had to cancel the class.

The two places where tensions ran highest were the cafeteria and dormitories, both of which were severely overcrowded. Endless lines formed at meals, and students with reputations as tough guys cut into lines. Dormitories had only a few showers, and hot water was available for only a few hours during the day, so students had to sign up ahead of time for showers. Here again, some students abused their rights, daring the student who lost his place to protest. Many of these tough students were known to carry knives; one informant told me of witnessing a knife-wielding bully chase another student through the dormitory into the fourth-floor mosque, where other students were praying, and stabbing him in the shoulder. School administrators generally kept their distance in these situations, in part at least because some of the worst violators of school rules were the sons of well-connected men whom the administrators could not afford to offend.[26]

If, as I argued in *Heroes of the Age,* becoming a disciple of a Sufi pir was for some a response to the heartlessness of the tribal world, joining a political party was for students to some degree an antidote to the friendlessness and anarchy of the university. Students who were even moderately inclined to religious feeling, who had prayed regularly at home and wanted to continue this practice at university, were impelled to seek the company of like-minded students not only because of the corruption and abuse they saw around them but also because of the petty annoyances of leftist students who reportedly took great pleasure in making fun of the customs of the devout. Niazi and other founding members of the Muslim Youth offered a bulwark against what appeared in the concentrated atmosphere of the university to be a tidal wave of atheistic behavior. Niazi, intelligent and charismatic, held daily meetings after prayers, during which he discussed with younger students sections of the Qur'an and hadith and helped them interpret the significance of these passages in light of current events. Initially, these meetings did not have a specific political content and were not sustained by any organizational apparatus. When campus elections were held, Muslim students at first did not have a specific party affiliation, referring to themselves rather as *bi-taraf,* or "nonaligned," but eventually the members of this group, recognizing their common interest in Islam, joined together as Sazman-i Jawanan-i Musulman—the Organization of Muslim Youth.

Accounts of the origins of the Muslim Youth Organization differ depending on the political affiliation of the speaker, but it is generally accepted that Muslim students began to meet on the campus of Kabul University in 1966 or 1967 and that a group of students representing different faculties within the university formally established the Muslim

Youth Organization in 1969. The founding members of the Muslim Youth were initially inspired by a group of professors in the Faculty of Theology, most importantly Ghulam Muhammad Niazi (not a relative of Abdur Rahim Niazi, though both were from the Niazi tribe), who had studied in Cairo in the 1950s and had come in contact with members of the Muslim Brotherhood during his stay there. Although Ghulam Muhammad Niazi and other professors did not take a direct role in student activities, they informed the students of movements going on in other parts of the Muslim world and provided them with a sense of how Islam could be made relevant to the social and political transformations everywhere apparent in the latter half of the twentieth century.[27]

This was an important requirement for many of the students, for as heady as it was to be at Kabul University during this period, it was also disorienting. Many of the students had never been far from their native villages before their arrival at the university, and for most of their lives Kabul itself had been little more than a distant rumor and a radio signal. In this context, many of the old ways—the customs and traditions that had bound together the villages from which most of them sprang—lost their vitality and their basic viability. What had given structure and meaning in the local community—the centrality of the kin group, the respect due senior agnates, the rivalry between cousins, the informality and warmth of the maternal hearth—were irrelevant in the university setting, where unrelated young people came together unannounced and unaware. In its earliest days, the Muslim Youth can be seen as a response to the experience of disorientation. In the beehive of a dormitory with twenty-five hundred denizens, groups of students sharing common interests began to gravitate to one another, and their association with one another helped stave off the loneliness and alienation that attended being strangers in a strange land. Significantly, the list of the founding members of the party included an even mix of Pakhtuns and Tajiks from a variety of provinces. Most of the students were Sunni, but there were a few Shi'a members as well, and this demographic mix speaks to the relative egalitarianism of the movement at this point as well as to its inclusiveness, both elements that would be lost as time went on.

In his life history of a religious scholar in Morocco, Dale Eickelman points out that some of the most significant educational experiences of his subject occurred outside the classroom in the peer learning circles that students formed among themselves.[28] The same could be said of Qazi Amin, and when I spoke with his contemporaries, the experiences they tended to emphasize as most memorable were also those they had in the company of their peers.[29] Even the stories of leftist provocation were told with a certain relish; it was clear that these incidents, which were recounted to indicate the immorality of the enemy, also were recalled with a sense of nostalgia. These provocations brought the movement into being, generated that first sense of righteous indignation and purposefulness, and led to a feeling of communal solidarity that the students had never felt before and that they had rarely felt since.[30]

CONFRONTATION, ARMED CONFLICT, AND EXILE, 1969–1978

(I): Do you remember any particular events from that period that you were involved in? Are there any clashes or demonstrations or other specific memories that you recall?

(QA): The first year, there was the problem of Asil [a leftist student] who was killed [by Muslim students] at the Ibn-i Sina High School. He was a student at Ibn-i Sina, and the Khalqis and Parchamis took charge of his funeral procession and carried his body around the city and brought him finally to the Eid Gah mosque. After this, demonstrations continued for some time, and the administration closed the university. As a result, we spent one more year in the program than was usual.

The next year, when the university started, another important event occurred. This event provoked the Muslims and caused the movement to become very strong, while the Khalqis and Parchamis were disgraced. There were some Russians who were teachers at the Polytechnic Institute. Their families also lived on the campus, and they showed their own films there. Engineer Habib-ur Rahman,[31] Engineer Matiullah, Engineer Azim, and Engineer Salam were all students at the Polytechnic at the time that the Russians showed a film there that was about godlessness [*bi khudayi*]. [In the film] there was a farmer who was plowing the land. He became thirsty, so he drinks some water and prays to God. After that, somebody else came along and helped him by giving him water and some other things. Then, this man asked the farmer, "Did God give you anything? Of course, it was I who gave you the water and helped you, so there is no God." During the screening of this film, while it was still running, Engineer Habib-ur Rahman threw something at the screen, and there was a confrontation. The film generated a lot of controversy, and the members of the circle stood against it. We criticized the showing of this kind of film, and we went to the parliament to protest. We also started protests at the university, and the Polytechnic students themselves demonstrated against showing this film.

About a year after this, another event occurred. During Ramazan, the communists threw the Qur'an from the window of a mosque that was on the fourth floor of a dormitory at the university. The next day, all the students saw the Qur'an lying on the road. The pages were torn, and it was covered with snow. This provoked the members of the movement. We felt the need for a more intensive struggle. In fact, we were revived by this action. On the occasion of such events, public meetings were always convened, and the late [Abdur Rahim] Niazi would deliver his speeches, which always inspired the young people to action.

In general, I was sympathetic to what was going on, but I only began to take an active role during an incident involving the Khalqis at the Polytechnic. It was the month of Ramazan, and the Khalqis had asked the government to keep the cafeteria open for students who did not want to keep the fast. But the government didn't dare to let it stay open. Besides that, during *iftar* [the ceremony that occurs at sunset each evening during the month of Ramazan, when Muslims break the fast], some of the Khalqis deliberately insulted students who were observing the fast. So the conflict started between those students who observed the fast and those who didn't.

(I): Did the top circle of the movement have relations at that time with people in any branch of the government, such as the military or any of the ministries?

(QA): In the beginning, our recruitment activities were confined to the university, but later, in 1970, it spread to all the schools in Kabul. For instance, I was responsible for organizing and inviting students at Khushhal Khan and Rahman Baba high schools. In this fashion, we divided all the high schools in Kabul, and everyone was working at a high school where he had some relationship and was training the students and organizing them into different cells [*hasta*]. We also divided up the provinces so that everyone was responsible for one or two. Everyone was aware where he should work, but it was just on the level of students and teachers. For instance, I went to Helmand and Qandahar several times for the sake of the movement.

(I): I have heard that your friend Maulavi Habib-ur Rahman was involved in the Pul-i Khishti demonstration that was organized by members of the ulama. Were you also involved in it, and what do you know about those events?

(QA): Maulavi Sahib didn't even speak there. He just tried to persuade them informally, but it was not under our control. All [the demonstrators] were Afghanistan's great ulama. We were just students at that time. We couldn't control them. After much effort, Abdur Rahim [Niazi] was finally allowed to deliver a speech there twice among the mullas. I think maybe Maulavi [Habib-ur Rahman] might also have delivered a speech there once. Maulavi Salam delivered a speech, so eventually we were able to preach our ideas among them and state some of our principles.[32]

Beginning in the early 1970s, the halcyon atmosphere of the first period of political activity evaporated and was replaced by a situation that was a great deal more tense and fractured. The first reason for this change was certainly the unexpected death, reportedly from leukemia, in 1970 of Abdur Rahim Niazi, the charismatic leader of the Muslim Youth. While a number of other students were as actively committed to the movement as Niazi, none commanded the respect that he enjoyed, and no one could muster the authority that he possessed in determining the party's direction. As a result of Niazi's death, leadership within the party became more fragmented, and factions began to develop around particular leaders and within the different university faculties. These splits were not serious until the political situation became increasingly tense and polarized, and the young student militants had to decide on a direction for their campus study group: Would the group remain as a student organization or become involved in national politics? If national politics was the proper forum for the group's activities, was their ultimate goal to influence debate on issues of national development or to win power for themselves? If their goal was to win power, should this goal be pursued through the parliamentary system or by alternative means, including the use of violence?

A second factor leading to the transformation in the party was the open hostility that existed between Muslims and Marxists on campus. Given their opposed ideological positions and their common objective of winning the hearts and minds of the student generation, animosity between Marxists and Muslims was inevitable, but the intensity of this feeling was undoubtedly exacerbated by a number of provocative actions initiated by campus leftists. In addition to the incidents already mentioned, I have been told other stories in which leftists ostentatiously ate food and smoked cigarettes next to Muslims during the month of fasting, kicked soccer balls at students who were praying outdoors, and defecated into the pots that students used for ritual ablution. Such provocations polarized the campus, leading even mildly religious students to feel as though they were under assault and motivating those who were politically inclined to action. Hekmatyar, who later became amir of Hizb-i Islami, described the situation this way:

> In the university, which was a great center of knowledge and where the future rulers of the country were trained, nobody could use the name of religion. Nobody there could wear national clothes. . . . Nobody could keep the fast. . . . Nobody could have a beard in the colleges, not even in the Faculty of Islamic Law. When those from the Faculty of Islamic Law and other colleges came into the dining halls, from one side and the other, students would ball up food and throw it at them and insult them. In the

high schools, the communists would ridicule anyone who had the feeling
of Islam, [saying] that they were "backward sheep" who would progress
as soon as they got to the university. They would tell them that when
they got to the center of knowledge and civilization, they would recognize
their path. There they wouldn't care anymore about praying, fasting, and
musulmani [Muslim practice].[33]

Provocations, it has already been noted, were not original to the university. Back in the 1940s, leftists had protested the building of the shrine for
the Prophet's hair in Ningrahar, and, in the late 1950s, wives of leftist
politicians began appearing in public without the veil as a direct challenge
to religious leaders who decried such ethical breaches.[34] Both these events
set off religious protests, including violent demonstrations in Qandahar in
response to the unveiling. One such episode occurred in 1969, when the
newspaper *Islah* published a cartoon viewed by religious leaders as disre-
spectful of the Prophet Muhammad. This cartoon depicted a man in an
Arab-style turban, accompanied by nine veiled women, being turned away
by a hotel manager who tells him: "Here there is no room for a man with
nine wives." Although not identified, the figure depicted in the cartoon was
recognized as the Prophet Muhammad, and his belittlement in the cartoon
was held up as an example of leftist sacrilege. A more significant outrage
occurred in March 1970, when the Marxist *Parcham* newspaper published
the poem "The Bugle of Revolution"; in it Lenin was eulogized using a
form of invocation (dorud) traditionally reserved solely for the Prophet
Muhammad.[35]

Where earlier provocations had resulted in scattered protests, outraged
mosque sermons, and delegations demanding audiences with the king, "The
Bugle of Revolution" inspired a more organized protest involving hundreds
Muslim clerics, Sufi pirs, and members of saintly families who congregated
in the Pul-i Khishti mosque in central Kabul to protest the poem and the
growing influence of leftists in Afghanistan. The demonstration was originally supported by the government as a way of indirectly dampening
increasingly militant leftist activities in the country. However, when the
protest dragged on for more than a month with no end in sight and began
to take an increasingly antigovernment direction, troops were sent into the
sacred precincts of the mosque to break up the demonstration; the soldiers
unceremoniously packed the protesting clerics on buses back to their
provincial homes and arrested some of the demonstration organizers.[36]

A few of the student leaders of the Muslim Youth Organization, such as
Abdur Rahim Niazi and Maulavi Habib-ur Rahman, were peripherally
involved in the Pul-i Khishti protest, but most of the members were

excluded from playing a significant role because—unlike these two—they didn't have the requisite madrasa training. This exclusion articulated a line of division within the Muslim political community that would loom increasingly large during the coming years—that between younger, secularly educated university and high school students and madrasa-trained mullas and maulavis. Likewise, the abortive Pul-i Khishti demonstration marked a turning point in the tactics of Muslim political activists. As members of the Muslim Youth Organization watched from outside as the mosque protest floundered and finally failed, many came to the conclusion that traditional religious leaders were unprepared for the changing political climate in Afghanistan, particularly the new modes of disseminating political propaganda and organizing popular movements that leftists parties were beginning to employ to great effect. In the opinion of many in the younger generation, demonstrations such as the one carried out at the Pul-i Khishti mosque only played into the hands of the government and the leftists, and the fact that the government had turned on the leaders of the demonstration (who had previously gained the tacit approval of the king) when the demonstration strayed beyond its official stated aims illustrated not only that the regime was untrustworthy but also that it was a major part of the problem. For weeks on end, the mullas and maulavis had made speeches to each other, while they waited for the government to respond. In the meantime, the king and his advisors were determining what action to take, and when they finally cracked down, the demonstration organizers had little popular support to draw on, no coordinated line of action to pursue, and finally no alternative other than getting on the bus and going home.

The Pul-i Khishti demonstration provided a fit ending to a half century of government co-optation of Muslim clerics. Beginning with Amir Habibullah, and with the exception of the decade-long reign of Amir Amanullah, the state's policy toward clerics and pirs had been one of appeasement, a policy that proved to be far more effective than either Abdur Rahman's style of confrontation or Amanullah's plan of radical reform. Since 1931, the government had placated its religious critics, giving them grants of aid and land, funding their schools, and providing them with a largely symbolic role as overseers of state morality and law via the jamiat-ul ulama—the official council of ulama. The effect of these concessions was not only to dampen the independent spirit of the religious class but also to blunt any effort on its part to establish independent organizations that would be in a position to criticize or counter government actions.

In this respect, the men of religion were considerably more vulnerable than even the tribes, for they had no corporate existence as a group except insofar as the government provided venues for collective action. Despite the frequent boasts that I heard in interviews with clerics as to the superior quality of Afghan madrasas, the reality was that these schools were scattered all over the country and had little connection with one another except in the haphazard peregrinations of students moving among them. In Afghanistan, no theological center of activity was equivalent to Qom in Iran or al-Azhar in Egypt, which made organizing difficult. In the more distant past, the dispersion of schools had also made state control over the religious class more difficult, as firebrands like the Mulla of Hadda and Mulla Mushk-i Alam, the leader of the Afghan resistance to the British in 1879, could use their students (*taliban*) as runners to connect them to their allies and deputies. However, the expansion of government authority throughout the country, the improvement of roads and communication, and the gradual co-optation of religious leaders by the government contributed to the decline of the religious class as active participants in the political process, a decline that culminated in the anemic protest at Pul-i Khishti.

Following the abortive demonstration, and probably inspired by it, the government continued its efforts to bring religion under control. In 1971, the government set up a new agency, the *riasat-i haj wa awqaf*, which was intended to centralize the financial control of mosques and shrines throughout the country in one agency. Before the establishment of this directorate, the Ministry of Culture and Information had exercised some control over the two most famous religious shrines, the beautiful blue and white tile tomb in Mazar-i Sharif where 'Ali, the cousin of the Prophet Muhammad and fourth caliph, is purported to be buried and the shrine in Qandahar housing a cloak of the Prophet. With the founding of the riasat-i haj wa awqaf, however, the government intended to assume financial control of other established religious shrines and mosques, while also taking responsibility for building new mosques and appointing and paying imams, *moazens* [those who call people to prayer], and other religious functionaries.[37] In the words of Kamal Shinwari, who was the director of the agency from 1972 until the Marxist revolution, "We had the goal of bringing all of the ulama into the government organization," while also assuming control of the endowments of the institutions they had previously run on their own.[38]

These efforts were undertaken with the approval of most of the clerics; they themselves participated in these initiatives and saw these measures as a way to ensure the financial well-being of religious institutions and religious personnel throughout the country. Prior to this point, many, if not most, mullas and maulavis had been dependent on the charitable contributions of local people, or they had been the hired help of wealthy landowners. While some shrines had endowments, often the only beneficiaries of a given shrine would be the descendants of the saint interred in its precincts, who would divide the income from associated lands and contributions left at the shrine among themselves. Few mullas or maulavis benefited from these arrangements, just as few mosques had endowments of land large enough to make them sustainable without additional assistance. So the desire of the ulama to regularize their income and make themselves less dependent on local people is understandable, but, at the same time, the fact that religious leaders could see their own best interests as allied with those of the government is a mark of how far they had moved in seventy years. It is difficult to imagine the Mulla of Hadda countenancing the establishment of the riasat-i haj wa awqaf unless it were independent of government oversight. As noted earlier in the chapter, the Mulla turned back to the government the sizeable parcel of land given to him by Amir Habibullah on the grounds that it was bait-ul mal, the property of the people, and thus not properly his to take (or the amir's to give). More to the point perhaps, the Mulla recognized that financial entanglements with the state limited the independence of religious leaders and made them less inclined to fulfill the role he had played for so many years as the moral guardian of the community.

Seventy years later, Afghanistan was a different place. The balance of power had shifted in favor of the state, and the ulama had new aspirations for financial and social security that overrode their ancient commitments to defend the faith against the perturbations of state rulers who lost their way. But the Muslim Youth didn't see it that way, and they didn't have the same priorities or the same professional interest in securing a livelihood as the ulama did. For them, the actions of the ulama were a betrayal, and it was up to them, so they believed, to stand fast as the true guardians of the faith. One former Muslim Youth member from Paktika Province described their view to me in an interview in 1986:

> Afghanistan was not a country without Islamic scholars. There were thousands of scholars, but we thought that when they didn't point out the people's needs, and when they didn't point out the traitors and the tyrant in the country, and they didn't point out the Soviet exploitation of Afghanistan, we thought that if people are hungry, they don't want to hear stories about cookies and banquets—they want food. That was the need of the time.[39]

With Marxists on the university campus speaking out against the injustices of the government and addressing the needs of the people, the Muslim

Youth leaders felt the need to demonstrate the relevance of Islam to the social problems of the country. The influence of Marxist ideology was readily apparent in a pamphlet written by Abdur Rahim Niazi in response to many questions he was hearing on what Islam had to offer in solving Afghanistan's economic problems and how an Islamic government would ensure social justice (*'adalat-i ejtema'i*) for its citizens.[40] While most of Niazi's pamphlet dealt with specific features of the Islamic economic system, such as *zakat* (religious tax) and *sud* (interest), the gist of his argument was that Afghanistan need not look to Marxism or any other foreign ideology to find the means of ensuring a better life for the poor:

> In Islamic law, the emphasis is so much on mercy that when a Muslim
> sees a needy person, he immediately feels that it is obligatory for him
> to help him, and he is ready to give his share to the poor. God said (in
> *surah dhariyat*, verse 19) that the needy have a share in the riches of the
> wealthy, and therefore God loves those who help their friends, neighbors,
> travelers, and other people.

According to Niazi, Islam had all the necessary answers to the problems of society; if the government would institute zakat, not only would poverty be eliminated, but funds would be left over for public-works projects. The government, however, had failed to live up to its responsibilities under Islamic law, and the result was that "the number of poor people is increasing day by day." On this point, "the Muslims and communists have little difference." Where the difference does intrude is in the manner of solving the problem, for "according to communist ideology, the [wealthy] class should be eliminated from society in order to pave the way for the communist revolution." The Prophet Muhammad, however, offered an alternative solution:

> Fourteen centuries back, Islam taught a very revolutionary and logical
> lesson for [achieving] revolution. God said to do jihad in the path of God
> with honesty. The establishment of an Islamic government requires that
> kind of jihad. . . . Today truth has been replaced by tyranny, and the only
> way that has been left is to invite [*dawat*] the people to truth and
> untiring militancy in this path.

In the face of threats from increasingly vocal Marxist radicals and a complacent, sporadically despotic state, the Muslim Youth expanded its attempts to recruit new members to its cause, especially in government offices and high schools in Kabul and the provincial capitals:

> For example, if I graduated and joined the Ministry of Education or the
> Ministry of Finance or Trade, I would form a cell over there. If there was
> somebody before me, I was introduced to him, or he was introduced to me

if he was junior to me. Since I was from the rural areas, I would approach family members and others from our area. If I knew there were fifteen people from our area in the city, I was approaching them—"Hello, how are you?" I was inviting them and providing materials. In this way, the party was organizing itself.[41]

In his interview with me, Qazi Amin mentioned some of the trips he made on behalf of the Muslim Youth, but I have also heard from others what it was like to be at the receiving end of such trips. One informant who lived in Kunduz, a provincial capital in northern Afghanistan, had his first contact with the Muslim Youth through a recent university graduate named "Mumin" (a pseudonym). This was in 1969–1970, while the informant was a student in secondary school. Everyday after class, Mumin waited outside for the informant and other students who were known to regularly attend mosque and therefore might be sympathetic to the Muslim Youth message. As Mumin got to know the students, he gradually began to talk to them about Islam and inquired about their attitudes toward a variety of political and social issues. Eventually, he offered the students a handwritten document that contained an explanation of modern scientific inventions from the point of view of the Qur'an and showed the ways in which the pursuit of technological progress was in keeping with scriptural belief.

Mumin was persuasive in conversation and impressed the students with his theological knowledge, which they believed was greater than that of the religion teachers they listened to in class. Over time, Mumin established solid relations with forty or fifty students from the high school, as well as from the local madrasa and the teacher-training school. Contacts with these students continued on a regular but informal basis for the first year, and every so often Mumin would supply the students with additional writings that they would then copy and distribute among their friends. Not until the second year did the informant become aware that Mumin was part of an organized political party. This revelation occurred in the spring of 1971, after local students belonging to the Marxist Khalq and Parcham parties held a public demonstration. From this point, Mumin began to operate more openly, bringing notes for the students to read and identifying the source of these writings as a group in Kabul named Jawanan-i Musulman—the Muslim Youth.

Having witnessed the humiliation suffered by the older clerics during the Pul-i Khishti demonstration, Muslim student leaders were determined not to endure the same fate, and they took elaborate measures to ensure that their nascent organization was not subverted or infiltrated. The former mid-level member of the Muslim Youth described the organization this way:

> First there was a central committee, and it came downward to small cells [hasta]. These were divided in Kabul and in the countryside. Each of the university students was responsible for one high school. Others were responsible for one district or for a street. All the students were responsible for different areas outside the campus, including schools, madrassas, mosques. Two might be responsible for a big high school like Rahman Baba. Within the school, leadership of the cell was according to the understanding of Islam and the activism of the people in that school.[42]

Division of the party into small cells guaranteed that lower-level recruits, about whom the party leadership knew relatively little, would know the names of only a handful of other members and that these recruits would come to know more members only as they were vetted up through the party hierarchy. Above the level of the primary cell, which usually had between five and ten members, there was the halqa, or circle, composed of the heads of a number of primary cells. The heads of each of these secondary circles were also members of a tertiary group known as the *hauza*. The local hauzas far removed from Kabul were generally connected to the capital through regional and provincial councils; each of these councils sent a representative to the next level. The provincial representative was a member of the central council (*shura*), which was made up primarily of the first group of student leaders from the university. These layers of segmental organization provided insulation; even if a cell were infiltrated, only that group would be compromised because members were unaware of the membership of other cells.

Advancement within the party was also monitored to ensure that those who rose in position reflected both the political philosophy and the moral tone expected of members. According to one high-ranking member of the Muslim Youth whom I interviewed in 1986, there were degrees of membership: "Each step is passed based on one's activism—the cell you belong to decides. The way you operate, the way you invite people [to join the party]. Personally, you could be watched by a member of the party. . . . I can give my personal view on a person's relations, life, attitude toward the country—all of these things count."[43]

Most of the members of the tertiary level—the hauza—were third- or fourth-degree members, and they were responsible for overseeing and ensuring the ideological and personal accountability of those below them in the party hierarchy. They were also responsible for nominating members for promotion; and they were required to sign each promotion form and ensure that the individual had performed in a way that merited advancement:

One condition was that you had to become a top student in school or university. It is a record that [in the late 1960s] numbers one to ten [in class rank at the university] were all members of the Muslim Youth. A second condition was that you had to memorize by heart each week a part of the Qur'an and hadith, and you had to write how many and what books you had studied.[44]

Members of the Muslim Youth carefully monitored each other's behavior and reported their findings to higher-ups within the party who made decisions regarding promotion. The individual under consideration would not necessarily know those who were involved in his promotion, or he might know them personally but did not know that they were high-ranking members of the party. "When you are promoted to the next step, you are informed, and then [the leader of your cell] gives you another responsibility."[45]

The Muslim Youth were continually on the lookout for new prospects but were wary of everyone and of the possibility of having the party infiltrated by Marxists or government agents.[46] One early party member, Sur Gul Spin, told me of the efforts made to check on the background of other members through their relatives, classmates, villagers back home. As he rose through the party ranks, he was given the responsibility of monitoring the behavior of the other forty-five students in his class: "If he belongs to another thinking, I can guess that this person is hard-core and this [one] is not hard-core, that [his way of thinking] is due to his brother. . . . We knew another person was regularly participating in the communist demonstrations, but just for fun. He didn't invite a single man to that party." While it was recognized that many students went to demonstrations because "they were the kind of place where you could talk about anything you wanted to, where you could yell 'bullshit' at anyone," this was an indulgence the party did not allow its own members "even secretly, even in your heart."[47]

While the party was obsessed with security, it did not back down from confrontation. The lesson that party leaders appear to have taken from the failed demonstration at Pul-i Khishti was not that demonstrations were unwise but that they had to be undertaken in a more calculated manner. In most cases, public protests by the Muslim Youth neither were targeted at nor demanded action by the state. Rather, they tended to be responses to actions of their Marxist rivals. Thus, when campus leftists initiated their various petty assaults on orthodoxy—showing offensive films, desecrating copies of the Qur'an, eating during Ramazan—the Muslim students took a more direct and violent line of action than their elders had at Pul-i Khishti or than they themselves had in the past. This line of action sometimes involved demonstrations, sometimes direct confrontations with the leftist authors of their discontent. These confrontations—some of which were initiated by the leftists, others by the Muslim students—led at first to scuffles and broken arms, later to broken heads, and finally to several deaths: in each case, according to informants, Marxists beaten or stabbed by Muslims.

The escalating combat between Marxists and Muslims culminated in May 1972 after a Western-trained professor at Kabul University reportedly denigrated the relevance of Islamic economic principles to contemporary problems. The classroom debate that ensued over these comments developed into a demonstration in which a member of the Maoist Shula-yi Jawed party was killed. The government responded by arresting a number of Muslim Youth leaders, including Hekmatyar, who had been one of the organizers of the demonstration. While these leaders were eventually released, the government was forever after wary of the potential threat from Muslim students. Well aware of the radical challenge that groups like the Muslim Brotherhood were making to the government in Egypt and aware as well of the influence that works by Muslim Brotherhood writers exerted on Muslim students at Kabul University, the government began to monitor the activities of the Muslim Youth in the last year of Zahir Shah's reign. Surveillance increased even further after Muhammad Daud's coup d'état in 1973, which led the Muslim Youth to move beyond recruitment and public protest to planning for armed confrontation with the government.

Daud's coup d'état also marked the emergence of the Muslim Youth from the protective chrysalis of the university. While the university setting was crucial to the development of the Muslim Youth, it also presented certain difficulties; in particular, after a period of intense involvement with the party, members would graduate and then have to go out and earn a living. Many graduates stayed in Kabul, most working in government ministries, but others ended up in the provinces, teaching school or working in regional government offices. This dispersal of party members offered opportunities for expanding the base of the party, but it also made coordination of activities far more difficult.

In Qazi Amin's case, graduation followed five months after Daud's coup d'état. Although he had hoped to return to Najm ul-Madares as a teacher, the Ministry of Education sent him to eastern Ningrahar Province in the winter of 1974 to teach first in a primary school and then in a secondary school in Surkh Rud. He remained there for a year and a half, during which he recruited on behalf of the party, both in Surkh Rud and in neighboring areas. Because of his status as a madrasa graduate and the son of an Islamic judge, Qazi Amin was especially useful to the party in dealing with traditional clerics, and consequently he was sent on missions to Qandahar and other regions to meet with religious scholars, as well as with students and teachers:

> I informed them about the non-Islamic policies of the Daud regime, and I told them that even though [Daud] proclaimed his regime as an Islamic republic, it was actually not Islamic at all. [I told them], "He is not a person who could bring Islam. He is pro-communist. The communists are involved in the regime and the hand of the Russians is behind all of them. The Russians want to vanquish and finish the Islamic movement through Daud's regime. Then they have a plan to bring communists directly into power." Some of the knowledgeable persons accepted these ideas. . . . Other brothers were involved in the same sort of activities in different provinces. We would establish some circles, meet with village chiefs and religious scholars, and put into effect some other programs as well.[48]

After he began teaching in 1974, Qazi Amin didn't return to Kabul and had only limited contact with party members in the capital, but by this time most of the top leaders either had been imprisoned or had fled to Peshawar. In the winter of 1975, he established relations with exiled party members, including his old friend Maulavi Habib-ur Rahman and Gulbuddin Hekmatyar, who were the senior members of the movement in Peshawar. That August, while Qazi Amin was still inside Afghanistan, party members, including Maulavi Habib-ur Rahman, led unsuccessful attacks on government installations in Panjshir, Surkh Rud, Paktia, Laghman, and other provinces. According to Qazi Amin, the party was forced to take this action because of the government's repression. Prior to the uprisings, more than 150 members had been arrested "without any reason. The only accusation against them was their membership in the Islamic movement. Until that time, we did not launch any attack or any other hostile action against the government. We didn't even spread slogans or night letters [*shabnama*] against the government. For no reason, [Daud] pulled people from mosques, teachers and students from schools, and arrested all of them."[49]

Though not directly involved in the planning or implementation of these raids, one of which occurred near his own home in Surkh Rud, Qazi Amin was implicated by association with some of those who had been arrested, and he escaped to the mountains. From there, he traveled by foot to Pakistan.

> When I reached Peshawar, Hekmatyar and [Burhanuddin] Rabbani
> [later head of the Jamiat-i Islami party] were both very sad and depressed.
> Hekmatyar became nervous and sick, and he had to go to Lahore to cure
> himself. They had been hopeful of bringing fundamental changes to the

government through these operations, but they failed. They expected the people to support the uprising, and they were hopeful that they would be able to continue the struggle against the government in this way. But contrary to their expectations, so many stalwarts of the party . . . were arrested by the government. Maulavi Habib-ur Rahman, for example, was arrested with twenty-five members of the movement. In the case of those members who managed to escape . . . the government put their close relatives in jail and tortured them. They tied their feet with rope and pulled them over the road from their houses up to the district administrator's office. They suffered very grave hardships and endured many kinds of cruelty.[50]

When Qazi Amin arrived in Peshawar, the movement was demoralized and directionless. The attacks had been intended to spark a nationwide uprising against Daud's government, to occur simultaneously with a military putsch in Kabul. The Kabul operation never got underway, and, instead of provoking a popular rebellion, the students in the countryside found themselves under attack from the very people they had hoped to rally to their cause.

Qazi Amin estimated that there were 120 families of refugees in Peshawar when he arrived, along with a few others in the tribal areas. During the next six months, another 1,200 families arrived from various parts of Afghanistan. For the most part, these refugees were the relatives of party members who had been arrested or killed for their antigovernment activities. Party leaders assigned Qazi Amin the job of securing tents, rations, and other basic necessities from the Pakistan government. While not exactly welcoming them, President Zulfiqar 'Ali Bhutto did recognize the potential value of these young zealots as a blunt instrument against Daud should the Afghan president decide once again to contest the political status of the tribal borderlands or create other difficulties. Consequently, Bhutto provided modest subsidies to the exiles, along with some out-of-date weapons and basic training in their use. Otherwise, the former students were on their own, with most living in dingy apartments and scraping by on their subsidies, whatever funds they were able to bring with them across the border, and additional assistance from sympathetic political groups in Pakistan, such as the Jama'at-i Islami Pakistan.

At the same time, and despite the setbacks, plans went forward to renew the struggle to overthrow the regime of Daud and to establish an Islamic government once and for all in Afghanistan. At the center of these efforts was Hekmatyar, the erstwhile engineering student who was the only founding member of the Muslim Youth Organization at large after the debacle of the summer of 1975. As discussed in the next chapter, Hekmatyar's leadership was controversial from the start. More than anyone else, he was responsible for converting the disjointed network of student study and protest groups into an authoritarian political party. More than anyone else, he was responsible for the party's uncompromising militancy and obstinate refusal to cede pride of place in the jihad to any other group, be it the tribes and regional solidarities that controlled the anti-Khalqi rebellion in its early days or the other political parties that set up shop in Peshawar following the Saur Revolution.

CONCLUSION

The story of Qazi Amin's coming of age bears a certain resemblance to the story previously told of Samiullah Safi's formative years. Both men had strong fathers who were immersed in venerated traditions that their sons initially sought to follow. But while both men were born into the world their fathers had known, that world changed as they came of age. One feature of that change was the unbalancing of the tripartite relationship of state, tribe, and Islam that had long been the foundation of Afghan political culture; in the second third of the twentieth century that relationship had begun to tip lopsidedly in favor of the state. Growing up, Qazi Amin and Samiullah Safi had an idealized faith respectively in Islam and tribal honor, but their experience and education led them both to believe that they could no longer continue on the paths laid out for them by their fathers. It was not enough to be a religious teacher or tribal chief. The expansion of the state made the very existence of those positions tenuous, and so both sought new venues within which to redirect the state's power. For Samiullah Safi, that venue was the parliament, which he viewed as the best place to push the state to become more responsive to the needs of the people. Going against the advice of his father, he ran for and was elected to parliament, but he found there a body of men all speaking for themselves with little commitment either to the institution itself or to the principles of democratic representation. When that institution was disbanded following Daud's coup d'état, Samiullah began a long period of inactivity that ended when a second Marxist coup d'état gave him a second chance at reconciling the disparate strands of his life.

Qazi Amin's story diverges from Samiullah's somewhat in that the venue he chose for keeping alive the faith of his fathers was a political party of student peers. Qazi Amin made this choice at a time when the ulama were generally complacent or ineffectual in the face of growing challenges to and indifference toward religion, particularly within the urban elite. In an earlier age, someone like Qazi Amin probably would have become the head of a madrasa, a judge, or a deputy to one of the major Sufi pirs in the country, but religious education and Sufism were both in decline when he was a young man. The great Islamic leaders of old were dead, and most of those who inherited their sanctity as birthright were either content with the wealth handed down to them or ensconced on the government payroll. The choice for Qazi Amin was either to take the job offered to him and ignore the larger problems he perceived in the country or to seek a new institutional setting within which to defend Islam. The interstitial space of the university campus allowed the formation of novel sorts of groupings—students of Islamic law with engineers, Pakhtuns from the border area with Tajiks from the north, Sunnis with Shi'as, and all of them young people, unrestricted by the usual protocols of deference to elders.

Kabul University offered a context for youthful political zeal different from any that had existed before; it is probably not an exaggeration to state that at no other time or place was such a diverse group of young Afghans able to meet together and to formulate its own ideas, rules of order, and plans for the future without any interference from those older than themselves. Some of the senior members of the Muslim Youth did have connections with faculty mentors. Abdur Rahim Niazi, in particular, was reported to have had close ties with Professor Ghulam Muhammad Niazi, who had spent some time in Egypt, where he had been acquainted with members of the Muslim Brotherhood, the prototype for many radical Islamic parties. However, presumably because they held government positions that could be taken away, Professor Niazi and other faculty members limited their role to private meetings with a few student leaders and never came out publicly in support of the student party. This reticence severely restricted their influence and also meant that as the confrontations on campus heated up, no moderating influence was available to push compromise or reconciliation. In certain respects, this experience was a liberating one, and it allowed new winds to blow into the ossified culture of Afghan politics. However, unhinged from traditional patterns of association, the student political parties were ultimately a disaster for Afghanistan, for as they were cut off from the past, living entirely in the cauldron of campus provocations and assaults, student radicals developed a political culture of self-righteous militancy untempered by crosscutting ties of kinship, cooperation, and respect that elsewhere kept political animosities in check.

The Muslim Youth, like their contemporaries in the leftist parties, abandoned (at least for a time) the ancient allegiances of tribe, ethnicity, language, and sect on which Afghan politics perennially had rested. In their place, young people took on new allegiances, professing adherence to ideological principles they had encountered only weeks or months before and swearing oaths of undying fealty to students a year or two older than themselves. These loyalties were kept alive through a paranoid fear of subversion. Only other members could be trusted; every other person was a potential spy, an enemy out to destroy the one true party of the faithful. Marxists and Muslims were tied together in ways they did not recognize at the time. Sworn enemies, they also needed—and ultimately came to be mirror images of—one another, linked together by their tactics, their fears, their confrontations, and their self-righteousness. Each believed that its enemies were wrong, that they alone held the key to Afghanistan's future. Each side also believed that violence in advancement and defense of a cause such as theirs was appropriate and ultimately necessary.

The religious moralism and suspicion that first took root in the soil of the new democracy at Kabul University reached its full flowering a decade later in Peshawar with the rise to power of Hizb-i Islami. The constant attention to the behavior of others that was evident in the first generation of Muslim student activists was extended in the second generation, as Hizb members watched how they and others dressed—Hizbis could be identified by the neatness of their clothing and the white skullcaps (*jaldar*) that most wore— how long they and others wore their hair and beards, and whether and how often they attended mosque and which mosque they frequented. In Kabul, there had been an element of play in the actions of the Muslim Youth. They were engaged in a game of "gotcha" with Marxist students that was played in the insulated confines of the university campus. After the coup in 1978, however, the game turned deadly serious, and the monitoring that went on in Peshawar was no longer associated just with party promotion but with disgrace and sometimes assassination.

The evolution of Qazi Amin's increasingly revolutionary persona can be glimpsed in the three photographs contained in Figure 11. The photographs are all studio shots taken at different stages of Qazi Amin's early life—the first when he was a taleb in his late teens at the Hadda madrasa; the second when he was a student in his early twenties at Kabul University; and the third when he was in his thirties and a leader of Hizb-i Islami. The three photographs, which Qazi Amin provided to me, are simple head shots of the type that could be used for an identity card. In the first, he looks like a typical madrasa student, with a sparse, patchy beard and cheap cotton turban. The second photograph shows a man more concerned with his appearance. The turban is gone. His hair is neatly combed and the beard trimmed close

to his face. The coat and tie were common in pictures of university students of that period, but the beard also tells us of his commitment to Islam, as more secular students almost always favored a mustache or clean-shaven look. In the third photograph, the suit coat remains, but the tie—which is identified with Western fashion—has been jettisoned. Though we cannot see the rest of his clothes, it is likely that the Western-style trousers he wore at the university have been replaced by traditional pantaloons (*shalwar*). On his head is the sort of karakul cap favored by mid-level Afghan government officials, which the man in the picture could be were it not for the full, untrimmed beard. This is the look Qazi Amin continued to favor in later years, except that the karakul cap was replaced by turbans—sometimes white, in the fashion of Muslim scholars, sometimes of the dark, striped sort worn by Afghan tribesmen (Fig. 12).

Perhaps more interesting in these photographs than the changes of look and style is the set of the eyes. The boy in the first photograph looks at the camera with guilelessness, his eyes wide; perhaps he is facing a lens for the first time. The young man in the second photograph seems at once more self-confident and earnest but also more affected and aware of his appearance. His back is noticeably straighter, and one suspects that he is looking not only at the camera but also at his future. The third man is identifiably the same person as in the other photographs, but he has gained a solidity that was absent before. That solidity derives partially from the fact that he is heavier now and has a longer, darker beard that curls out from his cheeks and down over his collar. It derives also from the lambskin cap, which seems

11. (left and opposite)   Qazi Amin
(courtesy of Qazi Amin).

12. (below)   Qazi Amin speaking at
the dedication of a new high school,
Kot, Ningrahar, post-1989 (courtesy
of Qazi Amin).

to push down on his head. But even more it comes from the look in his eyes—fierce, resolute, and unwavering. This is not a man who you would imagine spends a lot of time laughing. It is a man focused on the task in front of him, a man used to making decisions and ordering other men around. It is also a man of conviction—a man determined in his course of action, a revolutionary.

7 Fault Lines in the Afghan Jihad

When I interviewed Qazi Amin in 1984, we met in the nondescript, concrete building on the outskirts of Peshawar that he used for his personal office. There were many such buildings on the western fringe of Peshawar, which was in the midst of a massive construction boom, a result of the influx of arms, money, and drugs that followed in the wake of the Soviet invasion of Afghanistan and the migration of more then three million refugees to Pakistan. Qazi Amin's office was on the floor of a ground-level room looking out on a scraggly garden. There were no chairs or couches. He sat cross-legged on one of the three uncovered foam mattresses that lined the sides of the room. His briefcase doubled as his desk, and on a short pine table off to the side he kept stacks of books, mostly on religious subjects, including one that advised which suras of the Qur'an to recite for different disorders such as insomnia and marital discord. There was also a box of teacups and saucers ready for guests, a telephone close at hand, a bell that he used to summon his servant or assistant, and a notepad with Hizb-i Islami letterhead stationery and an official stamp, which he used to authenticate the letters and directives he sent out to various subordinates and associates. I also noted a large hole in the upper corner of one wall, I assumed for the eventual installation of an air conditioner. Construction in Pakistan was so frenzied at that time that builders rarely planned ahead or worried about the end use of their buildings. Consequently, in many of the homes and offices I visited, I found similar gaping holes made after the fact to accommodate wiring or gas fixtures or air-conditioning units.

When Qazi Amin was at home, his bodyguards lounged in the room next to the office, where one of his assistants could be found punching away at a Persian typewriter. Outside, the garden was filled with young Afghan men who milled about while awaiting the opportunity to meet with the leader.

Some would request his assistance in getting a ration card or an increase in their allotment of food supplies or a family member admitted to a hospital; others were there looking for a job or funds for one worthwhile project or another. In the compound of every major and minor leader in Peshawar, a similar scene took place every day, and Peshawar was full of leaders—from the heads of the Afghan parties to the directors of the parties' myriad committees, directorates, and offices. And there were the hard-eyed commanders, just in from the provinces and trailed by a pack of scruffy-looking mujahidin, making their way from office to office in search of the weapons and supplies they needed to go back for more fighting. Peshawar was full of leaders, but as everyone knew, no one was in charge.

In this chapter, I examine the evolution of the Islamic party infrastructure in Peshawar, focusing in particular on the transformation of the Muslim Youth Organization into Hizb-i Islami Afghanistan and the role of Hizb in fashioning the fragmented and vituperative refugee political culture of the mid-1980s. Trying to conduct fieldwork in this environment (for eighteen months from 1982 to 1984 and for six months in 1986), I found the profusion of parties puzzling, particularly since Islam had seemed such a taken-for-granted but politically insignificant part of Afghan society a decade earlier, when I lived in Kabul. I also found all the party business and the readiness of Afghans to speak of it, usually in disparaging terms, something of a bad joke and not easy to take seriously. On one level, it seemed like so much individual bickering and power grubbing—all sound and fury, signifying nothing. But it was there, the political culture of the moment, and I spent most of my time trying to make sense of it. In retrospect, I attribute greater importance to the political machinations swirling around me back then. Specifically, I see that they made possible the rise of the Taliban, for that movement was a direct response to the infighting within the Islamic resistance, which was becoming increasingly bitter during the period I was conducting research. The fissioning of the resistance climaxed after the Soviet pullout in 1989, when the parties were engaged in an armed struggle for control of Kabul. However, the process that culminated then had its origins in the period between the Marxist revolution of 1978 and the founding of the radical (seven-party) and moderate (three-party) alliances in September 1981. This was the formative period of the Islamic resistance—when the fault lines that later sundered it first revealed themselves—and it is vital to understand what transpired then in order to make sense of what happened later.

In preceding chapters, I discussed several factors in the early ascendance of Islam. Here, I take up the matter of how the Islamic jihad failed. Specifically, I am concerned with how there came to be ten separate parties in Peshawar, all claiming to represent Islam, all claiming to represent the best interests of Islam, all working to advance their own interests and to undermine the interests of their rivals.[1] In previous encounters between Islam and the state, a variety of religious figures had often been involved, but they generally were in agreement about the meaning of Islam and about the sect or school that was most entitled to paramount status. Thus, leaders like the Mulla of Hadda and Mulla Mushk-i Alam, who played a prominent role in the Second Anglo-Afghan War (1878–1880), could unite other religious figures behind them, in part because they thought of themselves and were thought of by others as scholars, Sufis, and reformers—not as potential kings. During the early stages of the counterrevolution against the Khalqi government, however, the façade of Islamic unity crumbled as philosophical differences became magnified and rivals competed for power among themselves with greater alacrity than they showed in their prosecution of the conflict with the Kabul regime.

Muslims generally agreed that a cornerstone of their faith is the principle of God's singularity. For Muslims, God is one, indivisible, and eternal, but the preeminent characteristics of the Islamic resistance in Afghanistan were multiplicity, fragmentation, and impermanence. The evolution of this disjuncture can be traced through a series of sequential ruptures that occurred between 1975 and 1980, in each of which an effort at unifying the resistance was followed by confrontation and the establishment of a new political party. The creation of new factions followed familiar patterns related to the particular nodes of Islamic authority that had long existed in Afghanistan as well as to more recent innovations. The flight to Peshawar brought together representatives of all the Sunni Islamic traditions active in Afghanistan, and while these representatives were all more or less dedicated to the cause of jihad, they had different approaches and often violent disagreements with one another over who should lead the jihad and how it should be conducted.[2] At the time, it seemed that many of these tussles were the result almost solely of personal ambition rather than of more meaningful social and political divisions, but it is clearer today—especially since the emergence of the Taliban—that these disputes had a larger significance than was then apparent. In what follows, I describe these divisions in the chronological order in which they occurred, the principal personalities involved, and the relationship of particular disputes and ruptures to the evolving structure of Islamic authority in Afghanistan.

THE LAST SUFI

Daud's coup d'état initiated a new era of politics in Afghanistan. Though groups like the Muslim Youth had been involved in violent demonstrations prior to the coup, the focus of most of their anger was the leftist student groups. From this point on, however, attention turned to the government itself, and the major concern became how to unseat President Daud himself. The Muslim Youth Organization was not alone in changing direction. Other underground Islamic political parties also began making plans to overthrow the government. These included three parties with strong links to the military officer corps that joined forces as Hizb-i Tauhid (the Monotheism Party) under the leadership of a Sufi pir named Maulana Muhammad Attaullah Faizani whose life story interweaves traditional and modern elements in a unique way. Born in 1924 in western Herat Province, Faizani grew up in a family of *miagan* (descendants of a venerated saint) and religious scholars, from whom he gained his primary education, and he later chose to attend the teacher-training college in Kabul.[3] Faizani began teaching in Herat in 1947 but quit after a few years, first to travel to other Muslim countries in search of Islamic knowledge and, then, for three years, reportedly to live a life of purification, fasting, and meditation in a secluded cave. After this period of ascetic retreat, Faizani resumed his traveling and ended up in Mazar-i Sharif, where he became enmeshed in his first political controversy after delivering a sermon in which he criticized the corrupt practices of clerics, government officials, and feudal landlords.

This incident led to the first of several arrests resulting from his defamation of those wielding power. Between prison stays, Faizani established a Sufi khanaqa, or center, near Pul-i Khumri in northern Baghlan Province, where he managed to secure a growing following, particularly among teachers, students, and mid-level military officers and government officials. He also attracted the attention of local clerics, who resented his popularity and accused him of claiming to have extraordinary spiritual powers. These accusations led to another arrest and a two-year prison term. Undeterred, he participated in the organization of the Pul-i Khishti demonstration shortly after his release in 1969, which resulted in his fifth stint in prison, this time for a year and a half. When he was released in 1970, Faizani remained in Kabul, where he set up a library near the Pul-i Khishti mosque and presided over weekly zikr ceremonies. Faizani's library and zikr circle attracted numerous visitors, including Muslim Youth leaders like Engineer Habib-ur Rahman and Maulavi Habib-ur Rahman, and many government officials and military officers. When Daud executed his coup d'état, Faizani was initially supportive, as he had long opposed the corruption of the monarchy, but he became increasingly pessimistic about the direction in which Daud was leading the government, and this pessimism led to his association with Hizb-i Tauhid. Despite the involvement of several high-ranking military officers, Hizb-i Tauhid was short-lived, as its plans for a coup d'état against the government were uncovered. Faizani was once again imprisoned, along with a number of his principal disciples and supporters, and he was still in prison when the Khalqis took power in 1978. Though his exact fate has never been ascertained (some disciples believe he is in occultation), it is probable that he was executed with other political prisoners before the Soviet invasion in 1979.

Maulana Faizani is one of the most interesting and enigmatic figures in contemporary Afghan history. In many respects, his life story is an updated version of the Mulla of Hadda's; the Sufi elements of his story are numerous—the period of youthful wandering followed by a lengthy retreat from society, the fearless disregard for secular authority, the clashes with traditional clerics and government officials, the claims of supernatural powers, the devotion of his disciples.[4] All these are standard features of saintly hagiography, but Faizani was a man of the modern age as well. Educated and knowledgeable about science and technology, he differed from many traditional scholars and Sufis in wanting to integrate spiritual and secular forms of knowledge. In a time of general decline for Sufism, when most of the established saintly families had lost their influence and clerics either ignored science or claimed it was an infidel trick, Faizani espoused a mystical theology that embraced science and technology as ways of understanding and appreciating God's creation.

For Faizani, science and politics were important and necessary activities, though he claimed that both were secondary to spiritual enlightenment, which had to precede and govern them. Only a person with knowledge of God could fully comprehend science's capabilities or the political needs of the moment, and the way to achieve that knowledge was first and foremost through study of the Qur'an and the Sufi practice of zikr. Even this process, though, was susceptible to refinement of a modern sort, as one of Faizani's disciples explained:

> In this age due to the progress and advance of science and other technological fields the spiritual methods have also changed. For instance, we are able to travel the distance [that used to take] one month in one or two hours. Similarly by adopting new methods we can gain spiritual understanding in a very short time. In this advanced age of science there is very little need for seclusion, and physical hardship. In old days it took many

years to attain self-purification. Nowadays we can gain the inner purification in a very short time, provided we put into practice the teachings of
Maulana Sahib [Faizani].[5]

Faizani was threatening to traditional clerics not only because of his syn-
thetic approach to spirituality and science but also because of his ecumeni-
cal openness to people from a variety of backgrounds. A native Pakhtu
speaker, he wrote mostly in Persian, and his followers included many Shiʾas
as well as Sunnis like himself. Hizb-i Tauhid, the party he helped to form
after Daud's coup, was equally inclusive, bringing together sectarian groups
that had formerly worked separately from one another.[6] After Faizani's
arrest, no other Afghan religious leader was able to unite Sunni and
ShiShiʿaa followers, and, with his arrest and the breakup of Hizb-i Tauhid,
activists from these two principal Islamic sects tended to go their separate
ways and have remained disunited to the present.[7] For a brief time, the
Muslim Youth did manage to hold the loyalty of some Shiʾa students, but
most of the prominent Shiʾas in the Muslim Youth also worked with Faizani
and were arrested with him after his failed coup attempt. Thereafter, the
Muslim Youth remained solidly Sunni in orientation and made few inroads
in Shiʾa areas. Some Shiʾas would later come to Peshawar seeking arms from
the Sunni parties in control there, but the alliances struck in this context
were strictly pragmatic. No leader since Faizani has been able to engender
true cross-sectarian loyalty, and these divisions are more pronounced now
than ever before.

Faizani probably enjoyed his greatest support among military officers.
He used the traditional zikr circle as an avenue not just for spiritual enlightenment but also for political organizing. In tapping into the officer corps in
this way, Faizani was following a longstanding tradition of Sufi association
with the military, a tradition that went back at least to the turn of the century and that had periodically generated considerable paranoia within the
government.[8] Indeed, one of the early points of contention between Amir
Amanullah and the Hazrat of Shor Bazaar and other prominent Sufi pirs in
the mid-1920s was the amir's attempt to forbid members of the military
from active participation in Sufi circles. Amanullah recognized the conflict
of loyalty that could emerge when officers swore fealty to both their secular leader and a spiritual mentor, a conflict that played itself out when the
Hazrat and other leaders called on their disciples within the military to take
up arms against the king. Many believe that Daud faced the same threat
from Faizani and his followers. Although, ultimately, Marxist cadres in the
military undid Daud, many believe that the Muslim officers were more

politically active—if also less fortunate—than the Marxists. The arrest of Faizani and many of his leading disciples forestalled this burgeoning movement, however, effectively crippling Muslim organizing efforts within the military and ultimately making it far easier for Hafizullah Amin to intensify his recruitment within the officer corps in the years leading up to the Saur Revolution.

Another feature of Faizani's leadership was his ability to appeal to younger people. Some of Faizani's surviving disciples contend that he was closely aligned with Abdur Rahim Niazi, the founder of the Muslim Youth Organization, and that it was Faizani who originally convinced Niazi to enroll in the university in order to recruit students away from Marxism to the Muslim cause. This assertion is impossible to prove, but there is evidence that Engineer Habib-ur Rahman, probably the leading member of the Muslim Youth after Niazi's death, was a Faizani ally. A number of informants have told me that Rahman was a frequent visitor to Faizani's library and zikr circle and was at least aware of, if not involved in, the organization of Hizb-i Tauhid's planned coup d'état. He was also among those arrested when the coup d'état was uncovered, and he was executed with other plotters in 1974.

After Engineer Habib-ur Rahman's death, the Muslim Youth turned away from alliances of this sort, keeping to themselves and trusting no one other than those whose loyalty to the party was assured. They also took to disparaging Faizani and his role in the Islamic movement. Thus, when I asked members of Hizb-i Islami who had previously been in the Muslim Youth about the activities of Maulana Faizani, I generally received condescending replies: Faizani was an old-style pir who had his disciples engage in the Sufi practice of repeatedly reciting God's name in zikr circles rather than organizing them politically:

> Faizani's approach to political things was different from that of the Muslim Youth. We were trying to challenge the communists right away in the university. We said that if we wait until every Afghan becomes a religious scholar, it will take ages, and then finally we will all become communists. So now is the time: if you don't stop the spread of communism on the university campus, you won't be able to stop it tomorrow. . . . Our belief was that the Russian plan was to bring communism through the educational institutions and to bring intellectual communism to Afghanistan. They were giving a lot of Afghans scholarships because of their long-run plans. . . . Hundreds of Faizani's own men went to the Soviet Union for training. When Daud was toppled [in 1978,] no one knew what had happened except the Muslim Youth, who explained to the people that it was a Soviet move.[9]

In seeking spiritual reform as a prelude to political reform, Faizani was in fact following a venerable Sufi adage that jihad against infidels or corrupt rulers was the "lesser" jihad compared with the "greater" spiritual jihad that the individual carried out against his own baser instincts and motivations (*nafs*). To the Muslim Youth, however, talk of "greater" and "lesser" jihads only mystified what was going on in the country, and this confusion made it easier for leftists to gain an advantage.

When I was conducting research in Peshawar in the mid-1980s, I could identify only two of Faizani's disciples who had escaped arrest. They had become active with other parties, not having the wherewithal or support to organize a movement of their own, but they maintained their loyalty to their absent spiritual mentor. Both disciples believed that Faizani was still alive, despite the prevalence of reports indicating that he had been executed either by President Daud or after the Khalqi takeover. One of the men told me that he thought Faizani was possibly in a state of spiritual occultation, waiting for the right moment to return.[10] The other man believed that Faizani might have been taken to the Soviet Union but that he could use his supernatural powers to come back whenever he chose. This disciple told me that Faizani was, in fact, the "deputy of the messiah of the end of time" (*khalifa-i mahdi akhir al-zaman*) and could not be contained, controlled, or killed by any secular power. So he and other true believers waited patiently for Faizani's reappearance, when his true status would be revealed and the mess in Peshawar would be set right.[11]

The most interesting aspect of these stories is how they connect to a venerated tradition of Sufi hagiography. In *Heroes of the Age*, I recount several stories regarding the Mulla of Hadda and his deputies that also involved miraculous escapes from prison and other acts of defiance against the state. Faizani's disciples kept that tradition alive, but in my experience they were the only ones to do so. In the many interviews I conducted, I never heard any stories like these concerning any other contemporary religious figure, though I knew that the stories themselves were still remembered from the past because I collected a large number about the Mulla of Hadda and his circle during this same period, as well as miracle stories about common mujahidin who had been martyred in the fighting.[12] It seemed that the kind of mystical power associated with the saints of the past and the veneration that went along with it were almost entirely absent from popular attitudes toward the leaders of this jihad and that Faizani was perhaps the last of the breed of old-style Sufi saints to whom were attributed supernatural deeds and powers. As discussed later in this chapter, heredity leaders of Sufi tariqats like Sibghatullah Mujaddidi and Sayyid Ahmad Gailani would emerge as significant players in the Peshawar milieu, but their leadership was based on their being offspring of famous pirs rather than on any mystical power or charisma of their own. Faizani, however, was a self-made Sufi from the premodern mold whose reputation rested on his personal magnetism and spirituality as well as his political activities, and no comparable figure has emerged since his arrest and disappearance.

— *//* —

Faizani is largely a forgotten figure today, but it is worth remembering him, if only to note what the Islamic jihad did not become. While there would be many subsequent attempts to establish a unified Islamic front in the wake of the Soviet invasion, Faizani's was the first and, in many respects, the most genuine, in that his following extended across regional, sectarian, class, and professional lines. It is impossible to know whether this alliance would have stayed together if Faizani had managed to escape to Pakistan. Probably its success would have depended on the survival of certain of his key disciples, notably General Mir Ahmad Shah Rizwani, his leading follower in the military, and Engineer Habib-ur Rahman, his leading ally within the Muslim Youth. With the arrest of Rizwani, networks within the military became severed. Rahman's arrest left the leadership of the Muslim Youth in the hands of Hekmatyar, who was not known to be interested in Sufism or sympathetic to alliances with other Islamic groups, preferring instead to stake out control of the jihad for the Muslim Youth alone.

Likewise, Faizani would probably have found Peshawar a less sympathetic place to operate than Kabul, and not just because of the fractious political climate that developed in Pakistan. Faizani was fluent in Persian, and though he himself was a Pakhtun from the Kakar tribe and had many Pakhtun followers, his core group of disciples was from Kabul and the Persian-speaking regions. Peshawar, however, was overwhelmingly, even belligerently Pakhtun, and Persian speakers felt themselves at a disadvantage there. Pakhtuns newly arrived in Kabul from the provinces were often made to feel that they were country bumpkins. However, Kabul was a more welcoming city than Peshawar, and even the roughest Pakhtun could eventually feel at home there. Indeed, several generations of rural Pakhtuns came of age in the tribal boarding schools of Kabul, learning Persian and becoming a part of the city's cosmopolitan culture. Peshawar was a less inclusive city that incubated Pakhtun chauvinism, which is a reason why one saw relatively few non-Pakhtun refugees on the streets of Peshawar during the 1980s. The need for weapons and supplies ensured that Tajik, Uzbek, and other non-Pakhtun mujahidin groups would come and pay their respects to the party bosses. However, they tended not to stay long, and they rarely brought their families with them; when they did, they usually settled them in refugee camps in the Mardan and Hazara districts, as far from Peshawar and the Pakhtun tribal areas as possible.

Faizani might have overcome the problem of language and ethnic background on the strength of his personality, but he would also have had to confront the fact that Sufism of the sort he practiced had little purchase in the refugee world created in Peshawar. During my research, I visited a few Sufi pirs who oversaw zikr circles, but these were generally low-key affairs, held sporadically in out-of-the-way camps and mosques. The only other pir who combined spirituality and politics and enjoyed general respect was Miagul Jan, the son of the Mulla of Tagab, who was one of the Mulla of Hadda's principal deputies. Many people told the story of how the communists unsuccessfully tried to bomb Miagul Jan in his mosque and how his disciples carried him on a bed all the way to Pakistan. The tone of these stories was invariably respectful, even sometimes rather awestruck, but as the story implies, Miagul Jan was an old man when he fled Afghanistan, and, shortly after his arrival in Pakistan, he left to spend his few remaining days in Mecca. In 1983, I attended the "turban-tying" ceremony (*dastarbandi*) by which his son was anointed as his successor. However, the son, while respected, clearly was not venerated with the same fervor as his father had been, and he did not have the kind of intensely devoted following his father enjoyed.

With the exception of Sibghatullah Mujaddidi and Sayyid Ahmad Gailani, who are discussed later in the chapter, none of the pirs in Peshawar had any significant role in the jihad, and it seemed to me that the personalistic ties of respect and deference that had traditionally bound disciples to their pirs no longer mattered as much as they once had, except to the few scattered souls who still found individual solace in Sufism.[13] A Sufi pir like the Mulla of Hadda developed over many years a base of support that allowed him to mobilize thousands of disciples to take part in any battle he thought worth fighting. These battles are what is remembered best about the Mulla and others like him, but it is forgotten that preceding these conflicts—and making them possible—were years of daily encounters between the master and his disciples. Devotees of the pir would travel long distances to his center, eat from his langar, and wait to sit in his presence in order to receive a few minutes of his time. In Peshawar, this kind of spiritual devotion was not in evidence, and party leaders like Hekmatyar ensured that a new model of relationship would take hold in its place—the model of the authoritarian political party.

THE RADICALS

Following the failure of the Faizani coup d'état and the subsequent arrests of numerous Muslim militants, leaders of the Muslim Youth Organization and other well-known Muslim figures fled to Peshawar. Among the refuge s were Qazi Amin's old friend and mentor Maulavi Habib-ur Rahman, Hekmatyar (Fig. 13), and one of their former professors at Kabul University, Ustad Burhanuddin Rabbani (Fig. 14). A Persian-speaking Tajik from northern Badakhshan Province, Rabbani had studied at madrasas in Afghanistan, graduated from the Faculty of Islamic Law in 1963, and then was employed to teach at the university. In 1966, he traveled to Egypt to study at al-Azhar, from which he received a master's degree in Islamic philosophy. While in Cairo, he became familiar with the activities of the Muslim Brotherhood and, on his return to Kabul, devoted himself to translating into Persian various works by Sayyid Qutb, the chief theoretician of that organization. He also resumed his position at the university and became closely associated with his fellow professor, Ghulam Muhammad Niazi, whom he served as secretary in 1969 and 1970. After Professor Niazi's imprisonment in 1974, the government reportedly sent police to arrest Rabbani at his campus office, but he was warned ahead of time and managed to flee to Peshawar, arriving there a few months after Hekmatyar, Maulavi Habib-ur Rahman, and other Muslim Youth leaders.

The most pressing issue for the refugees was deciding how to press their political agenda, and a split immediately developed between the younger group, which wanted to commence armed operations against the government, and Rabbani, who was more cautious in his approach and did not think the refugees were ready to begin an armed struggle. The dispute continued for some time, but while Rabbani was away in Saudi Arabia in the summer of 1975, the student group went ahead and initiated the abortive attacks that led to the arrest of many of the top student leaders. The failure of this plot decimated the Muslim Youth, as a number of the chief figures in the movement were arrested and later executed by the government.[14] Of equal importance, the uprisings cemented a lasting rupture between what was to become the Tajik-dominated wing of the party (which became known as Jamiat-i Islami Afghanistan) and the Pakhtun-majority wing (which was to become Hizb-i Islami Afghanistan). At the center of this dispute were Hekmatyar, who had been a strong advocate of the attacks, and Rabbani.

A Kharoti Pakhtun from northern Kunduz Province, Hekmatyar was a student in the School of Engineering at Kabul University when he became one of the founding members of the Muslim Youth Organization.[15]

13. Qazi Amin (right) with Engineer Gulbuddin Hekmatyar, Charasiab, post-1989 (courtesy of Qazi Amin).

Considered one of the most militant of all the Muslim activists, Hekmatyar was actively involved in many of the violent demonstrations that flared up on the campus of Kabul University in the early 1970s, including one in the spring of 1972 in which a member of the Maoist Eternal Flame party (Shula-yi Jawed) was killed. Whether he was responsible for this killing has been disputed, but there is little doubt as to his advocacy of violence in pursuit of political objectives. In the case of the uprisings carried out in 1975, criticism of Hekmatyar centers on the naïveté of the plan, its devastating impact on the party's leadership, and the fact that, while strongly supporting the attacks, Hekmatyar—almost alone among the party's student leaders—stayed in Peshawar rather than participate. Enemies of Hekmatyar have seen his noninvolvement as evidence that he wanted the uprisings to fail and its leaders to be captured so that he could consolidate his own power.

Another source of controversy and criticism of Hekmatyar concerns the purported existence of a military coup d'état that was supposed to happen concurrently with the attacks on rural government offices. According to one informant in Rabbani's party, those who were involved in the provincial attacks were told that once they had succeeded in securing their objectives,

14. Qazi Amin (with briefcase) with Professor Burhanuddin Rabbani (in dark suit coat), Saudi Arabia, n.d. (courtesy of Qazi Amin).

they were to listen on the radio for word of the progress of the Kabul coup attempt. If the coup succeeded, they were to stay in place. If it failed, they were to leave their positions and make their way back to Pakistan. Those who participated in the uprisings were assured that as soon as the troops in Kabul heard that the provincial operations had begun, they would immediately mobilize their own assaults. But in fact there is little evidence that a military coup d'état was under consideration or even conceivable following the arrest of Faizani's group. Engineer Habib-ur Rahman had been the Muslim Youth's chief contact with the military, along with Hekmatyar himself, and since Rahman's execution and Hekmatyar's flight to Pakistan, it appears that military recruitment and mobilization had effectively ceased. In the view of many of Hekmatyar's critics, the assumption that Muslim officers would mount an attack against the government when they heard word of the rural insurrections was no more than a wish, and on this feeble premise idealistic Muslim militants were sent off on their mission.

In their criticism of Rabbani, Hekmatyar loyalists contend that he was all along a moderate who had never had a significant role in the Islamic movement prior to his flight and therefore had no right to a leadership role in

Peshawar. Rabbani, it was charged, was an apologist for the government who supplied articles to government journals and associated with government officials. Some have even declared, without apparent evidence, that Rabbani informed friends in the government ahead of time of the planned uprisings and thereby contributed to their failure. Rabbani's involvement in the Islamic movement in Afghanistan prior to 1975 was a controversial issue, for precedence in the movement was one of the principal bases on which authority was premised. Hekmatyar's assertion of preeminence in the jihad was grounded in the early militancy of the Muslim Youth, originally against Zahir Shah and then against President Daud. Muslim Youth activists were the first to recognize the threat of Soviet communism in Afghanistan, and they had called for a jihad against the government before anyone else. On this basis and despite their youth and lack of Islamic credentials, they claimed the right to lead the resistance.

For Rabbani, what counted more than anything else was his close relationship with Professor Niazi, as well as his own early involvement in the Islamic movement inside Afghanistan. Because of Niazi's generally accepted status as the first Afghan to import the ideas of the Muslim Brotherhood in Egypt into Afghanistan, the question of who worked most closely with him prior to his arrest was a matter of great importance within the ranks of the Afghan Islamic leadership in Peshawar.[16] Members of Rabbani's Jamiat party claimed that Rabbani was Niazi's chief assistant, and while acknowledging that Rabbani's activities were necessarily carried out discreetly because of his position as a government employee, they asserted that he was actively involved with Niazi long before the founding of the Muslim Youth Organization. Further, they noted that Rabbani's role in translating works of Sayyid Qutb proved both his knowledge of and his commitment to Islamic reform, and they contended that he was selected as the leader of the original Jamiat-i Islami party in 1972 by a fifteen-member council that comprised "all active youths with leading members of Jamiat including Ghulam M. Niazi."[17] Hekmatyar and other members of the Muslim Youth discount this history, maintaining that the Jamiat party was founded in Peshawar only after the split between Hekmatyar and Rabbani and that the person closest to Professor Niazi was his student Abdur Rahim Niazi. The elder Niazi, they argued, was an enlightened man, but because of his position he would not take an active role in political activities. This role was assigned to the younger Niazi, through whose leadership the Muslim Youth Organization was founded and the Islamic movement was begun in Afghanistan. Rabbani, in this accounting, was a minor figure, a colleague of

Professor Niazi's in the Faculty of Islamic Law, but not himself a significant actor in the drama then beginning to unfold.

These claims and counterclaims will never be resolved conclusively since most of the principals are dead and those still alive are entangled in political arrangements that compromise their neutrality. However, the relative merits of the different positions aside, the dispute demonstrates the importance given to history and lineal succession as different parties jockeyed for position in Peshawar. In a politically turbulent and uncertain environment, Hekmatyar and Rabbani each made claims of precedence, rooting these assertions in their connection to venerated ancestors who were dead and could not contest claims made in their names. For Hekmatyar in particular, the issue of precedence was vitally important because he had little else to offer by way of justification for his leading the jihad. Still in his twenties, from an insignificant family and tribe, and without any substantial religious education or even a college degree, the only basis he could offer for leadership in the jihad was his connection to an obscure student group, most of whose members were now dead. Rabbani had better credentials. He was older, a respected scholar familiar with both the traditional madrasa and the university, a man of experience who had studied abroad and spoke numerous foreign languages.

The fact that Rabbani's partisans were forced to assert their leader's historical link to Niazi can be seen, at least in part, as an indication of Hekmatyar's success in dictating the terms of the debate over the right to leadership. It is also, however, a demonstration of the importance that lineality plays in Afghan culture. Lineality is the primary basis of tribal relations, just as it is in Sufi orders and madrasas, where claims to rights and privileges are premised on connections to respected mentors. In this light, the fact that both Hekmatyar and Rabbani wanted to prove their relationship not to a Sufi saint or a traditional religious scholar but to a little-known university professor speaks to the marginalization of the clerical establishment and the decline of the great saintly families. Regardless, this was one of the principal grounds on which Hekmatyar and Rabbani contested their claims to authority, and their inability to resolve their differences led to the first major rupture in the Peshawar-based community of Muslim refugees, as Hekmatyar and Rabbani became the heads of separate parties.[18]

This split occurred in the winter of 1976, at a time when Peshawar was beginning to fill up with Afghan religious leaders, among them Maulavi Jalaluddin Haqqani from Paktia, Maulavi Hussain from Pech, and Qazi Amin. The Afghan ulama in Peshawar were upset over the Hekmatyar-

Rabbani rupture and as Qazi Amin indicates, joined together to try to heal this rift in their ranks:

> We appointed a council of six people to try to find a compromise between Hekmatyar and Rabbani that would unite them. The council worked for about two months. The members of the council talked separately with each of them and asked them which one should be the leader. According to their own declarations, neither of them was ready to accept the other's leadership, so the neutral members of the delegation, who had more authority, proposed that there should be a third choice for amir. . . . The delegation said that they didn't want to choose the third person themselves. They had to confer with both sides to find a person that both of them would agree on. First, they asked Engineer Hekmatyar, and he mentioned two or three names. My name was among the names he mentioned. When they asked Rabbani to choose a possible third man, my name was again among the suggestions. Since my name was on the list of both of the opposed leaders, I was selected, and the dispute was solved.[19]

In this way on May 11, 1976, Qazi Amin was selected as the amir of the unified Islamic movement, which was given the name Hizb-i Islami Afghanistan. Both Hekmatyar and Rabbani agreed in the presence of the council to accept his leadership and merge their own factions within the unified party. Both were also included as members of the executive committee of this newly constituted party.[20] Though still small at this point, the Islamist movement that first developed at Kabul University seemed to have resolved its difficulties and put itself in a position to spearhead efforts against the Daud regime. Between them, Rabbani and Hekmatyar represented the faculty and student wings of the Islamist movement. That Rabbani was a Persian-speaking Tajik and Hekmatyar a Pakhtun was also significant for building a national front. So too was the fact that the executive council of the party included Maulavi Haqqani and Maulavi Nasrullah Mansur, who were more traditional clerics from Paktia Province, where earlier antigovernment movements had successfully developed, and Maulavi Hussein of Pech, the most important and visible representative of the reformist Panj Piri movement, which was influential in Kunar Province.

Qazi Amin's role as amir of the party is of particular interest here. Clearly a compromise candidate, Qazi Amin was not exclusively associated with any one group, and his lack of ties was his greatest advantage. In Kabul, he had been an important, but second-tier member of the Muslim Youth, more closely aligned with Maulavi Habib-ur Rahman than with Hekmatyar. Even though he was associated with the student wing of the movement, he was madrasa-educated and a graduate of the Faculty of Islamic Law, which undoubtedly made him more acceptable to Rabbani as well as to the clerics on the council. Finally, the fact that he was still living in Afghanistan during the uprisings of 1975 meant that he was not directly implicated in the still-bitter dispute over who was responsible for that disaster. What Qazi Amin was not, however, was a strong leader who brought strategic assets of his own to the party. Qazi Amin's role in the coalition was a traditional one for a cleric—that of the *stana*, or holy man, whose principal function was to mollify and mediate between the heavyweight factional leaders who otherwise would be at each other's throats. Qazi Amin was a fundamentally decent person who was not likely to play any tricks or push his own agenda on the council. Throughout the years of jihad, when treachery became standard operating procedure for many leaders, Qazi Amin maintained a reputation for trustworthiness, and this quality more than any other apparently gained for him the honor of being the first amir of Hizb-i Islami Afghanistan and the leader who issued the first formal declaration (*fitwa*) of jihad against the Afghan government. This declaration was distributed widely within Afghanistan in the last year of Daud's regime and spread the name of Hizb-i Islami throughout the country, so that when the Marxists succeeded in taking power in 1978, many ulama looked to this party and to Qazi Amin for leadership after they had fled to Pakistan.

During the time the party was united under Qazi Amin, the primary concerns were solidifying its organizational structure (a shura was established, articles of association and a manifesto were drafted, a party emblem was designed, and a newspaper was published), expanding its activities inside Afghanistan in order to establish more and more cells and branches, and attempting to generate financial support in the Arab Middle East—an activity in which Rabbani, with his command of Arabic, took the lead. The party also reportedly continued to pursue its political objective of overthrowing the government. The avenue of the military coup d'état was assayed unsuccessfully, but according to both Qazi Amin and Hekmatyar, the party did manage to dispatch hit squads to assassinate Afghan communist leaders.[21] Although most of the major leftist leaders were targeted, the only attack that ultimately proved successful was against the Parchami ideologue Mir Akbar Khyber. Ironically, this assassination precipitated the street demonstrations that led President Daud to arrest Taraki and Hafizullah Amin, who then launched the Saur Revolution in April 1978.[22] By this time, however, the united Hizb-i Islami under Qazi Amin's leadership had broken apart, with Rabbani establishing (in the fall of 1977) Jamiat-i Islami as a separate party and Qazi Amin and Hekmatyar staying in Hizb-i Islami.

A major point of contention between Rabbani and Hekmatyar was Rabbani's willingness to negotiate with the Afghan government. At the end of his tenure in power, President Daud was moving increasingly away from his Soviet allies and seeking new alliances with Saudi Arabia and the Shah of Iran. Rabbani spent much of the year prior to the Taraki coup in Saudi Arabia and reputedly was in contact with Daud's minister of justice, Wafiullah Sami'e, an old friend and former colleague of Rabbani's in the Faculty of Islamic Law. Rabbani's discussion with Sami'e supposedly concerned the release of imprisoned activists in Kabul as a sign of the regime's good faith. Despite this purported goal, however, which might have led to the release of many jailed members of the Muslim Youth, Hekmatyar opposed Rabbani's initiative on the grounds that it would diffuse the jihad and lead to Daud's remaining in power. Hekmatyar's opponents counter that Hekmatyar didn't want his own leadership undermined by the release of prisoners who had a better claim to leadership than his own. In any event, the effort—if it took place at all—proved futile, and the united Islamic front was already history well before the Marxists took power.

— ∥ —

The feud between Hekmatyar and Rabbani that began before the revolution proved to be one of the defining fault lines of the Afghan jihad and the subsequent civil war. Underlying this feud were the personal ambitions and animosities of the chief protagonists, but there were other factors as well—notably the generational divide that lay between them. Hekmatyar represented a younger generation, which came of age in the political confrontations that tore apart the Kabul University campus during the late 1960s and early 1970s. Hekmatyar's reality was shaped by his experiences as a member of the inner circle of the Muslim Youth, and, for him, all issues, relationships, and options were judged in relation to the party, its ideological tenets, and its organizational interests. Rabbani, however, grew up in a less polarized climate. Politics were subordinate to studies for most of his youth, and they took on importance only gradually as he was exposed to the Muslim Brotherhood in Egypt and then came back to Kabul to join colleagues in discussions about Afghanistan's future. These discussions were less tense and urgent for Rabbani, who found time to translate documents, teach, travel to foreign countries, and learn other languages. Rabbani ultimately was more open to compromise than Hekmatyar, in part at least because he had wider experience in and awareness of a world larger than Afghanistan. Like many university students, Hekmatyar lived in a world defined by personal experiences and peer relations. As his experiences became increasingly antagonistic and his peer relations narrowed to the confines of the party, Hekmatyar came to see all compromise as potentially threatening to the welfare of the party and his own leadership, and therefore he believed that it had to be opposed.

Another underlying factor in the feud between Rabbani and Hekmatyar was ethnicity. While it would be an overstatement to say that it was a cause of the feud, ethnic division within the resistance became one of the legacies of the dispute. In its first campus incarnation, the Muslim Youth Organization included Pakhtuns, Tajiks, and members of other ethnic groups, and the group around Professor Niazi was equally diverse. However, over time, Hizb and Jamiat, the two parties that claimed the mantle of the early organizing activity at Kabul University, became increasingly polarized along ethnic lines. During the Taraki and Amin period, Hizb and Jamiat had commanders on their rosters representing the range of ethnic groups found in Afghanistan. Thus, in Pakhtun areas like Kunar, Hizb and Jamiat mujahidin groups existed side by side in nearly every locality, and the same was true in Tajik-majority Kohistan, north of Kabul, and many other regions as well. However, that situation gradually changed during the course of the war, as Jamiat became increasingly associated with Tajiks and Hizb with Pakhtuns.

In certain respects, the division between Hizb and Jamiat can be compared with that between the Marxist Khalq and Parcham parties. In its early years, the PDPA had also included in its inner circle individuals from different ethnic and linguistic groups. Over time, this inclusiveness had broken down, and an atmosphere of distrust had taken hold. Like Hizb, Khalq recruited mostly among Pakhtuns and was the more militant of the two parties. Parcham's support came mainly from Tajiks, and it had a more experienced and moderate leadership, which was willing to compromise with the government in power to achieve its ends. As with Hizb and Jamiat, distrust within Marxist circles ultimately gave way to outright hostility and organizational schism, which helped obscure the common purpose the parties were striving for and ensured that neither would be able to get a solid hold on power for long.

One factor in the increasing ethnic polarization of the Islamic movement was the role of Ahmad Shah Massoud, the famous Jamiat commander in Panjshir Valley, who was minister of defense after the collapse of the Najibullah regime in 1992. Massoud was an early member of the Muslim Youth Organization, though not one of the inner circle. Like other members of the organization, he emigrated to Pakistan after Daud's coup and was one of those who went inside Afghanistan in 1975 to lead attacks against the government. His assault on the government offices in Panjshir failed, and a number of his compatriots were captured in the operation. Massoud, it appears, never fully forgave Hekmatyar for his role in these uprisings or trusted him again, and, after that time, Massoud generally stayed inside Afghanistan, rarely setting foot in Pakistan, in part because of his distrust of Hekmatyar. On his side, Hekmatyar showed a marked disdain for Massoud, as I discovered in an interview in 1983, when he derided the man the Western press was lauding as "the Lion of Panjshir."

THE CLERICS

The coming of the Khalqis brought with it a massive disgorgement of Afghan religious leaders over the border to Pakistan. Most of these leaders congregated in Peshawar and tried to make contact with the leadership of Hizb-i Islami, which they had heard of prior to their arrival because of the party's declaration of jihad and the clandestine distribution of publications critical of President Daud.[23] When they discovered that Hizb-i Islami had already split into two factions, newly arrived members of the ulama urged the principals to reunify, but Rabbani and Hekmatyar each refused to accept the other's party as the umbrella. The compromise that was arrived at this time was the creation of a new alliance that was to be called Harakat-i Inqilabi-yi Islami Afghanistan (the Revolutionary Islamic Movement of Afghanistan). After various candidates were proposed and rejected for the position of amir, the assembled members of the ulama decided in early September 1978 on Maulavi Muhammad Nabi Muhammadi as the leader of the new alliance.

Muhammad Nabi was a respected member of the ulama who had first come to public attention in 1969, when he was elected to the parliament from his home district of Barak-i Barak in Logar Province. As one of only a handful of religious scholars in the parliament, he took it upon himself to be a first line of defense against the Marxist deputies who constituted the most vociferous group in the parliament. Nabi's most famous experience in the parliament was the altercation with Babrak Karmal that led to Karmal's being hospitalized. When the parliament was dissolved by President Daud, Nabi returned to teaching in madrasas, first in Logar and then in Helmand, from where he emigrated to Quetta after the revolution. According to Muhammad Nabi, thirty Afghan religious scholars were in Quetta at that time, and they decided to send a delegation to Peshawar to obtain arms so that they could begin jihad in the southern part of the country. When the delegates arrived, they discovered that while neither Hizb nor Jamiat had extra weapons to provide, they were looking for a new leader to unify their parties, and both Hekmatyar and Rabbani accepted Nabi for the job.

Hekmatyar had known Nabi in Afghanistan. Unlike many members of the ulama who had been standoffish toward the Muslim Youth, Nabi had invited Hekmatyar and other leaders of the organization to graduation ceremonies at his madrasa in Logar, and when Hekmatyar was arrested, Nabi had tried to get him released. These prior contacts made Hekmatyar well-disposed toward Nabi, as did the fact that Maulana Maududi, who had been a longstanding supporter of the Muslim Youth Organization, urged Hekmatyar to accept Nabi as the leader of the alliance. These factors undoubtedly encouraged Hekmatyar to throw his support to the older cleric; but he also probably recognized that Nabi's status as a respected scholar and former parliamentary deputy would make him an acceptable compromise leader not only to the exiled ulama but also to the ordinary people inside Afghanistan whom the alliance needed to mobilize and lead.

In my interview with him in Peshawar in 1983, Nabi indicated that personally he had no interest in taking on this responsibility or even of staying in Peshawar, but he was forced to accept the position by his fellow clerics:

> A maulavi named Muhammad Gul, who was from Mashriqi and was an imam in Kabul, rose up, took hold of my hand, and said, "You look in the face of God and be afraid of God because they are disunited; they have destroyed themselves and destroyed the homeland. Today they form a union through you, and you say that you will think about it and give a positive or negative answer." He said to the meeting, "There is no negative answer. All of you raise your hands and pray that Maulavi Muhammad Nabi is amir."

Following Nabi's election, another informant told me:

> They announced that all the brothers of Hizb and Jamiat should come to the Masjid-i Madina in Sikandarpura [a mosque in one of the quarters of Peshawar] the next day. Then we all went and gathered, and all the members of Hizb and Jamiat declared their allegiance [bayat] to Maulavi Sahib Muhammad Nabi and gave their hands to him. [Dr. Musa] Tawana was the president of the conference and spoke as the representative of Jamiat. Engineer [Hekmatyar], Qazi Amin, and [Muhammad Jan] Ahmadzai also spoke, . . . and Muhammad Nabi gave his speech at the end. That day, there was so much crying and so much emotion from the people that the whole mosque trembled. With great affection and love, Maulavi Sahib Muhammad Nabi was selected as the president [ra'es] of the alliance. Tsaranwal Muhammad Rasul was so moved that he took out his pistol and called out that he would shoot anyone who broke the alliance.[24]

After this meeting, an office was opened, and all the committees of Hizb and Jamiat were officially disbanded or subsumed within Harakat. From this point on, every newly arrived refugee was referred directly to this office and was given clothing and a new pair of sandals and fifty rupees a month for expenses. Provincial committees were also established to coordinate resistance activities in each of the twenty-six provinces of Afghanistan. A number of experienced former military officers began to develop coordinated plans for the resistance. Symbolic of his new status, Nabi was taken to the Bala Hissar fort in Peshawar by Rabbani and Hekmatyar. There he was introduced to the Pakistani authorities in charge of Afghan refugee affairs as the elected leader of the Afghan resistance, who was henceforth in charge of relations with the Pakistani authorities and responsible for all assistance directed to the mujahidin.

Shortly after the establishment of Harakat, however, efforts began in earnest to undermine the alliance. Rumors began to spread that Nabi was incapable of organizing the party, that he hadn't done a day's work since the alliance was announced, and that his family members were draining the party coffers. During this period, a secret plan was also approved for an uprising by military officers in Qandahar, but the timing of the uprising was botched, information was leaked, and the government succeeded in capturing the officers involved in the plan. While the causes of this failure have never been adequately explained, many assume that the mix-up was brought about by either miscommunications within the leadership or outright sabotage by disaffected members of the party who wanted to see the alliance destroyed. Nabi himself was blamed by many of those involved in the Qandahar uprising. They had been told that Harakat had weapons and would support the operation, but support never appeared, and those involved were decimated. Nabi subsequently claimed that he had had no involvement in the order to begin the uprising in Qandahar, and he accused Hekmatyar and Rabbani of working behind his back.

About the same time, Hazrat Sibghatullah Mujaddidi, from the family of the famous Hazrat of Shor Bazaar, arrived in Peshawar, and Nabi asked him to join Harakat. Mujaddidi refused, however, setting up his own party instead, which Rabbani himself initially joined though he retained his membership in Harakat as well. Hekmatyar protested Rabbani's dual allegiance, and Rabbani eventually left Harakat to join Mujaddidi's party. Hekmatyar himself stayed in Harakat for a few more months. However, with Rabbani no longer a party to the alliance, Hekmatyar had no further obligation or reason to stay, and he soon abandoned Harakat to reestablish Hizb-i Islami.[25] In the following months, both Hekmatyar and Rabbani reportedly tried to convince Nabi to join their parties, but, with the encouragement of loyal ulama who refused to break their oaths of allegiance, Nabi decided to keep Harakat-i Inqilab-i Islami alive as a separate party to represent the Afghan madrasa-educated ulama. This party received strong backing and financial support from influential Pakistani clerics. Through this support, Harakat was able to rebound, with Nabi continuing as its head and Mansur serving as his deputy (mawen). In the new configuration of Peshawar parties, Harakat became known as the party of the ulama and religious students (taliban), the majority of whom joined its ranks and helped Harakat gain ground on Hizb and Jamiat in the competition to establish bases inside Afghanistan.

At the same time, what was to become a continuing dispute over the rightful leadership of Hizb-i Islami emerged between Qazi Amin and Hekmatyar. For several years, Hekmatyar had accepted Qazi Amin as the putative leader of Hizb in order to bolster the party's support among the ulama, with whom Qazi Amin continued to have good relations. With the establishment of Harakat as a separate ulama party, however, that pretense was no longer useful to Hekmatyar's purposes, and he demanded that the party have an election to choose its rightful leader. In a close vote, Hekmatyar won out over Qazi Amin, who then became Hekmatyar's deputy, a position that more accurately reflected the balance of power in the party. According to Qazi Amin, ulama tried to persuade him to leave Hizb after the election, and Nabi promised him a leadership position in Harakat if he joined. However, he decided to remain with Hekmatyar because, in his words, "I had a background in the Islamic movement and believed that in order to establish an Islamic government after jihad in Afghanistan, ulama alone can't run the affairs of the government."[26]

Another division occurred about this time that also affected Hizb-i Islami in its relations with the ulama. This split involved Maulavi Yunis Khales, another older cleric who—despite his age—had been aligned with the Muslim Youth Organization in the early 1970s. Educated in madrasas, he had spent part of his career as a civil servant in Kabul and part teaching in madrasas in his native Ningrahar Province. In addition to his ties to the Muslim Youth, he was also closely associated with Menhajuddin Gahez, who published the only independent Islamic newspaper, *Gahez*, during the late 1960s, when *Khalq*, *Parcham*, and other leftist and nationalist papers were stirring up so much controversy. Khales himself had been involved in political organizing during this period and wrote and translated several books on Islamic political philosophy, but he curtailed his activities and spent some time in Mecca after Gahez was assassinated by unknown assailants in 1970. Khales emigrated to Pakistan after his son, who was a member of the Muslim Youth, was arrested by the Daud government. He lived quietly for some time on the outskirts of Peshawar, serving as the imam of a mosque and running a shop in Land-i Kotal, outside of Peshawar, where he was when the Saur Revolution took place.

Initially, Khales played a minor role in party affairs because his son was still in prison and much of his family remained in Afghanistan. As other leaders were converging on Peshawar, he remained in his shop in an effort to persuade any spies who might be watching that he had given up politics and had become a simple shopkeeper. When the first split between Hekmatyar and Rabbani broke out, Qazi Amin and other clerics in the mediation group asked Khales to join them in their attempts to heal the breach, but Khales declined. Later, when Hizb and Jamiat were disbanded in favor of Harakat, Khales again refused to join, but this time he set aside his pose of detachment and formed a separate party with other madrasa-trained clerics, claiming for his party the name of Hizb-i Islami, which had been formally dropped when Harakat was formed. In an interview, Khales stated that he viewed the Hizb name, with which people were already familiar, as too valuable to abandon.[27] After the breakup of the Harakat alliance and the reestablishment of the original Hizb-i Islami under Hekmatyar and Qazi Amin, two parties continued to operate under this name—one in which younger students dominated and the other in which older clerics under Khales played the leading role.

Khales's reasons for refusing to join Harakat are obscure, and my own interview with him did not clarify matters. When I discussed the matter with Nabi, he indicated that he went to Khales to ask him to join Harakat, but Khales refused.[28] Khales, in response to the same question, stated, "I and some of my friends didn't accept him because he couldn't lead this union. He is a good scholar and can teach, but he can't do this work."[29] Khales may have had other reasons for his refusal, but it is also the case that, despite having secured the support of some excellent military commanders, Harakat had gained the reputation as one of the more corrupt and least well-organized parties, in part because of the abuses attributed to Nabi's son, who was his principal lieutenant. By contrast, Khales's group maintained a relatively positive reputation, mostly on the strength of its commanders, especially Abdul Haq in Kabul and Jalaluddin Haqqani in Paktia.

The relationship between Khales and Hekmatyar is also ambiguous. In part because of his son's involvement with the Muslim Youth Organization, Khales was more supportive of the students' efforts than were most older clerics, so much so in fact that Khales stored arms at his home in Ningrahar for use by Muslim Youth activists in the abortive uprisings in 1975.[30] Once in Peshawar, Khales quietly threw in his lot with Hizb-i Islami, before using the occasion of Nabi's ascendance to announce the formation of his own Hizb-i Islami. Khales had long been known for his independence and idiosyncrasies, but apparently the principal factor in this decision to establish his own Hizb-i Islami was his resentment at being subordinate to younger and less experienced men. Although he did not want to discuss the reasons for his split with Hizb in my interview with him, he did comment on Hekmatyar's lack of understanding of religious matters, a subject on which he had previously written a polemical pamphlet:

> The Muslim Youth wanted to do demonstrations and talk about the government, but we wanted to work deeply and bring about a theological revolution. Our work was ripe, but the work of the Muslim Youth was unripe, like young people themselves. The Muslim Youth would make up slogans just like the communists. [They would chant,] "Death to Zahir Shah," but they didn't know who would come after him if Zahir Shah was kicked out.[31]

To Khales, Hekmatyar and his followers were "unripe" (*kham*), and he questioned how Hekmatyar could claim to lead an Islamic jihad when he had only a rudimentary understanding of Islamic scripture. The term most commonly applied to Hekmatyar and the other erstwhile student revolutionaries by Khales and other older clerics was *maktabian,* or "schoolboys," which reflects the fact that most of them were young and had gone to state schools rather than madrasas. Some clerics were willing to forgive the maktabian their lack of training because their hearts at least were with Islam, but increasingly that sympathy was strained as the political environment in Peshawar became more polarized.

For their part, Hizb-i Islami adherents had a long list of complaints against Khales, Nabi, and other members of the ulama, beginning with their condoning of popular religious practices that had no basis in Islamic scripture. As various informants told me, the people had little understanding of Islam, and the ulama as a group did nothing to counteract that lack of knowledge. Islam in Afghanistan was confined to the mosque. A person would go there for prayers, but when he left the mosque, he would accept all kinds of laws that were against Islam. Likewise, they believed that most people used the Qur'an only for ritual and talismanic purposes. For example, when a person died, the family would invite a *qari* (someone who had memorized the Qur'an) to their home, and he would recite a few verses of the Qur'an. People also kept copies of the Qur'an in their houses for protection from fairies or jinns or so that a thief wouldn't steal something. Travelers embarking on a journey customarily passed under a copy of the Qur'an to ensure their safe return, and mothers placed verses of the Qur'an in lockets around their children's necks to keep them from physical harm and the evil eye. Aside from these ritualistic uses of the Qur'an, however, few people—so the Hizbis argued—knew anything of the sacred book's contents, and the ulama had to shoulder the blame for this state of affairs. They indulged the people in their superstitions and benefited economically from such abuses.

The Hizbis also condemned the backwardness of the ulama who, in the words of one informant, "just kept us busy with old philosophy."

> If our brothers talked with mullas about the scientific issues in the mosque, they would issue a fitwa of infidelity [takfir] against us. . . . They were severely antiscience. Even when they traveled in cars and planes, they would say that these were magic and that they would be destroyed once people hit them with swords. If we told them that America, the Soviet Union, and France had atomic bombs and could destroy the world, they would say that we were mad and told lies. If we told them that there was poverty and illiteracy in Afghanistan and urged them to learn about contemporary affairs, they would say that we had turned away from Islam.[32]

By contrast, Muslim Youth leaders were familiar with Western science and society, and, in the pamphlets they wrote and the speeches they delivered, they addressed scientific and social issues from an informed Islamic perspective that neither ignored nor condemned the intellectual and technological advances of the West. They were aware of the way leftists made fun of the "backwardness" of Islamic scholars and were intent on showing the compatibility of religion and science.

Another criticism of the ulama was their support of Zahir Shah when the Muslim Youth Organization was getting started. In the view of the Hizbis, the ulama's failure to recognize and respond to the infidelity of the monarchy created the need for the Muslim Youth to band together in the first place. Thus, citing one oft-mentioned example, a former member of the Muslim Youth noted how clerics employed by the government used Qur'anic passages to justify Zahir Shah's reign:

> Islam should be broadcast by the Department of Propaganda [tablighat], but the people who worked there used the Qur'an and hadith solely for the benefit of Zahir Shah and his government. For example, the Prophet (peace be upon him) said, "The Sultan is the shadow of God on the land." The ulama who worked for Zahir Shah would use this hadith to argue that Zahir Shah was "the shadow of God," but the purpose of this hadith is different. . . . The power and domination of God is the shadow on the land, not a person. The powers of God on the land are the Qur'an and

sunnat [religious obligations] established by the Prophet, [peace be upon Him]. Now, if the sultan or king is a follower of the Qur'an and hadith, God will assist him. If [God] is offended by him, then [the king] will be discredited. But, unfortunately, those ulama who worked in the government would say that Zahir Shah was the shadow on the land.[33]

Condemnations of government-employed ulama had a particular saliency in Peshawar since Khales had been an employee in a government ministry and Nabi had been a member of parliament who had accepted the king's sovereignty. As one former Muslim Youth activist noted, "What difference was there between Zahir Shah and Pharaoh? Pharaoh said, 'I am your God. I am the one that feeds you. I am the one that no one can question. You are my servants and must obey.' Zahir Shah also said, 'I am to be respected and cannot be held responsible. Anything I want, I will do.'"[34] At the same time, while the secularly educated Hizbis were quick to deride the ignorance and political cautiousness of the clerical class, they recognized that they had a problem in challenging their authority because the clerical class had one thing they were sorely lacking—working knowledge of Islamic scripture. Thus, while the younger activists could condemn the clerics for being backward and accepting un-Islamic practices back home, they were in a poor position to debate them on much of anything having to do with religion because of their own rudimentary familiarity with scriptural sources. By the time the Muslim Youth evolved into Hizb-i Islami, its adherents had been well schooled in revolutionary doctrines, but it was the older clerics who could quote line and verse of scripture and apply hadith to the variety of circumstances and disputes that arose on the battlefronts and in the Afghan diaspora. The clerics also bore the titles deriving from an Islamic education and enjoyed the respect of the people, and when it came time to issue a fitwa of jihad against the Khalqis, the bulk of the names on the document belonged to clerics. Theirs were the names people recognized and responded to, and they were the ones who knew the formal protocols of drafting and sending forth such a document.

Another of Khales's strengths in comparison with Hekmatyar was that he was as much a man of the tribe as he was a party leader. For Hekmatyar, the party was all-important, and as the events in Pech Valley illustrated, he and his subordinates never hesitated to undermine tribal alliances if it was advantageous for the party to do so. One of the marks of Khales's wing of Hizb-i Islami, conversely, was its ability to work with tribal leaders and to accommodate tribal customs, even if it meant contravening the formal dictates of Islamic law. I experienced this personally in the summer of 1984, when I visited mujahidin bases in Paktia Province that were run by Haqqani, Khales's chief deputy. Khales's local commanders worked closely with tribal leaders, sharing jurisdiction with them and allowing them to apply customary tribal law to resolve internal disputes. In areas controlled by Hekmatyar's Hizb, local commanders generally insisted that all disputes and criminal proceedings be handled according to Islamic law under the supervision of party leaders. Khales's commanders took a different approach, which helps to explain the considerable military and political success his groups enjoyed in the early 1980s in the areas under their jurisdiction; in comparison, the early victories of Hekmatyar's Hizb-i Islami were more modest.

THE GREAT SAINTS

As fractured as the political situation was by the winter of 1979, when Harakat and Khales's Hizb-i Islami were formed, it was about to get worse. This time, the principals were the scions of Afghanistan's two most prominent saintly families—Hazrat Sibghatullah Mujaddidi, the grandnephew of the Hazrat of Shor Bazaar, and Sayyid Ahmad Gailani, a descendant of the venerated twelfth-century Sufi saint 'Abd al-Qadir al-Jilani (d. 1166), known by many Sufi adherents as the *pir-i piran*—"the saint of the saints."[35] The involvement of these two men in the Islamic resistance began in the summer of 1978, when Mujaddidi, then living in exile in Copenhagen, traveled to Saudi Arabia to meet with Gailani, Rabbani, and a representative of Zahir Shah. Before going to Saudi Arabia, Mujaddidi had telephoned the former king to urge him to join him in Pakistan to rally the tribes against the Khalqi regime. In essence, it was 1930 all over again, when Sibghatullah's great uncle and Zahir Shah's father spearheaded the tribal assault on Kabul that deposed Bacha-i Saqao. This time, Sibghatullah would be playing the role of spiritual firebrand, and, like his famous forebear, he intended to be more than a figurehead:

> I contacted some leaders of the tribes—secretly. I called them to Peshawar. Some ulama from my own Jamiat-i Ulama Muhammadi [Society of Muhammadan Clerics]. They had come already. Some of them were here. . . . Then I went back. I contacted some friends in Saudi Arabia, Egypt—Afghanistan people. They were here, there, and everywhere—America, Europe. I said, "We have to arrange a meeting in Mecca. We came to Mecca—fifteen to twenty persons. Rabbani was also with us at that time. . . . And then we agreed that we should establish a front in this name—Jabha-yi Nejat-i Milli Afghanistan [Front for the National Salvation of Afghanistan]—and this front would be a platform for all the groups. . . . All the tribes, all the people must come together on one platform, under one umbrella.[36]

The result of the meeting was the formation of a new alliance (hereafter referred to as Jabha) with Mujaddidi as the amir and Rabbani serving as his deputy. Nabi and his deputy, Maulavi Mansur, initially agreed to fold their Harakat party into this new union, with each taking a seat on the council. Though not publicly involved, Zahir Shah was waiting in the wings, and his son-in-law and main advisor, Sardar Abdul Wali, was in close contact with Sibghatullah, pending the king's own appearance on the scene. Following the meeting in Mecca, Sibghatullah remained in Copenhagen, between trips to Pakistan, awaiting final permission from the Pakistan government to establish his base there. The Pakistanis, however, put him off for some time, probably because they saw the existing parties as more dependent and sub-servient to their wishes than a coalition involving Mujaddidi and the ex-king, both of whom had overseas backing and the ability to secure arms and resources on their own, without the help of the Pakistanis.

If this was the source of Pakistan's resistance to Mujaddidi's return, it was at least well reasoned, for no one was better positioned to break through the divisiveness that had prevented the formation of an Islamic alliance than Mujaddidi, members of whose family had been recognized as kingmakers for most of the modern history of Afghanistan. Descended from Sheikh Ahmad Sirhindi, the seventeenth-century mystic and philosopher, who is one of the central figures in the development of Sufism in the Indian sub-continent, the family claims to have come to Afghanistan originally at the behest of Ahmad Shah Abdali, the founder of the Afghan state, in the latter part of the eighteenth century.[37] Once ensconced, the family established an independent base of support, especially among the Pakhtun tribes of Paktia, Logar, and Ghazni. Members of the tribes in these areas became their disci-ples in the Naqshbandiya Sufi order.

The high-water mark of family political influence probably occurred in the late 1920s, when Fazl Umar Mujaddidi, known as the Hazrat of Shor Bazaar, helped to rally members of the ulama and several powerful Pakhtun tribes against the government of Amanullah. Given land, royal marriages, and influence in the councils of court following Nadir's victory, the family maintained its exalted position, but not its political edge. Most members of the extended family pursued secular careers in medicine, engineering, and business. Sibghatullah was an exception however. Born in 1925, he attended a secular high school in Kabul, but then chose to study Islamic law. Although he did not attend a formal madrasa, he was tutored in Islamic subjects at home and, through the intervention of his uncle, the former ambassador to Egypt, was admitted to al-Azhar University in Cairo, where he earned his degree in Islamic jurisprudence in 1953. Like Ghulam

Muhammad Niazi, who arrived in Cairo the year after him, Sibghatullah made his first forays into politics while in Cairo, meeting with Hasan al-Bana, Sayyid Qutb, and other leading figures in the Muslim Brotherhood and attending some of their meetings. After returning to Kabul, he taught at several secondary schools and the teacher-training college, and began meeting with like-minded scholars distressed by the government's policies, the increasing role of the Soviet Union in Afghan affairs, and the diminishing role of Islam in society generally. As a member of the Mujaddidi family and an effective speaker, Sibghatullah was one of the first Islamic leaders to attract the government's attention when he argued against Soviet involvement in Afghanistan. Since Prime Minister Daud was solidly aligned with the Soviets at that time and was busy wooing Soviet development assistance, Sibghatullah's pronouncements were embarrassing to the government, and in 1959 he was arrested on a charge of conspiring to assassinate Nikita Khrushchev during a state visit to Kabul. Despite his denials and the influence of his family, Sibghatullah, along with a number of family loyalists, was imprisoned for three and a half years, while other members of his family were prohibited from going outside the city to meet their disciples.

Sibghatullah's release from prison came at the beginning of a period of remarkable change in the Afghan state. In 1963, Prime Minister Daud was forced to resign his office after becoming enmeshed in an intractable dispute with the Pakistan government over the issue of sovereignty for the border tribes, and in 1964 Zahir Shah introduced the period of democratic liberalization. As a result of Zahir Shah's policy, there was the sudden relaxation of government control over political activity, the consequent emergence of previously covert or inchoate interest groups and political parties, and the establishment of a number of newspapers with widely disparate points of view. In this environment, the Hazrat family was coming increasingly to appear a throwback to an earlier era of political activism. The old Hazrat of Shor Bazaar had died in 1960, and his eldest son, Muhammad Ibrahim, had succeeded him as head of their Sufi order. While Muhammad Ibrahim took an active part in political affairs as the leader of the conservative faction in parliament and a loyal supporter of the monarchy, his influence with the emerging urban-based students, military officers, and government officials was negligible, and events such as the abortive Pul-i Khishti demonstration only reinforced the growing irrelevance of the family's traditional tribal/clerical coalition. The one member of the family with the credentials and capacity to take a leadership role in activist politics was Sibghatullah; but, despite his association with the Muslim Brotherhood and his stint in prison, he was denied membership in the Muslim Youth Organization when he applied and was thus effectively precluded from gaining access to the student population, which, as a teacher and activist, he considered his natural constituency. A second effort by Sibghatullah to develop a political party within the ranks of the ulama (Jamiat-i Ulama Muhammadi) also proved unsuccessful, although opposition in this case came not from the Muslim Youth but from his cousin Muhammad Ismail. The son of Muhammad Ibrahim, Muhammad Ismail seems to have viewed Sibghatullah's efforts as an attempt to usurp his role as heir apparent in the family, and he responded by forming a party of his own (Khodam ul-Forqan—Servants of the Qur'an), effectively negating the influence of both parties.[38] When Muhammad Daud overthrew Zahir Shah in 1973, Sibghatullah was attending an Islamic conference in Libya. Since he had long been at odds with President Daud, he chose to remain overseas with his immediate family, settling first in Saudi Arabia and later moving to Denmark, where he became the director of the Islamic center in Copenhagen. The head of the Hazrat family, Muhammad Ibrahim Mujaddidi, stayed on in Afghanistan with his family and appears not to have had any particular problems with the government but also not to have taken an active political role.

The other figure who appeared alongside Sibghatullah in 1979 at the founding of the Front for the National Salvation of Afghanistan in Saudi Arabia was Sayyid Ahmad Gailani, the second son of Naqib Sahib, a pir of the Qaderiya Order who was born in Baghdad. Naqib and his brother, Abdul Salam, both struck out for India early in the century, it being a common practice for the younger sons of renowned Sufi pirs to establish orders in new locations. Since he had had a Pakhtu-speaking tutor as a boy, Naqib was encouraged to move to Afghanistan but was initially prevented from doing so by Amir Abdur Rahman, who had enough problems with home-grown pirs without inviting an even more exalted personage from abroad to stir up additional intrigues. Consequently, Naqib lived in Quetta for a number of years before finally being invited to settle in Afghanistan in 1915, during the reign of Amir Habibullah, who welcomed him and provided an allowance and land in Kabul and eastern Ningrahar Province.[39]

Naqib died in 1943 and was succeeded by his eldest son, Sayyid ʿAli (known as Sher Agha), who had a reputation for dissolute behavior. Sayyid ʿAli's younger brother, Sayyid Ahmad Gailani, attended a private madrasa as a boy and later audited classes in the Faculty of Theology, where one of his classmates was Rabbani. Like most members of the Mujaddidi family of his generation, however, he turned from a career in religion to one in business, founding the Peugeot dealership in Afghanistan and spending much of his time in France and England. When Taraki came to power, he is reported to have tried to gain Sayyid Ahmad's support. Instead, Sayyid Ahmad arranged to flee with his family over the border to Pakistan, arriving early in 1979.

The first action undertaken by Mujaddidi's party was a nationwide uprising planned for mid-March 1979. Letters were sent to provincial leaders, front commanders, and sympathetic military officers informing them that they were to rise up simultaneously on the appointed day. Small-scale uprisings occurred in Jalalabad, Kunar, Nuristan, and Kabul, but the most serious incident was in Herat, where some two hundred thousand people are said to have rallied against the regime. For two days, anticommunist protesters stalked the street looking for Khalqis and Soviet advisors. Some were armed with weapons taken from government stockpiles, and it is said that at least fifty Soviets were killed during these attacks. When Afghan pilots refused to go into action against their own people, the Soviets dispatched aircraft from Tajikistan to bomb the rebels. Eventually, the Khalqi rulers managed to bring in loyal troops to suppress the insurrection, and the government is reported to have killed as many as thirty to forty thousand people in the process of restoring its authority over the city.[40] If similar uprisings had been ignited in other locations, the Khalqis might have been routed. But the insurrection in Herat was not associated with any more general mobilization, and the resistance in the city and surrounding areas was decimated.

According to Sibghatullah, he never intended for uprisings to occur in urban areas. His plan was for operations to begin in mountainous areas and later spread to the plains, and the abortive insurrection in Herat happened as a result of sabotage by factions within the alliance:

> Everyone agreed on this plan, and we chose the time. Two days before [the planned date], letters were delivered to all [front commanders inside Afghanistan], but unfortunately Jamiat—they did something dishonest with me. Because I was busy with all the other things, I signed the letters. All of these went out with my signature, all over Afghanistan. . . . I told them—for Herat, Khost, Qandahar, for these flat areas, don't deliver now. After our activity is very warm, very hot in the mountainous areas, then we shall start there. But, unfortunately, they sent out all the letters at one time. . . . And Herat people tell me, "When we saw your signature, we thought, 'Oh, this man is the right man. We shall start.'" They started, and in one day twenty-five thousand people were killed. This was all from Jamiat. This Sayyid Nurullah from Herat [was with] Jamiat. He sent this [letter], and I did not know it. I was surprised that Herat rose up. We did not inform them. After one year, when the Herat people came here, they said, "It was because of your order."[41]

Whatever the truth of this assertion, Mujaddidi's party lost much of its credibility as a result of the failed rebellion in Herat, and consequently it was in effect demoted from a unifying national front to one among the multitude of resistance parties.[42]

Gailani's National Islamic Front of Afghanistan (Mahaz-i Milli Islami Afghanistan) was established several months after Mujaddidi's party and, like his, gained its principal support from the devoted disciples of the family's Sufi tariqat. In Gailani's case, his base of support was strongest among Pakhtun tribesmen in Paktia, Paktika, and Ningrahar provinces. Gailani also had strong ties to Zahir Shah and his retainers. Since Gailani himself was an uncharismatic politician who didn't seem to harbor great political aspirations for himself, many assumed from the beginning that his party was a stand-in for the former king himself, a suspicion that was strengthened by the presence in Gailani's entourage of several politicians who had been prominent during Zahir Shah's reign.

— *||* —

If any leader might have appeared to be in the position to exert leadership over the whole Islamic resistance, it was certainly Sibghatullah Mujaddidi. His inability to accomplish what his great uncle had done forty years earlier was another blow to the ideal of creating a unified response to the Marxist takeover and guaranteed that the ensuing conflict would be a piecemeal and protracted affair. The Herat incident stands out as the immediate cause of Mujaddidi's decline, but the roots of his failure go much deeper, back ten years to his attempt to join the Muslim Youth Organization and perhaps ten years beyond that, to the first organized attempts to initiate a radical Islamist movement in Afghanistan following his and Ghulam Muhammad Niazi's return from Cairo in the late 1950s. We have incomplete information concerning these first meetings, and highly partisan information at that, but it does appear that Sibghatullah had an overbearing presence and did little to ingratiate himself with his fellow travelers in the Islamist camp. I derive this inference, in part, from statements made by Sibghatullah himself, who commented to me, for example, that while Niazi was "a nice man, a good man, a sincere man," he was "not a high-degree scholar. When I was speaking, he was silent. He said, 'Before you, I cannot speak.'"

Sibghatullah appears to have treated the student leaders of the Muslim Youth Organization with even greater condescension, taking credit for much of their work: "This youth [*jawanan*] activity was indirectly guided by me. [Abdur Rahim] Niazi was just like a student to me. He respected me so much. I told them, 'Please Jawanan, I have started this activity in the university indirectly from the outside.' I called these students whom I knew or who knew me. They came to my house. I taught them. I guided them."[43] For their part, former members of the Muslim Youth downplayed Mujaddidi's early activism and cited his family's connections to the royal family as the principal reason he was denied membership in the party. One can also suppose that the students might have resented Sibghatullah's superior attitude, and it is probably the case that leaders of the Muslim Youth recognized Sibghatullah as a threat to their own positions. Since Sibghatullah was older and far better trained in Islamic studies than members of the group, most of whom were studying non-Islamic subjects, the student leaders presumably realized that they would have had to defer to Sibghatullah not only as their elder but also as their better in Islamic matters.

When Sibghatullah appeared on the scene following the revolution, Hekmatyar and his Hizbis were not about to cede pride of place. Hekmatyar based his opposition on distrust of the Mujaddidi family and their connections with the king, but he also undoubtedly worried that Sibghatullah would make Hizb-i's gradual efforts at mobilizing cadres of mujahidin in different localities irrelevant. With his name recognition, Sibghatullah could potentially galvanize a nationwide uprising overnight. If that uprising were to succeed in sweeping out the government, a new moderate Islamic regime would likely come to power, and the Hizbis would find themselves again in the wilderness. For his part, Rabbani, who had been associated with Sibghatullah in the Islamic movement since the 1950s, was initially willing to work with him—whatever his personal misgivings. More than the unbending Hekmatyar, Rabbani appears to have recognized the potential value of Sibghatullah's standing as a member of the Mujaddidi family in rallying popular support, just as he also seems to have been more open to the possibility of working with the former king if it meant gaining an advantage over the Khalqis. Of all the leaders who emerged in this period, Rabbani seemed the most amenable to compromise and the most willing to share in the credit if it helped to accomplish the common objective. This is seen, for example, in his later readiness to cede the limelight to his famous commander Ahmad Shah Massoud through most of the 1980s. Perhaps, as Sibghatullah contended, the Jamiatis betrayed the plan of the uprisings and brought about the debacle in Herat, but just as likely it was the fault of Sibghatullah himself or of his subordinates. Given the disorganization to which his party was prone during the subsequent years of jihad, this supposition seems entirely plausible.

While Sayyid Ahmad was relatively less known to the Hizbis than

Sibghatullah, they viewed him in much the same light—as a proxy for Zahir Shah who would push Afghanistan back into the hands of the monarchy as soon as the communists were defeated. Like Sibghatullah, Sayyid Ahmad had marriage and social connections with the royal family, so such speculation was not entirely unfounded, but he was nevertheless quite different from Sibghatullah. While Sibghatullah had been committed from early in life to his role as a religious leader, Sayyid Ahmad, with his trim goatee and tailored clothes, always seemed to be playing a role that had been allotted to him and that he didn't necessarily enjoy. To his credit, he stayed with that role, even as many of his relatives emigrated to Europe and the United States, but he nevertheless seemed from the start less than suited to the political struggle that claimed him. Unlike Sibghatullah, who engendered resentment among some for being all too comfortable with the deference of others, Sayyid Ahmad strikes one as an easygoing, unassertive leader who does what he can without forcing anyone's hand. Regardless, in the final reckoning of the roles different leaders and parties played in the jihad, Sayyid Ahmad and his Mahaz party—though limited in influence mostly to the tribal borderlands—proved relatively effective, in part because of their willingness to work with local leaders without imposing a rigid set of doctrinal expectations on them. Likewise, Gailani and the people around him were not accused of the kind or degree of corruption that Mujaddidi's associates were.

Relative effectiveness aside, the larger question is why no one from the great saintly families emerged to lead the jihad. Part of the answer must be sought in the rivalries that beset Peshawar. Part also lies in specific events, such as the arrest and execution of Sibghatullah's uncle, Muhammad Ibrahim, and his family and the tragic accident of the Herat Uprising. More important, the failure of the great saintly families to play a role commensurate with their traditional standing in Afghan society speaks to the erosion of their position since the reign of Habibullah. In many respects, the peak of saintly political influence in modern times came in 1929, when the Hazrat of Shor Bazaar helped topple Bacha-i Saqao and placed Nadir Khan on the throne of Kabul. By this time, the members of some saintly families had already squandered their inherited prestige through dissolute behavior, and many others decided on their own to renounce the life of a pir for the secular opportunities that became increasingly available to the Kabul elite from the 1930s on. Sibghatullah cannot be associated with this development. Nor can he be cited as one who indulged in worldly pleasures. Still, he undoubtedly suffered as a result of this general development since few people beyond the traditional circle of his family's devotees were willing to suspend what they knew or suspected about the decline of saintly families in order to grant him the sort of allegiance that the Hazrat of Shor Bazaar would have expected as a matter of course. Those days were gone, and consequently Sibghatullah's destiny was to serve not as kingmaker but merely as another in a list of failed politicians who tried to mold the anticommunist resistance to his liking.

THE ABSENT KING

In the winter of 1980, following the Soviet invasion, an ambitious attempt was made to establish a unified resistance under the leadership of a national jirga that would operate outside the framework of the political parties. This effort was spearheaded by Umar Babrakzai from the Zadran tribe in Paktia Province, who had served as a judge before the war and was also well versed in tribal law. Babrakzai came from a renowned family in Paktia. His grandfather, Babrak Khan, had served Afghan kings, beginning with Abdur Rahman until his death defending Amanullah during the rebellion of Mulla-i Lang in 1924.[44]

The impetus for the creation of a national jirga began in 1979 in Miran Shah, where representatives from a number of Paktia tribes gathered to discuss the conduct of the jihad in their territory. Resistance against the government had begun in Paktia within days of the Khalqi coup. The mountainous terrain had allowed opponents of the regime to take control of most of the roads and villages and had forced government troops to hole up in the fortified town of Khost and a few outlying forts that had to be supplied by helicopter. Relative to other areas of the country, Paktia had tribes with well-developed legal codes and traditions of collective action in defense of its laws and customary practices. When the conflict with the government began, the tribes instituted their own procedures for ensuring order in their territories and succeeded in working cooperatively with the Islamic political parties that had established fronts in the province. Thus, in contrast to the situation in Pech, where tribal and party leaders were working to undermine each other, many tribal and party leaders in Paktia had come to accept a division of authority. Party leaders did not insist on adjudicating internal tribal disputes and often accepted the authority of the tribal police force—the *arbaki*—to enforce tribal law and apprehend lawbreakers. In response, the tribes allowed the parties (principally Gailani's Mahaz and Khales's Hizb under Haqqani) to establish bases, recruit local tribesmen, and conduct military operations.

The Paktia jirga that began meeting in Miran Shah in December 1979 was initially concerned with coordinating resistance activities in Paktia itself, but the relative harmony that had been forged in the province led Babrakzai and other Paktia leaders to believe that their experience might provide an example for the resistance movement generally. The Paktia jirga dispatched eighty or so delegates to Peshawar to speak with party leaders and to lay the groundwork for a national jirga. According to Babrakzai, the leaders unanimously agreed to the convening of a national jirga based on traditional tribal principles, and the Paktia leaders set up their own office in Peshawar.[45] During January and February 1980, they met in council with representatives from other areas—mostly elders from various refugee camps—to prepare the ground for the national *momasela* (provisional) jirga.[46] Nine hundred sixteen representatives convened in Peshawar on May 9. From these participants, two people were selected from each province, along with four representatives of the nomadic tribes, to serve on the "revolutionary council" (*shura-yi enqelab*), which would continue to meet regularly after the adjournment of the full jirga until an elected government could be established. The seven principal parties were also to have a representative on the revolutionary council, but, despite their initial support of the jirga, all the parties except Gailani's Mahaz decided to boycott the meeting. According to Babrakzai, the parties recognized that their influence would be considerably diluted in this public forum:

> In a jirga where only seven representatives of the parties were present, and sixty-eight representatives from the people of Afghanistan were present, the majority would naturally have been in favor of the tribe [qaum], and the decisions which would have been taken would have been outside the limits of the party [*hizbi*] system. . . . These parties saw that this would create new problems for them. A party system would have been changed to a comprehensive national system. When the parties studied the matter in-depth, they figured out that this would be against their beliefs.[47]

Having the support of only one party proved more detrimental than having the backing of none at all, for the jirga came to be viewed by many as a tool of Gailani's party. This perception was amplified when Sayyid Ahmad Gailani's nephew, Sayyid Hassan, was allowed to chair a session of the jirga, which led more party members to boycott the proceedings.[48] Ultimately, Gailani's role was not the issue for most of the party leaders. It was rather the conviction that Gailani was a stand-in for Zahir Shah and that the jirga itself was intended as a vehicle for bringing the former king back as the savior of a secularized resistance movement. A related factor in the ultimate failure of the jirga was the attitude of the Pakistani government, which withheld its support for the jirga because of its own uncertainty as to the consequences of the coalescence of the Afghan resistance. In particular, the Pakistanis appear to have been loath to witness the creation of a PLO-like supra-organization on Pakistani soil.[49] Such an organization could become independent of Pakistani control and—given its potential support among the border tribes—could create common cause with independent-minded Pakistani Pakhtuns along the frontier. In addition, President Zia ul-Haq, who was pushing a program of Islamization within his own country, had already thrown his support to the Islamic parties, especially Hizb-i Islami.

Without significant support from either the parties or the Pakistan government, the momasela jirga faded in importance even before it had adjourned. Despite this failure, however, the institution of the jirga had sufficiently hardy roots that a second attempt to convene an assembly was initiated fifteen months later in Baluchistan. This plan again received an enthusiastic response, and the jirga attracted more than three thousand Afghans. The main result of this jirga, which was again opposed by the Islamic parties and the Pakistan government, was to spotlight the intentions of Zahir Shah, who was proposed by the jirga as its national leader (*milli qa'id*).[50] Unlike his father, however, who came in person to the frontier to right the toppled throne, Zahir Shah dithered, sending forth proclamations supporting armed jihad conducted by a united front but never making any concerted attempt personally to enter the fray.[51] As a result of his inaction and the efforts of party leaders and Pakistani government officials, the second jirga, like the first, ended in failure.

— *II* —

The parties balked at accepting the jirgas for understandable reasons. Their leaders reasoned, probably accurately, that if the people of Afghanistan were able to choose the form in which they would conduct their war against the communist government, political parties would lose out—in all likelihood to some moderate coalition led by Zahir Shah and a collection of ex-ministers, courtiers, and mainstream religious figures like Gailani and Mujaddidi. The failure of the two jirgas, however, ensured that there would be no independent and united national front. It also brought an end to the one institution that Afghans had always been able to count on in times of national emergency to bring consensus and reconciliation among warring factions.

National jirgas had been convened periodically throughout modern Afghan history both to draft new constitutions and to provide leadership at times of crisis, such as before and after the country's several military con-

frontations with Great Britain in the nineteenth and early twentieth centuries. However, the most famous instance of a national jirga is the one that
selected Ahmad Shah to lead the Durrani confederacy in 1747. This is the
ur-event of Afghan nationalism and is described in the following passage
from an article that appeared in a 1963 volume of *Afghanistan*, a now-
defunct government-sponsored journal of culture and history:

> After the assassination of Nadir Shah [Afshar] in 1747, his vast empire
> began to splinter. The Afghan contingent, headed by Mir Afghan Noor
> Mohammed Ghilzai and Ahmad Khan Abdali, returned home. On reach-
> ing Kandahar, a tribal Jirga was held at the shrine of Sher-i-Surkh (Red
> Lion) to consider the future of the country. The chief question was who
> should be elected king. Among the aspirants there were many elderly
> chieftains of great power and influence. The Jirga met eight times without
> making any choice. On the ninth day so heated did the discussions and
> arguments become that recourse to arms seemed inevitable. Seeing this,
> Sabir Shah, a respectable divine, whom all tribes revered, proposed the
> name of young Ahmad Khan, who was hardly twenty-five and who had
> kept quiet during the whole of the session. . . . Seeing this all the contend-
> ing chiefs came forward to pay homage to him. Young Ahmad Shah, the
> future king of Afghanistan, raised by his own people to the highest hon-
> our and dignity, was seen to prove himself the most worthy of this
> trust.[52]

This account illustrates not only the crucial role that the institution of
the jirga played in Afghan history but also the traditional role assigned to
religious figures in political affairs. The "dervish" Sabir Shah is depicted
not as a participant in the proceedings but as a mediator, someone who
intervenes only as a last resort when "recourse to arms seemed inevitable."
Likewise, the story shows Ahmad Khan, later Ahmad Shah, as a quiet figure and not the strongest of the assembled chiefs. Ahmad Khan, in this
account, does not force himself on the assembly but is chosen, as much by
divine providence (in the figure of Sabir Shah) as by the assembly itself.
The absence of pomp and show also emphasizes that the king has been
"raised by his own people" to his position of honor and is not above them.
The new king is to be first among equals, and it is via the jirga that this
exemplary state of affairs is arrived at and the perils of both divisiveness
and tyranny are avoided. This particular rendition of Ahmad Shah's election comes from a government journal and has a decidedly hagiographic
slant, but the story nevertheless demonstrates the role of the jirga in
mediating among and binding together the three foci of Afghan political
culture—Islam, tribalism, and state rule. Without this assembly, with its
established rules and protocols, tribal chiefs posture and bully without

bending to the needs of the many; kings emerge from decimating battles— the strongest of the strong, but not necessarily the wisest of the wise; spiritual leaders keep to themselves, cultivating followings and sometimes rising up to cause their own disruptions but never being seen as potential rulers themselves. With the jirga, however, compromise becomes possible. Divergent interests are placated, and the best course is found for the community as a whole, even if it is not the course desired by the mightiest among those assembled.

Thus the origin myth of the jirga, but how different the outcome when the same route was tried in Peshawar and Quetta and how different the balance of power. This time, the tribal leaders were in the subordinate position. The fact that the movement for a jirga was led by Babrakzai, a lawyer educated in Europe, rather than a warrior chief, is one indication of change. More important, though, the Islamic leaders were now the "chiefs" contending for power, while the tribal leaders were in the dependent position, seeking compromise and reconciliation from their party patrons, who this time controlled the arms and were in a position to posture and bully. Consider as well the role of Sayyid Hasan Gailani, who, taking the chair during part of the first jirga, directly reversed the fabled role of Sabir Shah. Unlike Sabir Shah, who intervened at the last minute to prevent conflict and save the proceedings, Sayyid Hasan, with his unwise intervention, effectively undermined what was admittedly an already endangered process. Whether Sayyid Hasan's involvement in the jirga was an attempted "coup d'état" of the assembly, as some party stalwarts claimed, or merely a clumsy attempt to gain some fame for himself or something altogether more innocent still is a matter of debate. Either way, however, the overreaching entanglement of the Gailanis in the jirga provided a pretext for the other parties to pull out, and in so doing ensured not only that the jirga system would lose its effectiveness as a mechanism of dispute resolution but also that religious leaders, who had long played an important role in keeping the peace in Afghanistan, would henceforth be excluded from that role. Saints, mullas, and other religious figures had provided the service of reconciling enemies and bringing feuds to an end. However, with religious leaders of all kinds implicated as antagonists in the political fighting in Peshawar, they lost the neutrality and noncombatant status that allowed them to play that role—a role that no other group has filled or is likely to fill in the near future.

Another factor to consider is the role of Zahir Shah in these proceedings. Opponents of both the Peshawar and the Baluchistan jirgas believed that they were little more than maneuvers designed to bring Zahir Shah into the fray. This may or may not have been the case, but the vast majority of

Afghans would undoubtedly have embraced the decision of a national jirga that elected Zahir Shah as its leader. Afghans, like most people, are oriented toward the idea of a single national leader, and with the death of Muhammad Daud in the 1978 revolution, Zahir Shah was the only figure who still enjoyed a national reputation. One effect of his family's prolonged dynastic control was that Zahir Shah was thought of as a representative of the royal family rather than a particular tribe, region, or ethnic group. The Pakhtun tribal roots of the dynasty were less salient to most people than the fact of their extended rule, their residence in Kabul, and their assimilation to the Persian-speaking culture of the capital city. The various leaders contending for power in Peshawar had limited constituencies. Mujaddidi and Gailani had the advantage of being outside the ethnic and tribal matrix, and both had some name recognition throughout the country, but their traditional constituencies were still largely Pakhtun. Likewise, while the mullas and maulavis in Nabi's party were able to build a base of support outside their own native regions, neither he nor Khales was well known nationally. In the eyes of many, they were still "just" mullas, and they retained their strongest support in Pakhtun areas south of the Hindu Kush. This was also the case with Hekmatyar, but he was even more hampered in attracting a national following by his humble roots and lack of prior accomplishment. He was after all "just" a student who had never completed his schooling and who was referred to as "engineer" without having actually earned the credential. For his part, Rabbani was older and a professor as well as a religious scholar; but he was a Tajik, a group that had produced only one major national leader—the ill-fated Bacha-i Saqao—and he hailed from the province of Badakhshan, which was far removed from Kabul and relatively insignificant politically.

The location of all the major Sunni parties in Peshawar also limited their ability to extend their power beyond the eastern provinces of the country as a whole. Peshawar is unmistakably a Pakhtun city. The fact that the parties all had their base of operations there reinforced the sense of non-Pakhtun Afghans (who constitute roughly half the population) that the victory of any of these parties, except Jamiat, would inevitably bring with it the advent of the sort of Pakhtun dominance that the monarchy had managed to keep at bay. Ultimately, none of these parties won out, but, nevertheless, the jirga system was probably Afghanistan's last best hope for creating a nationwide framework of political rule. For all his evident weaknesses, Zahir Shah was the only leader capable of enlisting the loyalties of all the various ethnic and tribal groups in the country and of forestalling the kind of deep ethnic divide that has since evolved under the Taliban regime.

THE ARAB CONNECTION

The last major participant to join the Afghan exile political scene was Abdur Rasul Sayyaf, who arrived in Peshawar in 1980 after being released from prison in Kabul under a general amnesty declared by Babrak Karmal soon after he was brought to power by the Soviet invasion. Sayyaf was well known to many of the leaders in Peshawar as he too had been a professor in the Faculty of Islamic Law at Kabul University. Like his former colleagues, Professors Niazi and Rabbani, Sayyaf had spent time at al-Azhar University in Cairo, where he had also associated with members of the Muslim Brotherhood. In the Jamiat version of history, Sayyaf was elected as Rabbani's deputy (mawen) in 1972, the year in which Jamiatis say their party's constitution was drafted.[53] Sayyaf was then arrested after Daud's coup d'état and was still in prison when the Khalqis took power. It is believed that he escaped execution because he was a Kharoti Ghilzai and cousin of Hafizullah Amin; these connections kept him alive long enough to benefit from Babrak's gesture of clemency.[54]

At yet another meeting to form an alliance—this one inaugurated in response to the Soviet invasion and pressure from potential international donors who wanted the mujahidin to have a single front to facilitate the allocation of assistance—Sayyaf was put forward as a candidate for leadership over Sibghatullah Mujaddidi, who was also pushing hard for the job.[55] As a relative moderate and nationally known leader, Mujaddidi thought he could count on receiving the votes of the delegates from Gailani's Mahaz party, Nabi's Harakat, and his own Jabha, but his votes fell short, and Sayyaf was elected. Sayyaf's success was the result of his having been recently released from prison and his not having been implicated in the divisions and fiascoes of the preceding several years. Under Sayyaf's leadership, the Islamic Union for the Freedom of Afghanistan (Ettehad-i Islami bara-yi Azadi-yi Afghanistan) came into existence, and one of the new leader's first responsibilities was representing the Afghan mujahidin at an Islamic conference in Tayef, Saudi Arabia. One of Sayyaf's strengths was his fluent command of Arabic, and, in Qazi Amin's words, he greatly impressed his Arab audience, "dressed in his simple Afghan clothes and speaking eloquently in their own language."

From the outset, Sayyaf overshadowed the other Afghan leaders in the eyes of wealthy Arabs who were eager to bankroll the Afghan jihad. At a time when the mujahidin were still largely dependent on Pakistan for financial support, Sayyaf's performance at Tayef promised to open the spigot of Arab oil money; but the new alliance quickly became mired in controversy, brought about by the new wealth that Sayyaf had tapped and the jealousies it inspired. Quoting Qazi Amin:

> After this conference, some [Arab benefactors] took a personal interest in Sayyaf and gave him aid directly. As a result, the other leaders were frightened that Sayyaf was becoming more popular day by day. At the same time, Hekmatyar was also increasing his popularity, while leaders like Khales, Rabbani, Sibghatullah, and Effendi [Gailani] were not considered important. Sayyaf also was thinking, "These [other leaders] are just bothering me because the aid is coming directly to me." No one asked them, so all the aid was in his control.[56]

Bitterness over Sayyaf's handling of Arab funds, as well as accusations that he was secretly conspiring with Hekmatyar to undercut the moderate parties, soon led to the breakup of this newest alliance, with Sayyaf's party becoming the seventh independent political party—one that had virtually no fighting fronts but a great deal of money.[57]

Shortly after the collapse of Sayyaf's alliance, Sheikh Abdullah, the Commissioner of Afghan Refugees for the Government of Pakistan, who had general oversight over Afghan political activities in Peshawar, stepped in and announced that only the seven Islamic parties (the two Hizbs, Jamiat, Harakat, Jabha, Mahaz, and Sayyaf's new party) would be allowed to remain in operation. At that time, there were more than a hundred small parties with offices in Peshawar.[58] Some of these parties were nationalist in orientation; some centered around individual personalities; some were regional, tribal, and ethnic coalitions. The government's restricted recognition meant that only the designated Islamic parties would be authorized to receive assistance from Pakistan and other international donors, and all refugees would have to receive a membership card from one of these parties in order to live in registered camps and receive tents, rations, and other assistance. In response to this move, tribal leaders living in refugee camps near Peshawar formed jirgas in which they publicly announced that the Pakistan government could also outlaw the seven Islamic parties—that all the parties were operating out of self-interest and betraying the Afghan cause. The first of these jirgas, which about two hundred elders attended, was held in the Nasirbagh camp; the second, with more than three thousand participants, was at the Kachagarhi camp. After these jirgas, smaller groups continued to meet in different mosques and public parks in Peshawar, where they pressed their demands for an end to party bickering and threatened to turn in their party identification cards as a sign that they no longer recognized the parties' authority.

Simultaneously, a group of respected clerics calling themselves *ulama dayun* began meeting in the Mahabat Khan mosque in Peshawar and declared that they would not leave the sacred precinct until a real and abiding alliance was established. Reminding party leaders of the Prophet's injunction that if two Muslims met sword in hand with the intention of killing one another both would be condemned to eternal damnation, the clerics succeeded in getting the party leaders to agree to work together through a council of clerics representing each of the parties. Only Gailani in the beginning kept his party out of the new union, which was given the name Islamic Union of Afghanistan Mujahidin (Ettehad-i Islami Mujahidin Afghanistan). The founding accords of this newest alliance were signed on August 14, 1981, and it was soon agreed that each of the seven parties would receive fifteen seats on the alliance council. According to various informants, however, Sayyaf and Hekmatyar recognized that, as the most radical members of the alliance, they would be outnumbered in this forum, and they convinced Mansur, Nabi's deputy, to separate from Harakat and to set up his own party in order to increase their votes in the executive shura. At the same time, Mujaddidi and Nabi refused to accept Sayyaf as the leader of a party entitled to full representation on the council since he had few fronts and little evidence of popular support inside Afghanistan or within the refugee community. The result of this maneuvering was that by September, Gailani, Mujaddidi, and Nabi had all dropped out and formed a separate alliance also with the name Islamic Union of Afghanistan Mujahidin. This split led to the relatively long-lived division of the Islamic resistance into two wings. The more radical alliance, generally known as the "Seven Party Unity" (Ettehad-i Haft Gana), comprised both Hizb parties; Jamiat; two splinter factions from Harakat, one led by Mansur, the other by Maulavi Moazen; a minor splinter group from Mujaddidi's Jabha led by his former deputy, Maulavi Muhammad Mir; and Sayyaf's financially well-endowed but otherwise minor party. The moderate "Three Party Unity" (Ettehad-i Seh Gana) included Nabi's Harakat, Gailani's Mahaz, and Mujaddidi's Jabha.

These two alliances managed to stay intact until 1985, when they disbanded under pressure from the Saudi and Pakistani governments and recombined under the familiar name Islamic Union of Afghanistan Mujahidin. This new union was little more than a shell. Committees that had been unified within the alliances were dissolved, and each of the seven principal parties (the two Hizb-i Islamis, Jamiat, Harakat, Jabha, Mahaz, and Sayyaf's Ettehad) again took up its separate work. The ostensible reason for taking this step was that the international patrons of the mujahidin wanted the resistance to appear united at international conferences and meetings with statesmen. To this end, a rotating presidency was established, with

Rabbani as the first to occupy this position. But the new arrangement only exacerbated tensions and jealousies among the leaders for all the cooperation and unanimity they tried to present to outsiders.

For his part, Qazi Amin claims to have been so upset by the dissolution of the old alliance format that he resigned from Hizb-i Islami and broke off relations with all the parties, calling this "the third darkest day after the communist coup and Russian invasion." This statement was made many years after the fact (in 1996 to be exact), after the Soviet withdrawal and the collapse of the coalition government in Kabul that arose out of the Peshawar party alliances. In Qazi Amin's view, "There wouldn't have been such a disaster in later years, if the original alliance had been kept." Whatever the accuracy of this view and whatever other factors may have been involved in his decision, Qazi Amin did choose this moment to resign his position in Hizb-i Islami and to promote a small party of his own, which he named Daiya Ettehad-i Islami Mujahidin Afghanistan (Inviting Islamic Mujahidin of Afghanistan for Unity). Qazi Amin's party was never a factor in the fighting. Its principal objective was to militate for cooperation within the resistance, an objective that was to prove elusive until the Taliban militia came into existence with the explicit aim of putting an end to party abuses and bickering.

— // —

Of all the major leaders to emerge in Peshawar, Sayyaf had the fewest fronts, but his contribution to the direction of the jihad was significant because, more than anyone else, he was responsible for internationalizing the jihad, making it not just an affair among Afghans but a focal point of concern for Muslims around the world.[59] More than anyone else, he was responsible for bringing in not only Arab money but also Arab mujahidin who saw the conflict in Afghanistan as their jihad just as much as the Afghan people's. Although the impact of Arabs in the jihad was not felt in substantial ways for several years after the Soviet invasion, this tack in the jihad was signaled as early as 1981, when Sayyaf, speaking at a conference hosted by Jama'at-i Islami Pakistan, stated that "Afghanistan provided a school of Islamic jihad" that "would determine the future of the Muslim world."[60] Sayyaf was not alone in seeking to internationalize the jihad. Others, notably Maulavi Hussain from Pech Valley, also welcomed the Arab mujahidin and included them in their operations. However, Sayyaf was associated more than anyone else with these efforts, benefited more from them, and accepted the ideological transformations that Arabs insisted on as the price of their support.

With regard to the ideological effect of the Arab connection, a turning point occurred when Sayyaf announced that he would no longer be known as Abdur Rasul ("servant of the Prophet") Sayyaf but Abd al-Rab ("servant of God") Rasul Sayyaf. The change was much noted at the time within the Afghan community, as was the related phenomenon of Sayyaf's allowing his beard to grow to a rather extraordinary length. Both moves, people believed, reflected his coming under the sway of Arab Wahhabi supporters, who told him that to call oneself "the servant of the Prophet" was not in the spirit of monotheism (*tauhid*) since one should be only the servant of God, not of a human being, even one so exalted as the Prophet. Similarly, some scholars argued that, according to scripture, beards should be allowed to grow and not be trimmed close to the face, as was the custom for many Afghan men. Though personal in nature, these gestures had a general symbolic importance that was much commented on at the time. Sayyaf, it was said, was now so thoroughly aligned with the Arab Wahhabis that he was even willing to change his name and his appearance. Whether these alterations were from sincere conviction or mercenary interest was never certain, but people did notice that Arab money was making it possible for Sayyaf to build a large administrative, scholastic, and residential complex in Pabu, an hour east of Peshawar. Arab backing also enabled him to offer front commanders willing to join his party sophisticated weapons and abundant financial assistance, beyond what most other commanders were able to offer to their forces; these offers increased the suspicion of many Afghans that Sayyaf and a few others like Maulavi Hussain were intent on shaping Afghan culture and religion along Arab lines.[61]

Between 1984, when I left Peshawar after completing my dissertation research, and 1986, when I returned to conduct another six months of fieldwork, the biggest change I noted was the conspicuous presence of Arabs in Peshawar. During my earlier stay, there had been many foreigners, the vast majority of them Europeans and Americans who worked in nongovernmental organizations (NGOs) providing assistance to the Afghan refugees. The Arabs, even those working in NGOs of their own, were fewer in number and didn't mix much with the other foreigners. Nor did it appear that they had much to do with Afghans, except those leaders aligned with them and dependent on their financial backing. Despite their intense devotion to Islam, Afghans, by and large, had no great fondness for Arabs, and their experience of the volunteer mujahidin did not alter that impression. For the most part, Arabs were perceived as overbearing and insensitive to Afghan traditions. Where they were present, it was felt that the war efforts were altered and diminished. Arabs brought dissension with them, along with a ruthlessness that hadn't been there before. While noted for their martial skill and keenness for battle, Afghans tempered these characteristics with other concerns. Kinship, honor, respect for elders, compassion for the plight of women and children, recognition of the needs of civilian populations— all might affect the decisions of an Afghan commander considering his options, but Arabs—informants believe—had no such crosscutting loyalties or scruples. They were zealots who had come to Afghanistan to prove a point and build their movement, and they had no particular affection or respect for the people living in the country where they were fighting. The result of this attitude was to make the war both more impersonal and more polarized.

Just as the communists had changed the ideological equation when the status of the Soviets changed from backers to participants so the appearance of Arab mujahidin as full-scale combatants changed the tenor and complexion of the conflict from the other side. One aspect of this change was that many Arab volunteers had militant ideological convictions of their own that were often inimical to Afghan religious beliefs. Since the rise of Hizb-i Islami and Jamiat-i Islami, Afghans had become used to hearing some of their own politicians calling for the creation of an Islamic state along the lines formulated by the first Muslim rulers, but while they maintained a general tolerance, if not a fondness, for homegrown versions of Islamic radicalism, they were much less sympathetic to Arab ideologues, particularly those branded as Wahhabis.

Wahhabism not only rejected the validity of Sufism but also asserted that Muslims should rely solely on the Qur'an and the traditions of the Prophet as guides to everyday behavior and legal judgments. The majority of Afghans, including most of the ulama, believed in Sufism in principle, even if they condemned many Sufi pirs, and they also relied on and strongly espoused the Hanafi school of interpretation *(fiqh)* as the basis for its legal code and ritual practice. Because of these beliefs, Sayyaf and other leaders who were dependent on Arab aid asserted their continued commitment to Hanafi doctrine, if not to Sufism, in order not to compromise their position among the people. However, some Afghan leaders were genuinely committed to Wahhabi principles and broke away from the parties rather than compromise their beliefs. One such leader was the previously mentioned Maulavi Hussain, who left Hizb-i Islami in 1980 and established an independent base in Bajaur, where he welcomed many of the Arab volunteers who began arriving in the mid-1980s to participate in the Afghan jihad. Though referred to by others as a Wahhabi or Panj Piri, Hussain himself referred to his movement as Salafi, and under his leadership, the Salafis became a major force in Kunar until Hussain was killed, ironically by one of the Arab volunteers he had welcomed into his front.[62]

CONCLUSION

> One evening in 1983, I was leaving a house in the old part of Peshawar, and passed a blind beggar standing in the street. The beggar must have heard one of my companions address me, for he called out, "Doctor Sahib, come here!" When I walked over, the beggar informed me that he was collecting money for a new party of which he was the amir. He was calling his new party Hizb-i Chur o Chapawul-i Islami—the Party of Islamic Thieves and Robbers—and he asked me if I would be willing to make a contribution.[63]

The configuration of seven parties that emerged by 1980 was effectively the core group responsible for winning the war against the Soviet Union. These parties, along with several Shi'a parties linked to Iran, provided the organizational backing for the mujahidin who first forced the Soviets into the cities and finally convinced them by 1989 to cut their losses and withdraw across the border. These same seven parties also lost the peace that followed the Soviet withdrawal by continuing to bicker among themselves, thereby laying the groundwork for the Taliban takeover. The pattern of squabbling that began in the late 1970s persisted throughout the period of Soviet occupation and intensified after the withdrawal; this inability on the part of the resistance organizations to work together provided the opening for the Taliban to challenge and ultimately vanquish the established parties in most of the country.

Given the mixed legacy of victory over a superpower but final failure to conclude the peace, one is left wondering why. Why were the parties never able to find ground for common cause? Why, when all agreed on the ultimate goal of establishing an Islamic state in Afghanistan, could the ideological differences separating them not be overcome? There are, of course, many ways to approach these questions. One could focus on the role of outside governments—Pakistan, the United States, Iran, China, Saudi Arabia—in providing the resources that fueled the rivalries. It is an Afghan obsession to blame "secret hands working behind the curtain" for internal problems whose causes are difficult to assess. While often unjustified, laying blame on foreign interference is justified in this instance, for as much as outside financial, material, and logistical support made the mujahidin victory possible, it also profoundly exacerbated internal divisions in the resistance, particularly since resources were distributed disproportionately, with some parties receiving a great deal and some almost nothing at all.[64]

Another way to approach the rivalries that tore apart the various alliances is to try to assess the motivations and actions of individual actors. Hekmatyar, for example, was the first leader to establish a base in Peshawar, and he was undoubtedly involved in many of the ruptures that beset the resistance. But if Hekmatyar was more inflexible and more ruthless in pursuit of his ambition, the other leaders played their parts with almost equal avidity. Given the failure of the leaders to rise above personal ambitions and rivalries, one is left wondering what might have happened if, say, the two Niazis—Professor Ghulam Muhammad and his student protégé Abdur Rahim—had managed to survive and make their way to Peshawar. These two men were the recognized leaders of the two groups that became Jamiat and Hizb, and their commitment to the cause of creating a just Islamic society in Afghanistan was recognized by all, as was their knowledge of Islamic scripture. There was a bond between them, based on their longstanding relationship as teacher and student, that one supposes might have helped mitigate the generational and ethnic cleavages that made Jamiat and Hizb such bitter enemies. Both Hekmatyar and Rabbani were secondary figures in the early days. Hekmatyar's main role was as a rabble rouser who pushed the offensive against the leftist students on campus, and one imagines that if some of the other student leaders had survived, he would have ended up as the chief of military or logistical operations, but not as overall head of the party. Perhaps, if the Niazis or some other early party leaders—Maulavi Habib-ur Rahman, Engineer Habib-ur Rahman, Maulana Faizani—had survived, the ruptures that ended up crippling the resistance would have been avoided; but such was not to be.

The role of outside intervention and the personal characteristics of party leaders both are relevant factors for understanding the persistent pattern of discord in the jihad. However, of equal importance is the nature of the parties themselves and what might be called their structural incommensurability. In the first part of this book, I discussed the Marxist PDPA and its attempt at transforming Afghanistan. The PDPA, it was argued, was as much a dysfunctional family as a political party, at least at its upper reaches. Thus, Taraki—the childless older man—gathered around himself a circle of young men who were like children to him. One among them, Hafizullah Amin, assumed the role of favored son and, fueled by his own hubris and ambition, turned the father against his rival—the "bad" son, Babrak Karmal—before finally betraying the father in what amounted to an act of patricide. None of the parties in Peshawar lend themselves to so archetypal an interpretation, but, nevertheless, only one of the parties—Hizb-i Islami—was in the modern sense of the word a political party. The other organizations were hybrids, part party organization and part something else—depending on the backgrounds of the individuals involved. Thus, in addition to variations in ideology and tactics, the parties also differed in how they viewed the role of the leader and how they thought decisions should be made. In a sense, fabricating an alliance between parties in Peshawar would have been structurally equivalent to merging a U.S. political party with a religious sect and a Mafia family. Their ways of conducting business and their respective "corporate cultures" were so varied and so deeply rooted that conflicts among the parties were inevitable. Add to these differences in educational backgrounds, ethnicity, and language, generational divisions, the ambitiousness of the leaders, as well as the interference of outside powers, and it becomes more apparent why alliances in Peshawar were continually breaking up.

Consider in this regard Jabha and Mahaz, the parties of the two saints, Sibghatullah Mujaddidi and Sayyid Ahmad Gailani. Both Mujaddidi and Gailani came to Peshawar as de facto heads of Sufi orders, even though neither man had previously been deeply involved in Sufi activities.[65] One important feature of the Sufi order is personal contact between the pir and his disciples, for it is through the pir that the disciples gain both additional knowledge (through the bestowal of new zikr exercises) and mystical blessing (barakat). Because personal contact with the pir was expected, every petitioner needed to see the pir himself. Translated to the realm of political affairs, there was no way to delegate work or authority effectively, and the result was that the Jabha and Mahaz offices were often empty and the compounds where the pirs lived were nearly always full—with officials seeking the pir's signature on nearly every piece of paperwork, with commanders seeking weapons, and with common refugees seeking help in resolving financial, medical, and personal problems. Simultaneously, pirs were also expected to be generous patrons, and so, despite having little in the way of work, the pirs' offices had full complements of officials, mostly disciples and retainers who drew their salaries but did little beyond filling out their time cards and drinking tea.[66] Because of Gailani's base in Paktia and his close relationship with tribal khans from the areas of his support, his party more than Mujaddidi's reflected this connection. In Olivier Roy's words, "There was no party structure; the local khan had freedom of action and people obeyed a local influential leader and not the party. There was no political office, but a small court; weapons were distributed according to the recipient's personal relationship with Ahmad Gaylani."[67]

The clerical parties—Nabi's Harakat and Khales's Hizb—were less centralized than the Sufi parties. No special status was invested in the heads of these parties, and business did not have to go through them. Consequently, they tended to be somewhat more efficient and less subject to bottlenecks than the Sufi groups, where major and minor decisions always had to await approval from on high. Khales, in particular, had a number of trusted lieutenants and commanders (for example, his deputy, Haji Din Muhammad, and commanders Abdul Haq of Kabul and Maulavi Jalaluddin Haqqani of Paktia) who were able to act independently and effectively. In essence, the clerical parties were networks of maulavis and mullas, some of whom knew each other already, but all of whom had in common their educational experiences and their commitment to a particular vision of Qur'an-centered existence. If there was an "old boys' network" in Afghanistan, a network of men who didn't necessarily know each other individually but who acted on each other's behalf because they knew "where they were coming from," it was probably this group.

In addition, and in contrast to the Sufi parties, the clerics also had effective avenues of recruitment. Thus, while neither Gailani nor Mujaddidi had any way to recruit new devotees except through the resources they were prepared to hand out—the Sufi orders associated with their families being largely scattered or inactive—the clerical parties had madrasas, which enjoyed a booming renaissance during the jihad years. By 1984, there were 3.5 million refugees in Pakistan, and, beyond the primary schools available in the camps and a handful of secondary schools in Peshawar, the only educational alternative for refugees was to go to religious schools. Prior to the Marxist revolution, mullas and maulavis had limited prestige in Afghanistan. Mostly poor and lacking in influence, clerics generally did not inspire emulation, and few young people, except the genuinely devout, were attracted to religion as a career. With the resistance in the hands of religious parties, however, madrasas became a surer path to advancement than secular schools, whose graduates found a paucity of jobs available to them. The madrasa thus replaced the school as the place to go to get ahead, and the clerical parties first, and later the Taliban, benefited by having this institution at their disposal.

Sayyaf's Ettehad and Rabbani's Jamiat were anomalous in not being strongly grounded in a prior institutional culture. Both Sayyaf and Rabbani were university professors prior to becoming party heads, and their political orientations reflected their exposure to international currents beyond the ken of most Afghans. Sayyaf's association with Arab backers also meant that his party was the most flush with cash and the least characterizable in terms of structure or constituency. According to Roy, Sayyaf's party appealed mainly to marginal commanders and groups that had come into conflict with their superiors. Others who switched allegiance to Sayyaf had been "elbowed out by newcomers from the dominant party [in the region], or [were] very small ethnic groups seeking to preserve their identity. Finally, there are other much more dubious groups, who border on banditry, for whom it is essential to have weapons to avoid being brought to heel by the dominant party."[68]

Rabbani's party also had an amalgam of followers, although not so many of the opportunistic variety that was attracted to Sayyaf. While perhaps best known before the war as a translator of Sayyid Qutb, Rabbani also studied the traditional theological subjects associated with the clerical class, as well as early Sufi texts, and his party reflected its leader's catholicism in its willingness to embrace groups with diverse backgrounds and interests. Again quoting Roy, "The Jamiat was well placed at the meeting-point of three of the four networks which went to make up the Afghan resistance movement: the Islamists, the Sufis and the *mawlawi*. With the fourth network (the tribes) its position was much weaker, which explains why it found it so difficult to establish itself in the south."[69] Another source of Jamiat's success in developing fronts inside Afghanistan was the high quality of its commanders and the democratic and multiethnic character of many of its fronts. Among those with excellent reputations were both Zabiullah Khan, the Jamiat commander in Mazar-i Sharif until his death in 1985, and Toran Ismail Khan, the Jamiat commander in Herat.[70] The strength of these commanders and the resilience of their fronts stemmed in large part from their ability to work and coexist with local leaders without forcing people in their areas to adhere to a particular ideology. In this respect, Jamiat contrasts with both Harakat, some of whose commanders incurred resentment for their heavy-handed rule, and Hizb, which tended to divide the world between those who were and those who were not party members.

If Jamiat, reflecting its name, was more of an "association" than a formal political party, Hizb-i Islami was a political party in the modern and specifically Leninist sense. In keeping with this status, it proved the least cooperative group to work with at the party level in Peshawar and in the field, and it was also the most hierarchical, disciplined, and secretive. Unlike Rabbani and the other leaders, Hekmatyar came of age in and through the party, and while the other leaders were more likely to see the organizations they led as means to an end, for Hekmatyar the party was the end itself. One became aware of the difference between Hizb and the other Peshawar fronts the moment one walked into Hizb headquarters. In contrast to the other parties in Peshawar, Hizb appeared to be a highly efficient and streamlined organization. Hizb offices were staffed mostly by young, educated men (as opposed to the older clerics with sinecures who decorated the offices of the moderate parties), and they were usually buzzing with activity. Appointments were kept, schedules adhered to, and assignments completed. Rarely did one see the milling crowds outside the Hizb office or Hekmatyar's home that were so common outside the offices and homes of Mujaddidi, Gailani, and Nabi. While there was never any doubt who was in charge, Hekmatyar had competent people reporting to him and delegated to them many of the mundane responsibilities that other leaders had to fulfill personally.

The underside of Hizb efficiency was the self-righteous discipline of the members. The so-called schoolboys (maktabian) who worked in the Hizb offices were readily identifiable by the nearly identical clothes and caps they wore, their trim beards, and their haughty expressions. For members of most of the other parties, loyalty to their family and kin group was of greater personal importance than allegiance to the party. That was not the case with Hizbis, however, or at least it was not supposed to be. They were expected to hold the party above everything else; as a result, people not associated with the party didn't trust them and were unwilling to speak freely around them. In Peshawar in the mid-1980s, there were ubiquitous rumors about Hizb prisons and torture centers around the city and about how Hizb had "disappeared" this or that person. It was even said that the Pakistani authorities had once dredged a part of the Indus looking for the body of a drowning victim only to find a score of other bodies—all presumed to have been Afghans killed by Hizb. While those rumors were never verified to my knowledge, the very fact that suspicions always centered on Hekmatyar and his people is an indication of the distrust with which other Afghans viewed the party. So too is the fact that party battlefield collaborations rarely involved Hizb and that Hizb mujahidin groups got into internecine conflicts more consistently than the mujahidin associated with any other party. In the view of Hizbis, theirs was the only legitimate party, and alignments with other parties only compromised them and empowered their unworthy rivals.[71]

Underlying the self-righteousness and intolerance exhibited by Hizb was a profound insecurity, for, alone among the parties, Hizb lacked a firm grounding in Afghan society that could ensure its survival. Thus, unlike Gailani and Mujaddidi, Hekmatyar didn't have a base of disciples, and he also didn't have a network of clerics to build on, as Nabi and Khales did, or the sort of established position and role they had as interpreters to the people of Islamic scripture. He also lacked the kind of natural constituency Rabbani had with non-Pakhtuns and the outside financial resources that

Sayyaf had at his disposal to attract people to his cause. Basically, Hekmatyar had the party itself and the loyalty of young maktabis who, like their leader, had been alienated from the society they sought to transform. However, instead of trying to build alliances that might expand the base of his party, Hekmatyar worked to undermine his rivals, and his principal pre-occupation for much of the war was not defeating the regime in Kabul or forcing the Soviets to withdraw but rather positioning himself to win the end game that would eventually be played among the parties after the victory of the mujahidin.

Coda The Death of Majrooh

In April 1987, the Afghan Information Center (AIC) in Peshawar—the only independent Afghan source of news about the fighting inside Afghanistan—broke its general rule of avoiding news and commentaries on the political situation in Pakistan to note the groundswell of support for Zahir Shah among refugees and mujahidin. This news accompanied indications that the Soviets might at last be ready to leave the country. According to the AIC, support for the king—while most evident among Afghans from the southern provinces—was widespread throughout the refugee and mujahidin communities and came even from some Hizb-i Islami commanders whose endorsement directly contravened their party's official position:

> A large number of refugees from the camps as well as resistance commanders and fighters from all political organisations met in Miranshah, North Waziristan on April 11. People were shouting pro-Zahir Shah slogans. All the speakers at the meeting without exception made strong declarations in his favour. Even Amanullah Mahssur and Shahzada Massud[,] commanders of Hezb-e-Islami (Hekmatyar), commander Khan Gul Khan of Jamiat (Prof. Rabbani), Gulam Jan[,] a Jamiat commander in Samangan[,] and Sufi Abdurrouf[, Gailani] commander in Herat[,] delivered speeches and declared their support to the former king.[1]

This report went on to describe a meeting outside Quetta of some six thousand refugees and mujahidin from the four western provinces (Qandahar, Helmand, Zabul, and Uruzgan) at which the speakers "deplored the persisting disunity among the political leaders and criticised their inability to unite, and at the end all shouted: 'We want King Zahir Shah!'"[2]

To this point in the conflict, the director of the AIC, Professor Sayyid Bahauddin Majrooh, had maintained a determined neutrality on political questions (Fig. 15). Since founding the AIC and taking on the responsibility of editing its bulletin, Majrooh had avoided taking sides with respect to the Peshawar political parties. In the seventy-plus monthly bulletins published up to that time, the activities of the Peshawar leadership were referred to on only a half dozen occasions and then only to report without commentary a new alliance or similar event. The bulletin's focus through early 1987 had been almost exclusively on providing an accurate portrayal of the infighting and intrigues of the Kabul regime and the progress of the war itself, and Majrooh had endeavored to be as comprehensive as possible, including accounts of activities in the most distant provinces and from every party. He also featured interviews with well-regarded commanders, regardless of their party affiliation. In the course of these interviews and in some accounts of the military and strategic situation in different areas, fighting between parties was noted, usually without commentary, and it was also noted when different parties were cooperating with one another in the field. Since Hizb-i Islami was involved in most of the internecine battles within the mujahidin and was rarely involved in battlefield alliances, it received worse coverage in the bulletin than other parties, but the only direct criticism of the party was that expressed by commanders themselves in their interviews.[3]

If Majrooh's assumption of neutrality on the political questions of the war was in part a response to the polarization that existed in Peshawar, it had deeper roots as well. Majrooh's grandfather, Pacha Sahib-i Tigari was one of the principal deputies of the Mulla of Hadda, who set up residence in Upper Kunar, in the interstices between the Safi and Mohmand tribes. Neutrality was one of the services offered by Sufi pirs. In the combative world of tribal honor, they offered sanctuary and mediation when disputes and feuds became excessively burdensome. Majrooh's office in Peshawar was a contemporary variation on a Sufi khanaqa in the sense that all were welcome there. Commanders from different parties could come and tell their stories, and Majrooh earned their respect by keeping himself aloof from the party factionalism that dominated almost every other corner of the city.

Majrooh began to set aside his studied neutrality in the spring of 1987, when talk of an imminent Soviet withdrawal was causing Afghans in Pakistan and abroad to turn their attention to possible endgame scenarios. The article on popular support for Zahir Shah was one of the first indications of Majrooh's shift, and it was followed two issues later by a signed commentary titled "The Future Government of Afghanistan," in which he argued for the formation of a "united political leadership for the resistance."[4] Among the points Majrooh made in this article was that one of the casualties of the war was the traditional respect the Afghan people held for

15. Professor Bahauddin Majrooh (right) with Samiullah Safi, Peshawar, Pakistan, October 1980 (courtesy of Samiullah Safi).

the central government. Prior to 1978, popular insurgencies had rarely been directed against the central government but rather at local officials who had made themselves unpopular with the people. There were exceptions, such as the uprising against Amanullah, but even in such cases the sovereignty of the state had ultimately been reclaimed without significant opposition, and a legitimate ruler had been reinstalled on the throne.

All of this changed, however, when the Khalqis took power. For the first time, "the age-old magical charm" that had kept the population in thrall to the Kabul government was broken, and "rebellion against the central authority . . . was justified, disobedience became lawful[,] fighting the communists a religious and national duty."[5] While it had sustained more damage than at any other time in modern history, the magical charm, Majrooh argued, still had enough vitality to ensure that the leaders in Peshawar would be unable to secure power for themselves once the Soviets had withdrawn and the puppet regime had been overthrown:

> Paradoxically, the same factor . . . which has prevented the Kabul Marxist regime from establishing its authority over the country, is also working against the resistance political leaders. The latter are well respected as persons, and also for their role in the jihad; they are also expected to have a

role in the future political solution, but none of them is considered as a legitimate national leader able to re-establish the respect for a central authority. Anyone of them coming to power will be challenged and other mujahideen groups will find enough justification to fight against the central government.[6]

In Majrooh's view, the only solution to the leadership problem was for the country to accept as its ruler a man "having the aura of the central authority's magical charm around his person—someone like former King Zahir Shah—not attempting to restore the old family rule, but working with an entirely new team."[7] Majrooh may not have been entirely objective in his desire to see Zahir Shah's return to the political arena. His father, Shamsuddin Majrooh, had served as minister of justice under Zahir Shah and had been a member of the committee that drafted the 1964 constitution, which introduced democracy to Afghanistan. Majrooh himself had served as governor of Kapisa Province under Zahir Shah before returning to Kabul University, where he was a dean and professor of philosophy and literature. Despite his associations with the former king, Majrooh viewed the monarch's return as an interim step, a way of rallying the popular support needed to forestall a political free-for-all in the wake of the Soviet withdrawal. Zahir Shah was the only person everyone in the country knew who was not also tainted by association with one or another of the existent political parties. His passivity during the years of the war was in a sense his greatest strength because he didn't have anything in his record to explain— the abuses of his own regime being not only long ago but also trivial compared with what had happened since.

To gauge the level of support for the former king, Majrooh devoted the bulk of the following issue of the bulletin to a survey of Afghan refugees, which asked the question "Who would you like to be the national leader of Afghanistan?" The data-collection team put together by Majrooh contacted more than two thousand respondents in 106 of 249 camps, representing twenty-three of the twenty-eight provinces, the eight major ethnic groups, and all seven political parties. The result was that 72 percent of respondents wanted Zahir Shah as the national leader of Afghanistan. Only nine of the two thousand people surveyed, or 0.45 percent, wanted one of the leaders of the resistance parties in Peshawar, and a mere 12.5 percent indicated that they would like to see the establishment of "a pure Islamic state."[8]

Despite the limits and biases of a survey of this type, the overwhelming support expressed for Zahir Shah, combined with the direct rebuke of the resistance leaders, indicated that the majority of Afghans remained unmoved by the Islamic political rhetoric with which they had been relentlessly assailed for the better part of a decade. Zahir Shah's support may have been largely nostalgic in nature and reflective of his stated view that government should play a limited and nonintrusive role in people's lives. Or it may simply have stemmed from the fact that he was not part of the morass in Peshawar. Whatever the reasons, Majrooh demonstrated with a degree of empirical precision heretofore lacking what everyone had long assumed— namely, that the Afghan people, if given the option, would choose Zahir Shah as their ruler.

In response to calls for his return, Zahir Shah broke his usual silence on exile political affairs in a radio interview with the BBC World Service in which he stated his willingness to serve the Afghan people if called on to do so; he stressed that, if asked to return, he would under no circumstance seek the restoration of the monarchy. These assurances aside, Hizb-i Islami and other radical Islamic parties reiterated their absolute opposition to any negotiated settlement that would bring Zahir Shah back to Afghanistan, even if he were selected through a democratic election. Hekmatyar's position, as well as that of other radical leaders, was that Afghanistan should be an Islamic state and that the head of state should be selected by a council of qualified Islamic scholars and leaders from among those who had played an active part in the jihad. Since he had remained in Europe throughout the war and had made no sacrifices for the jihad, Zahir Shah was disqualified a priori from consideration. Majrooh's commentaries and refugee survey challenged that view and gave ammunition to those who sought a more moderate solution to the political crisis facing Afghanistan after the Soviet withdrawal.

While disunited among themselves, the Peshawar parties had nevertheless succeeded in dominating the political debate and excluding other interest groups and the people at large from participation in discussions about Afghanistan's future. Majrooh tried to break that monopoly and would pay dearly for doing so. Around 5 P.M. on February 11, 1988, gunmen rang the buzzer at his compound gate, and when Majrooh opened the door, they opened fire. The killer or killers apparently had been watching the movements in and out of the compound, for they waited until Majrooh's cook had gone to buy bread at a nearby bakery before ringing the bell. Majrooh had been expecting a visit from the chargé d'affaires of the French embassy in Islamabad, so one imagines that he must have been caught unawares when he opened the gate and saw through the evening dusk the Kalashnikov pointed at his chest. He probably had never seen his killer before, but, in any case, those responsible have never been identified. No person or group has ever stepped forward to claim responsibility, and no solid clues have ever been discovered to indicate why Majrooh was singled out, though few who were familiar with Peshawar were surprised. If anything, many who knew Majrooh were surprised that he had lasted in the city as long as he did.

Majrooh was representative of a type that had largely vanished from the Afghan community in Peshawar. Since he had received his Ph.D. in France, he undoubtedly could have emigrated there or to the United States or Great Britain or Germany. He spoke the languages of all of these places and had friends and admirers abroad who would have helped him secure the necessary papers. But aside from short trips overseas, Majrooh maintained his base in Peshawar and never seriously contemplated leaving. Like his Sufi grandfather perhaps, he seemed happiest and most complete in the thick of warring protagonists, for each of whom he offered equal access and service. His staying might also have had something to do with the profound sense of detachment and solitude one sensed in Majrooh's company. For nearly two years in the mid-1980s, he had been my neighbor, and I frequently dropped in on him at his office. Invariably anywhere from six to twelve men would be sitting around the living room smoking cigarettes and drinking tea, but Majrooh rarely joined them. He was almost always in the adjoining room, listening to the conversation as he typed up one of his stories.

Majrooh was senior in age and status to most of the men who congregated at the AIC office, but his separateness derived from deeper springs of isolation. His name itself was indicative; *majruh* was an appellation, or takhalus, meaning "wounded." The family had adopted the word as its surname years earlier at a time when educated elites in Kabul were fashioning new, more cosmopolitan names for themselves, distinct from the tribal and regional terms by which most people were known when they left their home areas. The term *majruh* has Sufi connotations, evoking the suffering of the believer separated from God, the Beloved, but the name was especially apt for Sayyid Bahauddin. A Parisian intellectual by temperament and training, as well as a Sufi poet, Majrooh was nowhere at home in the world, except perhaps when absorbed in his work. He had children, but no real family or home, having been estranged from two wives. Even his physical condition reflected his chosen name, for years earlier he had been involved in an automobile accident that left him with a permanent limp.

While he hated all that Peshawar had come to represent, Majrooh knew he would never be happier elsewhere, and he seemed even to take a certain perverse satisfaction in defying the moralists who dictated behavior to others. If he chose to smoke French cigarettes and enjoy an occasional glass of Scotch whiskey, that was his business, and he had no need to apologize for it. Majrooh knew his own mind and conducted himself as he pleased. As long as he provided the much-needed service of reporting the war and assisting Western journalists who wanted to see the war for themselves, important commanders and the more open-minded of the leaders were glad for his presence, even after he published an extended poetic allegory titled "The Ego Monster" (*azhdeha-yi khudi*), which told of a traveler journeying in a benighted land not unlike Afghanistan and Pakistan ruled over by tyrants not unlike the leaders in Kabul and Peshawar.

Apparently, Majrooh's decision to openly support the return of Zahir Shah changed the thinking of at least some party leaders as to Majrooh's continued usefulness to their version of the jihad. His proclamations that a wide array of commanders, including some from Hizb-i Islami, supported Zahir Shah's involvement in the peace negotiations undoubtedly made him seem not just expendable but also dangerous to the more radical leaders, particularly when it became known that Majrooh had also been meeting with Felix Ermacora, the United Nations Investigator for the Human Rights Commission, and appeared ready to play a prominent, personal role in U.N. efforts to mediate an end to the fighting. Majrooh possessed the pedigree to assume this role and might have been accepted as a mediator, despite his background as a Westernized intellectual, since most of those with established religious credentials had compromised their neutrality through their involvement with the various parties. Majrooh, the journalist, had not, and he had thus put himself in a position to play an important part in the upcoming negotiations, as his grandfather Pacha Sahib had done on many occasions in his native Kunar Valley and as religious figures have done throughout Afghanistan's history.

Majrooh certainly knew the risks he was incurring by his actions and recognized that he would face the wrath of party leaders; they had turned a blind eye to his presence in the past because they saw him as a benign presence but would be unlikely to do so now. That he was mindful of his jeopardy, however, makes his death no less tragic. The Soviets' announcement of their intention to withdraw from Afghanistan created a brief opportunity for commanders and party leaders and ordinary people to find common cause. Majrooh recognized that the chance was at hand and would soon be lost. This is why, I believe, he decided to break his customary silence on political issues to seek a solution based not on any residual loyalty to the old monarchy but rather on his understanding of Afghan culture and history. In past crises, Afghans had been able to use the institution of the jirga to meet together and choose one among them to rule. The point this time was not for Zahir Shah to reclaim his throne but for the old monarch who had stayed out of the fray for the previous decade to provide a symbol of national unity around which people could rally until a coalition government could be formed. Majrooh was enough of a realist to know that Zahir Shah had neither the charisma nor the vigor nor the strength of character to weld the nation back together as his father had after Amanullah's overthrow. However, he also knew that, if left unchecked, the parties would soon turn the country into carrion, and no other leader had sufficient stature to bring the people to him and, thereby, the parties to heel. It was a perilous wager, but one he chose to make. Lesser men have been called heroes.

8 Epilogue
Topakan and Taliban

QUETTA, Pakistan, November 7 [1994] (Reuters)—Islamic students have captured Afghanistan's second largest city, Kandahar, and freed a Pakistani trade caravan held by guerrillas, Pakistani official sources said Saturday.

They said the 30-truck convoy, held up by two guerrilla commanders Tuesday while on its way to Central Asia, reached Kandahar in southwest Afghanistan Friday when the Taleban student group took control of the city.

The Taleban fighters have also captured Kandahar airport and governor's house, the sources added.

More than 50 people have been killed in four days of clashes between the Taleban and guerrillas, the sources said, quoting reports they said they had received from the area.

The caravan, the first of several Pakistan plans to send to blaze the trail for regular commerce with former Soviet republics, left Baluchistan's provincial capital of Quetta Oct. 29 with gifts for Afghanistan and the two Central Asian republics of Turkmenistan and Uzbekistan.

The trucks were carrying rice, wheat, clothes, medicines, surgical instruments, and X-ray machines.

The party polarization and infighting that I had witnessed in the mid-1980s became even more severe following the Soviet withdrawal in February 1989, as leaders and groups jockeyed to dominate what was expected to be the short endgame to the war. To the surprise of almost everyone, however, the government of President Najibullah refused to fall even after the departure of Soviet troops; his survival was undoubtedly assisted by the failure of the resistance parties to work in a coordinated fashion. Nominally, the seven principal parties established a power-sharing interim government. This new government entity was supposed to establish a capital for itself in Jalalabad, the assumption being that under the combined force of the seven parties the city would quickly capitulate; but the attack failed to dislodge Najibullah's forces, and this failure exacerbated frictions within the resistance coalition, as local fronts—increasingly disconnected from central control—intensified their attacks against one another. Banditry also increased as the withdrawal of the Soviet forces led to a decline in financial assistance to the Peshawar parties and a concomitant reduction of support to local fronts; as a result, many individual commanders had to look to the people around them to provide the resources they needed. In local parlance, this period after the withdrawal of Soviet forces came to be known as *topakeyano daurai,* the time of the gunmen, the nomenclature reflecting the fact that, in people's eyes, the once venerated mujahidin, the warriors of God, had become simply men with guns, intent on their own selfish goals.

President Najibullah, who was still receiving financial help from Moscow, was also stepping up assistance to local militia and front commanders in an effort to undermine the parties' attempt to coordinate their activities. These efforts enabled Najibullah to hang on for several years, but his government finally fell in April 1992, amid a flurry of deal making involving party and former government and militia leaders. Thus, an arrangement among Ahmad Shah Massoud (Rabbani's deputy and the strongman in Panjshir Valley), Parchami leaders in Kabul, and Rashid Dostam (a powerful Uzbek militia leader and former general from northern Afghanistan) enabled Massoud to effect a bloodless takeover of Kabul and to assume the role of defense minister and strongman of the new government. Sibghatullah Mujaddidi assumed the presidency of the new Islamic government, with party leaders agreeing that the presidency and ministerial posts would rotate among them on a regular basis. This arrangement, not surprisingly, proved impractical, and the peace was predictably short-lived as leaders refused to relinquish their formal posts at the end of their allotted turns, and each tried to improve his military position at the expense of the others.

As before, Hekmatyar was among the most ruthless in his pursuit of power, and his Hizb party soon initiated street fighting in an effort to improve its position in the capital. In the bloody skirmishes that followed, old battle lines, most notably the longstanding antagonism between Massoud and Hekmatyar, were renewed, while new ones, such as that between the Shi'a Hizb-i Wahdat and Sayyaf's Saudi-supported Ittihad, were initiated. The primary victims were the residents of Kabul, thousands of whom fled the capital to escape the fighting and incessant rocket attacks.

Further conflict in the winter of 1993 led to the negotiation of a new power-sharing agreement between Rabbani and Hekmatyar that allowed Rabbani to stay on as president past his allotted term and made Hekmatyar prime minister. A sign of the precariousness of this arrangement, however, was that Hekmatyar, fearing for his safety, refused to go to the prime ministry in Kabul from his base in the suburb of Charasiab, while Rabbani was prevented on one occasion from meeting with Hekmatyar at his base by attacks against his convoy.

While the parties were at the center of the fighting in Kabul, one of the most pronounced developments of this period was the radical polarization of ethnic alignments, with Tajiks (including many who had been associated with the Parcham faction in Kabul) rallying to Rabbani and Massoud's cause, Hazaras to the Hizb-i Wahdat party, and Uzbeks to the militia force of Rashid Dostam. All these groups were fearful that, regardless of the talk of establishing a "true" Islamic government, Hekmatyar, Sayyaf, Khales, and the other principal party leaders, all Pakhtuns, would renew the time-honored practice of suppressing and exploiting the non-Pakhtun groups within Afghanistan's borders once they had power in their hands. At the same time, however, while ethnic alignments hardened, the party leaders themselves were as willing as ever to make opportunistic deals across ethnic boundaries to advance their personal positions and to exploit the vulnerabilities of their rivals. Thus, in February 1993, Massoud joined Sayyaf to attack the Shi'a Hazaras, who controlled the western suburbs of Kabul, while in January 1994 Hekmatyar joined forces with Dostam to try to unseat Rabbani and Massoud. This attack, which continued on and off throughout 1994, led to the flight of tens of thousands of residents from Kabul and was halted only when Hekmatyar himself was forced by the emergent Taliban militia to flee Charasiab and set up a new base at Sarobi, on the road between Kabul and Jalalabad.

The appearance of the Taliban in Qandahar and their rapid success in reaching the outskirts of Kabul caused Rabbani, Massoud, and Hekmatyar to come up with a new power-sharing agreement, which briefly kept the militia at bay, but by the fall of 1996 the Taliban had succeeded in dislodging the established Islamic political parties from Kabul and had forced all the party leaders to flee for their lives. Massoud was the only one of the old leaders to mount an effective resistance, but his base in the Panjshir mountains became increasingly isolated and his struggle seemingly ever more quixotic. The rest of the leaders had to content themselves with fulminating to the press, and when the press stopped listening, they mounted websites to continue their efforts to prove that they alone should rule Afghanistan.

EXPLAINING THE TALIBAN TAKEOVER

KABUL, Sept 27 [1996] (Reuters)—Afghanistan's Taleban Islamic militia appeared in full control of Kabul on Friday after entering the capital in tanks and on foot, witnesses said.

They said the streets were bustling with pedestrians, cyclists and cars, and shops and markets were open despite an Islamic holiday. Tanks had pulled back to the side streets although fighters were still visible at key points.

All key government installations appeared to be in Taleban hands including the Presidential Palace and the Ministries of Defence, Security and Foreign Affairs.

No government forces were visible on the city's streets.

Unusual activity was most obvious outside the presidential palace, where crowds had gathered to see the bodies of former President Najibullah and his brother Shahpur Ahmadzai hanging from a concrete traffic-control post.

"We killed him because [he] was the murderer of our people," Noor Hakmal, a Taleban commander who entered the city from Charasyab, south of Kabul, overnight, told Reuters.

Najibullah was ousted in 1992 when Islamic Mujahideen guerrilla forces closed in on Kabul after 14 years of civil war against a Soviet-backed communist government.

The Taleban met little resistance from government forces which had abandoned the city hours before.

Abdul Rahim Ghafoorzai, Afghanistan's deputy foreign minister, said at the United Nations in New York on Thursday that government forces had retreated to prevent civilian casualties.

The Islamic movement announced just hours after the takeover that an interim six-man ruling council would run the country.

A Taleban commander, who gave his name only as Musa, told Reuters the militia was using loudspeakers to tell civilians to go about their daily life as usual.

Musa said he hoped the new regime in Kabul would mean more plentiful food in the capital. But he added hundreds of thousands of civilians would remain vulnerable, particularly in the coming winter.

He said the International Committee of the Red Cross was asking Taleban to protect civilians and not to retaliate or carry out executions.

He said Taleban were not out for revenge.

"Taleban will not take revenge. We have no personal rancour. If the people find someone responsible for crimes in the past we will judge him according to Islamic law," he said.

Musa said Taleban fighters had occupied Afghan army headquarters in the northern suburb of Khairkhana, which was headquarters of government commander General Baba Jan.

He said Taleban forces were heading north from the Bagram airbase they captured last night. "We know the senior government leaders escaped from Kabul to the north," he said.

Musa said the Jala-us-Seraj base further north was still held by the government's top commander Ahmad Shah Massood but Taleban fighters were heading in that direction.

The emergence of the Taliban caught observers of the Afghan scene off-guard. Few people had heard much of this group before it suddenly started moving up from the south, and its immediate and rapid success in consolidating power in and around Qandahar and then in expanding its advance to the suburbs of Kabul was something that no other military force had been able to accomplish in the preceding eighteen years of war. The most common explanation one heard after the Taliban's first appearance was that they were the creation of the same Pakistani security forces—the Inter-Service Intelligence (ISI)—that had built up Hekmatyar and Hizb. One opinion has been that the failure of Hekmatyar to consolidate power led the leaders of ISI to fabricate a new entity to do their bidding, and the Taliban militia was the result. While Pakistan probably played a substantial role in organizing, arming, training, and financing the Taliban, the manpower and the motivation behind the movement cannot be explained away entirely as a Pakistani fabrication, and the ultimate meaning of the Taliban likewise defies so simple or so conspiratorial an explanation. While a comprehensive discussion of the origin of the Taliban is beyond the scope of the present work, I do want to consider the meaning of the Taliban in the context of the discussions in the preceding chapters, particularly the connection between the Taliban and the Islamic political parties that won the jihad yet lost the war and the more general implications of the Taliban in relation to Afghan political culture.

In analyzing the success of the Taliban, it is important to recognize that despite the apparent novelty of the movement, this was not the first time religious students (taliban) played an important role in political events. To the contrary, madrasa students were the principal sources for various political movements in the nineteenth and early twentieth centuries; they were viewed as especially dangerous by the British colonial authorities because they were so difficult to identify or hold accountable. For all the problems the tribes occasionally brought down on the Raj, they were nevertheless locatable on a map; they had villages that could be razed if need be; they had leaders with whom to negotiate and from whom to extract promises; and they had practical and material interests that provided a basis for getting along once the enthusiasms of any given moment had passed. Madrasa students, however, were from everywhere and nowhere; they were often destitute and generally had much more to gain by keeping people in an agitated state than by allowing a conflict to die down.[1]

The contemporary situation is different, but one point of commonality is that religious education once again became an important avenue of social mobility, especially for young male Afghan refugees. On the frontier, at the turn of the last century, becoming a taleb was one of the few ways an individual could improve his life fortunes, gain social respect, and escape the— for some—claustrophobic world of the tribe and the village. In Afghanistan prior to the war, the government sponsored tribal boarding schools, and many of the brightest and most ambitious young men from the border areas attended these schools with the hope of landing a government job after graduation. However, this possibility ended for most Afghans when the war began. Between three and four million people fled to Pakistan, and the vast majority ended up in refugee camps scattered up and down the frontier. Most of the camps had primary schools, and a few secondary schools were set up especially for Afghan refugees. But these schools had more to do with social control than with education, and few who attended them had their life chances expanded as a result. The same was not the case, however, for those who attended madrasas. As in the nineteenth century, a religious education once again became the surest avenue to social advancement. In the years before the war, madrasa graduates generally ended up in menial positions teaching children and taking care of village mosques, but in Pakistan, with the resistance parties in the hands of religious leaders, madrasa graduates had more numerous and lucrative options than ever before. Madrasas were also more vibrant and lively than secular schools and more connected to the world outside because the war, which defined people's lives, was seen as a religious struggle and those who graduated from madrasas were considered more likely to play significant roles in that struggle.

For all the power of the parties, religious schools were by no means simple indoctrination centers. Though party-supported madrasas tended to toe the party line, many other schools remained outside the orbit of politics, found their own financial sponsors, and maintained their independence from the parties. Consequently, through the 1980s and early 1990s, as the reputations of the Islamic political parties and their leaders steadily declined, madrasas kept alive the notion that Afghanistan could still become an ideal Islamic polity. This message held a special potency for veterans of the fighting, who had become disillusioned with the way the jihad was being conducted by the parties, as well as for young refugees who had grown up in camps and who witnessed firsthand the corrupt administration and moral malaise of refugee society.[2]

Those who refer to the Taliban as a creation of the Pakistan government often overlook the fact that the Taliban themselves were in a fundamental way Pakistani, or at least a hybrid of Afghans and Pakistanis. Unlike earlier generations, who were tied to village and tribe, the Taliban generation grew up in refugee camps in Pakistan with people from a variety of backgrounds, and many of them were orphans who had lost one or both parents in the war. In such a context, loyalty to place, to descent group, to tribal ancestor, even to family lost much of its former saliency. Religious schools built on this foundation, bringing together in one place young men from a variety of backgrounds, many of whom had never set foot in Afghanistan and therefore had only vague conceptions of what Afghanistan was like before the war. Like their teachers, most of the madrasa students were disillusioned with the infighting and corruption of the parties but still idealistic in outlook. Having spent months and years in quasi-monastic communities, the potential recruits were also naive in their understanding of the world and relatively untainted by the tribal, regional, ethnic, and party loyalties that conditioned and compromised the values of so many in the refuge universe. They were also, undoubtedly, eager to put into practice what they had been discussing in theory, and the emergence of the Taliban movement offered that opportunity.

One of the most remarkable features of the Taliban's drive to power was how little resistance they encountered up until the siege of Kabul itself. For nearly twenty years, efforts to establish a unified movement had failed, and the question that arises is why the Taliban were successful. In answering this question, one must take into consideration the fact that the early, easy Taliban successes were all in Pakhtun areas; the Taliban did not make significant inroads in non-Pakhtun regions without effort and bloodshed, as evidenced by their prolonged struggle with Massoud for control of the Tajik areas north of Kabul. Even with this caveat, however, the Taliban accomplishment is still considerable, for while Pakhtuns probably made up somewhat less than half of the prewar population of Afghanistan and have long been the most powerful ethnic group in the country, they are also famously fractious, and no party or movement had previously managed to bring so much of this large and disparate population under one political umbrella.

The Taliban's success in moving from madrasa to military movement stems in the first instance from the corruption that preceded them. Part of the Taliban mythology is that Mulla Umar committed himself to forming the Taliban one day when he came across a carload of people by the side of the road who'd been robbed, raped, and killed by former mujahidin who had taken to preying on the people in their area. Whether apocryphal or not, the story is believable within the experience of average Afghans, who came to see the Taliban as a deliverance from the anarchy that had befallen Afghanistan after the Soviet withdrawal.[3] Even before people knew who the Taliban were or what they represented, they were willing to give the Taliban the benefit of the doubt, and even if they were suspicious, they weren't willing to risk their own lives to defend those in charge against the Taliban assault.

Another factor in explaining the Taliban's success is that they consistently downplayed tribal or regional identities in favor of what might be called "village identity." As a Taliban spokesman stated to Western reporters in an interview, "Our culture has been greatly changed over the past 40 or 50 years, particularly in Kabul. In the villages the culture has not changed much. . . . The Taliban are trying to purify our culture. We are trying to re-establish a purist Islamic culture and tradition."[4] In identifying purist culture and tradition with the Islam of the village, the Taliban were indirectly condemning the Islam of the parties since most of the party leaders were products of Kabul University or had worked for state-sponsored institutions. They were also putting themselves on a par with the people whose support they had to enlist if their movement was going to be successful. The truth was that the Taliban themselves, having spent most of their lives in refugee camps, armed mujahidin groups, and religious madrasas, had little experience of villages, but this was still an effective position to take, given the nostalgia people felt for the world they remembered or at least imagined before the war.

An additional point in the Taliban's favor was the relative invisibility of their leadership. Although the Taliban was nominally headed by the rarely seen and seldom heard Mulla Umar, most decisions emanated from a council of Islamic clerics headquartered in Qandahar. No one knows much about these men, and they appear to have made it a point of policy to keep a low profile. One can only speculate on the motivation behind this strategy, but it seems reasonable to conclude that it might be related to the people's disillusionment with the all-too-visible leaders of the established religious parties, who did so much to divide the country. In this sense, the Taliban in their first period seemed to represent something like an anticharismatic movement; the emphasis was not on leaders and their promises but on the movement itself and its supposed rootedness in an idealized sort of ordinary village existence that had been absent for twenty years and that was longed for all the more for that reason. The fact that most of those who were recruited into the Taliban movement had little experience of the village life they idealized mattered less than the fact that the movement's leaders promised a return to this life and were distinctly different in their approach to politics than were the parties that had come before.

Perhaps the most significant reason for the Taliban's success though was simple exhaustion. As the Taliban movement began to pick up steam in 1995, their reputation for keeping security preceded them into each new area. Thus, for example, when they launched their attack on eastern Ningrahar Province, where roadblocks had become a fixture of everyday life and renegade mujahidin operated with impunity, the local population failed to support local commanders, even when they were from the same tribe or ethnic group; the people were simply tired of the status quo and willing to accept the new leadership, despite its promises of certain austerities and purist doctrines that deviated from established custom. While the Taliban did not gain mastery over the entire country, the roads in areas they did control were relatively safe. People were able to ride buses without fear of being searched at roadblocks, something they had been unable to do for years, and trucks carried goods without having to pay exorbitant road taxes. That may not sound like much of an accomplishment, and it is generally ignored in Western accounts, but after a decade of Soviet rule and more years of predation by former mujahidin commanders, basic security was a longed-for luxury and sufficient reason for many to offer their support to the new regime.

THE CHANGING PLACE OF ISLAM

KABUL, March 17 [1997] (Reuters)—Afghanistan's purist Taleban rulers pledged their support for a revival of Moslem and Afghan culture at a seminar in Kabul which concluded on Monday.

"I would like to give my assurances that I will do my best for the support of those involved in cultural spheres, the education of future generations, and for the preservation of our genuine culture," said a message from Taleban leader Mullah Mohammed Omar, read out at a two-day seminar on "Endeavours Directed at the Revitalisation of Islamic Culture." Omar's message also asked Afghans to reject foreign cultures.

"Everyone should reject foreign cultural influences and abide by their own cultural values," said the message.

On the podium behind the speakers hung a banner reinforcing the message: "The struggle against colonialist culture is the duty of every Moslem," it said.

Since first appearing in Afghanistan more than two years ago, the Taleban have forced women in territory under their control to wear the burqa, the traditional Afghan head-to-toe veil that has a small patch of gauze over the eyes. They have declared that Saudi-style veils, which do not cover the eyes, are not allowed.

There seems to be some confusion in the Taleban ranks on the over-
lapping of Islamic laws and traditional culture of southern Afghanistan,
home to most of the Taleban.

Although the edict concerning burqas was publicly justified by saying that Sharia, or Islamic law, demanded it, the head of the Taleban's
highest court told Reuters that Sharia allows women to bare their faces.

"Sharia allows women to have their faces unveiled as long as there is
no sign of agitation or lust on their faces. However we are now in an
emergency situation, so it is right that women should have their faces
covered," Mullah Abdul Ghaffour Sanani said.

Some Afghans have expressed concern that the Taleban were using
Sharia as an excuse to impose southern Afghan culture on this
ethnically and culturally diverse nation.

The tradition that women should not work and should stay at home,
which has been made law by the Taleban in areas they control, has
never been part of the northern Afghan way of life, although it is common in the southern provinces.

Although in Monday's message Omar pledged Taleban support for
the education of future generations, that support does not yet include
education for women.

Women were excluded from Kabul University when it was officially
re-opened last week.

The Minister for Higher Education told journalists that the
segregated education of women would begin when resources became
available, but that women would only be allowed to study certain
subjects.

"The main problem is a lack of resources. We need separate facilities
for girls and we do not have enough women teachers, but if we get the
resources, women's faculties in certain subjects will be allowed to open,"
said Higher Education Minister Maulawi Hamdullah Noumani.

"Although they may not be allowed to study engineering for example, they will be allowed to study medicine, home economics and teaching," he said.

There were 4,000 female students at the university before the
Taleban took over Kabul last September and closed the university.

While the reasons for their initial success may be debated, there is little
doubt that the Taliban have redefined the role of religion in Afghan political culture, particularly the relationship between religion, state, and tribe. In
an earlier age, Islam had played an interstitial role between the tribes and
the state. Having no coercive power of their own to wield, Muslim leaders
had to rely on their charisma and powers of persuasion to fuse tribal coalitions or, contrarily, to ingratiate themselves with and becomes allies or even

functionaries of the ruler. Muslim leaders existed on the in-between margins; on the one hand they pulled the tribes out of their insularity through a rhetoric of common submission and promises of eternal reward, and, on the other hand, they served as mediators and guarantors of state authority at the peripheries of government control. On those occasions when the ruler overstepped his authority, Muslim leaders were in a position to exaggerate and channel tribal energies outward rather than in the usual internecine directions. Likewise, when tribes became fractious, the ruler could recruit Muslim leaders with established followings in the tribes to help calm the storm of discontent or to redirect it against an enemy common to the tribes and the state; this enemy could be either another tribe or ethnic group (Hazaras and Uzbeks were the most frequent targets) or that other ruler over yonder (most often the British, but later also the Pakistanis). In all cases, Muslim leaders stood betwixt and between, possessing a forceful ideology but little power of their own.

In the middle decades of the twentieth century, the relationship of Islam, tribe, and state became more complex, but this basic structure remained the same. Religious leaders like the Hazrat of Shor Bazaar and Naqib Sahib continued to court tribal support, making periodic visits to the homelands of their supporters and welcoming delegations of visitors to their khanaqas; but they also accepted visits from the king and his ministers, along with occasional marriages with the royal family, and in some cases they held official positions within the court and government bureaucracy. The political tenor of these relationships became increasingly muted, particularly following the overthrow of Amanullah. Established religious families and lesser figures were pulled into the orbit of the state; madrasas and shrines were put on the dole; and new graduates of religious schools were given government sinecures. However, the possibilities for antagonism were never entirely eliminated, if only because no individual figure or family could represent Islam or hold a monopoly of power. Charismatic leaders could always appear unexpectedly and seemingly out of nowhere, as was the case with Maulana Faizani. In addition the advent of modern communication and transportation meant that Afghanistan, more than ever, was connected to broader currents of political activism that the government could not control, particularly with the expansion of secondary schools and universities, sympathetic places for radical political ideas from abroad to incubate and develop.

In the overheated environment of Peshawar, the multiple strands of Afghan religious political culture intertwined and cross-fertilized. Old-style clerics began imitating the young radicals by forming political parties of their own, while younger radicals educated in secular schools memorized the Qur'an and hadith to prove their own Islamic bona fides; but this cross-fertilization did not lead to a fusion of purpose and conduct, despite the obvious commonality of interest of the different factions and their declarations of common devotion to Islam. Rather, Peshawar became its own insulated world, cut off from the rest of Afghan society, a world that finally referred more to itself than to the struggle going on inside Afghanistan. The parties headquartered in Peshawar lost touch with the basic truth of Afghan history: that religious leaders don't have power of their own—they borrow it from others. In the past, religious leaders had gained authority through association with the tribes or the government in Kabul. This time, the parties gained leverage from the patronage of Pakistan, the United States, Saudi Arabia, and China, and they were successful as long as they had massive infusions of financial and military assistance from these sources. But with the departure of the Soviet Union, much of that assistance dried up, the parties had less to offer, and whatever credibility they still had with the people had largely withered because of their ruthless pursuit of their own political agendas.

The Taliban prospered at first because they seemed to renounce the ways of the parties. Their approach was different, and they seemed to care about and identify with the people. Unlike the parties, which could never surmount their individual political interests when given the opportunity to rule, the Taliban managed to form a government with a unified purpose and direction, and they have sustained much of this unity, or at least the appearance of unity, despite the severe economic and military challenges they have faced. In evaluating this accomplishment it is easy to ignore how novel the situation is in the *longue durée* of Afghan history. Although it has happened before in smaller contexts, the reign of the Taliban represents the first time, at least since the advent of the Afghan state under Ahmad Shah Abdali, that religion does not function as support for the ruler but is identical with state rule. Given the rough-and-ready rural background of the Taliban, from their top leaders to their rawest recruits, and the regime's self-conscious identification with an idealized "village" culture, one might even go so far as to argue that the Taliban victory has fused all three traditional legs of Afghan political culture—Islam, state, and tribe—and that being the case, one might have expected the Taliban to be more successful than it has proven to be in uniting the country in the wake of their relatively easy early triumphs.

THE FAILURE TO UNIFY AFGHANISTAN

MIRAN SHAH (North Waziristan), January 26 [1999] (NNI): An Afghan tribe in the western province of Khost has demanded of Taliban authorities to hand over the militia officials involved in the killing of several people last week. At least 6 persons, including a woman, were killed and 2 women injured in fighting between a local tribe and Taliban officials in Khost on Wednesday.

The fighting broke out when youth of Gurbuz tribe refused to obey Taliban's orders to stop playing a traditional "egg fighting" game, they said. Taliban officials stopped the children from the game, which they considered as un-Islamic.

Taliban had sent a jirga (team) of Pakistani religious scholars and Afghan elders to the Gurbuz tribe for resolution of the dispute but failed to reconcile the angry tribesmen. Taliban have rejected the demand to hand over their officials to the tribe.

The Gurbuz tribe, which had backed Taliban when they tried to capture the Khost province, has announced withdrawal of its support to the student militia's administration.

Ulema returned here from Afghanistan say tension has gripped the area following the incident and Taliban are facing problem to deal with the situation. Taliban, who control some 90 per cent of Afghanistan, enforced strict Islamic laws in the areas controlled by them.

Before the Soviet invasion, there had always been an adaptive side to Afghanistan's political incoherence, particularly given its location at the interstices of powerful empires in Iran, the Indian subcontinent, and Central Asia. As the British discovered to their dismay, securing the capital tended to enflame rather than behead the resistance. Captured kings were replaceable, and the presence in Kabul of a foreign host provided a context for desperate and mutually antagonistic tribes and ethnic groups to rally together, most often under the inspirational leadership of a Sufi saint or revered clerical leader. Then, once the foreign presence had been expelled, the steady state of balanced opposition between the central government, the tribes, and Islam could reassert itself, with a new king taking control of the capital, the tribes retiring to their homelands enriched with booty, and the saints and clerics returning to their schools and shrine centers shrouded in reverence.

The advantages of incoherence in relation to the external world are apparent, but perhaps incoherence has also been internally adaptive—perhaps the existence of separate realms of discourse and moral expectation has provided a degree of internal flexibility that has dampened more extreme turbulence within this multiethnic, linguistically heterogeneous, historically composite, and never entirely logical nation-state. In their zeal to over-

come the abuses of the previous twenty years and to create a new foundation for the country, the Taliban have instituted an uncompromising moral
severity and inflexibility that, abuses aside, does not mesh well with Afghan
sensibilities, especially the valorization of individual autonomy that is
shared across the ethnic and regional spectrum. Afghans rejected the
Marxist regime principally because they came to believe that Taraki, Amin,
and later Karmal were intent on imposing a foreign moral code on the country, and now many feel that the Taliban are trying to do the same thing—
this time instituting under the cover of "village morality" religious mores
that are more parochial and conservative than those of the vast majority of
Afghans, including most Afghans from rural areas. Ironically, the Qandahari
villages that Mulla Umar and other top Taliban officials come from are
famous throughout Afghanistan for their enjoyment of music, dancing, and
games of various sorts. One comes to the conclusion that the Taliban call for
a return to "village morality" has as little connection to real villages as the
Khalqi valorization of "downtrodden peasants" did to the struggles of actual
people. One also suspects that just as the isolation of Kabul-based Marxist
leaders from the lives of the rural poor led them to formulate unrealistic
social programs, so the cloistered society of the all-male madrasa has led the
Taliban to create an idealized vision of Afghan villages unmoderated by the
domestic influences of women, families, elders, and the everyday realities of
tilling fields, tending flocks, and raising children.

The Taliban failure to consolidate their early victories is most pronounced in non-Pakhtun areas, where the people see the emergence of the
Taliban as one more instance of Pakhtun hegemony. During the course of
the war, the non-Pakhtuns of the country, who control more than half the
land mass and constitute close to half the population, became disengaged
from their dependence on the central government and ever more distrustful of the parties in Peshawar. Back in the 1980s, when I spoke with Uzbek,
Tajik, or Hazara mujahidin who had journeyed to Peshawar to negotiate
with the parties for weapons, they always expressed wariness and suspicion
of what was going on around them. They walked the streets of Peshawar in
groups, not interacting much with Pakhtun Afghans and keeping to themselves. It seemed that they felt almost as alien in Peshawar as they would
have among the enemy in Kabul, where at least they would have encountered more people who looked like themselves and who spoke the same languages and dialects. While they still had need of the financial support
offered by the parties, the non-Pakhtun populations of Afghanistan became
more independent and self-assured over the course of the war. The parties
provided for certain of their needs, but they otherwise went about their

business, developing local organizations and institutions of their own and in some cases developing alternative avenues for the supply for weapons and ammunition.

Since the Taliban have come to power, non-Pakhtun groups have shown little willingness to relinquish their hard-earned autonomy, and the determination of the Taliban to impose their morality throughout the country has further alienated groups with different and often considerably more liberal traditions (for example, with regard to female veiling and the right of individuals to worship as often and with whom they please) than those of the conservative and conformist Taliban. With much of the population exhausted and impoverished from decades of war, distrustful of political leaders and of other ethnic groups, and, in many areas, suffering from prolonged drought and famine, it is not surprising that, with the exception of Massoud's continuing holdout in the Panjshir Valley, a widespread and sustained military challenge to the Taliban has not yet arisen. However, evidence of popular discontent is considerable. Stories regularly filter out of local disputes, such as the one in Gurbuz in 1999, involving villagers who fight back when local Taliban authorities try to tell them, for example, how to celebrate a marriage or a circumcision. Other cases are more serious, such as the 1997 uprising in Mazar-i Sharif, which left thousands dead and many more homeless. Similar incidents have occurred in Herat and the Hazarajat, as well as in Pakhtun areas like Kunar, where the people resent the Qandahari ascendance almost as much as Uzbeks, Tajiks, and Shi'a Hazaras do.

While the Taliban have generated hostility in Pakhtun areas, there is little doubt that antagonism to the regime is most concentrated in non-Pakhtun areas and that the regime has greatly exacerbated ethnic divisions within the country that were already made worse during the Soviet occupation. Thus, even before the Taliban came to power, one notable result of the war was the loss of an Afghan lingua franca. Before the war, young people throughout the country learned both Dari Persian and Pakhtu, but the collapse of the educational system and the exodus of mostly Pakhtun refugees to Pakistan and Iran mean that most of the younger generation of Afghans is more likely to speak only their native tongue or to have Urdu as a second language than to be conversant in the two Afghan national languages. When they first came to power, the Taliban claimed to represent all Afghans, and some Afghans I have spoken with believe that their public execution of former president Najibullah was a demonstration of their intention not to offer more favorable treatment to Pakhtuns.[5] Whatever the original ambitions, however, few doubt that divisions are stronger than ever—particularly between Persian and Pakhtu speakers. Some Afghans I have spoken with even contend that, were it not for the large numbers of Pakhtuns who were forcibly resettled in the north by the government since the time of Amir Abdur Rahman, Afghanistan would now be a divided country, with Pakhtuns ruling south of the Hindu Kush, Tajiks and Uzbeks contending for control of the north, and Hazaras holding out against both sides in the center.

One lesson from the Taliban experience is that a degree of political indeterminacy of the sort that had previously existed in Afghanistan may be necessary for effective rule, with respect to both forces outside the borders and the heterogeneous population within. Perhaps the triangulated political culture of the past, which had seemed incoherent and destructive of civil society, was actually its guarantor. More simply, perhaps people like their rulers to be separate from themselves and are not so eager to abandon the moral logic of opposition—of tribe/ethnic group and state, of "rough" village ways and "smooth" urban custom. The failure of the Taliban to consolidate their rule forces the question of whether their subjects want uniformity across social planes and to have their cities treated as though they were big villages. Afghan culture has long been defined by dynamic oppositions, not by transparency and sameness, and people generally might be more eager to explore the future than to accompany their rulers on their excursion into the past.

CONCLUSION

KABUL, January 25 [2001] (AP)—The Taliban religious police have jailed 22 hairdressers accused of propagating a western-style haircut referred to among young men in Kabul as "the Titanic," residents said Thursday. The hairstyle mimics that of actor Leonardo DiCaprio and the cut is named for the movie in which he starred.

Religious police deployed by the Taliban's Ministry of Vice and Virtue—responsible for imposing the religious militia's brand of Islamic rule—say the hairstyle is offensive, according to Mohammed Arif, a barber in Kabul.

The hairstyle allows hair on the forehead, which the Taliban say could interfere with a person's ability to say his prayers. Muslim prayers are said while bowing toward Mecca in Saudi Arabia, Islam's holiest site.

The arrests began last Saturday. Some 22 men have been arrested, Arif said.

It's not clear whether they will be punished or what the punishment might be. So far none of those arrested have been freed.

In the 95 percent of Afghanistan that they control, the Taliban have imposed a harsh brand of Islamic law that espouses public punishment for most offenses. The Taliban also ban most forms of light entertainment and demand men grow beards and pray in the mosque.

Arif said men secretly trim their beards, an offense according to the Taliban.

"They come very early in the morning or very late at night," he said. "It is done very secretly and only for friends," he said.

I began this book with a description of Lowell Thomas's trip in 1922, when the American showman set out to meet the Afghan king in "forbidden Afghanistan" and found instead a Hollywood stage set. Thomas encountered not an exotic Oriental despot but a progressive leader intent on dressing up his nation to prepare it for a different future than his people had ever imagined they might have. When I first lived in Afghanistan, I discovered that Amanullah's dream had not died with the overthrow of his regime five years after Thomas's visit. The students I met each day in class had absorbed something like his dream and wanted something like the future Amanullah had sought, and they too dressed for the occasion in cast-off Western clothing that seemed no less dignified for being second-hand.

Recently, I had the chance to view the film *Naim and Jabar*, discussed in the Introduction, which captures so well the sense of possibility that students felt before the revolution. It was the first time I had watched the film in a number of years, and I saw again the earnest longing of fourteen-year-old Naim, who wants so desperately to join his friend Jabar at the high school in Mazar-i Sharif. New details appeared to me with this viewing—such as Naim's response to the filmmaker's question of what he would do if he were admitted to the school ("I'd conquer Aq Kuprak," his home village) and what he'd do if he were rejected ("My heart will break, by God"). This time I noticed as well the blind and absolute faith that the two boys' fathers—both landless farmers and itinerant laborers—place in education as a path for their sons ("If I am down to my last crust, my children go to school"). And I saw more clearly than ever the look of desperation in Naim's face as it becomes clear to him that his desires will not be realized, that he will be getting on the truck to go back home to the village rather than starting school in the city. Still, the most poignant moment in the film was the one I discussed in the first chapter when Naim, wearing his new coat, casually removes his head covering after Jabar has whispered in his ear that his friends will think he is "a villager" if they see him wearing a turban. More than a quarter century later, that scene is sadder and more poignant than ever. If a butterfly beating its wings off the coast of Africa can, in theory, set off the chain of meteorological events that culminates in a hurricane in the Gulf of Mexico, could not a gesture like this be linked to the political maelstrom that followed?

In *Imagined Communities*, Benedict Anderson wrote of the pilgrimage to the city of village boys, all speaking different languages and wearing their regional costumes, all transiting through primary and secondary schools, where their separate dialects and costumes were melded into one and where they were transformed into functionaries of the state.[6] Afghanistan's progress in the last half century begins with the expansion of the state into ordinary lives, much as Anderson describes in Southeast Asia, and the early life histories of Nur Muhammad Taraki, Samiullah Safi, and Qazi Amin in their different ways all provide examples of the sort of nationalized youth about whom Anderson writes so eloquently. However, these men became not government functionaries but revolutionaries intent on disrupting and overturning the institutions of the state. Taraki, Safi, and Qazi Amin couldn't be more different in most respects. Their goals were contradictory, and they each detested what the others represented, yet their similarities are also profound—most important, their shared commitment to social progress as they each defined that ideal.

However impoverished he may have been as a child and however mistreated his family by feudal landlords, Taraki's vision of social justice seems to have owed less to personal experience than to his own flights of imagination and his reading of socialist theories that he spun together in his novels and speeches. When he suddenly and unexpectedly had the opportunity to resolve in real life the sorts of social dilemmas he lamented in his writings, Taraki proceeded with ill-considered haste. The decision to implement social reform on a host of fronts may have been due to Hafizullah Amin's influence, but Taraki's poor connection to social realities outside Kabul and perhaps his vanity kept him from objecting.

Samiullah Safi's notion of social justice seems separated from reality for different reasons. He was from the opposite end of the socioeconomic spectrum and learned his way in the world watching a father who, in his own valley, commanded fear rather than pity. In Safi's world, there was much talk of the equality of honor and the importance of personal autonomy, but equality of means was never a possibility. Men affected equality through their adherence to the tribal code, which Safi could exalt; however, his testimony reveals a man who remained troubled by the contradictions poverty posed to the values of his people. Safi also saw the great man, his father, wrenched from his valley and forced to suffer humiliations at the hands of a government that viewed his power and wealth with suspicion. This experience engendered indignation at government abuses and its failure to care for the people, but indignation only briefly found its channel, perhaps because Safi could never feel entirely at home in the presence of the strangers he called kinsmen.

In my meetings with Qazi Amin, social principles rarely came up—perhaps because I focused my questions on the events happening around me, as I tried to make sense of Peshawar politics. But I don't think this is the whole answer, for none of the leaders in Peshawar—or anyone else for that matter—spent much time worrying about principles. It always appeared that when leaders brought up abstract matters like what an Islamic state should stand for, how it should organize economic life and treat its people, they were doing so to gain an advantage over their rivals. These leaders were animated not by abstract matters but by the politically relevant questions of precedence (Who started the jihad and was therefore entitled to lead it?) and qualification (Did a madrasa education count more than a university one? Were maulavis or maktabis better suited to run the government?).

In this way, the impassioned debates of the 1960s over ideals and first principles were superseded by a more brutal concern for power, in pursuit of which the primary actors found themselves trusting those most like themselves regardless of their political beliefs. Thus, one of the saddest ironies of the Afghan conflict is that the contest of ideas between Marxist and Islamist ideologues ultimately mutated into an ethnic struggle between Pakhtun and non-Pakhtun. At the center of this development was the rivalry between Ahmad Shah Massoud and Gulbuddin Hekmatyar for preeminence in the resistance. As each sought advantage over the other, belief gave way to self-interest, and self-interest to compromise, with both leaders seeking alliances with former ideological enemies who would give them additional leverage and who could be trusted because they were something close to kin. Perhaps because his was the more precarious position, Massoud appears to have been the first to make this move; the alliances he forged with Tajik Parchamis in Kabul in turn led to the separate peace with the Soviet invaders that he began to negotiate in the late 1980s. When Hekmatyar saw Massoud first attracting Western aid and adulation and then making deals with the government in Kabul, he did everything in his power to undermine his rival and proved equally willing to broker his own deals with Pakhtun Khalqis who could help him move closer to his ultimate ambition of ruling Afghanistan.

The most gruesome irony of the partisan strife and bloodletting that bedeviled Afghanistan during the last three decades of the twentieth century is that the idealistic visions of progress that animated Afghan politics in the democratic period ended with the Taliban. Arresting men for growing their hair is an example chosen for its resonance with earlier examples where appearance also mattered, but it is only one of many reported instances in which the Taliban Bureau for the Promotion of Virtue and Prevention of Vice (amr bi al-ma'ruf wa nahi 'an al-monkar) imposed its moral vision of a future defined entirely by the past. Sadly, virtually the only reports that make it into Western media regarding Afghanistan have to do with public punishments for various offenses. One time the story is of women caught in public without their burqa veils; another time it is of men flogged for clipping their beards too short; the next is of thieves having their hands and feet surgically removed or of homosexuals having mud walls toppled on their backs for the crime of sodomy.

While Western media tend to forget the years of war, invasion, and predation that hardened the Taliban in their severity and also to ignore other, less sensational stories like the multiyear drought that has made vast stretches of the country uninhabitable or the success of the Taliban in lowering poppy production, the Taliban campaign for public morality is a significant story and deserves attention for what it tells us of the regime and its vision of society. And what we learn from these stories is not so much that the Taliban rule through fear but that they rule out of fear. The fear that grips the regime more than any other is the fear of having any intercourse with the larger world; and *intercourse*, with its sexual connotations, is the appropriate word to use in this context, for in the Taliban vision of the world all relations with outsiders, particularly non-Muslims, carry the taint of the licentious and forbidden.

If, as I have implied, Naim's disposable turban can be taken as an appropriate symbol for the fearlessness that fueled the revolutionary movements that collectively tore Afghanistan apart, then the indispensable burqa that is being reimposed on the women of Kabul is certainly the best symbol for the fearful spirit that animates the Taliban rulers today. The burqa tries to preserve a rigid divide between male and female, public and private. It seeks to manage threats to women's virtue by eliminating situations of insecurity and ambiguity. More intimately, it speaks to male anxieties over being shamed before peers and to men's need to maintain control over uncertain circumstances whatever the costs to themselves and their dependents; and in this respect, the hypermorality of the Taliban bears as much resemblance to the honor-based insecurities of Sultan Muhammad Khan as it does to the quotidian practices of village Islam, which the regime claims to represent. Taken as a more general symbol of Afghanistan under the Taliban, the burqa can be seen to embody a spirit opposite to the one the young people I met in 1975 possessed in such abundance. Those young people so wanted the world to open up for them, to offer them new experiences. Now the youthful faces of the Taliban, faces that have known mostly war, refugee camps, and the cloistered confines of all-male madrasas, stare back with unblinking negation. Nothing outside their own world is good, nothing outside their own experience and their scriptural lessons is worth emulating or caring about. The world for them is closed.

Stories like the one about "Titanic" haircuts offer some hope at least. In another context, a story of boys imitating a popular film star's hairstyle would hardly be news, but in present-day Afghanistan, where men are forced to wear black turbans to work and to keep their beards long and where every other form of nonconformity is a punishable offense, it is significant that boys the same age as many in the Taliban risk punishment to keep some exposure to the outside world alive. It is also sadly ironic that the film of the great ship that hit an iceberg and sank in the North Atlantic should be so popular in this landlocked desert nation that is itself like a great ship rocked by natural forces (repeated earthquakes, devastating droughts followed by bitter-cold winters, plagues of locusts) and buffeted by wave after wave of political turmoil.

The paramount question now is whether the Taliban vision is one that Afghans generally will embrace or at least accept. While the people's devotion to Islam is deep and abiding, it cannot be said that they are clamoring for a more orthodox approach to their faith, that they want to rid religious practices of customary overlays like shrine visitation, that they feel the government needs to intervene to make sure people attend the mosque on Fridays, or that they are as worried as their rulers about women's dress and men's turbans. The Taliban has premised its rule on precisely these matters, and from the moment the movement captured Kabul and, in its first public act, hung the castrated bodies of former President Najibullah and his brother from a traffic light in the city center, it has gone about its business in a public and often spectacular style. If this manner of exercising power resembles anything, it might—ironically—be the reign of Abdur Rahman, who likewise ruled with his whip hand and incurred the wrath of his subjects for his brutality. But as ruthless as he could be with those who challenged his power, Abdur Rahman also recognized the need to meet people's basic needs and to accept progress and technology where it could augment his authority and bring prosperity to his kingdom. To date, the Taliban have shown little of Abdur Rahman's larger vision for the nation's future to go along with their exercise of power, and so one suspects that their own tenure may be short-lived.

Speculation about the future aside, another question of special significance to my project concerns whether the Taliban victory represents a decisive break with the political culture of the past. The monarchy, at least in its recognized form, is gone, but the tribes may not be. They and other more remotely located ethnic groups (Hazaras in the center of the country, Turkmen and Uzbeks in the northwest, Tajiks in the northeast, Nuristanis on the eastern frontier) are pursuing their own goals and taking advantage of their opportunities while the Taliban continue to expend most of their energies subduing the immediate threat of Massoud. Borders these days are also porous. Commercial traffic of various sorts, much of it involving illegal drugs, weapons, and smuggled goods, flows in and out, and it is increasingly unclear whether it makes sense to speak of a coherent political structure of any sort. The future of Pakistan as a nation-state is also tenuous; the collapse of that country's governing structure would make Afghanistan's existence even more precarious and would perhaps lead to the complete disappearance of the boundaries separating the two countries, as well as those to the north and perhaps also to the west. Afghanistan would then effectively come to an end, and the rules of nation-state engagement that have held firm in the region for the last hundred years would cease to matter.

In key respects, conditions would be similar to those that Abdur Rahman confronted before he forged the Afghan state at the end of the nineteenth century; at that time power was not institutionally fixed in administrative structures and demarcated at external borders, but rather it radiated out from various charismatic centers. The cycle would thus begin again, but it would be fair to say that this age is not conducive to heroic action, as that time arguably was. While the political conditions might recapitulate those of an earlier era, things have changed. Weapons of personal destruction are more powerful and menacing, the means of communication and transportation are quicker and more efficient, competing forms of purist Islam and ethnic nationalism have coalesced and hardened against one another. All that can be said with certainty is that ordinary people now, as before and ever since, will more often be the victims of political change than the beneficiaries. That, sadly, is one facet of the situation that is unlikely to change whoever rules Afghanistan in the future.

Notes

1. INTRODUCTION

1. Thomas 1928. Unless indicated otherwise, all quotes in this section are taken from this work.

2. When Thomas first got to India, he seemed to have had it in mind to focus his story on a colonial officer, Major Francis Yeats-Brown of the Seventeenth Bengal Lancers, whom he had met during his travels. Yeats-Brown, or "Y. B." as Thomas called him, was the closest approximation to Lawrence that Thomas could come up with. Fluent in a number of local languages and reportedly prone to dressing up in native dress and disappearing for days at a time in the native suq, Yeats-Brown was also an aviator and war hero, having been shot down behind Turkish lines during the war. Like Lawrence, he had even performed undercover intelligence work, in his case, in the guise of a middle-class German woman living in Istanbul! Yeats-Brown was, in other words, Lawrence flambé, with a heavy sauce of Rudyard Kipling on top. Fortunately or unfortunately for Thomas's travelogue, Y. B. was unable to play a role in the Afghan adventure because of the refusal of the Afghan government to issue an entry visa to a British officer.

3. Thomas 1976, 248.

4. See Mack 1976 and Caton 1999.

5. Curzon 1923, 59.

2. LIVES OF THE PARTY

1. The PDPA was known in Persian as Hizb-i Democratik-i Khalq-i Afghanistan and in Pakhtu as da Afghanistan da Khalq o Democratik Gund.

2. Male 1982.

3. *Kabul Times*, May 4, 1978. The *Kabul Times* was a government-run newspaper. Grammatical errors in this and subsequent quotations from government publications are in the originals.

4. *Kabul Times*, August 16, 1978.

5. In a story published in the *Kabul Times* on December 13, 1978, the government claimed that Bacha-i Saqao was influenced by "Col. Lawrence" and "Moslem-looking farangis" posing as mullas, who inspired him to lead his rebellion against Amanullah. In an interesting addendum to the story of Lowell Thomas's visit to Kabul, Lawrence also made his way to the Afghan frontier in the late 1920s, in his case serving as an ordinary soldier in a British garrison. Lawrence had enlisted under an assumed name to escape the crush of publicity that followed him in England, but word got out that he was on the frontier, and it occasioned numerous rumors inside Afghanistan that he had somehow orchestrated Amanullah's overthrow.

6. "A Glance at Historic Crimes of Naderi Dynasty in Afghanistan," *Kabul Times,* May 4, 1978.

7. Nur Muhammad Taraki, speech delivered on the fifty-ninth anniversary of the Third Anglo-Afghan war, Radio Afghanistan, August 19, 1978; quoted in Foreign Broadcast Information Series (hereafter FBIS), South Asia Review, vol. 5, August 21, 1978, 52–56.

8. *Kabul Times,* May 4, 1978.

9. Hafizullah Amin, speech delivered at the opening ceremony of the Academy of Sciences of Afghanistan and reprinted in the *Pashto Quarterly* 2 (1–2) (Autumn–Winter 1978–1979): v–xxxii.

10. On the dangers of kibr, see Edwards 1996, ch. 2.

11. "The Biography of the Great Leader," reproduced "by popular demand" in the *Kabul Times,* October 30, 1978. It was also reprinted in the January 1979 issue of the *Afghanistan Council Newsletter* 7 (1): 30–32.

12. Edwards 1996, 51.

13. Ibid., 78–79.

14. According to Taraki's biography, "his outstanding works that greatly enthused the youth were as follows:

1. The Drugged Traveller, a revolutionary and class-conscious novel.
2. The White, a revolutionary and class conscious novel.
3. Sela (a lonely man in search of work) a revolutionary and class-conscious novel.
4. The Peasant's Daughter, a revolutionary and class-conscious short story.
5. The New Life, a profound appraisal of the three fundamental parts of the working class ideology namely economy, philosophy and scientific socialism."

15. Unrest of this sort was not limited to Kabul. In several provincial towns, demonstrations led to clashes between Marxist and Muslim students. One such confrontation occurred in the town of Gardez in Paktia Province in the winter of 1966. In that incident, Muslim students reportedly tied a cloth around a stray dog, wrote the name "Lenin" on it, then sent it toward the Marxist demonstrators. In response, the Marxist students wrote the words "mulla" and "Muhammad" on sheets and attached them to other dogs. This led to a fight involving many townspeople who pelted the students with stones and broke up the demonstration.

16. Quoted in Dupree 1980, 608.

17. See Chapter Six for a more detailed discussion of this protest.

18. Interview with Samiullah Safi, February 1983.

19. Dupree 1980, 615.

20. Interview with Qasim Baz Mangal, July 24, 1994. Qasim's father and brother both served as aides-de-camp to Daud.

21. From the many laudatory comments in the biography regarding Hafizullah Amin, one suspects that he was either the author or had considerable say in the final form of the work. If that is the case, one must wonder whether Amin might have included some of the biographical information to indirectly sabotage Taraki, even while referring to him repeatedly as "great leader."

22. See Edwards 1996, 78–79, 102–103.

23. Quoted in ibid., 111.

24. Robinson 1978, 111. For a fictional depiction of these nomads, see Rabindranath Tagore's short story "The Cabuliwallah."

25. "The Biography of the Great Leader."

26. The Taraki biography notes that "Babrak Karmal who was rumoured to have connections with the Royal Court imposed on the party in 1967 a division in accordance with the wishes of the ruling circles and a number of innocent and true patriots were led astray by him and thus kept away from Comrade Taraki according to the wishes of imperialism and the reactionary court."

27. Hyman 1984, 66. Another source with whom I have spoken, a former government official familiar with both Amin and Karmal, claims that Karmal had bad relations with his father and lived away from him from an early age.

28. See Dupree 1980, 615. The Taraki biography, published after the dismissal of Karmal and other Parchamis from senior positions, explained the initial PDPA rift in the following way: "Following the suspension of the Khalq, due to the presence of a number of elements with undesirable class connections and their political immaturity as far as the working class ideology was concerned and because they had failed to declare their stands, the ruling oppressive classes and circles had penetrated into the party cadres and consequently created some troubles for it."

29. The name *Amin* can be translated as "trustworthy." The term *la'in* rhymes with Amin and is used to refer to the angel, Satan, who was thrown out of heaven by God for his untrustworthiness.

30. Hyman 1984, 29.

31. Kakar 1978, 212.

32. Hyman 1984, 30.

33. Quoted in FBIS, South Asia Review, vol. 5, August 17, 1978, 51–54.

34. Proclamation reproduced in Curzon 1923. Translation by Nasim Stanazai and David Edwards.

35. See J. Anderson 1983 on the oppositional relationship of *qaum* (tribe) and *gund* (faction).

36. This is not the first time that this allegory has been played out in Afghanistan. Amanullah's story could also be told in a somewhat similar fash-

ion, though with these differences. In his case, the favored son (Amanullah) is lured into disloyalty to his father, Amir Habibullah, by his attraction to an alternative father figure, Mahmud Beg Tarzi, who became Amanullah's intellectual and political mentor. Through Tarzi, Amanullah gained his interest in reform and also began associating with courtiers, teachers, and foreign advisors who encouraged him to move away from his father and—in the view of some—plan his assassination in order to take control of the throne.

37. See Edwards 1996, 105–108.

38. The best example of the effort to rehabilitate Bacha-i Saqao's reputation is *Ayyari az Khorasan*, a privately published biography by Khalilullah Khalili. According to Khalili, Habibullah received the name Bacha-i Saqao (son of a water carrier) not because his father served in this lowly position but because he had once taken water to mujahidin fighting against the British during the Second Anglo-Afghan War. Khalili goes on to tell how Bacha-i Saqao was renowned as a horseman and wrestler and how he joined in the jihad against the Bolshevik conquest of Bukhara. His feats of bravery and skill as a soldier were legendary and caused poems and songs to be composed in his honor. Bacha-i Saqao's career as a bandit was brought about by circumstances in his homeland north of Kabul, where landlords oppressed the peasantry with impunity. Bacha-i Saqao became a bandit to defend the poor and attack the wealthy, but the government sided with the landlords against Bacha-i Saqao. Rather than being motivated by greed and opportunism, Bacha-i Saqao's attack against the regime of Amanullah was motivated by his anger over government oppression and the un-Islamic nature of the government reform program. After Bacha-i Saqao's death at the hands of Nadir, his memory was kept alive by the peasants he had helped. Stories continued to be told about his life, and miracles were commonly attributed to him. The truth of Khalili's account cannot be ascertained, but it is interesting how completely this telling of the story makes Bacha-i Saqao out to be a noble bandit of the type analyzed by Eric Hobsbawm (1959 and 1981). Khalili himself is worthy of a biography. Generally reckoned one of the premier Persian poets of the twentieth century, he was also a witness to and a participant in more events of recent Afghan history than any man of his generation, beginning in childhood when his father was an important official under Amir Habibullah. Coming from the same village as Bacha-i Saqao, he knew him from a young age and afterward was in his administration. Later, he served under Zahir Shah, at various times as a close advisor. Finally, in his old age, he became a refugee in Pakistan and continued to work as an advisor in the Jamiat-i Islami party of Professor Burhanuddin Rabbani until his death at eighty in 1987.

3. THE ARMATURE OF KHALQI POWER

1. From a proclamation by Amir Abdur Rahman; quoted in Edwards 1996, 78.

2. Quoted in Poullada 1973, 60.

3. On unveiling and other symbolic changes undertaken by Amanullah, see ibid. and Gregorian 1969.

4. For an account of the twisted tale of Nadir's assassination, see Dupree 1980, 474–475.

5. Nur Muhammad Taraki addressing a delegation of elders, June 5, 1978; quoted in FBIS, South Asia Review, vol. 5, June 6, 1978.

6. Two mutually comprehensible dialects of Pakhtu are spoken in Afghanistan. Pakhtu is spoken in the eastern part of the country; Pushtu is spoken in the south and west and was the dialect used by the royal family. The speakers of this language are referred to variously as Pakhtuns, Pushtuns, and Pathans.

7. Transcript of a Taraki press conference, *Kabul Times*, May 13, 1978. Taraki speaking to Behsud and Wardak elders, July 11, 1978; quoted in FBIS, South Asia Review, vol. 5, July 25, 1978.

8. See Stewart 1973 and Poullada 1973.

9. An article in the May 6, 1978 issue of the *Kabul Times* announced that "the people in different areas of Tirah in Pashtunistan . . . have wished for the health of Noor Mohammad Taraki," along with residents of Sultani Maseed and Waziristan in "Pashtunistan." The next day, elders from Shinwar, Utmanzai, Ahmadzai, Wazir, Daud, Beitni, Masid, Karam, Wazir, Khyber, Mangal, Bangash, Nawi, and Turi were all said to have praised the new regime, while Taraki met with more elders from other border tribes: Atmerkhel, Khwajazai, Khogakhel, Utmankhel, Mohmand, Kukikhel Afridi, and Ahmadzai Wazir.

The May 17 *Kabul Times* published separate photographs of Taraki and tribal elders from Ahmadzai and Wazir; Mohmand, Utmankhel, and Bajawar; and Afridi and Afridi Tirah.

Similarly, on May 21, more pictures appeared of Taraki with leaders from the Wazir, Masud, Daur, Madakhel, Pari Zamkani, Shinwar, and Taraki tribes. On May 22, a photo was published of Taraki with elders from the Zadran and with other Paktia elders, along with a second photo of him with elders from Badakhshan and Qandahar.

10. *Kabul Times*, May 20, 1978.

11. These meetings picked up again the following year, as antigovernment violence increased. From late April through November 1979, there were successive waves of meetings with *ulama* (religious authorities) and tribal elders, mostly from Paktia and Kunar, as well as Kohistanis from specified areas such as Mir Bachakot, Kalakan, and Panjshir—all famous for their past involvement in antigovernment insurgencies. After Taraki's assassination, in late September 1979, Amin staged a new round of meetings with tribal elders from both sides of the border.

12. *Kabul Times*, July 17, 1978.

13. Margaret Mills has pointed out that Afghans generally utilized a personal credit arrangement known as *gerau*, in which the borrower hands over a piece of real property to the lender in exchange for money. At the end of the designated term (usually seven years), the debtor gives back only the original sum, the lender's profit deriving from usufruct of the collateral property—not from

interest on the loaned money, which is illegal in Islam. In Mills's view, "the government's rationale for forgiving gerau after seven years was that the lender would already have gotten a usufruct equal to the cash value of the loan. Hence they tried to counter any allegation that release from gerau obligations amounted to the theft of the lender's principal" (personal communication, 2000).

14. *Kabul Times,* October 18, 1978. In justifying the government's promulgation of this decree, the *Kabul Times* in its July 19, 1978, issue noted that conditions had worsened for the average peasant because of "his persistent observation of unhealthy customs and traditions, such as holding lavish feasts for circumcision, paying of dowry, and large wedding and engagement ceremonies, huge expenditures on funeral and mourning ceremonies and the like." Social pressure "compels numerous peasants to resort to borrowing on interest from the usurers or soliciting advances and loans from the landlords, which binds him to the land virtually the whole of his life, with little hope for being relieved from the burden of loans and mounting interest."

15. Ibid.

16. *Kabul Times,* October 3 and October 18, 1978.

17. *Kabul Times,* October 18, 1978.

18. *Kabul Times,* July 18 and August 6, 1978.

19. *Kabul Times,* November 4, 1978, and January 31, 1979.

20. *Kabul Times,* February 13, 1979.

21. *Kabul Times,* June 30, 1979.

22. Interview with Sayyid Mahmud Hasrat, March 31, 1983.

23. Margaret Mills has aptly noted that Afghans didn't generally view fifteen to thirty jeribs of land as excessive wealth, in part at least because they understood the fragile nature of the agricultural economy. "People well knew that 'just enough' land would become 'not enough' during regular, periodic droughts—that they would need to borrow again. . . . *Gerau's* seven-year cycle in a way took account of periodic crop failures and surpluses" and provided "a bridge strategy that any small landowner had to know well" (personal communications, 2000). The failure of the Khalqi regime to appreciate the importance of these arrangements to those trying to survive in a marginal environment and its failure to institute an alternative source of credit after abolishing the existing system were important factors in the loss of support for the government.

24. *Kabul Times,* April 22, 1979.

25. The first example of this kind of photograph appeared in the June 17, 1979, issue of the *Kabul Times.*

26. Taraki in an address to citizens of Behsud and Wardak Province, July 11, 1978; quoted in FBIS, South Asia Review, vol. 5, July 25, 1978.

27. See Anderson 1978.

28. *Kabul Times,* May 4, 1978.

29. See Edwards 1993a.

30. One example of the regime's support for Pushtunistan (or Pakhtunistan) was the celebration in late August 1978 of Pushtunistan Day. The *Kabul Times*

on that day published an illustration of the red flag of Pushtunistan on its front page, along with pictures of Abdul Ghafar Khan and his son Khan Abdul Wali Khan, long-time Pakhtun nationalist leaders from the Pakistani side of the border. In addition, various Pushtun and Baluchi "freedom fighters" were also lauded. *Kabul Times*, August 30, 1978.

31. *Kabul Times*, June 13, 1978.

32. *Kabul Times*, August 6, 1978.

33. FBIS, South Asia Review, vol. 5, August 17, 1978.

34. *Kabul Times*, June 4, 1979.

35. *Kabul Times*, May 23, 1979.

36. *Kabul Times*, April 1, 1979.

37. See Edwards 1996 and Ahmed 1976.

38. Quoted in Stewart 1973, 59.

39. Quoted in Lewis 1998, 95.

40. *Kabul Times*, May 16, 1979; reprinted in the *Afghanistan Council Newsletter* 7, no. 3 (June 1979).

41. *Kabul Times*, June 18, 1979.

42. *Kabul Times*, August 15, 1979.

43. On the PDPA's use of terror, see Kakar 1995.

44. See Girardet 1985, 107–110.

45. Gregory Massell (1974) has discussed earlier attempts by the Soviets in Central Asia to create a "surrogate proletariat" through the liberation of women. See also Bacon (1980 [1966]).

46. In the 1970s prior to the revolution, far more scholarly works were published on Buddhism in ancient Afghanistan than on Islam in contemporary Afghanistan. Robert Canfield (1973) wrote a paper on Shi'a/Ismaili relations in Bamiyan Province; Louis Dupree (1966 and 1967) wrote a few articles on Islam; and there were some descriptive works on *khanaqa*s (centers of activity associated with Sufi pirs) in western Afghanistan, but little else. This lack of publications reflects the shared sense of scholars, diplomats, and other observers that Islam was no longer an effective form of political mobilization.

CODA: THE DEATH OF A PRESIDENT

1. *Kabul Times*, October 10, 1979.

2. Kakar 1995, 35, 36.

3. *Kabul New Times*, January 23, 1980; reprinted in *Afghanistan Council Newsletter* 8, no. 2 (March 1980).

4. *Kabul New Times*, headline of January 1, 1980: "Sanguinary Amin Band Ousted, United PDPA Ends Reign of Terror: Murderer Meets His Fate."

5. *Kabul New Times*, March 30, 1980.

4. A SON OF SAFI

1. Interview with Samiullah Safi, February 14, 1983. I conducted a total of

twelve hours of interviews with Samiullah spread over six sessions between February 14 and March 23. The longest of the sessions by far was the first, which lasted for six hours and included most of the family and personal history included in this chapter. Subsequent sessions added a few new stories, clarified elements and chronology that were unclear from the first session, and included a great deal of editorializing on the situation in Peshawar. Following the conclusion of our taping sessions, I saw Samiullah occasionally but usually in groups with other people, and we had no further extended conversations, although we have corresponded since the publication of my first book.

2. In *Heroes of the Age*, I referred to Samiullah Safi as "Safi," which is the term many of his friends used when speaking of him. Commonly, however, they addressed him to his face with the honorific "Wakil," and I use that term here to avoid confusing his name with the many references to the Safi tribe that occur in Part Two.

3. Interview, February 14, 1983.

4. Different people cite different reasons for the outbreak of hostilities. Safi himself blamed the abuses of government soldiers, who would harass local people, steal chickens, confiscate cooking oil and other valuables under the pretext of collecting a grazing tax, and force people to cut firewood and deliver it to government offices.

5. According to Aman-ul Mulk, who was one of the leaders of the Safis during the uprising, Safi tribesmen served together prior to the uprising and were posted in Jalalabad, near their own homeland (interview, January 1983). For general information on military conscription, see Kakar 1979 and Gregorian 1969.

6. Interview, February 14, 1983.

7. Ibid.

8. See Edwards 1996, 73–77, for a story in which this equation is explicitly made.

9. Interview, February 14, 1983.

10. Ibid.

11. N. Tapper 1983.

12. While exiled members of the tribe were initially unified in their determination not to accept land from the government, their consensus began to break down as more and more families decided to take the land while it was available. Sultan Muhammad and his brothers and sons continued to refuse however, and while this obstinacy can be interpreted in moral terms, it was also undoubtedly the case that—as major landowners in the Pech Valley—they had more to lose by giving up their claim to their original lands. Despite their refusal to accept the offer, the government turned over land to Sultan Muhammad and his brothers, with Sultan Muhammad receiving property in Shebargan and his brothers receiving their share in Balkh. Wakil claimed not to know how much land the government deeded to them. The land was parceled out by local officials and then turned over to tenant farmers who actually worked the land. Each year, the tenants brought the owner's share of the produce to the government, and

the government turned over the profits to the prisoners: "We never went to see the land, nor asked about it since my father's will was not to take any land here. It was up to the government if they wanted to give us an allowance or bring a portion of the production of the land. It was up to the government." This situation continued for more than a decade, until the family was allowed to move to Kabul after the introduction of democratic reforms in 1964. Interestingly, in the course of his archaeological and ethnographic work in the town of Aq Kupruk in Balkh Province, Louis Dupree encountered a Safi family who had been relocated after the uprising. According to Dupree 1970, the family had intermarried with Tajiks in the area and referred to themselves locally as Tajiks, though they called themselves Pakhtuns when they traveled to Mazar-i Sharif. While the Safi family was alone in Aq Kupruk, Dupree indicates that they enjoyed disproportionate influence, probably in part because government officials in the area were also Pakhtuns. Unfortunately, he does not say whether it was also because they were given a substantial amount of land, but that conclusion might be assumed from Dupree's comment that the Safi leader in Aq Kupruk had formed an ethnically heterogeneous "gang" in the town, an enterprise that would have required substantial resources.

13. As the following story illustrates, the prison in Herat had a lasting impact on Wakil, and his experiences there help to explain his later concern for social reform:

> In the courtyard of the prison, in the late afternoon, some of the prisoners would be cooking in their pots over charcoal fires. They would cook meat, greens, vegetables, and whatever else they could lay their hands on. Those who had them would sit in front of their pots with sticks in their hands. They would sit like this: the pot would be in front of them, the stick would be in their hands, and they'd sit close to the pot, crouched over it, watching. I would see the other prisoners watching those who were cooking.
>
> Their asses and other parts of their body would be naked, and you could see them. They would be wearing only a few pieces of clothing, and you got the impression that, like, a crazy man has arrived, and you'd think that it was some kind of monster you were watching. That's what someone would think. From a distance, they would sit like this, staring at the pots, hungry. Watching. Like this.
>
> Each of [the cooks] was in a struggle, a competition; ... if [his] eye turned from the pot in one direction, someone would mount an attack on the pot from the other side. So, he would continually look around him while stirring the pot. He would make sure that nothing happened, all the while keeping the stick in his hand. This was an ongoing situation, but once I witnessed an altercation. It was like this.
>
> Three or four people were sitting near a cooking fire when one of these hungry prisoners succeeded in carrying off one of these pots. It was a red pot. There was meat and other things in it, and the other hungry prisoners, all of them grabbed it and burned their mouths on it, and by the time they let the pot go, it was empty, and there was nothing left of the meat. I will never forget this.

14. In Pakhtun society, a boy's patrilateral first cousin (his father's brother's son, or *tarbur*) is considered his natural and inevitable rival. In relation to the

tarbur a boy first strives for laurels within the family, and through the tarbur he learns of the essentially antagonistic nature of social relations in the world at large.

15. Interview, February 14, 1983.

16. Ibid.

17. Ibid. It is worth noting the similarity between Wakil's speech and his father's reported address to his kinsmen and tenant farmers in which he enlisted their support for his plan to ambush his father's killers (see Edwards 1996, 39 and 66). In both cases, the speaker assured his listeners that his course of action was dictated by a concern for honor rather than self-interest and that, in offering their assistance, his listeners' autonomy of action would in no way be compromised.

18. Interview, February 14, 1983.

19. There is, of course, an unanticipated irony in this statement given the fact that mullas would soon come to power in the country as a whole. However, in the context in which it was uttered, the meaning was that an unopposed candidacy would be demeaning to the tribe (from the traditional tribal point of view, only a debased group would send a mulla to Kabul), as well as to Wakil himself.

20. Interview, February 14, 1983.

21. Ibid.

22. See Dupree 1980, 652–654, 753–754.

23. This argument recapitulates that made by Louis Dupree, who was resident in Kabul during most of the democratic era: "Many Afghans . . . including some of the king's closest advisers in the royal family, argued that if parties became legal the left would become stronger and threaten the monarchy. But de facto, if not de jure, political parties already existed on the left and right and, at the very least, promulgation of the Political Parties Law may have drawn moderate activists from both extremes, and forced the comfortable stagnates of the growing urban middle class to join responsible groups. Then party discipline and an acceptable spoils system (essential to democracy, if kept within culturally allowable bounds of deviance) could have helped political parties define their positions vis-à-vis any existing government. The government, for its part, could have become integrated with the party system and formed its own platform for action" (Dupree 1980, 753).

24. Interview, February 14, 1983.

25. Ibid.

26. Wakil told me of a number of secret encounters he had with Kalakani during the time the Khalqis were chasing him down. He also commented on how impressed he was by the risks people took to protect Kalakani from the authorities and noted that even some of the police officers who had been dispatched to capture Kalakani ended up protecting him because of their deep regard for the man. Despite such efforts, however, Kalakani was eventually captured and executed by the Khalqi regime.

27. Interview, February 14, 1983.

28. Wakil's conjecture as to what his father's response to Amin might have been reminds me of how Sultan Muhammad responded to the news that his mother had taken revenge for his father's murder (Edwards 1996, 37–38, 56–63). In that situation, as in Wakil's, the son could take no pleasure in the act of vengeance, for he had not participated in bringing it about. In both cases, the act of vengeance was seen by the son as illegitimate, and it served to remind him of his own inaction and the tenuousness of his identity until he had proven his right to call himself his father's son.

29. Sahre, n.d.

30. Edwards 1996, 216.

31. Ibid.

5. ANATOMY OF A TRIBAL UPRISING

1. Samiullah Safi interview, February 14, 1983. Unless otherwise indicated, all quotations in this chapter are from this interview.

2. See Robertson 1974 [1896] and Jones 1974 for historical background on Kafir/Safi relations.

3. I have heard from many Afghans that they were confused when they first heard the Khalqis use the exclamation "hurrah," which had no roots in Afghan cultural practice and which presumably the Khalqis borrowed from the Soviets. Various theories arose in rural areas as to what "hurrah" might mean. Among these theories was the notion that it was the name of Lenin's wife and that they were being encouraged to shout her praises as well as those of Lenin himself.

4. During the Safi War in 1945–1946, similar rumors circulated through the Pech Valley that women would be shipped off to Kabul to become prostitutes.

5. Sahre, n.d. The quotations are taken from Sahre's manuscript; the categories are my own.

6. See Girardet 1985, 107–110.

7. See Pitt-Rivers 1966 and Bourdieu 1966.

8. At the time of the insurgency in Pech, a separate uprising was going on in the Kamdesh Valley of Nuristan, which is the northern extension of the Kunar Valley. These two uprisings, one coming from the west and one from the north, both threatened the provincial capital of Chagha Serai. For information on the Kamdesh uprising, see Strand 1984.

9. Shahmahmood Miakhel, personal communication, August 10, 2001.

10. Sahre, n.d., and in an interview conducted in Peshawar, May 21, 1984.

11. Edwards 1996, 196.

12. Sahre, n.d..

13. Interview with Commander Abdur Rauf, Peshawar, September 29, 1983.

14. Delawar Sahre's account of the Asmar incident confirms that of Samiullah Safi. He also indicates in his report that at a meeting in Nuristan in mid-July tribal leaders decided to make a final attempt to reunify the jihad and agreed to send a delegation to Utapur to meet Maulavi Hussain. The Hizb leader would

not agree to participate in a non-party-based alliance, however, particularly after the rival, and more moderate, Jamiat party agreed to join.

15. On the symbolic significance of taking away a man's weapon, see Edwards 1996, 73–77.

16. Another commander I spoke with from the neighboring valley of Deh Wuz, who was also involved in the negotiations with Rauf and the planned attack on Chagha Serai, supports Rauf's version of events. In an interview conducted in 1984, this commander told me that the Hizb-i Islami mujahidin purposely deceived Rauf and plundered his troops.

17. Interview with Maulavi Hussain, Peshawar, May 2, 1984.

18. The Maududi referred to is Maulana Maududi, the founder of the Jamiat-i Islami political party, which took much the same line as the Ikhwan ul-Muslimin and played much the same political role in Pakistan as the Ikhwan played in Egypt.

CODA: THE DEATH OF A SAFI DAUGHTER

1. Interview, February 14, 1983.

2. Ibid.

3. Ibid.

4. This theme is developed further in Edwards 1996.

5. The practice of having women and mullas acting as emissaries between warring parties is an established tradition among Pakhtuns and other tribal people in the Middle East, but Wakil in essence rejects the application of this custom to this situation, telling the women that they are all one tribe and under the same threat and that they all must be willing to sacrifice to preserve their honor.

6. MUSLIM YOUTH

1. This speech was recorded on a tape cassette given to me in the fall of 1983 by an Afghan informant who was unaware of when, where, or to whom the speech was delivered.

2. Olivier Roy noted that in 1980 most foreign observers would have agreed "with varying degrees of reluctance that the Hizb was the backbone of the resistance" (Roy 1986, 134).

3. While the age difference between Wakil and Qazi Amin was slight, it was not insignificant. When Wakil was a student, political organizing on campus was still fairly covert, and confrontations between Muslim and leftist students were still restrained. Such restraint was no longer in evidence by the time Qazi Amin began his university career, and this lack of restraint undoubtedly influenced the choices that he made and that were forced on him.

4. Interview, May 29, 1986.

5. Edwards 1996.

6. When Hadda Sahib made his first appearance at court, Habibullah is said

to have offered a dramatic gesture of respect to symbolize his favorable attitude toward Islam:

> When Sahib-i Hadda went to the court of Amir Habibullah Khan for the funeral [*fateha*] of Abdur Rahman, Amir Habibullah, Nasrullah Khan [Habibullah's younger brother], Inayatullah Khan [Habibullah's eldest son], and other ministers were standing to receive him when he came with his deputies. Since Amir Habibullah Khan was worried about this meeting, he offered his seat to him, and Sahib-i Hadda sat there [on the throne]. After he had recited two or three verses of the Qur'an, he forgave Habibullah Khan and prayed for the prosperity of Afghanistan and Islam. When he left the court, he told one of his disciples that he had brought some water and had washed his feet in front of the Amir and his ministers. Someone asked him why he wanted to wash his feet. He replied that it was because the court had become colored by the blood of Muslims and his feet had become *bi namazi* (polluted and unacceptable for prayer).

This account was told to me by Khalilullah Khalili. Ustad Khalili was a particularly useful informant on matters having to do with the evolution of the state during the twentieth century. His father, Mustufi Mirza Muhammad Hussain Khan, occupied a high position in Habibullah's cabinet [*mustaufi ul-mamalek*], and Khalili himself served as one of the principal ministers in the short-lived administration of Bacha-i Saqao and later became a close confidant of Zahir Shah.

7. 1 kharwar = 80 ser. 1 Kabul ser = 7 kilograms.

8. These figures come from interviews conducted with offspring of Sufi Sahib and Pacha Sahib, as well as from government decrees (*firman*) in their possession.

9. One expression of this new strategy can be seen in the elaboration of national and specifically monarchical rituals under Habibullah. At his coronation, for example, the amir eschewed royal for Islamic symbolism by having the *khan mulla*, the chief religious figure in the court, perform the act of installation in the style of the Sufi *dastarbandi* (ceremony of succession) rather than in a more regal manner. Thus, just as a pir has a white cotton turban wrapped around his head when he succeeds to the head of a Sufi order, so Habibullah adopted the same simple ceremony for his own investiture. Thereafter, the khan mulla emphasized the religious character of the ritual by presenting the new ruler with a copy of the Qur'an, some relics of the Prophet Muhammad, and a flag from the tomb of an Afghan saint.

Vartan Gregorian points out that Habibullah instituted a new Afghan holiday, National Unity Day, intended to commemorate the conquest of former Kafiristan: "The holiday, which was celebrated annually with much pomp and ceremony, had both a religious and a political character, honoring at the same time Afghan unity and the divinely ordained Afghan monarchy. . . . In this light, the conquest of Kafiristan was hailed as a triumph of Islam over foreign intriguers and Christian missionaries, aliens who had been determined to convert the Kafirs and thereby subvert the territorial integrity of Afghanistan" (1969, 181–182).

10. During the course of my interviews in Peshawar, I heard frequent complaints about the decadence and corruption of various deputies and their offspring, and when I inquired why Sufism had declined in importance, the most frequent response I received had to do with the way in which different pirs had abandoned the pious lifestyle and lost the respect of the people.

11. On the 1897 uprisings, see Edwards 1996 and Ahmed 1976.

12. The deputies who participated in the 1919 jihad included Pacha Sahib Islampur, Haji Sahib Turangzai, the Mulla of Chaknawar, and Mia Sahib of Sarkano.

13. Abdur Razaq instituted a number of logistical innovations to help counteract the weaknesses of the tribal system of warfare. Among these innovations were a rotation system that ensured that every tribal section would have men present at the front at all times, a plan for ensuring adequate food at the front, the establishment of command centers at designated locations, and the establishment of transport groups to get supplies to the troops. For details on this campaign and on Razaq's life, see Zalmai 1967.

14. The war, which is known in Afghanistan as the jang-i istiqlal, or the war of independence, was a short-lived and mostly half-hearted affair on both sides. With the exception of the Afghan attack on the British garrison at Thal, where a "lucky" cannon shot exploded an ammunition dump (Khalilullah Khalili, interview, April 26, 1983), the fighting proved inconclusive. However, the Afghans did receive concessions from the British that allowed them a degree of independence in the conduct of their foreign affairs, and, as a result, they considered the desultory campaign a victory.

15. See Kushkaki 1921, 205–208.

16. On the reign of Amanullah and the abortive reform program that led to his overthrow, see Gregorian 1969, Poullada 1973, and Stewart 1973.

17. Interview with Maulavi Ahmad Gul Rohani, son of Ustad Sahib of Hadda. Prime Minister Hashim Khan, the brother of Nadir Khan, acted as the chief policymaker and regent for King Zahir Shah from Nadir's death in 1933 until 1946, when his brother, Shahmahmood Khan, took over.

18. Qazi Amin knew the most about the Shinwari upheaval, which he said centered around Shinwari leader Muhammad Afzal's right to keep fifty militiamen whose salaries were paid by the government. Qazi Amin believed that Afzal was holding out for increased privileges from the government, and when he didn't get his way, he attacked the local government base and set up his own government. Because his father had lived a long time in the Shinwari area, he was in a position to mediate between the government and Afzal, who eventually gave up his opposition. According to Qazi Amin's description, the government's treatment of Afzal and his family has similarities to the treatment of Sultan Muhammad Khan and his family after the Safi uprising: "He was in prison a short time, and after that he couldn't go back to Shinwar. The government gave them houses and plenty of property in Kabul. It was good for them to some extent because they were living in good conditions in Kabul, and they could

educate their children there. Now all their children are educated. When democracy came in 1964, they were also allowed to return to their own area."

19. Zikr is the principal ceremony associated with Sufism. Disciples gather in a circle around their pir and chant in unison a phrase from the Qur'an. As disciples advance in their spiritual understanding, their pir gives them new phrases to learn and chant.

20. Interview, May 29, 1986.

21. The success of a shrine complex has less to do with a saint's accomplishments in life than it does with his accomplishments after death, and the most successful shrines have usually been those that have managed to create a name for themselves curing one or another of the major illnesses and setbacks that befall people —be it infertility, snakebite, or scrofula. Despite the Mulla's many miracles in life, his shrine at Hadda apparently never earned a reputation for engendering miracles after his death, and the flow of pilgrims visiting Hadda gradually began to decline. As it did, the interest the mulla's deputies took in the center seems to have decreased as well. At least that was the case with Pacha Sahib of Islampur, whom Hadda Sahib himself had designated as the keeper of the langar. For reasons that remain unclear, Pacha Sahib relinquished his title to the langar and turned over its keys to Ustad Sahib, who was the only one of Hadda Sahib's principal deputies to stay on in Hadda after his death and who already had been given responsibility for maintaining the library. Over time, the langar ceased regular operations, and the only other activity at Hadda's center that appears to have continued was a yearly reading of the Qur'an during the month of Ramazan (which was significant not only as the month of fasting in the Islamic calendar but also for being the anniversary of the Mulla's death).

22. The government-sponsored madrasas in Afghanistan were Madrasa-yi Abu Hanifa (Kabul), Dar ul-Ulm-i Arabi (Kabul), Dar ul-Ulm-i Rohani (Paktia), Fakhr ul-Madares (Herat), Madrasa-yi Jama-i Sharif (Herat), Najm ul-Madares (Ningrahar), Madrasa-i Mohammadia (Qandahar), Dar ul-Ulm-i Asadia (Balkh), Dar ul-Ulum-i Abu Muslim (Faryab), and Dar ul-Ulum-i Takharistan (Kunduz). During my interviews, informants offered dates ranging from 1931 to 1944 for the founding of the madrasa at Hadda. I have not been able to clarify which of these dates is correct, although I tend to believe the testimony of one particularly reliable informant, who stated that the Hadda madrasa was built in 1937.

23. The three biweekly newspapers published in 1951–1952 were *Watan* (Homeland), *Angar* (Burning Ember), and *Nida'-yi Khalq* (Voice of the Masses); Dupree 1980, 495; Bradsher 1985, 38; and Reardon 1969, 169–170.

24. See Dupree 1980, 495–496.

25. Interview, April 23, 1984.

26. Nasim Stanazai, interview, Peshawar, July 7, 1992. The same and similar stories were told to me by a number of former university students. The details sometimes differed, but the theme of antagonistic relations was always the same.

27. One of the issues that Afghans of different political persuasions debate is the exact role of Ghulam Muhammad Niazi and other professors in the development of the Muslim Youth. Thus, members of Jamiat-i Islami Afghanistan, which is headed by Burhanuddin Rabbani, a former professor at Kabul University and a colleague of Niazi's, say that the professors were secretly overseeing the Muslim students' activities, first through Abdur Rahim Niazi and then through Engineer Habib-ur Rahman. The position of Hizb-i Islami, however, is that the professors chose to avoid direct involvement in student politics for fear of losing their sinecures. Since most of my informants are members of Hizb-i Islami, the interpretation offered here is more reflective of the Hizb-i Islami view of history. For an interpretation of Muslim Youth history that is more in keeping with the Jamiat-i Islami version, see Roy 1986, 69–83.

28. Eickelman 1985.

29. When my informants spoke of the classroom, it was generally to note the very different techniques that the foreign instructors brought to Afghanistan, such as the system of professors lecturing and students taking notes, and also the relative informality of many of the foreign instructors and their openness to debate and discussion—qualities that were apparently not often found in Afghan teachers, who tended to be more authoritarian in their dealings with students.

30. The Moroccan peer learning circles discussed by Eickelman differ from those that I studied in that they appear to have been significantly more "preprofessional" than their Afghan counterparts. Thus, the Moroccan peer learning circles served as a context in which young scholars acquired "the additional knowledge considered essential for men of learning and the practice necessary to develop competent rhetorical style." In Kabul University circa 1968, however, the peer learning circle functioned less as a forum for fashioning polished scholars than as a place of protection and instruction for young Muslims who felt alone in the impersonal environment of the university and beleaguered by the rising tide of leftist activism on campus. Many of those who attended these meetings had little background in formal Islamic studies, but they did share a sense that Islam and the traditional values associated with it were in peril.

31. Engineer Habib-ur Rahman and Maulavi Habib-ur Rahman were both founding members of the Muslim Youth Organization.

32. Interview, April 23, 1984.

33. This quote is from the cassette cited in Note 1 above.

34. One finds occasional reports from this period of religious clerics throwing acid in the faces of unveiled women whom they encountered on the streets of Kabul. I have never been able to ascertain whether these stories were true or whether they were examples of antireligious propaganda disseminated by leftists.

35. The poem to the glory of the "land of Lenin" and the "miracles of the life-bearing revolution" ended with these lines:

For this matchless achievement
We send DORUD to that pioneer party,

And to the heroic people.
We send DORUD to that great leader,
The Great Lenin.

Quoted in Dupree 1970, 23.

36. Among the leaders of the demonstration were Miagul Jan, the son of the Mulla of Tagab, Maulavi Miskin from north of Kabul, and Mir Abdul Satar Hashimi from Logar. Among those I interviewed who were involved in the Pul-i Khishti demonstration were Hazrat Sibghatullah Mujaddidi; Maulavi Habibullah, a.k.a. Kuchi Maulavi from Logar; Maulavi Fazl Hadi from the Shinwari district of Ningrahar; Maulavi Wala Jan Wasseq from the Khogiani district of Ningrahar; Maulavi Amirzada from Laghman; and Maulavi Abdul Ahad Yaqubi from Helmand. Most leaders were not treated harshly when the demonstration was broken up, but Maulavi Wasseq, who was a government official at the time of his involvement in the demonstration, claims to have been imprisoned for almost three years. He told me that for one month of his imprisonment he had a skewer thrust through his tongue as punishment for his outspokenness.

37. Some positions, including caretaker of some shrines, were hereditary, and those holding them couldn't be dismissed by the government. In such cases, one-tenth of the income from the shrine generally went to the caretaker, while the other nine-tenths went to the shrine itself. Under the riasat-i haj wa awqaf, the government took the nine-tenths portion of the income and allowed the caretakers to keep their tenth.

38. Interview, March 22, 1984. Also according to Shinwari, another initiative of the riasat-i haj wa awqaf was the centralization of control over the annual pilgrimage (haj) to Mecca. From this point on, the agency was to designate how many and who would be allowed to go on pilgrimage each year, while also arranging transportation, collecting fees from the pilgrims, and handling all the government paperwork. In 1972, eighteen thousand Afghans were allowed to go on haj.

39. Interview with Sur Gul Spin, Peshawar, May 25, 1986.

40. The only copy of Niazi's pamphlet I have been able to find is a reprinted version that appeared in the Hizb-i Islami newspaper *al-Sobh* (no. 23, March 1986). The pamphlet, titled "The Importance of Economy in Islam and Communism" (*ahmat-i eqtisad dar islam wo komunism*), was originally published in Pakistan in 1970 around the time of Niazi's death. See also Edwards 1993b.

41. Interview with Sur Gul Spin, Peshawar, May 25, 1986.

42. Ibid.

43. The levels of membership were formally designated as sympathizer (*ham nawai*), supporter (*hamkar*), candidate (*candid*), and member (*ruqan*). Interview with Sur Gul Spin, May 25, 1986.

44. Ibid.

45. Ibid.

46. Fear of infiltration was not unwarranted. According to a number of former Muslim Youth members, a student named Moqtadar, who had been accepted into the organization, provided information on the party's leadership

and activities to the Ministry of Information. He and other government informers were blamed by some for the arrests of Engineer Habib-ur Rahman and the
failure of the uprisings in 1975.

47. Interview with Sur Gul Spin, May 25, 1986.

48. Interview, April 23, 1984.

49. Ibid. See Dupree 1978, 2–7, for an eyewitness account of the insurgency
in Panjshir. Dupree, who happened to be in Panjshir when the Muslim Youth
attacked, describes the confusion of the moment, the naïveté of the insurgents,
and the rumors that circulated after the fact.

50. Ibid.

7. FAULT LINES IN THE AFGHAN JIHAD

1. The ten parties I refer to were all associated with the Sunni sect of Islam.
There were also a number of Shi'a parties that represented the 10 percent of the
population that professed and practiced Shi'a principles. These Shi'a parties were
headquartered in the central Hazarajat region of Afghanistan and received most
of their assistance from Iran. See Canfield 1973, Edwards 1986b, Roy 1986, and
Mousavi 1998.

2. Although the Peshawar refugee settlements contained representatives of
all the major Islamic traditions, they contained relatively few Shi'a and Ismaili
leaders. Shi'a leaders in particular tended to gravitate to Iran, while Peshawar
remained the center of the Sunni majority, and it is the Sunni leadership with
which I am primarily concerned here.

3. My information on Maulana Faizani has a hagiographic quality to it
because it comes primarily from two of his disciples (Mirajan Saheqi and Rohullah), whom I interviewed in Peshawar in 1983–1984.

4. Faizani's disciples recounted a number of Faizani's miracles and told of the
strange occurrences and premonitions that accompanied his birth. Rohullah also
noted that Faizani received his instruction in tasawuf directly from the saints
(*awaliya*) and four companions of the Prophet (*char yar kubar*) and that the
Prophet himself "tied his waist" and "selected him for an important task." Interview, September 4, 1983.

5. From a photocopy of the introduction to Faizani's "Why Do We Read the
Books of the Koranic School," by Mirajan Saheqi (Shah 1983, 10).

6. The three parties that joined together were Madrasa-i Qur'an, under
Faizani; Paiman-i Islami, under Mir 'Ali Gauhar; and Qiyyam-i Islami, under
General Mir Ahmad Shah Rizwani. Hizb-i Tauhid, the united party, was also
known as Madrasa-i Tauhid.

7. Although Faizani himself was a Sunni from Herat in western Afghanistan, he was close to Sayyid Ismail Balkhi, a prominent Shi'a spiritual figure and
political activist who had been involved in an attempted coup d'état against
Prime Minister Shah Mahmud Khan in 1949. Balkhi was arrested for his role in
this plot and remained in prison until the advent of democracy in 1964, but
many of his followers continued their political activities, a number under the

leadership of Faizani. On the evolution of Shi'a political protest through the mid-1980s, see Edwards 1986b and Mousavi 1998.

8. In explaining Faizani's popularity with military officers, one informant indicated that because they often lived in isolated, out-of-the-way bases and had to spend long hours in the middle of the night on watch, officers had plenty of time to practice zikr. Another informant argued that most officers were politically neutral (bi-taraf) and found Faizani's tendency to prioritize spirituality over politics to be a more sympathetic approach than the more militant orientations of other groups.

9. Interview with Sur Gul Spin, May 25, 1986.

10. Interview with Rohullah, September 4, 1983.

11. Interview with Mirajan Saheqi, October 3, 1983. See also Edwards 1986b.

12. Most of the miracle stories told of the contemporary period involved signs of special grace associated not with leaders but with devout mujahidin killed in battle. A common theme was the perfumed smell arising from the corpse of a martyr, and sometimes it was said that angels had been seen hovering around the grave of a martyr.

13. Olivier Roy has noted that a number of Sufi commanders were prominent in the jihad inside Afghanistan, particularly in the western and northern regions of the country less closely associated with the situation in Peshawar; Roy 1986, 112–116.

14. Among those captured were Saifuddin Nasratyar in Herat, Khawja Mahfuz in Panjshir, and Dr. Umar in Badakhshan.

15. Though he is referred to as "Engineer," Hekmatyar never completed his studies because of his involvement in political activities.

16. As is discussed in a later section, the other Afghan with a claim to being the first to import the ideas of the Muslim Brotherhood was Hazrat Sibghatullah Mujaddidi.

17. Interview with Wasil Nur, October 8, 1983.

18. Another, more important point of dispute between Hekmatyar and Rabbani involved Hekmatyar's arrest and execution of Jan Muhammad, an ally and friend of Rabbani's. Few people would discuss this matter with me, in part because it was so controversial and also because few people knew much about it. However, the version of events that appears most reliable to me is as follows. Following the failed attacks of 1975, several factions developed in Peshawar, one of which was led by Hekmatyar and the other by Jan Muhammad. Jan Muhammad was from Kunar and part of a group known as the Council of Kunar, which included Maulavi Hussain from Pech Valley and Kashmir Khan from Shigal. Hussain, the story goes, wanted to send an antigovernment night letter (shabnama) inside Afghanistan, a move that Jan Muhammad and other members of the council opposed. However, Hussain went ahead with the plan, and two of his relatives were captured with the night letter in their possession. Hussain accused Jan Muhammad of having informed the government of the

plan. Jan Muhammad was taken into custody by Hekmatyar's group, confessed under torture, and was later executed.

19. Interview with Qazi Amin, April 23, 1984.

20. Other members of the executive council included Maulavi Nasrullah Mansur, Maulavi Jalaluddin Haqqani, Maulavi Hussain (Jamil-ur-Rahman), and Haji Din Muhammad (brother of Commander Abdul Haq and later the deputy to Maulavi Yunus Khales).

21. Qazi Amin told me that Hizb-i Islami planned "three or four coup d'états" against Daud prior to the Saur Revolution (interview, April 23, 1984).

22. Hekmatyar claimed in an interview with me in 1983 that Khyber's assassination was the doing of Hizbi guerrillas. This claim has not been confirmed, and others claim that Daud himself ordered the killing.

23. For an example of one of these publications, see Edwards 1993b.

24. Interview with Wasil Nur, October 8, 1983.

25. According to one informant, after the establishment of Harakat, Nabi insisted that the leaders of Jamiat and Hizb turn over to him all party documents, information about fronts, and other materials. Both Hekmatyar and Rabbani refused, however, and approximately two months after the initiation of Harakat, Hekmatyar's faction staged a coup d'état, occupying the Harakat offices and confiscating safes containing the financial resources of the alliance. Some say that Nabi was also briefly held prisoner until the Pakistan government intervened and ordered his release. Thereafter, Nabi remained at home, deciding on his course of action, while the separate offices of Hizb-i Islami and Jamiat-i Islami were reorganized, both sharing in the spoils taken from Harakat. Interview with Wasil Nur, October 8, 1983.

26. Interview with Qazi Amin, April 23, 1984.

27. Interview with Yunus Khales, April 22, 1984.

28. Interview with Muhammad Nabi Muhammadi, April 25, 1984.

29. Interview with Yunus Khales, 1983.

30. Khales's contact with the Muslim Youth was initiated through Engineer Habib-ur Rahman as well as through his own son, Muhammad Nasim, a madrasa teacher and organization member who was arrested about the same time as Habib-ur Rahman and, like him, is presumed to have been executed.

31. Interview with Yunus Khales, April 22, 1984.

32. Interview with Zemarak Abed, Muslim Youth member from Wardak Province, May 5, 1984.

33. Ibid.

34. Ibid.

35. See Trimingham 1971.

36. Interview, September 12, 1983.

37. See Edwards 1993a, 171. The name "Mujaddidi" derives from Sheikh Ahmad Sirhindi's honorific title, *mujaddid-i alf-i thani* (renewer of the second millennium).

38. Most family members and loyalists would not discuss the apparent rivalry between the two Mujaddidi cousins. However, reasons did exist for bit-

terness between the two wings of the family, especially considering that the leadership of the family had been assumed by the descendants of Fazl Umar (Ibrahim's father), even though Sibghatullah's grandfather (Fazl Muhammad, the elder brother of Fazl Umar) was the senior member of the family. Although he did not confirm my suspicion that there was bitterness over this usurpation, Sibghatullah did tell me in an interview on September 12, 1983, that his cousin was jealous of him and had founded his party simply to prevent Sibghatullah from encroaching on his position with the ulama. He also expressed the belief that his cousin's murder and his own survival were not accidental: "Because I was pure, my heart was pure and I was sincere in my purpose, God protect[ed] me, save[d] me with all my children, family, I came here from abroad, and they were all captured. Some may be killed, some may be in jails up to now. This was really a great fault of family policy. I advised them; I requested them when I started my activities here in Peshawar; I told them, 'Please, I am secretly coming here.' Nobody knew I was here. I sent a man [to tell them], 'You must emigrate to Pakistan because I must start. I can't stop for you.' They said, 'No one will tell us anything. We are happy.'"

39. According to the family history, Naqib refused these gifts because they were public property (bait ul-mal) and insisted on paying for them from his own resources. Whether true or not, the account echoes a similar story told of the Mulla of Hadda when he was offered land by Habibullah a few years earlier. It also tells us that Naqib had both independent resources to draw on and the wisdom to realize that dependence on the government would likely compromise his position.

40. Girardet 1985, 115.

41. Interview, September 12, 1983.

42. The parties worked their separate wiles after this until the summer of 1979, when the garrison at Asmar was looted by Hizb-i Islami. This incident created a stir among the other parties, which joined together under the name Paiman-i Islami, but this alliance was also short-lived, breaking up within three months.

43. Interview, September 12, 1983.

44. In a strange reversal for Babrak Khan, who gave his own life to preserve the state, one of his two sons was held responsible (the circumstances and reasons remain murky) for the assassination of Pakistani Prime Minister Liaqat 'Ali Khan. His involvement in this episode has never been adequately explained.

45. Interview, June 12, 1984.

46. One of the decisions of this initial council was to call the proposed jirga a momasela (provisional) rather than a loya ("great," or national) jirga since it would be convened outside the country and circumstances prevented the holding of formal elections to decide who should sit on the council.

47. Interview, January 1983.

48. Kakar 1995, 100.

49. Ibid.

50. Ibid., 101.

51. Ibid., 103. In fairness, Zahir Shah was also not welcomed by the Pakistani authorities, and some of the Islamic parties in all likelihood would have done anything in their power to prevent him from setting up a base of operations in Pakistan. Both the Pakistanis and the Afghan resistance parties recognized Zahir Shah's popularity within the refugee population and inside the country.

52. Ali 1963, 16.

53. Roy 1986, 73.

54. It is also said that after Amin's own death members of his family emigrated to Peshawar and took up residence with Sayyaf, proving perhaps that even among the more zealous ideologues blood and honor retained some meaning.

55. This alliance included all the parties except Hekmatyar's Hizb-i Islami.

56. Qazi Amin, interview, April 23, 1984.

57. Roy 1986, 123.

58. Khan 1981.

59. While Sayyaf had relatively few fronts, he did attract some first-rate commanders, including Abdul Salam Roketi from Zabul, Amir from Khanabad, and Saznur from Ningrahar.

60. *Afghan Information Center Bulletin*, no. 9, January 1982, 10. Sayyaf took the notion that Afghanistan should provide "a school of Islamic jihad" quite literally; he established for Afghan refugees an Islamic university in exile that also included Arabs in its student body.

61. Hussain, like Sayyaf, changed his name during this time. Known widely in Kunar as Maulavi Hussain or as Panj Pir Maulavi, for his advocacy of Panj Piri doctrines, he came to be known as Maulavi Jamil-ur-Rahman because the name Hussain was associated with Shi'a Islam and was not popular in Arab circles.

62. Most people assume that Hizb was behind Hussain's assassination. However, some well-placed informants expressed the view that Pakistan's Inter-Service Intelligence, which coordinated most aspects of Pakistan's involvement with the Afghan resistance, was behind the killing because Hussain had announced the formation of an Islamic state in Kunar and had clashed with Pakistani militia groups along the border.

63. Personal communication, Dr. Zahir Ghazi Alam, 1986.

64. Yousaf and Adkin 1992, 105.

65. Ibrahim Mujaddidi had been the *pir-i tariqat* of the Mujaddidi family, while Nur Agha Gailani had been most actively involved in his family.

66. The advantage that accrued to both Mujaddidi and Gailani was that each began with a loyal following, mostly in the tribal areas, but both had difficulty moving beyond this initial base of support, especially since they were given a smaller percentage of total funds than the other parties were. Mujaddidi's problems were also compounded by the fact that many of his family's disciples were Ghilzai Pakhtun from Logar, Ghazni, Zabul, and Qandahar; this area had a high concentration of mullas and maulavis, many of whom joined Harakat, particularly when it became clear that Mujaddidi's party had relatively little in the way

of resources. By contrast, Gailani's strongest support was in Paktia, where clerics as a rule had less influence.

67. Roy 1986, 135.

68. Ibid.

69. Ibid., 131. The *Afghan Information Center Bulletin* noted in 1983 that while Rabbani was "one of the prominent figures of the young revolutionary Islamic movement," he had established his reputation as a leader "in a traditional way," and his doing so had encouraged some local Sufi leaders and brotherhoods in the northern provinces to join his movement; *Afghan Information Center Bulletin*, nos. 32–33, November–December 1983, 18.

70. *Afghan Information Center Bulletin*, no. 21, December 1982, 14.

71. The *Afghan Information Center Bulletin* cites a number of examples of Hizb conflicts or noninvolvement (or both) with other fronts in Tagab (no. 26, May 1983, 7), Wardak (no. 26, May 1983, 7), Panjshir (no. 27, June 1983, 7), Maidan (no. 34, January 1984, 14), Kunduz (no. 34, January 1984, 15), and Kabul (no. 35, February 1984, 10).

CODA: THE DEATH OF MAJROOH

1. *Afghan Information Center Bulletin*, no. 73, April 1987, 4–5.

2. Ibid., 5

3. If there was any bias in the bulletin, it was not toward the moderate parties but rather toward Jamiat, in part because Majrooh, who had studied in France, had close ties with a number of French journalists and researchers, who were the most active and courageous group covering the war. These individuals, including Oliver Roy, Jean-Jose Puig, and others, often traveled inside Afghanistan with Jamiat units and usually provided reports for the bulletin on their return. Through these reports, Jamiat received more attention than other parties, and a number of Jamiat commanders, including Ismail Khan in Herat, Zabiullah Khan in Mazar-i Sharif, and especially Ahmad Shah Massoud in Panjshir, were lionized, while commanders from other parties labored in relative obscurity. For his part, however, Majrooh appears to have tried to correct for the French bias toward Jamiat commanders by sending his own reporters out to provide coverage of other groups and by conducting interviews himself with commanders from other parties, including Qari Taj Muhammad (Harakat) from Ghazni, Amin Wardak (Mahaz) from Wardak, Maulavi Jalaluddin Haqqani (Khales) from Paktia, and Maulavi Shafiullah (Harakat) and Abdul Haq (Khales) from Kabul.

4. Sayyid Bahauddin Majrooh, "The Future Government of Afghanistan," *Afghan Information Center Bulletin*, no. 75, June 1987, 2.

5. Ibid., 5.

6. Ibid.

7. Ibid.

8. *Afghan Information Center Bulletin*, no. 76, July 1987, 2–8.

8. EPILOGUE

1. The authors of a 1901 British report on the tribes of Dir, Swat, and Bajaur discussed the role of madrasa students in inciting popular discontent in the following terms (McMahon and Ramsay 1981 [1901], 22–23):

> Worse even than the bigger men are the Talib-ul-ilm (seekers of knowledge). These are men, chiefly young men, who contemplate following the religious profession. They flock to the shrines of the country and attach themselves to some religious leader, ostensibly for religious education. Their number far exceeds those required to fill up vacancies in village mullahships and other ecclesiastic appointments, and they are reduced to seek other means of livelihood. They are at the bottom of all the mischief in the country, the instigators and often the perpetrators of the bulk of the crime. They use their religious status to live free on the people, who are too superstitious to turn them out, even when they destroy the peace of the family circle.

2. For a contemporary depiction of talebs as vituperative as that of McMahon and Ramsay, see Goldberg 2000.

3. During a trip through eastern Afghanistan in 1995, a year prior to the Taliban takeover in the region, I witnessed the conditions that the Taliban complained about and cited as justification for its existence. On that occasion, I was accompanied by a number of armed men and so was relatively safe, but wherever we traveled we had to pass through improvised roadblocks where vehicles were stopped and forced to pay tolls. Local commanders drove around in expensive four-wheel-drive cars and trucks and were clearly enriching themselves as the mass of people scraped by. While I never encountered or heard of an incident as brutal as the one Mulla Umar is said to have come across, it was clear from what I saw that the country was in a state of nearly complete anarchy—a state that had little to do with the Islamic principles on which the war against the Soviets had been premised.

4. Interview with Maulawi Rafiullah Muazin, C-reuters@clarinet.net, March 29, 1997.

5. Whether it was officially sanctioned or not is unclear, but the act of removing President Najibullah and his brother from the United Nations compound where they had been given refuge and stringing their mutilated bodies from a traffic light in downtown Kabul was seen as a dramatic repudiation of the previous Islamic regime, which had allowed Najibullah to stay put. Afghans understood that the Taliban were not just executing a Marxist; Najibullah was also a prominent member of the Ahmadzai Pakhtun tribe, and people saw the incident as an example of the Pakhtun Taliban being willing to risk the enmity of a powerful tribe in order to fulfill their vow to rid the country of the immoral, whoever and wherever they might be. Thus, while the act was gruesome, it had symbolic value as a unifying gesture. Whatever utility it might have had at the time has since been squandered, however, as non-Pakhtuns have come to see the Taliban as another variation on the theme of Pakhtun political domination.

6. B. Anderson 1983, ch. 4.

Glossary

This work includes stories, texts, and commentaries translated from both Pakhtu and Afghan Persian (Dari). Most of the words included in this glossary are found in both languages. In those cases where a word is unique to Pakhtu, I have added the designation (P). Following each word (as it appears in the text), I have provided in parentheses a transliteration with appropriate diacritical marks. The system of transliteration used here is that employed for Persian by the *International Journal of Middle East Studies*. Pakhtu has several letters and sounds that are not found in Persian. These include four retroflex phonemes (indicated by d, n, r, & t) and two additional consonants (indicated by kh and tz). Pakhtu also has a complex system of endings that I have not tried to reproduce here.

'ADALAT ('adālat) justice
A'ENA (a'enah) charity, donation
AKHUND (akhûnd) religious scholar, used also for someone who replaces an imam of a mosque
ALAQADARI ('alâqadârî) rural administrative district
AMIR (âmir) commander, ruler, king, used also for the chief of a political party or group
AMR BIL MA'RUF (amr bil ma'rûf) Arabic phrase referring to the act of calling people to proper faith and action and promoting virtue
BAIT UL-MAL (bayt ul mâl) property of the people
BAYAT (ba'at) oath of allegiance
BE ABRU (bî âbrû) dishonored, disgraced
BE GHAIRATI (bî ghaîratî) cowardly
BIDAT (bidā't) innovation
BI KHUDAYI (bî khudâyî) "without God," atheism

BI-TARAF (bî taraf) nonaligned

CHANDA (chanda) religious alms, charity, used principally in Pakistan

DARAJA (darajah) rank, degree, class

DARBAR (darbar) court

DAR UL-ULUM (dar ul ilûm) teacher-training college

DASTARBANDI (dastarbandî) ceremony of succession

DAWA (dawa) prayer

DEHQAN (dehqân) peasant, tenant farmer

DIN (dîn) religion

DO'A (do'a) oath

DODAI (dûdai) (P) food

DRUND (drûnd) (P) heavy, great, consequential

DUSHMAN (dushman) enemy

FARANGI (ferengî) foreigner, European

FIRMAN (firmân) proclamation, command, order

FITNA (fitnah) sedition, discord

FITWA (fitwā) religious decree

GHAIRAT (ghaîrat) courage, zeal, bravery

GHARUR (ghorûr) pride, vanity

GUND (gûnd) faction

GUNDI (gûndî) factionalism

HADITH (hadîth) traditions and sayings associated with the life of the Prophet Muhammad

HAJI (hajî) honorific for a man who has completed the pilgrimage to Mecca

HALQA (halqah) circle, used both for a group of people who meet to perform ZIKR and for a group of political activists who meet to discuss ideology and plan tactics

HAMSAYA (hamsâyah) tenant farmer, someone dependent on another for his livelihood

HARAM (haram) domestic area, off-limits, forbidden

HASTA (hastah) "cell," used by political parties, including the Muslim Youth Organization, to designate the smallest unit of the organization

HAUZA (haûzah) used by political parties, including the Muslim Youth Organization, to designate the more inclusive organizational level above the cell

HAYSIAT (haysîat) prestige

HEMAT (hemat) honor, magnanimity

HUJRA (hûjrah) guest house

IFTAR (iftar) the ceremony that occurs at sunset each evening during the month of Ramazan, when Muslims break the fast

IKHWANI (ikhwani) "brother," sometimes used by opponents of radical Islamic parties to describe these parties' members; taken from the Muslim Brotherhood (Ikhwan ul-Muslimin) in Egypt

INQILAB (inqilab) revolution

JALDAR (jaldar) skullcap

JAZA (jazah) punishment

JERIB (jirîb) unit of land measurement (2,000 square meters)

JIHAD (jihad) effort, struggle on behalf of Islam; holy war

JIRGA (jirgah) tribal council or assembly

KAFIR (kâfir) nonbeliever

KALAMA (kalamah) profession of faith—"There is no god but Allah, and Muhammad is His Prophet"

KALI (kalī) (P) clothing

KHAIRAT (khîrat) charity

KHAM (kham) unripe

KHAN (khan) title/honorific used for the leader of a tribal group

KHANAQA (khânaqâh) center of activity associated with a Sufi PIR

KHARWAR (kharwar) unit of weight (80 SER)

KIBR (kibr) pride, arrogance, insolence

KOR (kûr) (P) home

KUFR (kufr) infidelity

LANGAR (langar) eating area for disciples and visitors to a Sufi PIR or associated with a saint's tomb

LASHKAR (lashkar *or* lakhkar) army

LOYA JIRGA (loyah jîrgah) national council

LUCHAK (lûchak) (P) naked; shameless

MADRASA (madrasah) religious school

MAKTABIAN (maktabîyan) schoolboys

MASAWAT (masawat) equality

MASHREQI (mashreqî) eastern border region of the country, especially Kunar, Ningrahar, and Laghman

MASUNIYAT (masûniyat) security

MAULANA (mûlânâ) an advanced religious scholar, similar to MAULAVI (although more often associated with those whose training has been in India or Pakistan)

MAULAVI (maulavî) an advanced religious scholar, similar to MAULANA

MAWEN (mawen) deputy

MLATAR (malâtar) (P) supporters, usually kinsmen who "bind their waists together"

MOMASELA JIRGA (momaselah jîrgah) provisional national jirga

MUJAHID (mûjahed) one who pursues JIHAD, holy warrior

MUJAHIDIN (mûjahidîn) those who pursue JIHAD, holy warriors

MULLA (mullâ) a man who earns all or part of his income supervising a mosque, teaching religious lessons, or otherwise engaging in religious activities

MUNSHI (munshî) secretary, writer, clerk

MUSULMANI (mûsulmanî) Muslim practice

NAFS (nafs) self, soul, passions, senses, carnal desire

NAJAWANI (najawanî) cowardly

NAMAZ (namâz) prayer

NAMINEK (naminek) reputation

NAMUS (nâmûs) honor, that which a man possesses that cannot be violated

NANG (nang) honor; reputation, esteem

NASIB (nasîb) share, portion

NI'MAT (ni'mat) blessing, riches, favor

PAIGHUR (paîghûr) (P) taunt, reproach

PAKHTUN (pakhtûn) one who speaks the Pakhtu (Pashto) language and who claims descent in one of the commonly recognized lines of the Pakhtun tribe

PIR (pîr) master of a Sufi order

QAHRAMAN (qahramân) hero, champion

QANUN (qanûn) law

QAUM (qaûm) tribe

QAZI (qâzi) judge

QIBLA (qiblah) direction of Mecca, toward which Muslims face during prayer

QUR'AN (qurân) word of God revealed to the Prophet Muhammad

RAHM (rahm) compassion

RAMAZAN (ramazân) ninth month in the lunar calendar, the Islamic month of fasting

ROZA (rozah) fasting

SAFA (safah) pure

SAHIB (sâheb) honorific meaning master or sir

SARDAR (sardar) prince

SATR (satr) seclusion

SAYYID (sayyid) descendant of the Prophet Muhammad

SER (ser) unit of weight

SHABNAMA (shabnamah) "night letter," political tract distributed covertly

SHAHID (shahîd) martyr

SHAHIDAN (shahîdan) martyrs

SHARI'A (shari'a) religious law

SHUJA'AT (shijâhat) bravery

SHURA (shurah) council

SIAL (sîal) (P) a rival; someone of equal status

SILSILA (silsilah) chain, series, order, hierarchical organization

STANA (stanah) holy man

SUD (sûd) profit, benefit, interest

SUFI (sûfî) a person devoted to the mystical path (TASAWUF)

SUNNAT (sunnat) tradition, customary or expected; circumcision

SUTRA (sûtrah) clean

TABLIGHAT (tablîghat) propaganda

TAKFIR (takfîr) infidelity

TALEB (tâlab) religious student, seeker of sacred knowledge

TALIBAN (taliban) religious students

TARBUR (tarbûr) patrilateral parallel cousin, one's father's brother's son; rival

TARIQAT (tarîqat) Sufi order

TASAWUF (tasawuf) Sufism

ULAMA ('ulama') religious authorities

WAHHABI (wahabî) term of disparagement for those who profess beliefs similar to those of the Arab religious reformer Abdul Wahhab; also known as Panj Piri and Salafi

WAKIL (wakîl) parliamentary representative

WOLESWAL (wuleswal) district administrator

WOLESWALI (wuleswalî) district

WULJA (wuljah) booty

ZAKAT (zakât) religious tax incumbent on all Muslims

ZIKR (zikr) mystical act associated with Sufism involving the repeated recitation of sacred phrases

Bibliography

Adamec, Ludwig. 1975. *Historical and Political Who's Who of Afghanistan.* Graz, Austria: Akademische Druck-u.

Ahady, Anwar-ul-haq. 1998, "Saudi Arabia, Iran and the Conflict in Afghanistan." In William Maley, ed., *Fundamentalism Reborn? Afghanistan and the Taliban.* New York: New York University Press.

Ahmed, Akbar S. 1976. *Millennium and Charisma among Pathans: A Critical Essay in Social Anthropology.* London: Routledge.

Ali, Muhammad. 1963. "Ahmad Shah Baba Father of the Nation." *Afghanistan* 18 (2).

Anderson, Benedict. 1983. *Imagined Communities: Reflections on the Origin and Spread of Nationalism.* London: Verso.

Anderson, Jon. 1975. "Tribe and Community among Ghilzai Pashtun." *Anthropos* 70: 576–600.

———. "'There Are No Knows Anymore': Economic Development and Social Change in Afghanistan." *Middle East Journal* 32 (2).

———. 1983. "Khan and Khel: Dialectics of Pakhtun Tribalism." In Richard Tapper, ed., *The Conflict of Tribe and State in Iran and Afghanistan.* New York: St. Martin's Press.

———. 1984. "How Afghans Define Themselves in Relation to Islam." In M. Nazif Shahrani and Robert L. Canfield, eds., *Revolutions and Rebellions in Afghanistan.* Berkeley, Calif.: Institute for International Studies.

Antoun, Richard T. 1989. *Muslim Preacher in the Modern World: A Jordanian Case Study in Comparative Perspective.* Princeton, N.J.: Princeton University Press.

Anwar, Raja. 1988. *The Tragedy of Afghanistan: A First-hand Account.* London: Verso.

Arnold, Anthony. 1981. *Afghanistan: The Soviet Invasion in Perspective.* Stanford, Calif.: Hoover Institution Press.

Bacon, Elizabeth E. 1980 [1966]. *Central Asians under Russian Rule: A Study in Culture Change.* Ithaca, N.Y.: Cornell University Press.

Barfield, Thomas J. 1984. "Weak Links in a Rusty Chain: Structural Weaknesses in Afghanistan's Provincial Government Administration." In M. Nazif Shahrani and Robert L. Canfield, eds., *Revolutions and Rebellions in Afghanistan: Anthropological Perspectives.* Berkeley, Calif.: University of California Press.

Barth, Fredrik. 1959. *Political Leadership among Swat Pathans.* London: Athlone Press.

———. 1987. "Cultural Wellsprings of Resistance." In Rosanne Klass, ed., *Afghanistan: The Great Game.* New York: Freedom House.

Bourdieu, Pierre. 1966. "The Sentiment of Honour in Kabyle Society." In J. G. Peristiany, ed., *Honour and Shame: The Values of Mediterranean Society.* Chicago: University of Chicago Press.

Bradsher, Henry. 1985. *Afghanistan and the Soviet Union.* Durham, N.C.: Duke University Press.

Canfield, Robert L. 1973. *Faction and Conversion in a Plural Society: Religious Alignments in the Hindu Kush.* Anthropological Paper 50. Ann Arbor: University of Michigan Museum of Anthropology.

Caroe, Olaf. 1965. *The Pathans.* London: Macmillan.

Caton, Steven C. 1999. *Lawrence of Arabia: A Film's Anthropology.* Berkeley: University of California Press.

Christensen, Asgar. 1980. "The Pashtuns of Kunar: Tribe, Class and Community Organization." *Afghanistan Journal* 7 (3).

———. 1982. "Agnates, Affines and Allies: Patterns of Marriage among Pakhtun in Kunar, North-East Afghanistan." *Folk,* no. 24.

———. 1988. "When Muslim Identity Has Different Meanings: Religion and Politics in Contemporary Afghanistan." In Klaus Ferdinand and Mehdi Mozaffari, eds., *Islam: State and Society.* London: Curzon Press.

Crapanzano, Vincent. 1980. *Tuhami: Portrait of a Moroccan.* Chicago: University of Chicago Press.

Curzon, George. 1923. *Tales of Travel.* New York: George H. Doran.

Davis, Anthony. 1998. "How the Taliban Became a Military Force." In William Maley, ed., *Fundamentalism Reborn? Afghanistan and the Taliban.* New York: New York University Press.

Denzin, Norman. 1989. *Interpretive Biography.* Newbury Park, Calif.: Sage.

Dupree, Louis. 1966. "Islam in Politics: Afghanistan." *Muslim World* 56 (4).

———. 1967. "The Political Uses of Religion: Afghanistan." In K. H. Silver, ed., *Churches and States.* New York: American Universities Field Staff.

———. 1970. "Aq Kupruk: A Town in North Afghanistan." In Louise E. Sweet, ed., *Peoples and Cultures of the Middle East.* Garden City, N.Y.: Natural History Press.

———. 1978. "Toward Representative Government in Afghanistan. Part I: The First Five Steps." *American Universities Field Staff Reports,* no. 1.

———. 1979a. "Afghanistan under the Khalq." *Problems of Communism,* July–August.

————. 1979b. "Red Flag over the Hindu Kush. Part I: Leftist Movements in Afghanistan." *American Universities Field Staff Reports,* no. 44.

————. 1980. *Afghanistan.* 3d ed. Princeton, N.J.: Princeton University Press.

————. 1984. "Tribal Warfare in Afghanistan and Pakistan: A Reflection of the Segmentary Lineage System." In Akbar S. Ahmed and David M. Hart, eds., *Islam in Tribal Societies: From the Atlas to the Indus.* London: Routledge.

Edwards, David B. 1986a. "Charismatic Leadership and Political Process in Afghanistan." *Central Asian Survey* 5 (3/4).

————. 1986b. "The Evolution of Shi'i Political Dissent in Afghanistan." In Juan R. I. Cole and Nikki R. Keddie, eds., *Shi'ism and Social Protest.* New Haven, Conn.: Yale University Press.

————. 1987. "Origins of the Anti-Soviet Jihad." In Grant M. Farr and John G. Merriam, eds., *Afghan Resistance: The Politics of Survival.* Boulder, Colo.: Westview Press.

————. 1990. "Frontiers, Boundaries and Frames: The Marginal Identity of Afghan Refugees." In Akbar S. Ahmed, ed., *Pakistan: The Social Science Perspective.* Karachi: Oxford University Press.

————. 1993a. "The Political Lives of Afghan Saints: The Case of the Hazrats of Shor Bazaar." In Carl W. Ernst, ed., *Manifestations of Sainthood in Islam.* Istanbul: Éditions Isis.

————. 1993b. "Summoning Muslims: Print, Politics, and Religious Ideology in Afghanistan." *Journal of Asian Studies* 52 (3).

————. 1993c. "Words in the Balance: The Poetics of Political Dissent in Afghanistan." In Dale Eickelman, ed., *Russia's Muslim Frontiers: New Directions in Cross-Cultural Analysis.* Bloomington: Indiana University Press.

————. 1995. "Print Islam: Religion, Revolution, and the Media in Afghanistan." *Anthropological Quarterly* 68 (3).

————. 1996. *Heroes of the Age: Moral Fault Lines on the Afghan Frontier.* Berkeley: University of California Press.

————. 1998. "Learning from the Swat Pathans: Political Leadership in Afghanistan, 1978–1997." *American Ethnologist* 25 (4).

Eickelman, Dale F. 1978. "The Art of Memory: Islamic Education and Its Social Reproduction." *Comparative Studies in Society and History* 20 (4).

————. 1985. *Knowledge and Power in Morocco: The Education of a Twentieth Century Notable.* Princeton, N.J.: Princeton University Press.

Fullerton, John. N.d. *The Soviet Occupation of Afghanistan.* Hong Kong: Far Eastern Economic Review.

Geertz, Clifford. 1968. *Islam Observed: Religious Development in Morocco and Indonesia.* Chicago: University of Chicago Press.

————. 1983. "Centers, Kings, and Charisma." In Clifford Geertz, ed., *Local Knowledge: Further Essays in Interpretive Anthropology.* New York: Basic Books.

Ghani, Ashraf. 1987. "Islam and Counter-revolutionary Movements." In John L. Esposito, ed., *Islam in Asia.* Oxford: Oxford University Press.

Ghobar, Mir Ghulam Muhammad. 1967. *Afghanistan dar Masir-i Tarikh.* Kabul: Government Printing House.

Girardet, Edward. 1985. *Afghanistan: The Soviet War.* New York: St. Martin's Press.

Goldberg, Jeffrey. 2000. "Inside Jihad U.: The Education of a Holy Warrior." *New York Times Magazine,* June 25.

Gregorian, Vartan. 1969. *The Emergence of Modern Afghanistan: Politics of Reform and Modernization 1880–1946.* Stanford, Calif.: Stanford University Press.

Hobsbawm, E. J. 1959. *Primitive Rebels: Studies in Archaic Forms of Social Movement in the 19th and 20th Centuries.* New York: Norton.

———. *Bandits.* New York: Pantheon Books.

Hyman, Anthony. 1984. *Afghanistan under Soviet Domination.* London: Macmillan.

Jones, Schuyler. 1974. *Men of Influence in Nuristan: A Study of Social Control and Dispute Settlement in Waigal Valley, Afghanistan.* London: Seminar Press.

Kakar, Hasan. 1978. "The Fall of the Afghan Monarchy in 1973." *International Journal of Middle East Studies* 9.

———. 1979. *Government and Society in Afghanistan: The Reign of Amir 'Abd al-Rahman Khan.* Austin: University of Texas Press.

———. 1995. *Afghanistan: The Soviet Invasion and the Afghan Response, 1979–1982.* Berkeley: University of California Press.

Katz, David J. 1984. "Responses to Central Authority in Nuristan: The Case of the Vaygal Valley Kalasha." In M. Nazif Shahrani and Robert L. Canfield, eds., *Revolutions and Rebellions in Afghanistan: Anthropological Perspectives.* Berkeley: University of California Press.

Keiser, Lincoln. 1984. "The Rebellion in Darra-i Nur." In M. Nazif Shahrani and Robert L. Canfield, eds., *Revolutions and Rebellions in Afghanistan: Anthropological Perspectives.* Berkeley: University of California Press.

———. 1991. *Friend by Day, Enemy by Night.* Fort Worth, Tex.: Holt, Rinehart and Winston.

Khan, Azmat Hayat. 1981. "Afghan Resistance and National Leadership." *Central Asia* 9 (Winter).

———. 1993. "Factional Organisation of the Afghan Mujahideens in Peshawar." In Fazal-ur-Rehim Marwat and Syed Wiqar Ali Shah Kakakhel, eds., *Afghanistan and the Frontier.* Peshawar: Emjay Books.

Khan, Muhammad Anwar. 1993. "The Emergence of Religious Parties in Afghanistan." In Fazal-ur-Rehim Marwat and Syed Wiqar Ali Shah Kakakhel, eds., *Afghanistan and the Frontier.* Peshawar: Emjay Books.

Kushkaki, B. 1921. *Nadir-i Afghan.* Kabul: Government Press.

Lewis, Bernard. 1988. *The Political Language of Islam.* Chicago: University of Chicago Press.

Mack, John. 1976. *A Prince of Our Disorder: The Life of T. E. Lawrence.* Boston: Little, Brown.

Magnus, Ralph and Eden Naby. 1998. *Afghanistan: Mullah, Marx, and Mujahid.* Boulder, Colo.: Westview Press.

Majrooh, Sayyid Bahouddin. N.d. "Education in Afghanistan: Past and Present." Unpublished manuscript, Afghan Information Center, Peshawar.

Male, Beverley. 1982. *Revolutionary Afghanistan.* London: Croom Helm.

Maley, William. 1998. "Introduction: Interpreting the Taliban." In William Maley, ed., *Fundamentalism Reborn? Afghanistan and the Taliban.* New York: New York University Press.

Marsden, Peter. 1998. *The Taliban: War, Religion and the New Order in Afghanistan.* London: Zed Books.

Massell, Gregory J. 1974. *The Surrogate Proletariat: Moslem Women and Revolutionary Strategies in Soviet Central Asia 1919–1929.* Princeton, N.J.: Princeton University Press.

Matinuddin, Kamal. 1999. *The Taliban Phenomenon: Afghanistan 1994–1997.* Karachi: Oxford University Press.

McChesney, Robert D. 1999. *Kabul under Siege: Fayz Muhammad's Account of the 1929 Uprising.* Princeton, N.J.: Markus Wiener.

McMahon, A. H., and A. D. G. Ramsay. 1981 [1901]. *Report on the Tribes of Dir, Swat and Bajour Together with the Utman-Khel and Sam Ranizai.* Peshawar: Saeed Book Bank.

Merk, W. R. H. 1984 [1898]. *The Mohmands.* Lahore: Vanguard Books.

Metcalf, Barbara D. 1978. "The Madrasa at Deoband: A Model for Religious Education in Modern India." *Modern Asian Studies* 12 (1).

Mills, Margaret. 1991. *Rhetoric and Politics in Afghan Traditional Storytelling.* Philadelphia: University of Pennsylvania Press.

Mitchell, Richard. 1969. *The Society of the Muslim Brothers.* London: Oxford University Press.

Mottahedeh, Roy P. 1985. *The Mantle of the Prophet: Religion and Politics in Iran.* New York: Pantheon Books.

Mousavi, S. A. 1998. *The Hazaras of Afghanistan: An Historical, Cultural, Economic and Political Study.* Surrey, England: Curzon Press.

Nicholson, Reynold A,. ed., 1981 [1898]. *Selected Poems from the Dīvāni Shams Tabrīz.* Lahore: Sang-e-Meel.

Peacock, James L., and Dorothy C. Holland. 1993. "The Narrated Self: Life Stories in Process." *Ethos* 21 (4).

Peters, Rudolph. 1979. *Islam and Colonialism: The Doctrine of Jihad in Modern History.* The Hague: Mouton.

Pitt-Rivers, Julian. 1966. "Honour and Social Status." In J. G. Peristiany, ed., *Honour and Shame: The Values of Mediterranean Society.* Chicago: University of Chicago Press.

Poullada, Leon. 1973. *Reform and Rebellion in Afghanistan, 1919–1929.* Ithaca, N.Y.: Cornell University Press.

Rashid, Ahmed. 1998. "Pakistan and the Taliban." In William Maley, ed., *Fundamentalism Reborn? Afghanistan and the Taliban.* New York: New York University Press.

———. 2000. *Taliban: Militant Islam, Oil and Fundamentalism in Central Asia*. New Haven, Conn.: Yale University Press.

Reardon, P. J. 1969. "Modernization and Reform: The Contemporary Endeavors." In G. Grassmuck, L. Adamec, and F. Irwin, eds., *Afghanistan: Some New Approaches*. Ann Arbor: University of Michigan Press.

Robertson, George S. 1974 [1896]. *The Kafirs of the Hindu Kush*. Karachi: Oxford University Press.

Robinson, Capt. J. A. 1978 [1934]. *Notes on Nomad Tribes of Eastern Afghanistan*. Quetta, Pakistan: Nisa Traders.

Roy, Olivier. 1983. "Sufism in the Afghan Resistance." *Central Asian Survey* 2 (4).

———. 1986. *Islam and Resistance in Afghanistan*. Cambridge: Cambridge University Press.

———. 1994a. *The Failure of Political Islam*. Cambridge, Mass.: Harvard University Press.

———. 1994b. "The New Political Elite of Afghanistan." In Myron Weiner and Ali Banuazizi, eds., *The Politics of Social Transformation in Afghanistan, Iran, and Pakistan*. Syracuse, N.Y.: Syracuse University Press.

———. 1998. "Has Islamism a Future in Afghanistan?" In William Maley, ed., *Fundamentalism Reborn? Afghanistan and the Taliban*. New York: New York University Press.

Rubin, Barnett R. 1995a. *The Fragmentation of Afghanistan: State Formation and Collapse in the International System*. New Haven, Conn.: Yale University Press.

———. 1995b. *The Search for Peace in Afghanistan: From Buffer State to Failed State*. New Haven, Conn.: Yale University Press.

Sahre, Delawar. N.d. "The Uprising in Kunar." Unpublished manuscript.

Saikal, Amin. 1998. "The Rabbani Government, 1992–1996." In William Maley, ed., *Fundamentalism Reborn? Afghanistan and the Taliban*. New York: New York University Press.

Salik, S. A. 1953. *The Saint of Jilan (Ghaus-ul-Azam)*. Lahore: Ashraf.

Shah, Bahadur, ed. 1983. "Why Do We Read the Books of the Koranic School by Maulana Muhammad Attaullah Faizani." Unpublished manuscript.

Shahrani, M. Nazif. 1984. "Introduction: Marxist 'Revolution' and Islamic Resistance in Afghanistan." In M. Nazif Shahrani and Robert L. Canfield, eds., *Revolutions and Rebellions in Afghanistan: Anthropological Perspectives*. Berkeley: University of California Press.

———. 1986. "State Building and Social Fragmentation in Afghanistan: A Historical Perspective." In Ali Banuazizi and Myron Weiner, eds., *The State, Religion, and Ethnic Politics: Afghanistan, Iran, and Pakistan*. Syracuse, N.Y.: Syracuse University Press.

———. 1998. "The Future of the State and the Structure of Community Governance in Afghanistan." In William Maley, ed., *Fundamentalism Reborn? Afghanistan and the Taliban*. New York: New York University Press.

Shahrani, M. Nazif, and Robert L. Canfield, eds. 1984. *Revolutions and Rebel-*

lions in Afghanistan: Anthropological Perspectives. Berkeley: University of California Press.

Sivan, Emmanuel. 1985. *Radical Islam: Medieval Theology and Modern Politics.* New Haven, Conn.: Yale University Press.

Stewart, Rhea T. 1973. *Fire in Afghanistan 1914–1929: Faith, Hope and the British Empire.* Garden City, N.Y.: Doubleday.

Strand, Richard F. 1984. "The Evolution of Anti-Communist Resistance in Eastern Nuristan." In M. Nazif Shahrani and Robert L. Canfield, eds., *Revolutions and Rebellions in Afghanistan: Anthropological Perspectives.* Berkeley: University of California Press.

Tapper, Nancy. 1983. "Abd al-Rahman's North-West Frontier: The Pashtun Colonisation of Afghan Turkistan." In Richard Tapper, ed., *The Conflict of Tribe and State in Iran and Afghanistan.* New York: St. Martin's Press.

Tapper, Richard. 1983. "Introduction." In Richard Tapper, ed., *The Conflict of Tribe and State in Iran and Afghanistan.* New York: St. Martin's Press.

Thomas, Lowell. 1925. *Beyond Khyber Pass.* New York: Century.

————. 1928. *Adventures in Afghanistan for Boys.* New York: Century.

————. 1976. *Good Evening, Everybody: From Cripple Creek to Samarkand.* New York: Morrow.

Trimingham, J. Spencer. 1971. *The Sufi Orders of Islam.* Oxford: Clarendon Press.

Urban, Mark. 1988. *War in Afghanistan.* London: Macmillan.

Yousaf, Mohammad, and Mark Adkin. 1992. *The Bear Trap: Afghanistan's Untold Story.* Lahore: Jang.

Zalmai, Mohammad Wali. 1967. *Mujahid-i Afghan.* Kabul: Government Printing House.

Index

Abdul Salam, 255

Abdur Rahman Khan, Amir, 26, 37, 44, 76, 186, 255; autobiography, 53; final days, 91, 92; on jihad, 78–79; proclamations and pronouncements, 34, 50–52; rhetoric of honor, 52; on rulers and sovereignty, 57–58; ruthless suppression of enemies, 82, 111–12, 307

Abdur Razaq Khan, Haji, 187, 322n18

adultery. See Safi daughter, death of a

Afghan Information Center (AIC), 166, 279–80

Afghanistan, 1–2; "forbidden," 1; in 1975, 10–16; dissatisfaction in (1975), 13–16; map of eastern, 101; from nineteenth-century kingdom to twentieth-century nation-state, 188; "old boys' network" in, 275; political incoherence of, adaptive aspects of, 299–300

Afghanistan prestige, as inherited asset, 115–16

Afghan political culture, three foci of, 263

Afghans, as "freedom fighters" vs. "terrorists," 17

Afzal, Muhammad, 322n18

Ahmad Khan Abdali, 263

Ahmad Shah Abdali, 45, 253

Ahmad Shah Durrani, 263

Amanullah Khan, Amir, 9, 253, 311–12n36; assumption of power, 64; clothing and appearance, 4–10, 13; contention between Hazrat of Shor Bazaar and, 230; declaration of jihad against British, 79–80, 187; downfall and overthrow of, 29, 55, 56, 76, 103, 189; economic and social reforms, 58–61; and education, 55; Lowell Thomas and, 2–7; photograph of, 60; as populist ruler, 10, 60; possible role in assassination

of father, 64; relations with others, 59, 60; as ruler, 2–3, 8, 10, 44, 59; speeches, 30–31, 79; transformation of, 10; Western writers on, 7–8

Amin. See Hafizullah Amin

Anderson, Benedict, 304

Anglo-Afghan War of 1919, 187, 188, 322n14. See also jihad(s), against British

Aqcha Poor, 14–16

Asmar, mutiny at, 155–58

Babrakzai, Umar, 260, 261

Bacha-i Saqao, 29, 34, 54, 265, 312n38

Bhutto, Zulfiqar 'Ali, 76, 218

bin Laden, Osama, 17

bismillah, 40, 91, 144

British, jihad against, 64, 79–80, 147, 152, 187

British imperialism, 29, 78

"Bugle of Revolution, The" (Bariq Shafi), 39, 208

Chagha Serai, assault on, 145, 147, 155, 157–59

Chase, Harry, 4–6

clerics/clerical parties, 244–52, 274–75, 298. See also Harakat; Hizb; Jamiat ul-Ulama Muhammadi

Daiya Ettehad-i Islami Mujahidin Afghanistan (Inviting Mujahidin of the Islamic Union for Unity), 269

Daud, Muhammad, 13, 48, 49, 62–63, 230–31, 244; anti-insurgency activities, 29–30; appointed prime minister, 36, 194; arrest of Taraki and Hafizullah Amin, 241; assassination of, 28–29, 85, 124, 125, 231–32; backing of Pakhtunistan, 76;

Compositor: BookMatters
Text: 10/13 Aldus
Display: Aldus
Printer: Sheridan Books, Inc.
Binder: Sheridan Books, Inc.